Writing Essays about Literature

A GUIDE AND STYLE SHEET

EIGHTH EDITION

Kelley Griffith

University of North Carolina at Greensboro

WADSWORTH
CENGAGE Learning

Australia • Brazil • Japan • Korea • Mexico • Singapore • Spain • United Kingdom • United States

For Gareth, Bronwen, and their families

Writing Essays about Literature: A Guide and Style Sheet, Eighth Edition
Kelley Griffith

Senior Publisher: Lyn Uhl

Publisher: Michael Rosenberg

Developmental Editor: Mary Beth Walden

Assistant Editor: Jillian D'Urso

Editorial Assistant: Erin Pass

Media Editor: Amy Gibbons

Marketing Manager: Christina Shea

Marketing Coordinator: Ryan Ahern

Marketing Communications Manager: Laura Localio

Sr. Art Director: Cate Barr

Production Service: PrePressPMG, Sini Sivaraman

Manufacturing Manager: Denise Powers

Sr. Rights Acquisitions Manager, Text: Katie Huha

Rights Acquisitions Manager, Image: John Hill

Cover Designer: Dare Porter, Real Time Design

Compositor: PrePressPMG

For product information and technology assistance, contact us at **Cengage Learning Customer & Sales Support, 1-800-354-9706.**
For permission to use material from this text or product, submit all requests online at **www.cengage.com/permissions.**
Further permissions questions can be e-mailed to **permissionrequest@cengage.com.**

Library of Congress Control Number: 2009938507

ISBN-13: 978-1-4282-9041-9

ISBN-10: 1-4282-9041-9

Wadsworth
20 Channel Center Street
Boston, MA 02210
USA

Cengage Learning is a leading provider of customized learning solutions with office locations around the globe, including Singapore, the United Kingdom, Australia, Mexico, Brazil, and Japan. Locate your local office at **www.cengage.com/global.**

Cengage Learning products are represented in Canada by Nelson Education, Ltd.

To learn more about Wadsworth, visit **www.cengage.com/wadsworth.**

Purchase any of our products at your local college store or at our preferred online store **www.CengageBrain.com.**

Printed in Canada
1 2 3 4 5 6 7 13 12 11 10 09

CONTENTS

PART TWO: Writing about Literature   223

7 Writing about Literature   225

8 Choosing Topics   229

PREFACE

I wrote the first edition of this book in response to questions students asked when I assigned essays about literature: "What should I look for?" "What's an essay?" "How long should it be?" "Do we have to use outside sources?" "How should I document sources?" Many students had little experience writing essays, not only about literature but about anything. They struggled to get started. This book was my answer to their questions. I meant it to be informative and very practical. It gave a brief introduction to the study of literature, defined key terms, explained details of usage (the "style sheet" part of the book), and included sample student essays.

Writing Essays about Literature: A Guide and Style Sheet has evolved over the years, and this, the eighth edition, still strives to answer questions students raise about studying and writing about literature. Part one (Interpreting Literature, chapters 1 through 6) provides extensive guidance about reading literature. Chapter 1 poses the questions that undergird the entire book: What is "meaning" in literature? How can we interpret literature to find meanings in it? Chapters 2 through 5 answer those questions with a formalist approach to analyzing literature. These chapters define the elements of literature itself (chapter 2), then of fiction (chapter 3), drama (chapter 4), and poetry (chapter 5). They provide heuristics—questions, "Thinking on Paper" exercises, and "Now It's Your Turn" assignments—that prompt students to work on their own, to come up with their own interpretations. Chapter 6 places the formalist approach within the larger framework of literary theory and invites students to enrich their interpretations with study outside the text.

Part two (Writing about Literature) offers guidance for writing. Chapter 7, the introduction to part two, poses the question, How can we write about literature? Although the main focus of part two is the interpretive essay, chapter 7 and subsequent chapters also discuss more "personal" kinds of writing, such as free writing, notes, and journals. Chapters 8 through 10 are arranged according to the four stages of the writing process: inventing, drafting, revising, and editing. Chapter 8 (Choosing Topics) suggests strategies for generating topics. Chapter 9 (Drafting the Essay) emphasizes argumentation in essays about literature. It covers strategies for reasoning, organizing, and developing essays from early to final drafts.

Chapters 10 and 11 are the "style sheet" part of the book. Both chapters include guidelines in keeping with the latest edition of the *MLA Handbook for Writers of Research Papers* (7th ed., 2009). Chapter 10 (Revising and Editing) provides advice about revising, rules for quotations and other matters of usage, and guidelines for the essay's appearance and format. Chapter 11 explains what research papers are, how to find information and opinions, how to incorporate them into essays, and how to document sources using the MLA style. The book concludes with chapter 12 (Taking Essay Tests) and chapter 13 (Sample Essays). In this final chapter, there are four essays—one on a poem, one on a short story, one on a play, and one on a novel.

Much is new and changed in this edition.

GREATER EMPHASIS ON MEANING IN LITERATURE

Although students' quest for "meaning" in literature has always been a focus in this book, I have emphasized it even more for this edition. In revising chapter 1, I wrestled with the question of what "meaning" in literature is and where one finds it. Here I attempt to define "meaning." I tie the material in subsequent chapters to this definition.

COMPLETE REVISION OF THE CHAPTER ON DRAMA

In revising this chapter I have retained the focus on potential performances as a device for exploring meanings in plays. I have rearranged sections, expanded some, and included new ones (on costume, for example).

COMPLETE REVISION OF THE CHAPTER ON THEORY

When I first wrote what is now Chapter 6 (Specialized Approaches to Interpreting Literature), I thought a brief overview of literary theory might be interesting to students, especially those who want to study literature beyond a formalist approach. After several editions I realized I wanted to do more than just report on literary theory. I wanted to suggest how students might actually use it. For this edition, then, I continue to place theory within a larger structure—all the "places" one might focus to find meaning in literature. These places are the author, the work, the reader, and the universe outside the work (all of reality). At the end of each of these sections, I have attached "applications" sections, in which I suggest how these theoretical approaches might provide avenues for finding meaning. Finally, I have expanded discussions of some theoretical approaches, notably the one on reader-response criticism. Throughout I have tried to explain all the theories accurately and clearly.

UPDATING OF GUIDELINES AND RESOURCES

I have revised the book, including especially the sections on usage and documentary style, according to the latest edition of the *MLA Handbook for Writers of Research Papers* (7th ed., 2009). This edition of the *Handbook* includes significant changes in documentary style from previous editions, mainly because of advancing computer technology. For example, the *Handbook* now assumes that all student writing will be done on a computer and printed so that it looks like a published document. As a result, the *Handbook* now asks that titles be italicized, not underlined. The *Handbook* also asks that all citations include the mode of publication ("print," "Web," etc.). In other words, no longer is it assumed that the default publication is print. Finally, with the advanced capabilities of search engines, no longer do citations need the URLs of Web sites. Just the title of the site will do. Web sites, as we know, come and go. I have checked all print and Web resources listed in the book. As of this writing, they all exist.

AN APPENDIX CONTAINING WHOLE WORKS OF LITERATURE

With one exception, all works of literature that are subjects of student essays have been moved to an appendix. Since I refer to these works throughout the book, placing them in an appendix makes them easier to find. The exception is book-length works, notably the *Odyssey* and *Adam Bede*, which are too long for inclusion here.

AN ADDITIONAL COMPLETE SHORT STORY

Ernest Hemingway's "Hills Like White Elephants," which I discuss at some length in the chapter on fiction, is now included in the Appendix.

OTHER CHANGES

A miscellany of changes is as follows:

- The addition of "Now It's Your Turn" prompts in Chapter 2.
- The division of Chapter 5 (on poetry) into four distinct sections: 1) Sense in Poetry, 2) Sound in Poetry, 3) Structure, and 4) Sight (visual qualities of poetry).
- In Chapter 8 (Choosing Topics), a section on using graphics to generate and organize ideas.
- Reorganized and renamed categories in Chapters 10 (on revising and editing) and 11 (documentation) for clarity.
- Revised definitions in Chapter 11 of primary and secondary research and sources.
- Throughout the book, the addition of examples from contemporary authors and recently published works.

This book can serve related purposes. Teachers can use it as a textbook in introductory courses and as a supplement in advanced ones. Students can use it on their own as an introduction to the study of literature, as a guide to writing about literature, and as a reference manual.

I have written this book out of a long-standing and continuing love for literature. My hope is that the book's information and suggestions will help readers get as much pleasure from literature as it has given me. I welcome comments and suggestions. My e-mail address is <kelley_griffith@uncg.edu>.

ACKNOWLEDGMENTS

I owe many people gratitude for their help. I am indebted to the writers whose works I have consulted. For past editions, very helpful were the insightful comments of Laurence Perrine, Frank Garratt (*Tacoma Community College*), George Gleason (*Southwest Missouri State University*), John Hanes (*Duquesne University*), Jacqueline Hartwich (*Bellevue Community College*), Irving Howe (*Hunter College*), Edward Pixley (*State University of New York at Oneonta*), Dexter Westrum (*Ottawa University*), Jeff Bagato (*Virginia Polytechnic Institute*), Helen O'Grady (*University of Wyoming*), Karen Meyers (*University of North Carolina at Greensboro*), William Tucker (*University of North Carolina at Greensboro*), Walter Beale (*University of North Carolina at Greensboro*), Thomas C. Bonner (*Midlands Technical College*), Nancy Hume (*Essex Community College*), Gretchen Lutz (*San Jacinto College*), Robbie Clifton Pinter (*Belmont University*), Wallace Watson (*Duquesne University*), Judy Brown (*University of British Columbia*), Gaye Elder (*Abraham Baldwin Agricultural College*), Albert J. Griffith (*Our Lady of the Lake University*), James M. Hutchisson (*The Citadel*), Ellen N. Moody (*George Mason University*), John David Moore (*Eastern Illinois University*), Tyler Smith (*Midlands Technical College*), Judith Corbin (*Eastern Illinois*), P. R. Dansby (*San Jacinto College*), Jim Dervin (*Winston-Salem State University*), Isabella DiBari (*Diablo Valley College*), Bruce Gans (*Wright College*), and Becky Roberts (*Mt. San Antonio College*). John Carroll (*California State University–Stanislaus*), William Davis (*College of Notre Dame of Maryland*), Glenn Hutchinson

(*University of North Carolina–Charlotte*), Homer Kemp (*Tennessee Technological University*), Lisa Ray (*Thomas Nelson Community College*), Ronn Silverstein (*Florida International University*), and Roberta Stagnaro (*San Diego State University*).

For this edition I am grateful for the valuable suggestions of Leisa Belleau (*University of Southern Indiana*), Sheryl Chisamore (*SUNY Ulster Community College*), and Lynn Severson (*Bismarck State College*).

At Cengage Wadsworth, I thank Mary Beth Walden, who oversaw the editing of the book, gave me valuable insights, and kept me on schedule. I would also like to thank Michael Rosenberg, publisher, and Sini Sivaraman, production project manager, who helped produce this book.

Finally, I am deeply grateful to my family for the support and encouragement they always give me.

INTRODUCTION

Literature is all around us. We find it in school courses, where we study masterpieces of the past. We run into it in drugstores, where best sellers occupy long ranks of shelves. We experience it in the poetry slams of coffee houses and night spots. The devices of literature show up in popular media. Hip-hop music incorporates its rhythms and rhymes. Movies and television shows co-opt its mythic stories and characters. Web sites reinvent its plot strategies. Artists enhance its psychological explorations with powerful visuals. Politicians clothe themselves in its images of authority. Every day, even when we aren't aware of it, literature gives our lives zest and imparts its wisdom.

Like all art, literature gives pleasure. Its magic transports us from the "real" world to remote and enjoyable places. We can experience this quality without thinking about it. But literature also poses intellectual challenges that do demand thought. For most readers, grappling with these challenges enhances the pleasure of literature. By studying literature, we "see" more of it to appreciate. We learn that, far from being remote from life, literature often reflects the real world and helps us locate our places in it.

This book addresses two questions: (1) How can we read literature? and (2) How can we write about it? These questions are interrelated. We have to read literature skillfully to write about it. In turn, writing about it increases our understanding of it.

There are many ways to read and write about literature. This book focuses on one way—interpretation. *Interpretation* is the act of making sense of something, of establishing its meaning. When we interpret literature, we explore its meaning. To do this well, we employ strategies of discovery, analysis, and reasoning. Exploring those strategies—for reading and writing—is the subject of this book.

Part One of the book takes up the first question, how to read. Chapter 1 discusses the nature and location of "meaning" in literature and follows up with strategies for interpreting literature. The rest of Part One concentrates on "places" to look for meaning: the properties of literature itself (Chapter 2) and of fiction (Chapter 3), drama (Chapter 4), and poetry (Chapter 5). Chapter 6, the concluding chapter of Part One, examines specialized strategies of interpretation, each of which illuminates potential sources of meaning.

Part Two considers the question of how to write about "meanings" in literature. Its organization tracks the process many writers follow: inventing (deciding what to write about), drafting (writing first drafts), revising (writing more drafts), and editing (producing a final draft for "publication"). Throughout Part Two, and most notably in the final chapter, samples of student writing illustrate interpretative writing.

Although each part of the book follows an orderly path—a step-by-step process for reading and writing—you can also use the book as a handbook. Part One covers such things as the elements of literature and of genres (fiction, drama, and poetry), as well as theoretical approaches such as historicism, formalism, structuralism, poststructuralism, new historicism, and feminist and gender criticism. Part Two gives information about such things as generating topics, organizing essays, using logic, doing research, documenting sources, handling quotations, and taking tests. The location of all of this material is easy to find, especially when you use the Index of Concepts and Terms located at the back of the book. If you do not remember where a definition or explanation is, just look it up in the Glossary and in that index.

We begin, then, with reading.

PART ONE

Interpreting Literature

Strategies for Interpreting Literature

WHY DO PEOPLE READ LITERATURE?

We read literature for pleasure and for meaning—because it is fun and because it speaks to us about important things.

Reading for fun.   When we read purely for pleasure, we do not usually care what the work means. We just want to escape from the concerns of the day and let the work perform its magic on us. You may remember your first great reading experience, when you were so caught up in a work that you were oblivious to everything else. Reading just for pleasure is like that. We sit down with a book and say to ourselves, "I don't want to think. I just want to enjoy."

Reading for meaning.   But on a more thoughtful level, reading for pleasure and reading for meaning are related. Part of the pleasure of reading comes from the meanings it gives us. On first reading a novel by Raymond Chandler,* the American author who helped invent the hard-boiled detective novel, we may be gripped by the suspenseful plot. We eagerly turn pages just to find out what will

*Dates of authors' lives and publication dates of works cited in this book can be found in the author-title index at the back of the book.

happen next. But upon rereading the novel, and especially reading other works by Chandler—like *The Big Sleep* (1939), *Farewell, My Lovely* (1940), and *The Long Goodbye* (1954) —we discover a thematic and artistic richness we may not have noticed before: how he uses conventions of the detective story—wise guy dialogue, intrigue, suspense, urban settings, stereotypical characters, a melancholy hero— to render a moral dimension to his fictional world. We notice his poetic language, his mastery of tone, his insights about American cities and obsessions, about high life and low life, wealth and poverty, and innocence and crime. As we continue to read Chandler, we move from one level of enjoyment—reading for "escape"—to another—reading for meaning. Or, put another way, we read not just for pleasure and meaning but for pleasure *because* of meaning.

WHAT IS MEANING?

In this book we will explore how to uncover possible meanings in works of literature and how to write about them. What is "meaning" and where do you find it in works of literature? The *Oxford English Dictionary* defines *meaning* as 1) the "sense or signification of a word, sentence, etc." and as 2) the "significance, purpose, underlying truth, etc., of something." Taken together, these definitions suggest three levels of meaning in works of literature. All are related to one another and are intertwined.

The Language and Details of a Work

The first level is the most basic "meaning" in literature: understanding the words and sentences of the text and, by extension, all the details that allow you to know who is who, what's going on, and where and when the action takes place.

For some works, this is easy; the words, sentences, and details are accessible and understandable. But for other works, getting the words and facts straight may not be so simple. The poetry of seventeenth-century authors like John Donne and George Herbert is notoriously dense and requires close study to understand. Modernist and Post-Modernist authors such as T. S. Eliot, Virginia Woolf, James Joyce, Thomas Pynchon, and Toni Morrison employ innovative techniques that obscure the details of their works. The language of Chaucer and Shakespeare is not quite our language. To understand it we have to rely on glosses (definitions) that editors often place at the bottom of the page. In short, we sometimes have to work hard—to look up words, unscramble twisted sentences, reread—just to recognize the facts of literary works.

The Larger Parts of a Work

A second level of meaning is ideas that emerge from connections among the larger parts of the work. These "parts" are the nuts and bolts of literature. They exist in and among literary conventions like characterization, plot, setting, word sounds, metaphor, symbol, allusion, and irony. The difference between this level of meaning and the first is that instead of just understanding the language and getting the facts straight you are developing ideas about how larger aspects of the work make sense and how they relate to one another.

Francine Prose, the contemporary American fiction writer, gives an example of this kind of meaning in *Reading Like a Writer* (2006), her guide to reading and writing fiction:

> When I was a high school junior, our English teacher assigned a term paper on the theme of blindness in *Oedipus Rex* and *King Lear*. We were supposed to go through the two tragedies and circle every reference to eyes, light, darkness, and vision, then draw some conclusion on which we would base our final essay.
>
> It all seemed so dull, so mechanical. We felt we were way beyond it. Without this tedious, time-consuming exercise, all of us knew that blindness played a starring role in both dramas.
>
> Still, we liked our English teacher, and we wanted to please him. And searching for every relevant word turned out to have an enjoyable treasure-hunt aspect, a *Where's Waldo?* detective thriller. Once we started looking for eyes, we found them everywhere, glinting at us, winking from every page.
>
> Long before the blinding of Oedipus or Gloucester, the language of vision and its opposite was preparing us, consciously or unconsciously, for those violent mutilations. It asked us to consider what it meant to be clear-sighted or obtuse, shortsighted or prescient, to heed the signs and warnings, to see or deny what was right in front of one's eyes. Teiresias, Oedipus, Goneril, Kent—all of them could be defined by the sincerity or falseness with which they mused or ranted on the subject of literal or metaphorical blindness.
>
> It was fun to trace those patterns and to make those connections. It was like cracking a code that the playwright had embedded in the text, a riddle that existed just for me to decipher. I felt as if I were engaged

in some intimate communication with the writer, as if the ghosts of Sophocles and Shakespeare had been waiting patiently all those centuries for a bookish sixteen-year-old to come along and find them (4–5).

In this example, the "part" is the numerous references to seeing and blindness that thread through the two works. Other examples arise from questions like these: Why do characters do what they do? How does one event in the distant past influence events in the present? Why do characters love or hate a particular place? What effect does a condition (wealth, poverty, war, heavy responsibility, parenthood, peer pressure) have on characters? What causes characters to fail or succeed? Why does a particular image or idea keep appearing?

All of the student essays printed in this book raise questions such as these about aspects of works of literature. The answers the writers give establish meanings in the works. The students' answers are not definitive. Other readers, including yourself, may have other answers, answers that are possibly more convincing. But the students' answers mark a "conversation" between the work and writer that we, as readers of the works and the essays, can join. The essays appear in the following chapters: on Homer's *Odyssey* (Chapter 8), on Frost's "The Death of the Hired Man" (Chapter 10), on Shelley's *Frankenstein* (Chapter 11), on Lawrence's "The Rocking-Horse Winner" (Chapter 12), on Robinson's "Richard Cory" (Chapter 13), on Poe's "The Cask of Amontillado" (Chapter 13), on Glaspell's *Trifles* (Chapter 13), and on Eliot's *Adam Bede* (Chapter 13).

The Work and the World Outside the Work

The first two levels of meaning have to do with meaning within the work. In contrast, the third level of meaning connects the work—either in part or as a whole—the work and the world outside the work.

This level of meaning can occur in at least two ways. First, the work mirrors (reflects) aspects of the outside world. Say, for example, you have worked as a line cook. If you see that a novel you are reading accurately depicts what it's like to be a line cook, then the novel is meaningful to you because it does. People often read works of literature, especially novels, for just this kind of meaning. Rohinton Mistry's novel *A Fine Balance* (1995) teaches us about poverty in modern-day India. Louise Erdrich's *Love Medicine* (1993) tells us about life on Native American reservations. Naguib Mahfouz's

Palace Walk (1956) reflects Muslim life in Egypt. Anzia Yezierska's *Bread Givers* (1925) teaches us about Jewish life on the Lower-East Side of Manhattan. O. E. Rölvaag's *Giants in the Earth* (1924) makes us feel what it was like to be a pioneer farmer on the American prairie. Other examples of this kind of mirroring are accurate portrayals of psychological states, family situations, historical events and characters, and the workings of institutions.

A second way that works of literature connect to the outside world is through themes. *Themes* are the ideas works express—or seem to express—about "reality," about our world. Sometimes themes can be stated simply and directly, as in the "morals" attached to the ends of Aesop's fables: "Better no rule than cruel rule" (25), "Union gives strength" (87), "The gods help them that help themselves" (98). But the themes of most works of literature are too complex to be stated so concisely and neatly. An example of a work that states a theme fairly clearly and directly is Shakespeare's Sonnet 116 (printed in full on p. 153). The sonnet seems to answer the question, what is love? But the sonnet doesn't explicitly say what love is. It speaks in metaphors. It isn't hard to figure out what the metaphors mean, but the sonnet is like most works of literature. It conveys themes indirectly.

You can locate possible themes in several places. Sometimes narrators or speakers say things that can be taken as themes, as does the speaker of Sonnet 116. Sometimes characters, especially the ones we admire (or the author favors), will do the same. Another place to look is in topics of works; that is, what they are about. You can be pretty sure that if authors make their topics obvious, then they have something to say about them. Sometimes authors announce their topics in places like titles and chapter headings: *Pride and Prejudice* (1813, Jane Austen), *Great Expectations* (1860–61, Charles Dickens), *War and Peace* (1865–69, Leo Tolstoy), *Crime and Punishment* (1866, Fyodor Dostoevsky), *Things Fall Apart* (1958, Chinua Achebe), *Atonement* (2001, Ian McEwan), *The Outsiders* (1967, S. E. Hinton), *The Unbearable Lightness of Being* (1984, Milan Kundera). Other works, even though they may not have give-away titles, are clearly "about" certain issues. Margaret Edson's play *Wit* (1999) is about coping with cancer. Mark Haddon's novel *The Curious Incident of the Dog in the Night-Time* (2003) is about autism. Margaret Atwood's novel *The Handmaid's Tale* (1985) is about societies that oppress women. All of these works may be about other things as well, but these topics are so obviously present that they are likely places to find themes.

How do we discover meaning in works of literature? We do so through interpretation.

WHAT IS INTERPRETATION?

Definition. *Interpretation* is a process. It is the process of examining the details of works of literature in order to make sense of them, to explore their meanings. John Ellis, the literary theorist, describes the goals and process of interpretation in this way: interpretation "is a hypothesis about the most general organization and coherence of all the elements that form a literary text." This "organization and coherence" emerges from a "synthesis" between a work's themes and its details. "The most satisfying interpretation," he says, "will be that which is the most inclusive. The procedure of investigation will be that of any inquiry: a continual move between general notions of the coherence of the text, and consideration of the function within the whole of particular parts of it. General conceptions will change in the light of particular observations, and new particular observations will then become necessary in the light of the changed conceptions" (202).

Interpretation as process. Ellis is saying here that as we read a work for the first time, we encounter details of a work and develop hunches about how they relate to one another, what they mean. As we continue to read, we encounter more details. These may confirm our hunches or cause us to replace them with new ones. Once we have finished reading the work, we review and study the work to decide which hypotheses (hunches) are best supported by the most details. Those hypotheses, Ellis says, constitute the best interpretations. Interpretation, in other words, is a quest for meanings manifested by a work's details. To be believable, **interpretations must emerge from the details of the work**. If we encounter details that contradict our interpretations, we must adjust the interpretations to accommodate those details.

Interpretation is something we do with more than just literature. It is an unavoidable process in any thinking person's life: Why is Miriam angry with me? Why did Jonathan go to pieces when he took the test? Would this job be better for me than that one? How will my blowup with Lucy affect our relationship? Is the defendant guilty? Should the federal government rescue failing banks? What were the causes of World War II? Do human beings have free will?

Answering questions like these, from the trivial to the profound, requires interpretation.

A crime scene, for example, demands a similar interpretive process as a work of literature. You, the detective, have just arrived at the scene of the crime. As you examine the details of the scene, you formulate hypotheses about what happened and who is responsible. With the discovery of new evidence, you adjust your hypotheses until, having sifted through all the evidence, you decide who committed the crime. A key difference between crime scenes and works of literature, however, is that literature has authors. Criminals may be "authors" of a sort; they create the crime scene, but they do not want us to know what they have done. Authors, in contrast, want to reach us.

The communication process.   The following diagram represents this process of communication:

Authors want to say something. They express these things in works of literature. They "send" the works to us, their readers. We read ("receive") the works.

As receivers, our challenge is to make sense of what the authors send us. But this challenge is complicated by the nature of literature. Instead of just telling us what they want to say, authors use "literary" devices—metaphor, symbol, plot, connotation, rhyme, meter, and so forth—to convey their ideas. Such devices communicate meaning indirectly. They force us to figure out authors' ideas. It is as if an author says to us, "I want to state my ideas about something, but instead of saying them straight out, I will tell a story and let you figure out what I'm trying to say." Or the author says, "The woman I'm in love with is wonderful, but instead of telling you directly how this is so, I'm going to say, 'My love is like a red, red rose.'" Or the author will hide behind a narrator or speaker (a persona) who may not speak for the author, whose ideas and personality may be different from the author's. Or authors may not be fully conscious of meanings that emerge in their work. As a result, these meanings might be underdeveloped, even contradictory. Most authors impose the task of "figuring out" on us, the readers. Such a task requires interpretation. The craft of interpreting literature is called *literary criticism.* Anyone who interprets literature is a literary critic.

HOW DO WE INTERPRET?

Interpretation of works of literature is the process of thinking about their details in order to see how the details interconnect and what ideas they might convey. Interpretation requires us to read actively rather than passively. When we read purely for fun, we are "passive," letting the work wash over us, not trying to figure it out. But when we interpret, we pay close attention to the potential meaning of details. We might even imagine the author as a wily rascal who uses literary devices to manipulate our emotions and our beliefs. Do we agree with the ideas authors foist on us? Should we resist them? How should we respond to a work that is entertaining and well done but whose ideas seem reprehensible?

The following are suggestions about how to be active, interpreting readers.

1. **Get the facts straight.** As we say above, understanding the language and details of a work is the most basic level of meaning in works of literature. Recognizing and understanding the *facts* of a work is the fundamental first step in interpreting anything. When we read, we should look up words we do not know. We should track down allusions (references to myths, religious texts, historical and biographical events, other works of literature). We should read carefully and more than once.

2. **Connect the work with yourself.** For each of us, the most important meanings of works of literature will arise from our own experience and beliefs. No matter how great and famous and revered a work may be, unless we can connect it to our own experiences and interests, it will not live for us.

   Use the "connection" strategy to project yourself into works of literature, especially ones that at first seem foreign to you. Ask questions like these: "How would I live under these circumstances?" "What would I do if I were a character in the work facing the same pressures and choices?" "What limitations or freedoms exist for these characters that do or do not exist for me?" "Which characters do I admire?" "Which ones make me uncomfortable?" "Can I identify with the setting of the action, with where and when it occurs?"

   The writings of the New England Puritans, for example, may seem remote and forbidding. But imagine yourself in the Puritan world. Capture its connection to your life. How would you think and feel had you lived then—about your family, the wilderness around you, the difficulty of scraping out a living, the harsh winters, the imperatives of your religion? What would your psychological state—emotional conflicts and tensions—have been? Authors like Nathaniel Hawthorne (in his novel *The Scarlet Letter,* 1850); Arthur Miller (in his play *The Crucible,* 1954); and Maryse Condé (in her novel *I, Tituba, Black Witch of Salem,* 1986) have done just this—projected themselves into Puritan culture and produced intriguing rethinkings of it.

3. **Develop hypotheses as you read.** As John Ellis says in the passage on page 8, when we read works of literature, even for the first time, we generate ideas about them. The "hypothesis" strategy makes this action intentional and constant. As you read, raise questions about what the details mean: Why does a particular character act the way she does? What ideas does a character espouse? Why does the author keep using a particular image? rhyme scheme? metrical pattern? As you read, do not feel that you have to give final answers to these questions. Plan to come back to them later. Such questions and tentative answers get us thinking, help us pick up important details that pop up later, and make reviewing the work easier.

4. **Write as you read.** Writing generates ideas and helps you think creatively. By putting concepts in your own words, you make them your own and embed them in your memory. If you own copies of works of literature, write in them: underline passages, circle words, draw arrows from one passage to another. In the margins, write questions, summaries, definitions, topics that the author addresses, and tentative interpretations. If something is repeated in a work, note where it first appears (for example, "see page 123") and make comparisons later. Such notations help you generate ideas about what you are reading. Your markings are huge timesavers when you review the work for tests and writing projects. They show you where key phrases and events are, without your having to reread or search through the work.

5. **Reread the work.** Once you have read the whole work, go back over it—review it, read it again, study it. Now you can consider the choices the author has made. Authors always select what goes into works and what they leave out. Especially important is the way authors end works. Up to the ending, a work can typically take several paths. Authors choose their endings and thus

signal their ideas about what the parts of the work add up to, what they mean. What endings, then, might have been possible? How apt does the chosen ending seem to you? Why do you think the author chose it? In addition to the ending, what other choices has the author made that seem significant or intriguing?

6. **Talk back to the work.** Peter Barry suggests that readers should "enter into a kind of dialogue" with works they read. Reading, he says, can be "a form of conversation between reader and writer" (35). This doesn't mean you can say anything you want about what the author may have meant. The "conversation," Barry says, "is initiated, and largely directed, by the author" (35–36). But you can express your opinions about aspects of a work and choices authors make. Is one section especially poignant or plea-surable? Then, say so—in your head or with a written note. Is the writing confusing? Is a character especially creepy or unconvinc-ing? Is the plot too predictable? Is it pleasurably suspenseful? Talking and writing back engages you with the techniques and thus the possible meanings of the work.

7. **Learn from the interpretations of others.** Although we read alone, interpretation is most fruitful as a shared activity, some-thing we do with others. Knowing what others think helps us decide what we think. One critic claimed that even blurbs on book jackets helped him get his bearings in a work. By learning from the insights and knowledge of others, we place ourselves in a dialogue with them. We listen, agree, disagree, share, and thereby clarify what we believe. Interpretations by professional critics are readily available in books and articles. Equally stim-ulating are the ideas of people we know—friends, classmates, teachers, colleagues. These people are often nearby, ready to share what they think. When teachers talk about works in class, mark the passages they discuss and make notes about what they say.

8. **Analyze works of literature.** We say above that the "larger parts" of works of literature convey meaning. They are the most obvi-ous and immediately accessible aspects of work, especially when we read it for the first time. Understanding what the parts are and how they work, then, provides a gateway to the meanings of the work. Analysis is the way to gain this understanding.

To *analyze* is to examine the "parts" of something and discover the relationships among them. Analysis is a powerful, necessary strategy for generating and communicating interpretations of any-thing, not just literature. If you sell computers, you will do it better if you analyze them—know how they work and what they can do, thus what they "mean" (how they can help your customers). The same is true for interpreting literature. Being able to analyze litera-ture helps us see how each "part" can generate meaning and how it contributes to the meanings of the whole work.

In the next chapter, we will consider the "parts" of literature itself and how they help us interpret.

Checklist for Interpreting Literature

- Understand the language and details of the work. Clarify any confusion about what goes on in the work.

- Use your imagination to relate the work to your experiences.

- As you read, develop hunches (hypotheses) about mean-ings in the work.

- If you own the work, mark in it (underline, draw arrows, etc.) and write comments in the margin to help you gen-erate ideas and remember key passages when you review the work.

- Engage in a "conversation" with the work. Feel free to talk back to it, to challenge and disagree with choices the author has made.

- Review or, even better, reread the work.

- Seek out ideas of others—critics, teachers, and other students. Compare your ideas with theirs.

Works Cited

Aesop's Fables: Selected and Told Anew by Joseph Jacobs. Illus. David Levine. New York: Capricorn Press, 1984. Print.

Barry, Peter. *English in Practice: In Pursuit of English Studies*. London: Arnold, 2003. Print

Ellis, John. *The Theory of Literary Criticism: A Logical Analysis*. Berkeley: U of California P, 1974. Print.

"Meaning." *Oxford English Dictionary. OED Online.* Library, University of North Carolina, Greensboro. 2009. Web. 2 June 2009.

Prose, Francine. *Reading Like a Writer: A Guide for People Who Love Books and for Those Who Want to Write Them.* New York: HarperCollins, 2006. Print.

2

What Is Literature?

Is a Batman comic book "literature"? What about a physics textbook? a restaurant menu? a university catalog? a television sitcom? a political speech? the letters we write home?

   Back in about the middle of the twentieth century, critics thought they knew what literature was and thus the answer to such questions. The so-called New Critics, who flourished in the United States from the 1920s until the 1960s, believed that literature had certain properties that experts trained in the writing and studying of literature could identify—such things as imagery, metaphor, meter, rhyme, irony, and plot. The New Critics confidently identified and evaluated works of literature, elevating the "great" works of literature to high status. Literature for them consisted, with but few exceptions, of poetry, drama, and fiction and would definitely *not* have included the kinds of writing listed in the paragraph above.

Problems with older definitions.   Beginning in the 1960s, however, critics questioned the concept of literature expounded by the New Critics. The New Critics, they noted, seemed narrow in policing the literary *canon*—that unofficial collection of works that critics deem worthy of admiration and study. The New Critics were mostly male and interested mainly in Western literature and culture, and the works they admired were written for the most part by males who wrote within the European literary tradition. Largely excluded from the canon were works by females, persons of color, and persons who lived outside Europe. Excluded, also, were the genres (kinds) of "literature" that such outsiders preferred. Because women often lacked access to the means of publishing, many wrote in genres that would not normally be published: letters, diaries, journals, memoirs, autobiographies. Why, critics asked, were these genres not "literature"? Because people of color were often politically active, they wrote in genres that furthered political ends: speeches, autobiographies, essays. Why were these not thought of as "literature"? And because some people belonged to "traditional" cultures, their works were often meant to be spoken, not written. Were these works not "literature"?

Recent definitions.   As a result of such questions and the emergence of new theories about language, critics wrestled anew with the question, "What is literature?" At stake were a number of related issues: Which works would get published? Which works were available—in textbooks and paperbacks—to be taught? If we compare textbook anthologies of English and American literature published circa 1960 with those published today, we can see that the canon now embraces a much broader variety of authors, works, and genres.

Such a comparison reveals how much the concept of "literature" has changed in the past fifty years. Some theorists have challenged even the concept of literature. John Ellis argues that literature is not definable by properties, such as rhyme, meter, plot, setting, and characterization. "Nonliterary" works often have such properties—advertisements, the lyrics to popular songs, jokes, graffiti. Rather, the definition of literature is like that of weeds. Just as weeds are "plants we do not wish to cultivate" (38), so literature is identifiable by how people use it. People use works of literature not for utilitarian purposes—to get something done—but as objects of enjoyment in themselves. Ellis says that a work becomes literature when it is no longer "specifically relevant to the immediate context of its origin" (44). If a physics textbook is no longer read for information about physics but instead is read for some other reason—say, the elegance of its prose style—then it transcends the "immediate context of its origin" and becomes literature.

Terry Eagleton, another contemporary critic, claims that literature is a social construct; that is, that the concept of "literature" is created by society: "Literature, in the sense of a set of works of assured and unalterable value, distinguished by certain shared inherent properties, does not exist" (11). Literature—and the literary "canon"—are constructs, established by society: "Anything can be literature, and anything which is regarded as unalterably and unquestionably literature—Shakespeare, for example—can cease to be literature" (10).

Ellis and Eagleton represent a skeptical reaction to the categorical pronouncements of the New Critics, whose definitions excluded many works we value today. Nonetheless, as interpreters of literature, it is helpful for us to know about properties traditionally identified with literature. Not every work may contain all of these, but most will have one or more of them. The value for us as interpreters is that these characteristics are "places" to look for meaning in literature.

LITERATURE IS LANGUAGE

The word *literature* has traditionally meant written—as opposed to spoken—works. But today, given the broadened meaning of the word, it includes oral as well as written works. The works of Homer (c. 800 BCE) emerged from an oral tradition. The author "Homer," whether a single individual or a group of people, may even have been illiterate and spoken his works to a scribe, who wrote them down. What Homer and other oral storytellers have in common with writers is language. The medium of literature, whether oral or written, is language. This raises questions about the "literariness" of media that rely heavily on other means of communication: film, dance, physical theater (mime, slapstick, farce), graphic (pictorial) narrative, musical plays. Most critics believe that language is a key aspect of literature and that there has to be enough language in a work for it to be considered literature.

Denotation and connotation.   Some theorists claim that authors of literature use language in special ways. One of those ways, according to René Wellek, is an emphasis on connotative rather than denotative meanings of words. Scientists, for example, use language for its *denotative* value, its ability to provide signs (words) that mean one thing only. For scientists, the thing the sign represents—the *referent*—is more important than the sign itself. Any sign will do, as long as it represents the referent clearly and exactly (11). Because emotions render meanings imprecise, scientists strive to use signs that eliminate the emotional, the irrational, the subjective. Writers of literature, in contrast, use language *connotatively*—to bring into play all the emotional associations words may have.

Connotation is the meaning that words have in addition to their explicit referents. An example of connotation is the word *mother*, whose denotation is simply "female parent" but whose connotations include such qualities as protection, warmth, unqualified love, tenderness, devotion, mercy, intercession, home, childhood, the happy past. Even scientific language becomes connotative once it enters everyday speech. When we see Albert Einstein's equation $E = mc^2$, we no longer think just of "Energy equals mass times the speed of light squared" but of mushroom clouds and ruined cities. Or the term *DNA*, which denotes the genetic code of life, connotes the alteration of species or the freeing of innocent people from death row. Some kinds of literature (poetry, for example) rely more heavily on connotation than others. Realistic novels, in contrast, may contain precise denotative descriptions of physical objects. Most authors of literature are sensitive to the emotional nuances of words.

Defamiliarization. The Russian Formalists, a group of theorists who flourished in the Soviet Union in the 1920s, claimed another use of language as a defining quality of literature. The key to literature, they said, is "literary" language, language that calls attention to itself as different from ordinary, everyday language. The term for this quality, invented by Viktor Shklovsky, is *defamiliarization* (literally, "making strange"). "The technique of art," he said, "is to make objects 'unfamiliar,' to make forms difficult, to increase the difficulty and length of perception, because the process of perception is an aesthetic end in itself and must be prolonged" (quoted in Selden 31). Shklovsky's idea of defamiliarization can apply not just to language but other aspects of literary form—plot, for example, or techniques of drama.

The principle of defamiliarization is to *foreground*—give prominence to—something in the work of literature that departs from everyday use or familiar artistic conventions. When authors foreground language, they in effect say, "Hey! Look at my language! See how different it is from ordinary language!" They focus on language for itself. They are fascinated by its sounds, its rhythms, even its appearance on the page. Sometimes they become so interested in these qualities that they subordinate meaning to them.

Some nursery rhymes, for example, exhibit a delight in language that virtually eliminates meaning, like this one, "Swan":

> Swan, swan, over the sea:
> Swim, swan, swim!
> Swan, swan, back again;
> Well swum, swan!

Here, the anonymous author revels in the repetition of sounds that key off the word *swan*. People who use language in everyday, non-literary speech and writing also show sensitivity to its sounds and subjective qualities, but writers of literature exploit these qualities more fully, more consciously, and more systematically.

QUESTIONS

Language is one of the "places" we can look for meaning in literature. Be alert to how writers convey ideas in their subtle and complex language.

1. How does an author use language to signal ideas?

2. What seems significant about such things as the author's choice of words *(diction)*, ways of constructing sentences *(syntax)*, word sounds, repetitions of key words and phrases, archaisms of diction or syntax (as in language that echoes the King James Bible or Shakespeare)?

3. Does an author's use of language—prose or poetic style—seem unique; that is, so striking that no other author writes that way?

NOW IT'S YOUR TURN

Compare the language of "The Cask of Amontillado" and either "Yours" or "Hills Like White Elephants," all short stories printed in the Appendix. What are the differences? Are there similarities? Is the language fitting for each story? Some works have a distinctive style of language. An example is A. A. Milne's Winnie the Pooh stories (1926–28), whose humor emerges partly from the way Milne uses language. Characterize the style of one of these stories or of another work you know well.

LITERATURE IS FICTIONAL

We commonly use the term *fiction* to describe prose works that tell a story about events that never happened in real life (for example, fairy tales, short stories, and novels). In fact, however, many works of literature are "fictional" in the sense that something in them lets readers know that they are different from real life.

Invented material. A work can be fictional in two ways. First, authors make up—imagine—some or all of the material. This property explains why literature is often referred to as "imaginative literature"; it features invented material that does not exist in the real world. In fantasy fiction, for example, human beings fly, perform magic, remain young, travel through time, metamorphose, and live happily ever after. But even historical fiction, which relies on actual events, is fictional. It includes characters, dialogue, events, and settings that never existed. The three main characters of Hilary Mantel's 1992 novel *A Place of Greater Safety*—Camille Desmoulins, Maximilien Robespierre, and Georges-Jacques Danton—were real people. But the author, while following the outline of their participation in the French Revolution, makes up much of what they do and say.

Stylized material. Second, the fictionality of literature lies also in the artistic control the writer exercises over the work. This artistic control has the effect of stylizing the materials of the work and thus setting it apart from the real. This effect occurs even when the material does accurately mirror the facts of real life or when it states ideas that can be verified in actual experience. Such works would include autobiographies like those by Benjamin Franklin and Frederick Douglass and "true crime" narratives like Truman Capote's *In Cold Blood* (1966) and Norman Mailer's *The Executioner's Song* (1979).

Compare, for example, how a newspaper reporter and a poet would describe the same event. Assume that both would describe the event accurately. The reporter would make his or her account correspond as exactly as possible to the event. Just like the poet, the reporter "controls" his or her account by arranging events in order, by choosing apt words, by leaving out details. There is an art to what the reporter does. But the reporter wants us to experience the details of the event, not the report of it. The poet, in contrast, makes his or her *poem* the object of experience. Through the play of language, selection of details, inclusion of metaphor, irony, and imagery, the poet makes the work an artifact, an object of enjoyment and contemplation in itself.

Consider Walt Whitman's "Cavalry Crossing a Ford" a poetic account of an event he no doubt witnessed during the American Civil War:

CAVALRY CROSSING A FORD

Walt Whitman

A line in long array where they wind betwixt green islands,
They take a serpentine course, their arms flash in the sun—hark
    to the musical clank,
Behold the silvery river, in it the splashing horses loitering stop
    to drink,
Behold the brown-faced men, each group, each person a picture,
    the negligent rest on the saddles,
Some emerge on the opposite bank, others are just entering the
    ford—while,
Scarlet and blue and snowy white,
The guidon flags flutter gayly in the wind.   1867

Although there are no end rhymes or regular metrical patterns in this poem—it is free verse—readers sense, even if they are not sure why, that this is a work of literature. The way it looks—lines separated, not run together, as they would be in prose—signal its difference from utilitarian writing. Also, such devices as unusual word choice ("array," "betwixt," "behold," "guidon"), alliteration ("flags flutter"), repeated vowel sounds ("silvery river," "horses loitering"), repeated phrases ("Behold the silvery river," "Behold the brown-faced men"), and colorful imagery ("Scarlet and blue and snowy white") call attention to *how* Whitman describes the event, to the poem itself. In this way, the work becomes "fictional." It transcends the event described. Long after people have forgotten the event, they will take pleasure in the poem.

Stylized nonfiction. Even works that are not supposedly fictional, that purport to be about real people and events, become "fictional" by means of literary devices. Two well-known autobiographical examples are Henry David Thoreau's *Walden* (1854) and Richard Wright's *Black Boy* (1945). Thoreau really did live in a cabin at Walden Pond (in Concord, Massachusetts), and we can be fairly sure the events he records in *Walden* did happen. But Thoreau does so many "literary" things with those events that he causes us to conceive of them in aesthetic and thematic terms. His prose style is highly stylized and "poetic." He emphasizes his own feelings. He collapses the two years he actually spent at Walden into one year, and organizes that year around the four seasons of the year, thus giving the book a kind of "plot." He retells events to illustrate philosophical themes. The text is heavily metaphoric and symbolic.

As with Thoreau, Richard Wright records events that actually happened to him growing up in Arkansas and Chicago. But here, too, the author employs "literary" devices to make these events vivid. He conveys his intense feelings through first person narration. His language is charged with emotion. He constructs "novelistic" scenes that have extensive dialogue and minute descriptions of physical actions and details. These scenes are almost certainly "fictional," because it is unlikely the author could have remembered the exact words these people said and the physical details he records. We can believe the scenes happened, but Wright fills in details to give them aesthetic impact.

The fictional quality of literature, then, is a second "place" to look for meaning in literature. The fantasy element in literature is fun in itself, but fiction grants authors the option to fill in gaps that always exist in historical events, to make connections that historians cannot. The stylized quality of literature often underscores ideas. Whitman's "Cavalry Crossing a Ford" conveys the impression of lightheartedness, vigor, and gaiety, largely through his selection of details of color, sound, and light.

QUESTIONS

1. What seems "fictional" about the work, whether imagined or stylized?
2. What ideas do those qualities suggest?

NOW IT'S YOUR TURN

Three famous nonfiction works that deal with the Holocaust are Primo Levi's *Survival in Auschwitz* (1958), Anne Frank's *Diary of a Young Girl* (Definitive Edition, 1995), and Thomas Keneally's *Schindler's List* (1982). They all present facts but are stylized in various ways. Explore how this is true in one or more of them. Or do the same with another work or works—newspaper reports, feature articles in newspapers and magazines, memoirs, accounts of historical events, and so forth.

LITERATURE IS TRUE

Factual accuracy. Even though works of literature are "fictional," they have the capacity for being "true." This paradox creates one of the most pleasurable tensions in literature: its imaginative and stylized properties (fictionality) against its representation of the human condition (truth). There are at least three ways that literature can be true. First, literature can be true to the facts of reality, as in descriptions of real people, places, and events—Napoleon's defeat at Waterloo, the operations of a coal mine, the building of the Brooklyn Bridge, the details of human anatomy, the biology of a forest.

Directly stated ideas. More important, literature can be true by communicating ideas about life. The model we presented in Chapter 1 is relevant here:

Authors have ideas they want to communicate to readers. They embed them in works of literature and "send" the works to readers. We can most readily spot this purpose when authors or their surrogates (narrators or characters who seem to speak for the authors) directly state their ideas, as in this poem, "My Friend, the Things That Do Attain," by Henry Howard, Earl of Surrey:

MY FRIEND, THE THINGS THAT DO ATTAIN

Henry Howard, Earl of Surrey

My friend, the things that do attain
The happy life be these, I find:
The riches left, not got with pain;
The fruitful ground; the quiet mind;

The equal friend; no grudge, no strife;
No charge of rule, nor governance;
Without disease, the healthy life;
The household of continuance;

> The mean° diet, no dainty fare;   *°simple*
> Wisdom joined with simpleness;
> The night discharged of all care,
> Where wine the wit may not oppress:
>
> The faithful wife, without debate°;   *°argument*
> Such sleeps as may beguile the night;
> Content thyself with thine estate,
> Neither wish death, nor fear his might.   1547

Here the poet tells us straight out his ideas about how to live the "happy life." Even when authors employ obvious elements of fantasy, they can state their ideas directly. Aesop's animal characters are like no animals in real life: They reason, talk, and act like human beings. But the author uses these fantastic characters to state "morals," shrewd commentaries on the human experience.

Indirectly stated ideas. More typically, however, authors refrain from directly stating their ideas. Instead, they present them indirectly by means of literary conventions such as plot, metaphor, symbol, irony, musical language, and suspense. All the details of a work make up an imaginary "world" that is based on the author's ideas about the real world.

The world of George Orwell's *Nineteen Eighty-Four* (1948), for example, is filled with crumbling buildings, frightened people, children who betray their parents to the police, procedures whereby truth is systematically altered, masses of people trapped by their ignorance and selfishness, and officials who justify any deed to achieve power. It is a world without love, compassion, justice, joy, tradition, altruism, idealism, or hope. The facts of this world are patently imaginary—Orwell placed them in the future—but we infer from them that Orwell had a pessimistic view of human nature and human institutions. We sense that he is warning us: the terrible society in *Nineteen Eighty-Four* has already existed in places like Nazi Germany and Stalinist Russia and could spread to other places as well.

Typical characters, probable actions. Since most works of literature tell stories, two prominent conventions for communicating ideas are *typical characters* and *probable actions*. You may have heard the phrase "stranger than fiction," as if the characters and events in works of fiction are abnormal and bizarre. But, ironically, it is real life that gives us freakish events and inexplicable people.

In contrast, authors impose order on the chaos of real life. To do this, they present characters who typify real people, and they recount actions that would probably happen in real life. J. R. R. Tolkien, for example, offers an array of fantasy creatures and kingdoms in *The Hobbit* (1937) and its sequel, *The Lord of the Rings* (1954–55). Yet his characters, whatever they may look like, represent recognizable types of people. The protagonists, Bilbo and Frodo Baggins, for example, typify those gentle, kindly people who would prefer to live in domestic obscurity but who instead play heroic roles in cataclysmic dramas. And the way they behave is probable because it fits the types of people they are. They do not suddenly become supermen with supernatural powers. Like average people, they are vulnerable to superior strength and to their own fears. They succeed because they exhibit the strengths of average people: perseverance, shrewdness, unselfishness, courage, and honesty.

Allegory.   So prominent in literature are typical characters and probable actions that most works of literature are to some extent allegorical. *Allegory* is a kind of literature in which concrete things—characters, events, and objects—represent ideas. Here is a very short allegory:

> Fear knocked at the door.
> Faith answered.
> There was no one there.

In this story, the character "Fear" stands for the idea of fear, and the character "Faith" is equivalent to the idea of faith. The setting of the story is a house, which symbolizes our psychological selves. Fear's knocking at the door shows an emotion that everyone experiences. Faith's opening the door shows a possible response to fear. The "moral" of the story, implied in the conclusion, is that we should all have faith because faith makes fear disappear.

   In longer allegories, such as John Bunyan's *Pilgrim's Progress* (1678), Edmund Spenser's *The Faerie Queen* (1590–96), the anonymous medieval play *Everyman* (c.1485), and Norton Juster's *The Phantom Tollbooth* (1961), the characters, places, and events are more complexly developed but nonetheless, as in this allegory, have names that directly indicate the ideas they represent. But even in works that are not blatantly allegorical, the characters, locations, and events are so typical and probable, that they could almost be given names to represent ideas: Hamlet could be named "Melancholy,"

Othello could be called "Jealousy," Ophelia "Innocence," Romeo "Love Sickness," Iago "Sinisterness," and so forth. We can infer the worldviews represented in works by their "allegorical" qualities—typical characters, suggestive places, and probable actions.

Literature as expression. The near-allegorical quality of literature underscores its expressiveness. Literature is always an expression of the individuals who compose it. Their personalities, emotions, styles, tastes, and beliefs are bound up in their works. As interpreters, our task is to determine objectively what the ideas of a given work may be. We do not, however, have to agree with them. Orwell's worldview is very different from Tolkien's. Orwell shows an average man rebelling against political oppression but failing miserably to do anything about it. He is weak, ineffectual, and controlled by forces outside himself. In Orwell's world, good loses because people are too stupid or greedy or weak to overcome evil. Like Orwell, Tolkien also shows the weakness of average people, but in his worldview, the average person is innately good and potentially strong. Such individuals can band together with others and overthrow evil. Orwell is pessimistic about human nature and the future of humanity; Tolkien is optimistic.

Literature as experiential. Still another kind of "truth" conveyed by literature is the experience of reality. Whatever the experience might be—white-water rafting, losing a loved one, falling in love, going hungry, overcoming a handicap, coming of age—authors put us in the midst of it, make us feel it. Such feelings can teach us about experiences we have never gone through.

Scientists, for example, do not often write novels about their research, but one who did was Björn Kurtén, the Swedish paleontologist. His novel *Dance of the Tiger: A Novel of the Ice Age* (1980) features the interaction of *Homo sapiens* and Neanderthal peoples during the Ice Age. Kurtén has published many scholarly books on Ice Age peoples. "Why," he asks in his preface, "write a novel about prehistoric man?"

> In the last three decades, it has been my privilege to be immersed in the life of the Ice Age. More and more, I have felt there is much to be told that simply cannot be formulated in scientific reports. How did it feel to live then? How did the world look to you? What were your beliefs? Above all, what was it like to meet humans not of your own species? That is an experience denied to us, for we are all Homo sapiens (xxiii).

In his novel, Kurtén brings Ice Age people to life. Through the thoughts, conflicts, and daily activities of his characters, we *feel* what it was like to live 35,000 years ago.

Another example is Jessamyn West's novel *The Massacre at Fall Creek* (1975). In the afterword she says she was intrigued by an event that occurred in Indiana in 1824. A white judge and jury convicted four white men of killing Indians, and the men were hanged. Although this event marked the first time in United States history that white men convicted other white men for killing Indians, West could find little information about it. She wondered: What was it like to be convicted for something previously condoned? How did the Indians and whites feel about the event? West's novel is her answer to these questions. Drawing upon her understanding of what most people would go through under those circumstances, she shows us what they *probably* experienced. Furthermore, she causes us to *feel* what they experienced. We live through the gruesome killings. We share the fear of Indian reprisal. We see the callousness of Indian killers. We experience the dawning consciousness of some whites that Indians are human and have rights. We suffer the alienation caused by taking unpopular moral stands. We inhale the circus-like atmosphere of the hangings. With the judge, we puzzle over ambiguous ethical dilemmas. We stand on the scaffold with the condemned.

QUESTIONS

The truth of literature is the most important "place" to look for meaning in literature. The following questions encapsulate the points we have made here about truth in literature.

1. What ideas are directly stated—by characters, by narrators?

2. How are the characters typical of human behavior? What ideas do they espouse or seem to represent? Which characters—and thus the ideas associated with them—predominate at the end of the work?

3. What ideas are associated with places and other physical properties?

4. Authors sometimes signal ideas through devices like titles, names, and epigraphs. (An *epigraph* is a pertinent quotation put at the beginning of a work or chapter.) Examples of suggestive titles are *The Grapes of Wrath* (taken from a line in "The Battle Hymn of the Republic"), *All the King's Men* (from the nursery rhyme "Humpty-Dumpty"), *Pride*

and Prejudice, Great Expectations, and *Measure for Measure.* What ideas seem embedded in titles, chapter heads, epigraphs, names, and other direct indications of authors' ideas?

5. What do other works by the author suggest about possible meanings in this work?

6. As with Björn Kurtén and Jessamyn West (discussed above), authors sometimes comment on their own work. What light does such comment shed on ideas in the work?

7. What feelings does the work elicit in each of us? What do we experience in the work that we have never gone through? What have we experienced that the work brings powerfully to life?

NOW IT'S YOUR TURN

Numerous works of literature have been banned by institutions, schools, libraries, and governments. Such organizations have deemed the ideas or details of these works—the "truths" in them—to be dangerous. You can find titles of banned works and sometimes the works themselves on the Internet by searching your Web browser for "banned books." You will find the usual suspects, works like D. H. Lawrence's *Lady Chatterley's Lover* (1928), James Joyce's *Ulysses* (1922), Mark Twain's *Adventures of Huckleberry Finn* (1884). But you will also find "Little Red Riding Hood," the Bible, and more recently J. K. Rowling's Harry Potter series (1995–2007), Judy Blume's *Forever* (1975), Katherine Peterson's *Bridge to Tarabithia* (1977), Khaled Hosseini's *The Kite Runner* (2003), Madeleine L'Engle's *A Wrinkle in Time* (1962), S. E. Hinton's *The Outsiders* (1967), Martin Handford's *Where's Waldo?* (1987), and Philip Pullman's fantasy trilogy *His Dark Materials* (1995–2000). Two especially informative Web sites are published by the University of Pennsylvania (http://onlinebooks.library.upenn.edu/banned-books.html) and by the American Library Association ("http://www.ala.org/ala/issuesadvocacy"). These sites contain lists of banned works as well as information about them.

Use these or other resources to choose a banned work that interests you. Explain why, when, and by whom the work was banned. Describe the "truths" in it that caused its banning. Offer your opinion about how reasonable or unreasonable the banning was.

LITERATURE IS AESTHETIC

Order and form in literature. Literature is *aesthetic*; it gives pleasure. The aesthetic quality of literature—its "beauty"—is hard to define and describe. In a sense, it just *is*. Like various other art forms—music, patterns of color in paintings, photographs of sunsets, dance—literature is an end in itself.

The pleasure of literature rests in the way authors use literary conventions, such as metaphor, plot, symbolism, irony, suspense, and poetic language. Taken together, they constitute the *form* of the work, the order authors impose on their material. Such order is not typical of real life. In real life, events can be random, disconnected, and inconsequential. Problems can remain unresolved. The murderer may not be caught, the cruel parent may continue to be cruel, the economic crisis may persist, the poor but honest youth may not be rewarded. We cannot be aware of all the things that happen to us, much less remember them. Nor do we always know which events are important, which trivial. But literature can give order to events in the form of a *plot*. Unimportant events are excluded, cause-and-effect relationships established, conflicts resolved. Events are arranged in logical order so that they form a sequence with a beginning, a middle, and an end. Plot is but one of a multitude of ways that artists give order to material. They may also arrange language into patterns, reduce characters to recognizable types, connect details to ideas, elegantly describe settings. In works of literature, all of the elements combine to form an *overall* order, an *overall* coherence.

The aesthetic quality of literature is thus another "place" to look for meaning in literature. Experiencing the beauty of literature may itself be a kind of meaning. But the aesthetic qualities of literature are bound up with the other kind of meaning, the ideas conveyed by a work. Authors use pleasurable conventions to enhance and communicate ideas.

QUESTIONS

1. What conventions (of language, plot, characterization, etc.) does the author use to give us pleasure?

2. Why does the author's manipulation of these conventions affect us so strongly?

3. How does the author use pleasurable conventions to communicate ideas and make them appealing?

NOW IT'S YOUR TURN

Choose one of your favorite works of literature. Identify the aesthetic qualities in it that you find especially appealing. Explain why you like this work so much.

LITERATURE IS INTERTEXTUAL

Genre. Literature is intertextual: It relates to other works of literature, it incorporates established literary conventions, and it belongs to at least one genre of literature. Genre is a French word that means "type" or "kind." Literary genres are identifiable by their literary conventions. Conventions are features of literature, whether of language, subject matter, themes, or form, that readers can easily recognize.

Consider the intertextualityof these two poems. The second, by Sir Walter Raleigh, is a response to the first, by Christopher Marlowe.

THE PASSIONATE SHEPHERD TO HIS LOVE

Come live with me and be my love,
And we will all the pleasures prove
That valleys, groves, hills, and fields,
Woods, or steepy mountain yields.

And we will sit upon the rocks,
Seeing the shepherds feed their flocks,
By shallow rivers to whose falls
Melodious birds sing madrigals.

And I will make thee beds of roses
And a thousand fragrant posies,
A cap of flowers, and a kirtle
Embroidered all with leaves of myrtle;

A gown made of the finest wool
Which from our pretty lambs we pull;
Fair lined slippers for the cold,
With buckles of the purest gold;

THE NYMPH'S REPLY TO THE SHEPHERD

If all the world and love were young,
And truth in every shepherd's tongue,
These pretty pleasures might me move
To live with thee and be thy love.

Time drives the flocks from field to fold
When rivers rage and rocks grow cold,
And Philomel becometh dumb;
The rest complains of cares to come.

The flowers do fade, and wanton fields
To wayward winter reckoning yields;
A honey tongue, a heart of gall,
Is fancy's spring, but sorrow's fall.

Thy gowns, thy shoes, thy beds of roses,
Thy cap, thy kirtle, and thy posies
Soon break, soon wither, soon forgotten—
In folly ripe, in reason rotten.

A belt of straw and ivy buds,
With coral clasps and amber studs:
And if these pleasures may thee move,
Come live with me, and be my love.

The shepherds' swains shall dance and sing
For thy delight each May morning:
If these delights thy mind may move,
Then live with me and be my love.

—*Christopher Marlowe, 1600*

Thy belt of straw and ivy buds,
Thy coral clasps and amber studs,
All these in me no means can move
To come to thee and be thy love.

But could youth last and love still breed,
Had joys no date nor age no need,
Then these delights my mind might move
To live with thee and be thy love.

—*Sir Walter Raleigh, c. 1600*

These poems are intertextual in the three ways mentioned above. First, Raleigh's poem is an almost line-for-line response to Marlowe's. We can understand Marlowe's poem without knowing Raleigh's, but we would miss a lot in Raleigh's poem if we did not know Marlowe's. Second, Marlowe's poem belongs to a genre called pastoral poetry. Third, Marlowe incorporated the conventions of the pastoral genre: a peaceful, simple rural setting; carefree shepherds (the word *pastor* means "shepherd"); a season of eternal spring; an absence of the difficulties of life—hard work, disease, harsh weather, betrayal; lovers who talk genially about love; and a playful, witty, charming poetic style. Raleigh knows the conventions of pastoral poetry so well that he can challenge their basic assumptions. These two poems are more specifically contrasted in the following questions.

QUESTIONS

The intertextuality of literature is a rich source of meaning for the interpretation of individual works. We can pose questions that help us mine this meaning.

1. **What can we learn about a work by considering works related to it?** Authors often have specific works of literature in mind when they compose their own. Sometimes they signal this by means of *allusions:* explicit references to other works. Such allusions are always invitations to compare the author's work with the other works. Dante, for example, by featuring the Latin poet Virgil as a prominent character in *The Divine Comedy*, signals that Virgil's writings and especially *The Aeneid* were significant for his work.

    Another example is Marisha Pessl's novel *Special Topics in Calamity Physics* (2006). The narrator and putative author, Blue Van Meer, is a senior in a private high school. The novel is intensely intertextual. The author casts the novel in the form of a very familiar genre, the detective story. The "mystery," announced at the beginning, is, Who murdered Blue's teacher and mentor, Hannah Schneider? Not only does the narrator constantly refer to cultural events, pop stars, movies, and works of literature, the title of each chapter is a famous literary work followed by its author's name. As we read, we see that the content of each chapter is linked to the titles. The narrator/author challenges us to figure out what the connections are. Why, we wonder, does she do this? Does the intertextuality mean anything? We are led to think that, yes, it does. But what?

Sometimes authors make no overt references to other works, but we infer from the work itself or learn from outside sources, that the author drew from other works. We know, for example, that Dostoevsky was influenced by the works of Charles Dickens, but he does not necessarily say so in his novels. Whether or not authors tell us what other works serve as their reference points, we can ask what ideas and artistic devices from these other works are applicable to the work under study. Raleigh, in "The Nymph's Reply to the Shepherd," openly invites us to compare his poem to Marlowe's. When we do, we see the stark difference between his ideas and Marlowe's.

2. **Can we understand the genre in which the work is written?** Genres are indispensable for both writers and readers of literature. Alastair Fowler, in his comprehensive treatment of genre, *Kinds of Literature: An Introduction to the Theory of Genres and Modes* (1982), says that genres are similar to language. The conventions of each genre constitute a "grammar" that allows us to "read" the genre and works written in it (20). Just as we must learn the structure of a language in order to read it, so must we learn the conventions of genres in order to read literature.

People learn popular genres as they grow up—by being read to, watching television, going to movies. But some genres require special training to understand. One reason is that genres are products of particular cultures and times. We can read narrative fiction, for example, because we know its conventions. But a culture could conceivably have no tradition of fiction. If so, its members would find fiction baffling, just as people brought up in the Western tradition usually find Japanese Noh plays and Kabuki theater puzzling. Another reason is that genres change over time or cease to exist. We may encounter genres even in our own language that puzzle us because we do not know them. To read some works of literature, we have to *recover* their genres. Pastoral poetry, a genre that was enormously popular in Christopher Marlowe's day, is virtually dead as a genre today. To recover it, we can read other poems in the pastoral tradition. And we can refer to historical works, such as M. H. Abrams and Geoffrey Galt Harpham's excellent *A Glossary of Literary Terms* (2009) for information about pastoral poetry and other unfamiliar genres.

3. **What values does the genre convey?** Genres are cultural phenomena. In contrast to individual works, they emerge from many authors and reflect the interests, ways of life, and values of particular cultures.

Detective fiction, for example, became a recognizable genre in the nineteenth century. Critics contend that its conventions mirror the values, troubles, and circumstances of Western culture in the nineteenth century. The detective hero, for example—Edgar Allan Poe's Dupin, Arthur Conan Doyle's Sherlock Holmes—represented Western culture's enormous respect for science. These detectives are dispassionate, analytical, and brilliant. Holmes, in fact, publishes treatises on forensic science. The setting of detective fiction was typically the great industrial cities, which were by-products of nineteenth-century capitalism. These cities, with their mazelike streets and heterogeneous populations, were perfect environments for intrigue and crime. Dupin works in Paris, Holmes in London. The crime was almost always murder or threat of murder. The pursuit and punishment of the murderer upheld the nineteenth century's respect for the individual. The murderer destroys the individual's most valuable possession, life itself. But the murderer destroys more than just lives. At stake also were the institutions held dear in the nineteenth century—the family, religious communities, boards of trade, governmental agencies, universities. The detective, by capturing the murderer, purges these institutions of those who would corrupt and destroy them.

Other genres reflect their own cultural contexts. The epic trumpets heroic deeds and national solidarity. The medieval romance inculcates a code of chivalry. Why, then, did the author choose to compose in this genre? What ideas associated with the genre carry over to this work?

4. **Why is or was the genre appealing?** It is a cold, rainy night. You are home, and on vacation. Everyone else in the house has gone to bed. You have been saving Stephen King's latest gothic thriller for just such a time. Perfect. You settle in for two hours of uninterrupted escape. The book, of course, need not be horror. It could be science fiction, romance, western, detective, adventure, spy, thriller. Maybe you do not care who the author is. You just picked the book off the shelf because it belongs to a genre you like.

When we do this—read something because it is a *kind* of literature—we have succumbed to the pleasures of genre. The reasons we like certain genres are part of the "meaning" of what we read—the pleasures the genres give as well as the ideas they convey. We can pinpoint that meaning by investigating the appeal of genres. Why do we and other people like them?

The same question applies to genres from the past. We can discern meanings authors may have intended by asking why people liked the genres in which the authors wrote. Authors and readers of pastoral poetry during Christopher Marlowe's time lived in the city. They liked pastoral poetry because the fantasy of an idealized rural life, with pretty scenes, images, and language, allowed them to escape the grimy, dangerous, and changing cities where they lived.

5. **How does the author challenge or change the genre?** Before authors can compose a work of literature, they have to know its genre well. But when they compose, they almost always rebel against generic formulas. Alistair Fowler describes the process in this way: The "writer who cares most about originality has the keenest interest in genre. Only by knowing the beaten track, after all, can he be sure of leaving it" (32). Because authors and readers hunger for innovation, every literary work, Fowler says, "changes the genre it relates to." Consequently, "all genres are continuously undergoing metamorphosis. This, indeed, is the principal way in which literature itself changes" (23). An example of a recent "new" genre is "magic realism," a form of fiction that has been popularized by Latin American authors such as Gabriel García Márquez (*One Hundred Years of Solitude*, 1970), Isabel Allende (*The House of the Spirits*, 1985), and Laura Esquivel (*Like Water for Chocolate*, 1992). Combining the characteristics of two genres—realistic fiction and fairy tale—these authors couch trenchant political and social criticism within the delights of erotic romance and supernatural happenings.

Most authors alter the formulas of genres on purpose. What shifts in values and aesthetic effects do these changes indicate? Raleigh, by having his female character challenge Marlowe's shepherd by referring to the harsh realities of life, cleverly changes the pastoral genre into a new genre, one we might call the antipastoral. He criticizes not only the ideas that undergird pastoral poetry but the pastoral genre itself.

6. **How do individual conventions of a genre add meaning to a work?** Alistair Fowler says that the framework of all literary genres is three huge, amorphous categories: fiction, drama, and poetry (5). Within these genres are numerous subgenres. *Subgenres*, Fowler says,

"have the common features of a kind—external forms and all—and, over and above these, add special substantive features" (112). Pastoral poetry, for example, has the overall characteristics of "poetry" but, as we have noted above, has other characteristics that make it a distinctive subgenre of poetry.

Our assumption in the next three chapters is that authors deliberately choose the genres in which they write. We will examine how the conventions of genres work and how they communicate ideas. Like the properties of literature discussed in this chapter—language, fictionality, truth, aesthetics, and intertextuality—each literary convention is a "place" to look for meaning in works of literature.

Now It's Your Turn

Describe the conventions of a popular genre of literature that interests you. Explain why you think so many people like it. Identify the audience for this genre (the people who like it the best). Explain how recent authors have challenged and altered the conventions of the genre. Speculate about where you think this genre is going, what it might be like in the future.

An example of a long-standing very popular genre of fiction is the vampire story. The first published literary version of this story was Heinrich August Ossenfelder's poem The Vampire (1748). (Folklore about vampires had existed for hundreds of years prior to this work.) The work that set the conventions of the story for modern times was Bram Stoker's *Dracula* (1897). Anne Rice's Vampire Chronicles series (1976–2003) rejuvenated and began to change the genre. John Ajvide Lindqvist's *Let the Right One In* (2004) and Stephenie Meyer's *Twilight* (2005) and its sequels have altered the genre further, introducing the vampire love story and "good" vampires. As with any popular genre, we can ask: What is the appeal of this genre? What are its conventions? What conventions have changed? Which ones remain the same?

Checklist for the Elements of Literature

- Note the qualities of language that make the work you're studying "literary." (Literature is language, pages 17–19.)

- Spot the ways in which the author uses invented materials. (Literature is fictional, page 20.)

- Explore how the author stylizes the work to make it seem "fictional." (Literature is fictional, pages 20–23.)

- Underline those places where narrators or characters state ideas directly. (Literature is true, pages 23–24.)

- Explore how the work might be allegorical—how characters, actions, and physical details embody ideas. (Literature is true, pages 25–26.)

- Explain how the characters are typical or atypical of real human beings. (Literature is true, pages 24–25.)

- Show how the events and actions of characters are probable or improbable. (Literature is true, pages 24–25.)

- Indicate how the work makes you experience its subject matter. (Literature is true, pages 26–27.)

- Explain how the work gives you pleasure. If it does not, say why. (Literature is aesthetic, pages 29–30.)

- Compare works that are alluded to in the work or that are similar to it. (Literature is intertextual, pages 30–35.)

- Identify the genre of the work. (Literature is intertextual, pages 30–35.)

- Note how the work abides by and departs from the conventions of the genre. (Literature is intertextual, pages 30–35.)

- Speculate about why the author chose this genre to present the ideas of the work. (Literature is intertextual, pages 30–35.)

Works Cited

Abrams, M. H., and Geoffrey Galt Harpham. *A Glossary of Literary Terms*. 9th ed. Boston: Wadsworth Cengage Learning, 2009. Print.

Eagleton, Terry. *Literary Theory: An Introduction*. Minneapolis: U of Minnesota P, 1983. Print.

Ellis, John. *The Theory of Literary Criticism: A Logical Analysis*. Berkeley: U of California P, 1974. Print.

Fowler, Alastair. *An Introduction to the Theory of Genres and Modes*. Cambridge: Harvard UP, 1982. Print.

Kurtén, Björn. *Dance of the Tiger: A Novel of the Ice Age.* New York: Pantheon, 1980. Print.

Pessl, Marisha. *Special Topics in Calamity Physics.* New York: Penguin, 2006. Print.

Selden, Raman, and Peter Widdowson. *A Reader's Guide to Contemporary Literary Theory.* 3rd ed. Lexington: U of Kentucky P, 1993. Print.

Wellek, René, and Austin Warren. *Theory of Literature.* New York: Harcourt, 1942. Print.

West, Jessamyn. *The Massacre at Fall Creek.* New York: Harcourt, 1975. Print.

3

Interpreting Fiction

This chapter begins an analysis of the three major *genres* of literature: fiction, drama, and poetry. Our purpose in this and the next two chapters is to show how elements of the three very broad genres (kinds) of literature provide opportunities for interpretation. After the discussions of each element, you will find questions and suggestions for exploring on your own. In this chapter, we take up the most popular genre today, fiction.

THE ELEMENTS OF FICTION

Fiction belongs to a large category of communication called narrative. *Narrative* is the telling of a story, a recounting of events in time. The distinguishing characteristic of narrative is the presence of a teller, a narrator. The "teller" can be any medium through which a story is revealed. Images (films, cartoons, paintings), bodily movements (dance, mime), sounds (singing, musical instruments)—all of these tell stories. The kind of narrative most people associate with literature is fiction. In contrast to nonfiction narrative (biography, memoir, autobiography, history), *narrative fiction,* whether written in poetry or prose, features a telling of made-up events. We now take up those conventions and aspects—elements—that typify narrative fiction.

Theme

Definition. *Themes* are ideas about life outside the work—about the real world, our world—that we draw from works of literature— not just from fiction but from literature in all genres. The following discussion continues the treatment of *truth in literature* begun in Chapter 2. Here we offer guidelines for stating themes and strategies for identifying them.

Guidelines for stating and describing theme

1. **Subject and theme.** Although the terms *subject* and *theme* are often used interchangeably, they are different. The *subject* is what you or others think the work is about. You can state the subject in a word or phrase: "The subject of Shakespeare's Sonnet 116 is love." In contrast, theme is what the work *says* about the subject. Stating a theme requires a complete sentence, sometimes several sentences: "A theme of Sonnet 116 is, 'Love remains constant even when assaulted by tempestuous events or by time.'"

2. **Reference to reality outside the work.** A theme applies to the world outside the work. The claim, "Rapid change in Rip Van Winkle's environment threatens his identity," is thoughtful and interesting, but it does not state a theme. It applies only to something inside the work, in this case, the character Rip Van Winkle.

   Instead, state themes so they refer to reality outside the work: "Rip Van Winkle's experience shows that environment threatens the identity of *many people*." Like all claims about theme, this one seizes upon concrete situations within the work to make generalizations about reality outside the work. Literature thus becomes a form of "philosophy"—universal wisdom about the nature of the world.

3. **Theme as dilemma.** Themes may present intellectual dilemmas rather than "messages" that neatly solve the dilemmas. Robert Penn Warren's novel *All the King's Men* (1946),* for example, raises the problem of morality in politics. How, the novel seems to ask, can political leaders in a democratic society do good when citizens are apathetic and easily misled? The character who embodies this question is a well-meaning and gifted politician who uses corrupt and violent means to attain good ends. By telling

---

*Publication dates of works of literature cited in this book and dates of authors' lives can be found in the author-title index at the back of the book.

his story, Warren dramatizes the question. But he never really answers it. You cannot pull a neat moral out of the story of this character's rise and fall. Rather, to state the "theme" of this novel—or one theme—you need to summarize as accurately as you can the problem Warren presents in the way he presents it. You could explain how the problem is worked out in this one character's life, but you could not necessarily generalize from that to all people's lives. Or the generalization might be that politics is morally contradictory, never simply right or wrong.

4. **Multiple themes.** In many works, especially complex ones, there may be several, even contradictory themes. A subject of Tolstoy's *Anna Karenina* (1875–78) is sacred love versus profane love. But another, equally important subject is social entrapment. One theme of *Anna Karenina*, then, seems to be that people should not abandon "sacred" commitments, such as marriage and parenthood, for extramarital "loves," no matter how passionate and deeply felt they may be. This theme emerges from Anna's desertion of her husband and child for Count Vronsky. An alternate theme is that people, through little fault of their own, can become trapped in painful, long-lasting, and destructive relationships that they want desperately to escape. This theme emerges from Anna's marriage. When she was very young, Anna married an older man whom she now realizes is too petty, prim, and self-absorbed to satisfy her generous and passionate nature. So discordant is her relationship with her husband that it seems no less "immoral" than her affair with Vronsky. Tolstoy, in other words, draws complex, even contradictory lessons from Anna's adultery. She is not simply the sinful person, she is also the driven person. This combination of traits characterizes the condition of many people.

5. **A lack of themes.** Some works may seem to have no clear themes. They may display images, actions, atmosphere, and characters that have no apparent relationship to the world outside the works. Or their ideas may be incompletely developed. Don't feel, then, that you have to state themes in a work when you think they don't exist.

6. **A work's themes vs. our values.** When writing about a work's themes, our task is to represent them fairly—with well-supported explanations of what we think they are. To do this, however, is not the same as to agree with them. You are always free to disagree with authors' world views.

7. **Themes and the author.** Are the themes we detect in a literary work equivalent to the author's ideas? Wayne C. Booth says no, they are not the same. In *The Rhetoric of Fiction* (1961), he argues passionately for the existence of themes in works of literature. A work embodies a "value system which gives it its meaning" (112). The author's "voice," which establishes this value system, "is never really silenced. It is, in fact, one of the things we read fiction for" (60). But Booth makes a now well-known distinction between "real" authors and "implied" authors. He reasons that real authors are rhetoricians. They craft works of literature to persuade us of their values. In order to persuade, they project an idealized concept of themselves in each of their works. Booth calls this idealized author, manifested by the work, the *implied author*: "The 'implied author' chooses, consciously or unconsciously, what we read; we infer him as an ideal, literary, created version of the real man; he is the sum of his own choices" (73–75).

Booth seems to imply that we can set aside the real author and, instead, attribute the values of a work to an implied author, whose existence we glean from the work itself. The "Jane Austen" of her novels is not the real Jane Austen but the "implied" author, unique to each novel.

But we might counter Booth's argument by saying that the identity of any human being is multiple. We all play different roles in life. We are different as family members from how we are at school or work. When we make sales pitches or political speeches, we advance versions of ourselves that we hope will sit well with our audience. Why aren't these "selves" all real, all part of our identity? Why can't we assume that the "self" an author projects in a literary work is an aspect of the real author, just as the selves each one of us manifests in different situations is an aspect of our real selves?

Learning about authors' lives and concerns, furthermore, often provides insight into the meanings of their works. Sometimes authors even comment on their works. In a lecture at Hollins College, the American author Flannery O'Connor explained some of the ideas she had in mind when she wrote her short story "A Good Man Is Hard to Find" (1955). Her elucidation of this story is highly compelling. She added that "there are perhaps other ways than my own in which this story could be read, but none other by which it could have been written" (109). In other words, when we see connections between authors and their works, we don't lock out other interpretations. But we can at least see connections between ideas held by the real author and themes in the work.

QUESTIONS ABOUT THEME (STRATEGIES FOR IDENTIFYING THEMES)

Two broad questions about theme are: What subjects does the work address? What does the work seem to say about them—what are its themes? The following are some strategies for answering these questions:

1. **Comments made by narrators and characters.** Sometimes narrators and characters state one or more of a work's themes. In the final chapter of Hawthorne's *The Scarlet Letter* (1850), the narrator says, "Among many morals which press upon us from the poor minister's miserable experience, we put only this into a sentence: 'Be true! Be true! Be true! Show freely to the world, if not your worst, yet some trait whereby the worst may be inferred!'"

   How believable are such statements? If they square with the philosophical and moral concepts of the work, then you can claim them as compelling themes. If they are mouthed by untrustworthy speakers or are contradicted by evidence, they are questionable— that is, not supported—as themes. Further questions include: Do the narrator and characters state other possible themes? Do other aspects of the work suggest themes? Do any themes seem to contradict one another—as in Tolstoy's *Anna Karenina* mentioned above (see p. 41)?

2. **Areas of philosophical inquiry.** Philosophers and theologians have for generations raised questions about the human experience. You can seize upon these to interpret works of literature. Here are four rich areas of inquiry:

   Human nature. What image of humankind emerges from the work? Are people, for example, generally good? deeply flawed?

   The nature of society. Does the author portray a particular society or social scheme as life-enhancing or life-destroying? Are characters we care about in conflict with their society? Do they want to escape from it? What causes and perpetuates this society? If the society is flawed, how is it flawed?

   Human freedom. What control over their lives do the characters have? Do they make choices in complete freedom? Are they driven by forces beyond their control? Does Providence or some grand scheme govern history, or is history simply random and arbitrary?

Ethics. What are the moral conflicts in the work? Are they clear cut or ambiguous? That is, is it clear to us exactly what is right and exactly what is wrong? When moral conflicts are ambiguous in a work, right often opposes *right*, not wrong. What rights are in opposition to one another? If right opposes wrong, does right win in the end? To what extent are characters to blame for their actions?

3. **Moral center.** Another strategy for discovering a work's themes is to answer this question: Who, if anyone, serves as the *moral center* of the work? The *moral center* is the one person whom the author vests with right action and right thought (that is, what the *author* seems to think is right action and right thought), the one character who seems clearly "good" and who often serves to judge other characters.

Not every work has a moral center; but in the works that do, its center can lead you to some of the work's themes. In Dickens's *Great Expectations* (1860–61), for example, the moral center is Biddy, the girl who comes to Pip's sister's household as a servant. She is a touchstone of goodness for Pip. When he strays from the path of right conduct, Biddy and his remembrance of her helps bring him back to it. *Great Expectations* is largely about morality (subject). By studying Biddy we uncover some of Dickens's ideas about morality (theme).

When identifying a work's moral center, answer questions such as these: How can we tell that this person is the moral center? What values does the moral center embody? Is the moral center flawed in any way that might diminish his or her authority? What effect does the moral center have on the other characters and on us?

THINKING ON PAPER ABOUT THEME

List the subject or subjects of the work. For each subject, see if you can state a theme. Put a check next to the ones that seem most important.

1. Explain how the title, subtitle, epigraph, chapter titles, and names of characters may suggest themes.

2. Describe the work's depiction of human behavior.

3. Describe the work's depiction of society. Show its representation of social ills and how they might be corrected or addressed.

4. List moral issues raised by the work.

5. If a character seems to function as a moral center, list his or her traits.

6. Mark statements by the narrator or characters that seem to state themes.

NOW IT'S YOUR TURN

Explain one or more of the themes in Mary Robison's "Yours" (printed in the Appendix), "The Daemon Lover" (pages 155–56), or Frost's "The Death of the Hired Man" (printed in the Appendix).

Point of View

Definition. *Point of view* is the narrator's relationship to the world of the work. The term is a metaphor that indicates the location (point) from which the narrator sees (views) everything in the narrative. Another term that some critics prefer is *perspective.* Authors employ four basic points of view.

Third-person omniscient point of view. In the *third-person omniscient* position, a narrator from "outside" the story world tells the story. This point of view is "third person" because the narrator refers to all the characters in the third person, as "he" and "she." It is "omniscient" because the narrator assumes near complete knowledge of the characters' actions, thoughts, and locations. Omniscient narrators move at will between places, historical periods, and characters. They sometimes even speak directly to the reader. Needless to say, their godlike knowledge exceeds what any of us knows about the real world. It is as if the omniscient narrator hovers above the story world, seeing and hearing everything, including characters' thoughts. Many famous eighteenth- and nineteenth-century novels use an omniscient perspective. Examples are Hawthorne's *The Scarlet Letter* (1850), Hardy's *Tess of the D'Urbervilles* (1891), Fielding's *Tom Jones* (1749), and Eliot's *Adam Bede* (1859).

Third-person limited point of view. As with omniscient narrators, narrators of the *third-person limited point of view* refer to characters as "he" and "she," and still have more knowledge of the fictional world than we do of our worlds. But they restrict (limit) their perspective to the mind of one character. This character may be either a main or peripheral character. Names for this character are *central consciousness*, *reflector*, and *filter*. A plot device that often accompanies this point of view is the character's gradual discovery of some truth that climaxes with an epiphany. (See page 61 for an explanation of *epiphany*.) Examples of third-person limited perspective are Hawthorne's "Young Goodman Brown" (1835), Stephen Crane's "The Open Boat" (1898), and James Joyce's "Araby" (1914).

Sometimes the author restricts this point of view so severely that we see everything solely through the mind of a single character, like sunlight filtered through a stained glass window. Henry James experimented with such severe restrictions in his later fiction, as in "The Beast in the Jungle" (1903) and *The Ambassadors* (1903). Usually, however, the limited point of view is a mixture of omniscient and limited. In Jane Austen's *Pride and Prejudice* (1813), for example, the narrator manifests an omniscient perspective but, for the most part, gives us the thoughts of just one character, Elizabeth Bennet.

Third-person objective (dramatic) point of view. Narrators in the *objective point of view* refer to characters in the third person and display omniscient knowledge of places, times, and events. They do not, however, enter the minds of any character. We see the characters as we do people in real life or as we might observe them in a play (thus the term "dramatic"). We learn about them from what they say and do, how they look, and what other characters say about them. But we do not learn what they think unless they tell us. Examples are Ernest Hemingway's "Hills Like White Elephants" (1927) and "The Killers" (1927), Stephen Crane's "The Blue Hotel" (1899), and Shirley Jackson's "The Lottery" (1948).

First-person point of view. In the *first-person point of view*, one of the characters tells the story and uses the first-person pronoun, "I." In the third-person limited point of view, the narrator reveals anything about one character—even things characters may be dimly aware of. But here the narration is restricted to what one character *says* he or she observes. The narrator may be a major character located at the center of events or a minor character who observes the action from the sidelines. The character's narration may be about events that have recently occurred (Twain's *Huckleberry Finn* [1884], Fitzgerald's *The Great Gatsby* [1925]) or about events that happened well in the past (Dickens's *Great Expectations* [1860–61], Poe's "The Cask of Amontillado" [1846]). An unusual use of first-person point of view is the epistolary narrative, which reveals action through letters. (An *epistle* is a letter; *epistolary* means "written in letters.") Samuel Richardson's *Pamela* (1740–41), Henry James's "A Bundle of Letters" (1878), Choderlos de Laclos's *Dangerous Liaisons* (1782), and Alice Walker's *The Color Purple* (1982) are all epistolary narratives.

Tone. Tone is an aspect of point of view since it has a great deal to do with the narrator. *Tone* is the narrator's predominant attitude toward the subject, whether that subject is a place, event, character, or idea. The narrator conveys his or her attitude through the way narrative devices are handled, including choice of words. Sometimes the narrators state point blank how they feel about a subject; more often, the narrator's attitude is conveyed indirectly. Jack Burden, the narrator of Robert Penn Warren's *All the King's Men* (1946), maintains a flippant and cynical tone through most of the narration. Jake Barnes, the narrator of Hemingway's *The Sun Also Rises* (1926), manifests a stoical, hard-boiled tone. Dr. Watson, the narrator of the Sherlock Holmes stories, displays a bemused, surprised tone.

Multiple points of view. Authors sometimes include several points of view in the same work. Dickens in *Bleak House* (1852–53) shuttles back and forth between a first-person narrative and an omniscient narrative. We see that the first-person narrator has a more limited view of things than the omniscient narrator. Point of view here becomes a means of developing characters and of making points about the limits of human perception.

Reliability of narrators and centers of consciousness. Some narrators and *centers of consciousness* are more reliable than others. You can almost always trust omniscient narrators. But be suspicious of first-person narrators and characters who serve as centers of consciousness. These characters may distort what they tell us or observe. They may be self-deceived, or untruthful, or gullible, or mentally troubled, or limited in understanding (children, for example), or self-serving.

In *The Adventures of Huckleberry Finn* (1884), there is a marked difference between the narrator's (Huck's) naïve view of reality and the author's more sophisticated and realistic view. When Huck sees the Grangerford house, he says, "It was a mighty nice family, and a mighty nice house, too. I hadn't seen no house out in the country before that was so nice and had so much style." He proceeds to describe the interior with awe and reverence. Although Huck is impressed with the furnishings, Twain clearly is not. We recognize Twain's attitude from the details Huck provides: the unread books, the reproductions of sentimental paintings, the damaged imitation fruit, the crockery animals, the broken clock, the painted hearth, the tablecloth "made out of beautiful oilcloth," the piano "that had tin pans in it" (85–88). Huck also shows his admiration for Emmeline Grangerford's poetry by reproducing some of it to share with us (87–88). But we see, as Twain wants us to see, that the poetry is terrible.

Finally, Huck is awestruck by the family's aristocratic bearing: "Col. Grangerford was a gentleman, you see. He was a gentleman all over; and so was his family. He was well born. . . . He didn't have to tell anybody to mind their manners—everybody was always good mannered where he was" (89). Yet he fails to see, as Twain and we see, the ironic contrast between the family's good manners and its irrational and murderous feud with another family. Twain's handling of point of view in this novel helps develop both character and theme. By presenting Huck's credulous view of things, it develops Huck as an essentially naïve and innocent person. By ironically contrasting Twain's view to Huck's, it underscores the author's harsher and more pessimistic perception of "reality."

The student essay on Poe's "The Cask of Amontillado" (pages 402–407) explores another example of a possibly unreliable narrator. Do you agree with the author's assessment?

Narratees.   When we define *narrative* as a story told by a teller (narrator), we assume the existence of an audience—one or more people who listen to or read it. The term for this audience is *narratee(s)*. In first-person narratives, the audience may be specified. Chaucer's *The Canterbury Tales* (c. 1387) presents a motley collection of people who, while making the pilgrimage to Canterbury, tell one another tales. Marlow, the narrator of Joseph Conrad's *Heart of Darkness* (1902), tells his story to men sitting in a living room. The duke in Browning's "My Last Duchess" (pages 129–30) addresses an ambassador from another family. But often the narratee of first-person narratives is not specified. Who is Huck's audience (in Twain's *The Adventures of Huckleberry Finn*)? Huck has apparently written the story. To whom is he writing? Charlotte Brontë's narrator Jane Eyre addresses a narratee whom she calls "Reader." Whom does she have in mind? Why is she writing this story?

The identity, character traits, motives, and inclinations of the audience for first-person narratives often illuminates other elements in the story, especially the narrator. The narratee of Poe's "The Cask of Amontillado" (printed in the Appendix) is referred to only as "you" and is not identified or described. But, as the student essay on this story indicates (printed in chapter 13), speculating about who this person is and why Montresor tells him the story, leads to provocative ideas about Montresor and his expectations.

The narratee of third-person works is harder to discern. Third-person narrators may indicate, directly or indirectly, an audience—people, for example, who until now have been ignorant about certain experiences, such as slavery, apartheid, imprisonment, and warfare. The narrator may seem to have an identifiable audience in mind—people with specialized knowledge, with certain political views, with a particular social bias, with certain experiences. An example is the author of the Old English epic *Beowulf* (c. 750 CE), who assumes his audience is familiar with the history and legends of sixth-century Scandinavian tribes. The author seems also to assume that his audience includes Christians who would favorably compare their religion to that of the pagan characters.

Works may have multiple narratees. Folk epics like *Beowulf* and *The Odyssey* have at least three categories of narratee. One is the characters who listen to other characters tell stories. Another is the audience for the oral versions of the epics, before the epic was written down. A third is the audience for the written version. Speculation about the settings, occasions, and audiences of such narratives often throws light on possible meanings of the work.

Narrators and authors. Is a narrator of a work of fiction equivalent to the author? First-person narrators are clearly not the author. They may resemble the author, but they are nonetheless fictional. Otherwise the work would be nonfiction—a memoir or autobiography. More problematic are third-person narrators, especially omniscient narrators, who seem to have the same knowledge as authors. Suzanne Keen says that the "temptation with omniscient narrators is to equate them and their opinions with their creators, a move that is rarely justified and often misleading" (38). She argues that we should see *all* narrators, even ones that refer to themselves as the work's creator, as fictional. They are as much "characters" in the story as the other characters.

QUESTIONS ABOUT POINT OF VIEW

1. Why did the author choose the work's point of view? How would the story be changed or affected by a different point of view?

2. What effect does the point of view have on us? If, for example, the point of view is first person, how does this character (rather than another character) affect our reception of the story? How would the story be different if told by another character? If the point of view is objective (dramatic), what do we gain or lose by not being able to enter the characters' minds?

3. If the work includes more than one point of view, how are they different? Why does the author use each one?

4. How reliable is the narrator? If a narrator is unreliable, how can you tell what the truth is?

5. What do we learn about human perception from the author's handling of point of view? Henry James's third-person limited point of view, for example, often shows people to be blind to the needs and desires of other people and blind to their own nature as well.

6. Who is the narratee (listener or reader)? Is it one person or a group of people inside the story? What characterizes this audience? Why does the narrator tell the story to this audience? If the narratee is not inside the story, does the author or narrator seem to have a special audience in mind? What characterizes this audience?

THINKING ON PAPER ABOUT POINT OF VIEW

1. Identify the point of view of the narrative. Choose a character who is not the narrator, one who interests you. Explain how the narrative would be different if that character were the narrator.

2. Mark places where the narrator or central consciousness differs from our view of reality or fails to see important truths that we or other characters see.

3. Mark places that are particularly expressive of the narrator's tone. List the characteristics of tone.

NOW IT'S YOUR TURN

Explain what the point of view is in Mary Robison's "Yours" (printed in the Appendix). Explore how her choice and use of point of view affects other elements in the story—characters, actions, and themes.

Plot

Definition.   *Events* are things that happen in a narrative—actions, statements, thoughts, and feelings. In a general sense, the word *plot* means events of a narrative. When someone asks you to tell them the plot of a work, they usually want you to say what happened.

The terms *plot* and *story* are often used interchangeably in this general sense. But in literary studies the terms have more restrictive meanings. The critic and fiction writer E. M. Forster in *Aspects of the Novel* (1954) distinguishes between plot and story. A "story," he says, is "a narrative of events arranged in their time-sequence. A plot is also a narrative of events, the emphasis falling on causality. 'The king died and then the queen died' is a story. 'The king died, and then the queen died of grief' is a plot. The time-sequence is preserved, but the sense of causality overshadows it" (86).

Expanding on Forster's distinction, we propose two concepts of events in fictional narratives: plot and story.

1. **Plot.** *Plot* consists of three things. First, it is the work itself, the author's arrangement of events from the first page to the last. By reading the work, we experience the events as the author has arranged them. Second, plot includes the linkage of events by cause and effect. This is Forster's concept of plot. An inevitable by-product of cause and effect is conflict—between characters, between characters and their environments, inside the minds of characters. Third, plot is the author's presentation of events so as to engage readers intellectually and emotionally. Authors do this through such devices as pacing, intense conflict, surprise, rising action, climax, withheld information, and foreshadowing of later events.

2. **Story.** The *story* is all the events we encounter in the narrative, arranged in the order of their occurrence. Again, this is Forster's concept of story. Sometimes the arrangement of events in the plot and story are the same. We read the events in chronological order. Usually, however, authors arrange events out of chronological sequence. We learn about past and future events by means of *flashbacks* and *flash-forwards*. We cannot assemble the events into their chronological order until we have read the plot. And usually we cannot see patterns of cause and effect or, at least, speculate about them until we understand the chronological sequence of events.

A classic example of the difference between plot and story is the detective narrative. First we read the work, the events as the author gives them to us: A murder occurs; a detective uncovers clues; the detective investigates suspects; puzzling events occur; the murderer is exposed; finally, the detective reveals the causes of the murder. As we read, flashbacks inform us of events preceding the murder. The author employs suspense and mystery to keep us turning the pages. Having read the work, we can now place everything that happens in the narrative—the "story"—into chronological order. Once we have done that, we can establish the chain of causes and effects that leads up to the murder.

Numerous theorists of narrative treat the function of events in fiction. Two clearly presented discussions are Suzanne Keen's *Narrative Form* (2003, 73–77) and the entry under "plot" in Ross Murfin and Supryia Ray's *The Bedford Glossary of Critical and Literary Terms* (286–88).

Plot patterns

A traditional pattern. Although authors arrange events into many patterns, a traditional and well-known pattern is illustrated by the *Freytag pyramid:*

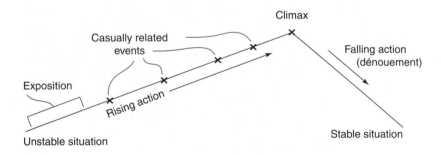

This diagram was developed by the German critic Gustav Freytag in 1863 to illustrate a typical five-act tragedy (114–5). But it applies to many, perhaps most, works of fiction.

At the beginning of this pattern is an *unstable situation,* a conflict that sets the plot in motion. The narrator's *exposition* here explains the nature of the conflict. He or she introduces the characters, describes the setting, and provides historical background. The narrator next introduces a series of *events,* all related by cause. One event may cause another event, which in turn causes another event, which causes the next event (husband gets angry with wife, who gets angry with kids, who get angry with dog, who sulks in the basement). Or several events may be linked to the same cause (a series of deaths at the beach, all caused by a monstrous shark).

Whatever the causal relationship among events, each event intensifies the conflict so that the plot "rises" toward a *climax*.

The climax is the most intense event in the narrative. The rest of the story—the *falling action*—is usually brief. It contains events that are much less intense than the climax and that lead toward the resolution of the conflict and toward a *stable situation* at the end. Another term for falling action is *dénouement*, a French word meaning "unraveling."

An example of the Freytag pyramid is the stereotypical fairy tale in which the youngest son must seek his fortune (unstable situation: He has no source of income, no home). He goes into a far country whose king is offering a prize, the hand of his daughter, to anyone who can accomplish three tasks. The hero completes all three (rising action and climax: Each task is increasingly difficult, but the third is a humdinger and is therefore the climax). The remaining part of the story may contain obstacles, but they are easily overcome. The king praises the hero but does not want his daughter to marry a commoner. The hero reveals that he is not, as he seems, a mere peasant but the son of a nobleman (falling action/dénouement: The conflicts now are minor and easily resolved). The hero marries the princess and lives happily ever after (stable situation: The hero has eliminated the initial conflict; he now has a wife, a source of income, and a home).

Other plot patterns.   Other plot patterns are possible. A work might have muted conflicts and so many digressions that it seems only to meander toward an understated climax. Or the work may be open-ended and thus have unresolved conflicts and no climax. Or the work may have multiple plots, some of which may be left unresolved. A famous example of a meandering, open-ended novel is the English author Laurence Sterne's *Tristram Shandy*. Sterne published this multivolume novel over a number of years (1759–1767) and died before he brought it to closure.

Multiple plot lines.   A narrative may have more than one plot line. A *plot line* is a single chain of events linked by cause and effect. In the detective narrative, the events that cause the murder constitute one plot line. But another one might be the love relationship between the detective and another character. The events leading up to the outcome of their relationship make up a second plot line that may or may not intersect with the murder plot line. If the murderer threatens the detective's love interest, or if the love interest helps capture the murderer, or if the love interest is the murderer, then the two plot lines are related. Our task as interpreters is to discern the various plot lines and explain how they relate.

Beginnings and endings

Beginnings. The plot and the story, as we have said, are different. Sometimes the plot follows the chronological order of the story. In that case, the beginning of the plot is the same as the beginning of the story. But often the plot starts with a later event. Only after reading for a while do you learn when the sequence of events that constitute the story begins. An often cited example is the *in medias res* (in the middle of things) device of epics like *The Odyssey* (c. 800 BCE), *The Iliad* (c. 800 BCE), and *The Aeneid* (29–19 BCE). In *The Odyssey*, the plot begins with Athena's plea to Zeus to allow Odysseus to go home. Calypso has been keeping him on her island against his will. This is the unstable situation that opens the plot, the last bit of unfinished business of the Trojan War. But the story of *The Odyssey* begins ten years before this, when Odysseus and his countrymen leave Troy. We don't learn about these events until later, when Odysseus recounts them. After Odysseus tells his tale, the author returns us to the present.

It sometimes requires interpretation to establish the beginning of a plot, the key event that sets in motion the chain of causes and effects that constitute the plot. When does the plot of *The Odyssey* really begin? When Odysseus and his men set sail from Troy? When they incur the wrath of powerful gods? During the war? A certain or fairly certain answer to such a question may not be clear.

Endings. Endings propel us to read narratives. We want to know how they will end. The plot of a narrative is like a pathway that constantly branches in two or more directions. As we read, we know those branches are there. We read on because we want to see which ones authors will take. This is especially true toward the end. As we read, we intuit the different ways the plot can end. We resist certain endings—the hero's defeat, the hero and heroine's permanent separation, the innocent child's death. But since *we* can't end the narrative, we keep reading to see what the author will do.

Authors choose endings. By so doing, they signal ideas about their narratives. Studying the endings of narratives helps uncover those ideas. To do this, think of other ways the author might have ended the narrative. Why didn't the author choose any of those? Some endings may not feel right to you. In the nineteenth century, readers expected novelists to provide happy endings. Sometimes these endings seem forced, given the causes and effects of the plot. Charles Dickens, for example, wrote two endings for *Great Expectations* (1860–61). In the ending he wrote first, Pip and Estella part, never to marry. But upon the insistence of a friend, Dickens provided a "happy" ending—the one published at the time—in which Pip and Estella will marry. Now we have both endings. Which is better? How does each ending influence our interpretations of the novel? Jane Austen provides a happy ending to *Pride and Prejudice* (1813), Elizabeth's marriage to Darcy. But what if Elizabeth had not married him? How would that unhappy and perhaps more realistic ending color our understanding of the novel?

Usually the plot and story of a narrative conclude at the same time. But sometimes the conclusion is open-ended: the conflicts of the plot are left unresolved. This time, you really are left on your own. You have to provide your own ending.

Internal and external conflict. Conflict is an essential element of plot. Without conflict we would not want to keep reading. The greater the conflict, the more intense our desire to know what happens next.

There are two general categories of conflict: external and internal. *Internal conflicts* take place within the minds of characters. An example is the good person who wrestles inwardly with temptation. *External conflicts* take place between individuals or between individuals and the world external to individuals (the forces of nature, human-created objects, and environments). The climactic shootout in an American western is an example of a physical, external conflict. But not all external conflicts are physical or violent. A verbal disagreement between two people is also an external conflict.

Protagonist and antagonist. The forces in a conflict are usually embodied by characters, the most relevant being the protagonist and the antagonist. The term *protagonist* usually means "main character," but think of the protagonist also as someone who fights *for* something. The *antagonist* is the opponent of the protagonist; the antagonist is usually a person, but can also be a nonhuman force or even an aspect of the protagonist—his or her tendency toward evil and self-destruction, for example. Although a protagonist sometimes fights for evil—Macbeth, for example—we usually empathize with the protagonist and find the antagonist unsympathetic.

Embedded stories and frame stories. *Embedded stories* are narratives that appear within the work and that digress from the main plot line—or seem to. Typically the main narration stops while a character tells a story, sometimes a long story. When you come across these, you might wonder, Why doesn't the author get on with it? Why do I have to read this "extra" story? Near the beginning of *The Odyssey*, for example, Odysseus escapes to the kingdom of Phaeacia. While there he tells a whopper of a story. This long embedded story—actually, a series of stories—recounts Odysseus's adventures since he left Troy ten years before. Other works that feature embedded stories are the Old English epic *Beowulf* (c. 750), Cervantes's *Don Quixote* (1605, 1615), Madame de Lafayette's *The Princesse de Clèves* (1678), and Herman Melville's *Moby-Dick* (1851).

Embedded stories may seem irrelevant, but in these works and many others, they serve important functions: They can reveal information about the past. They can predict the future. They can provide valuable information about characters and settings. They can parallel events and characters in the main plot. They can establish themes. Take, for example, the embedded stories in *Beowulf*. The main plot of *Beowulf* is straightforward: the hero fights three monsters: Grendel, Grendel's mother, and a dragon. But woven into this plot are embedded stories about Scandinavian history. When we take the trouble to understand these stories, *Beowulf* becomes a richer, more interesting work. The apparently simple tale of Beowulf's heroic deeds belongs to a much more complex and troubling story that began before Beowulf's birth and will continue after his death.

Frame stories "surround"—provide a frame for—other stories in the work. In Boccaccio's *Decameron* (1349–51), ten people travel from Florence to escape the plague that ravages the city. When they arrive at their country destination, they agree to tell stories that will center on different topics. Each person will tell ten stories (the "deca" in the title means "ten"). Between each grouping of ten stories, the author returns to the frame story, telling us what the characters do and say and what the next topic will be. After all the stories are told, the characters return to Florence. Mary Shelley's *Frankenstein* (1818) also begins and ends with a frame story—Robert Walton's account of his exploration in the Arctic seas and his meeting with the monster and Victor Frankenstein. Frankenstein, upon arriving on Walton's ship, tells his story—the primary story of the novel—of how he created the monster.

Frame stories are similar to embedded stories in that they often relate meaningfully to the other story or stories in the narrative.

The topics and stories of *The Decameron* comment on the circumstances of the plague. Frankenstein's story, because it parallel's Walton's, calls into question Walton's motivations and goals. The stories in Chaucer's *Canterbury Tales* reflect the traits of their tellers and of the medieval society they typify.

Summary narration and scenic narration. Two devices that affect the speed and focus of plots are summary narration and scenic narration. *Summary narration* relates (sums up) events that take place over a period of time, as in this example from Pushkin's story "The Queen of Spades" (1834):

> From that time forward not a day passed without the young officer [Hermann] making his appearance under the window at the customary hour, and between him and her [Lizaveta] there was established a sort of mute acquaintance. . . . After about a week she commenced to smile at him. (8)

Scenic narration presents events in real time. An event takes about as long to read as it takes to happen. Scenic narration typically features dialogue, as in this example, also from "The Queen of Spades":

> Three days afterwards, a bright-eyed young girl from a milliner's establishment brought Lizaveta a letter. Lizaveta opened it with great uneasiness, fearing that it was a demand for money, when suddenly she recognized Hermann's handwriting.
>
> "You have made a mistake, my dear," she said. "this letter is not for me."
>
> "Oh, yes, it is for you," replied the girl, smiling very knowingly. "Have the goodness to read it."
>
> Lizaveta glanced at the letter. Hermann requested an interview.
>
> "It cannot be," she cried, alarmed at the audacious request, and the manner in which it was made. "This letter is certainly not for me."
>
> And she tore it into fragments. (11)

Summary and scenic narration affect readers in different ways. Summary narration provides emotional distance from events and speeds up the passage of time. Scenic narration is more vivid and emotionally involving. It slows down the passage of time. Authors typically alternate between the two: speeding up time here, slowing it down there; giving us distance from events here, drawing us into them there. Such alternation establishes a kind of rhythm in the unfolding of a plot. Some short works are solely one scene, as in Frost's "The Death of the Hired Man" and Robison's "Yours" (both printed in the Appendix).

QUESTIONS ABOUT PLOT: CONFLICT

1. What conflicts does the work dramatize?
2. What is the main conflict? What are minor conflicts? How are all or most of the conflicts related?
3. What causes the conflicts?
4. Which conflicts are external, which internal?
5. Who is the protagonist? Who or what is the antagonist?
6. What qualities or values are associated with each side of the conflict?
7. Where does the climax occur?
8. How is the main conflict resolved? Which conflicts go unresolved?

An example of how questions about conflict help interpret fiction is Ernest Hemingway's short story "Hills Like White Elephants" (1927). The complete story is printed in the Appendix.

"Hills Like White Elephants" consists almost entirely of a dialogue between a young woman and man who are waiting for a train at a tiny station in the Spanish countryside. We learn that they have traveled widely and are lovers—but they are in conflict. About what? The conflict they bring out into the open and discuss aloud concerns an abortion. The woman is pregnant. The man urges her to have an abortion. He keeps telling her that the abortion will be "simple," "perfectly natural," will make them "all right" and "happy." But she resists. She asks if after the abortion "things will be like they were and you'll love me" (275). She says that they "could get along" without the abortion (277).

Gradually we realize that although the immediate conflict is about the abortion, there is an unspoken conflict over the nature of their relationship. The man wants the abortion because it will allow him to continue the rootless and uncommitted relationship he has enjoyed with the woman up to now. The woman wants a more stable relationship, one that having the child would affirm, one that she has apparently believed the man wanted too. Hemingway resolves the conflict by having the woman realize, in the face of the man's continued insistence on the abortion, that the relationship she wants with the man is impossible.

Examining the story's main conflict in this way helps reveal important things about the story. At first glance, it seems to have little "action," but examining the conflict reveals what its action is. Studying the conflict also helps illuminate the characters: The man is selfish and obstinate; the woman is idealistic and somewhat innocent. Analyzing the conflict points to a possible meaning of the story. The author (or narrator) doesn't have to take sides in conflicts between characters. But here Hemingway seems to support the woman's view of the way a loving relationship should be. He makes her the protagonist, the more sympathetic character of the two. A theme of the story seems to emerge from this conflict, something like that committed love (settling down, permanence, family) is superior to rootless, uncommitted love.

Other Questions about Plot

1. How are the "story" and "plot" different? Why does the author arrange events out of chronological order? Can you retell the story in chronological order? Does the plot have gaps—events that are omitted or only hinted at in the text. In "Hills Like White Elephants," for example, we have to guess information about the couple's relationship before the plot begins.

2. If the work has multiple plot lines, what links them together?

3. If the work has embedded or frame stories, how are they related to the main stories?

4. When does the author use summary narration and scenic narration? Is the work primarily one or the other? How do the two kinds of narration complement one another?

5. Does the ending follow logically from the plot? Can you think of a better or equally good ending?

Thinking on Paper about Plot

1. On one side of a piece of paper, list the external conflicts of the work. On the other side, list the internal conflicts. Draw a line between the external and internal conflicts that seem related.

2. List the key conflicts. For each conflict, list the ways in which the conflict has been resolved, if it has.

3. Describe the turning point or climax. Explain what conflicts are resolved. List the conflicts that are left unresolved.

4. Summarize what happens in a unit of the work (chapter, section, scene) that seems to mark a turning point. Explain what the turning point is.

5. List the qualities of the protagonist and antagonist.

6. Describe the qualities that make the situation at the beginning unstable. Describe the qualities that make the conclusion stable.

7. List the causes of the unstable situations at the beginning and throughout the work.

8. Compare the arrangement of events in the plot and the story. Speculate about why the author arranges the plot this way.

9. Using the graph of the Freytag pyramid as a model, draw a graph of the plot. If it's different from the Freytag pyramid, draw the graph to reflect those differences.

10. If there is more than one plot line, describe each one. Indicate how the plot lines are related and how they intersect at the end.

11. Mark passages of summary narration and scenic narration. Explain why the narrator shifts from one to the other.

12. Write a different ending for the narrative.

Now It's Your Turn

Discuss the presentation of events in Robison's "Yours" (printed in the Appendix). What are the conflicts? Does the Freytag pyramid work for this story? Can you reconstruct the "story" of the work? How is the "plot" different from the "story"?

Characterization

Definition. Characters are the people in narratives, and *characterization* is the author's presentation and development of the traits of characters. Sometimes, as in fantasy fiction, the characters are not people. They may be animals, robots, or creatures from outer space, but the author endows them with human abilities and human psychological traits. They really are people in all but outward form.

Flat and round characters. There are two broad categories of character development: simple and complex. E. M. Forster in *Aspects of the Novel* coined alternate terms for these same categories: *flat* (simple) and *round* (complex) characters (67–78). Flat characters have only one or two personality traits and are often recognizable as stereotypes—the shrewish wife, the lazy husband, the egomaniac, the stupid athlete, the shyster, the miser, the redneck, the bum, the dishonest used-car salesman, the prim aristocrat, the Wall Street hustler, the absent-minded professor. Round characters have multiple personality traits and are thus more like real people. They are harder to understand and more intriguing than flat characters. No single description or interpretation can fully contain them. An example of a flat character is Washington Irving's Ichabod Crane, the vain and superstitious schoolmaster of "The Legend of Sleepy Hollow" (1819). An example of a round character is Shakespeare's Hamlet. To an extent, all literary characters are stereotypes. Even Hamlet is a type, the "melancholy man." But round characters have many more traits than just those associated with their general type. Because it takes time to develop round characters convincingly, they are more often found in longer works than in shorter ones.

Static and dynamic characters.   Characters who remain the same throughout a work are *static*. Those who change are *dynamic characters*. Usually, round characters change and flat characters remain the same, but not always. Shakespeare's Sir John Falstaff in *Henry IV, Part I* (1598) and *Part II* (1600), a round character, is nonetheless static. Dynamic characters, especially main characters, typically grow in understanding. The climax of this growth is sometimes an *epiphany*, a term that James Joyce used to describe a sudden revelation of truth experienced by a character. The term comes from the New Testament and describes the Wise Men's first perception of Christ's divinity. Joyce applied it to fictional characters. His own characters, like Gabriel Conroy in "The Dead" (1914), perfectly illustrate the concept. Often, as in "The Dead," the epiphany coincides with the climax of the plot.

Direct and indirect revelation.   Authors reveal what characters are like in two ways: directly and indirectly. In the *direct* method, the narrator simply tells readers what the character is like, as Jane Austen's narrator does in *Pride and Prejudice* (1813):

> She [Mrs. Bennet] was a woman of mean understanding, little information, and uncertain temper. When she was discontented she fancied herself nervous. The business of her life was to get her daughters married; its solace was visiting and news. (3)

When the method of revealing characters is *indirect*, however, authors show us, rather than tell us, what characters are like through dialogue, external details (dress, bearing, looks), and characters' thoughts, speech, and deeds.

Representing characters' thoughts. One of the signal methods of modern fiction is access to characters' minds. Before about the seventeenth century, epics, romances, tales, and other forms of fiction did not do this, at least not extensively. Such access is something we cannot have in real life. Real people may tell us what they think. We can guess from their facial expressions what they think. We know what *we* think—usually. But we cannot enter other people's minds. Surely one of the great appeals of modern fiction is that it allows us to do just this.

The presentation of thoughts in first-person narratives is no different from real life. The narrators—characters in the works—tell us what they think, just as real people do. But third-person narrators place us inside characters' minds. Suzanne Keen describes three ways third-person narrators do this (59–63). In the first, *reported thought* (her term is "psycho-narration"), narrators use their own words to summarize characters' thoughts. An example is this passage from *Pride and Prejudice*, describing Elizabeth Bennet's thoughts:

> She perfectly remembered everything that had passed in conversation between Wickham and herself, in their first evening at Mr. Philips's. Many of his expressions were still fresh in her memory. She was now struck with the impropriety of such communications to a stranger, and wondered it had escaped her before. (143)

Reported thought allows narrators to probe "thoughts"—levels of consciousness—that characters may not fully recognize, as in this passage from Madame de Lafayette's *The Princesse de Clèves* (1678):

> It is impossible to describe the pain she [the Princess of Clèves] felt on realizing, as a result of what her mother had just told her, how much the Duc de Nemours meant to her: she had not yet dared admit it to herself. She saw then that the feelings she had for him were those that M. de Clèves had so often required of her, and she felt the full shame of experiencing them for someone other than a husband who deserved them. (56)

Here, and throughout the novel, the narrator presents the Princess's interior struggle between her love for the Duc de Nemours and her duty to her husband, the Prince of Clèves. Her feelings on these occasions often seem less than conscious thoughts. When the narrator says, for example, that the Princess "had not yet dared admit it to herself," the narrator seems to know more about the Princess's mind than she knows.

In the second way of representing characters' thoughts, *quoted monologue,* narrators cast thoughts in the characters' own words. "These thoughts," Keen says, "though unspoken, are written in such a way that they could plausibly be spoken aloud without violating the reader's sense of grammatical speech" (61). We can be sure that the characters are fully aware of these thoughts because the characters "say" them. Narrators may or may not place quotation marks around the characters thoughts. Either way, the thoughts are a quotation. Here is an example from *Pride and Prejudice* that uses quotation marks:

> "And of this place," thought she [Elizabeth Bennet], "I might have been mistress! With these rooms I might now have been familiarly acquainted! Instead of viewing them as a stranger, I might have rejoiced in them as my own, and welcomed to them as visitors my uncle and aunt." (168)

The following example, from Virginia Woolf's story "Mrs. Dalloway in Bond Street" (1923), omits quotation marks:

> Of course, she [Clarissa Dalloway] thought, walking on, Milly is about my age—fifty—fifty-two. So it is probable that. Hugh's manner had said so, said it perfectly—dear old Hugh, thought Mrs. Dalloway, remembering with amusement, with gratitude, with emotion, how shy, like a brother—one would rather die than speak to one's brother—Hugh had always been, when he was at Oxford, and came over, and perhaps one of them (drat the thing!) Couldn't ride. (20)

In this passage the thoughts are clearly the words Mrs. Dalloway would actually use.

A third method of presenting characters' thoughts, *narrated monologue,* is similar to quoted monologue in that the words are "spoken" by a character, but the narrator states them in the past tense and refers to the character in the third person. As in the following example, from Richard Wright's story "The Man Who Was Almost a Man" (1939), narrated monologue is usually mixed in with reported thought and quoted monologue. The underlined sentences are narrated monologue:

> That night Dave did not sleep. He was glad that he had gotten out of killing the mule so easily, but he was hurt. Something hot seemed to turn over inside him each time he remembered how they had laughed. He tossed on his bed, feeling his hard pillow. N Pa says he's gonna beat me . . . He remembered other beatings, and his back quivered. Naw, naw, Ah sho don wan im t beat me tha way no mo. Dam em all! <u>Nobody ever gave him anything. All he did was work.</u> They treat me like a mule, n then they beat me. He gritted his teeth. N Ma had t tell on me. . . . Dammit, he'd done it! He fired again. Blooooom! He smiled. *Blooooom! Blooooom! Click, click.* <u>There!</u> It was empty. <u>If anybody could shoot a gun, he could.</u> He put the gun into his hip pocket and started across the fields. (25–26)

Another term for narrated monologue is *free indirect discourse*.

Stream of consciousness. *Stream of consciousness* is a narrative device whereby authors place us within different levels of characters' conscious minds. "Consciousness," Robert Humphrey says (in *Stream of Consciousness in the Modern Novel*, 1954), "indicates the entire area of mental attention, from preconsciousness on through the levels of mind up to and including the highest one of rational, communicable awareness" (2). Stream of consciousness narration typically deals with "those levels that are more inchoate than rational verbalization—those levels on the margin of attention" (2–3). These "prespeech levels of consciousness are not censored, rationally controlled, or logically ordered" (3). William James, in his influential treatise *Principles of Psychology* (1890), coined the phrase, "stream of consciousness." The mind, he said, is like a river with debris—thoughts—floating on the surface. The thoughts are not necessarily related to one another.

Ever since James published this work, authors—Dorothy Richardson, Virginia Woolf, Gertrude Stein, James Joyce, William Faulkner, and numerous others—have devised methods to represent the apparently incoherent flow of prespeech thoughts. Sometimes their methods take the form of quoted monologue:

> Through the fence, between the curling flower spaces, I could see them hitting. They were coming toward where the flag was and I went along the fence.

In this, the opening lines of William Faulkner's *The Sound and the Fury* (1929), we are inside the mind of Benjy Compson, a grown man who has the mind of a three-year-old. Although Benjy is "speaking," he is not capable of speaking aloud this way. Rather, his interior "speech" is Faulkner's method of rendering his stream of consciousness.

Stream of consciousness can also take the form of reported thought or a combination of reported thought and quoted monologue, as in this example from Katherine Anne Porter's story "The Jilting of Granny Weatherall" (1930):

> She meant to wave good-by, but it was too much trouble. Her eyes closed of themselves, it was like a dark curtain drawn around the bed. The pillow rose and floated under her, pleasant as a hammock in a light wind. She listened to the leaves rustling outside the window. No, somebody was swishing newspapers: no, Cornelia and Doctor Harry were whispering together. She leaped broad awake, thinking they whispered in her ear. (122)

In this example the "stream" of consciousness flows through the mind of a dying woman, Granny Weatherall, whose thoughts are incoherent and fragmented. The narrator includes not just "words" in her mind but sensuous experiences as well—images and sounds. Sometimes, as in this passage, the stream of consciousness represents characters' hallucinations and dreams.

In real life, the prespeech thought of people may indeed be irrational and disconnected. But in stream of consciousness narration, the images and thoughts only seem to be incoherent. Ironically, authors take great pains to establish logical connections between their characters' prespeech thoughts. Benjy Compon's narration, for example, features confusing shifts between present and past events and from one past event to another past event. It leaves out information—that, for example, the "hitting" in the opening sentence is done by men playing golf. It focuses on images and smells—his sister's muddy drawers, her smell, objects of nature—that at first seem without meaning. It sets us down in the middle of Benjy's mind without any preparation or explanation. We have to figure things out as we go. But once we do figure them out, we see that every time shift, every image, every thought fits together into a coherent and brilliantly conceived whole. Stream of consciousness narratives are puzzlelike. Part of the fun of interpreting them is solving the puzzle.

Questions about Characters

The main questions about characters are two: What is the character like? What are the character's traits?

Consider the example of the woman in Hemingway's "Hills Like White Elephants," discussed previously. Hemingway drops hints that indicate something about her personality. She compares the Spanish hills to white elephants, a comparison that at first seems capricious but later suggests an imaginative, even artistic, quality that the man cannot comprehend. After she senses the man's true motivation for wanting the abortion, she looks out over the fields of ripe grain, the trees, the river, and the mountains beyond, and tells the man that "we could have all this" but that "every day we make it more impossible." She seems to connect the appreciation of nature—the sympathy they could feel for it together—with the moral quality of their relationship. But because their relationship must remain superficial, she says that the landscape "isn't ours any more" (276). Once again, the man lacks the imagination to make the connection, and he fails to grasp her moral point.

Hemingway seems to admire the woman's ability to make these comparisons. It underscores her more obvious and admirable desire for a profound and lasting relationship. Another thing we learn about the woman is that she is a dynamic character. At the beginning of the story, she does not fully recognize the falseness of her relationship with the man. She seems genuinely to hope for something better. By the end of the story, she knows the truth and, from all appearances, has changed as a result. At the beginning she is innocent and dependent upon the man for her happiness; by the end she has lost her innocence and has become independent.

Other Questions

1. Are the characters flat or round? What types do they represent? What makes them complex? Do they have traits that contradict one another and therefore cause internal conflicts?

2. Are they dynamic or static? What, if anything, changes about them? What steps do they go through to change?

3. What problems do they have? How do they attempt to solve them? Are they sad, happy, or in between?

4. Do they experience epiphanies? When, why, and what do their epiphanies reveal—to themselves, to us? Does what they learn help or hinder them? Is the epiphany the climax of the work? Does it mark a turning point in the plot or character's life? What further actions does the epiphany cause?

5. How do the characters relate to one another?

6. How do we learn about their inner lives—their conscious and unconscious thoughts, their ambitions, their ideas? Do they have speech mannerisms, gestures, or modes of dress that reveal their inner selves? What narrative devices does the author employ to render characters' thoughts?

THINKING ON PAPER ABOUT CHARACTERIZATION

1. List the traits of the main characters in the story.

2. Describe the ways the author reveals traits of a character.

3. Write a description of a complex character. Explain what makes the character "complex."

4. Describe the emotional reaction a character has to an important event or events.

5. Write a paragraph explaining how and why a character changes.

6. Describe the scene in which a character has an epiphany. Explain what happens and what the character comes to see.

7. Mark the places in which the narrator or characters make revealing statements about a character.

8. Show how the author represents characters' thoughts. Write a paragraph that describes a character's inner life.

9. Speculate about what will happen to the characters after the story ends.

NOW IT'S YOUR TURN

Describe the two characters in Robison's "Yours" (printed in the Appendix). Consider how everything we learn about them—their looks, ages, clothing, circumstances, statements, other people's reactions to them, attitude to each other, treatment of each other, narrator's comments—adds to your understanding of their nature.

What do you infer about them? Are there different ways to see them? Once you have done your analysis, share it with someone else who has done the same assignment. Are your assessments the same?

Setting

Definition. *Setting* includes several closely related aspects of a work of fiction. First, setting is the physical, sensuous world of the work. Second, it is the time in which the action of the work takes place. And third, it is the social environment of the characters: the manners, customs, and moral values that govern the characters' society. A fourth aspect—"atmosphere"—is largely, but not entirely, an effect of setting.

QUESTIONS ABOUT PLACE

Facts about place. *First get the details of the physical setting clear in your mind.*

1. Where does the action take place? On what planet, in what country, in what locale?

2. What sensuous qualities does the author give to the setting? That is, what does it look like, sound like, feel like?

3. Do you receive a dominant impression about the setting? What is the impression, and what caused it?

Interpretation of place. Once you have the basic facts clear, move on to questions about place. What relationship does place have to characterization and to theme? In some fiction, geographical location seems to have no effect on characters. Indoors or out, in one locale or another, they behave the same. In other works, such as those by Thomas Hardy or Joseph Conrad, place profoundly affects the characters.

In Hamlin Garland's story "Among the Corn Rows" (1891), the narrator shows how environment influences a character's decision. The setting is a farm in the American Midwest:

> A cornfield in July is a hot place. The soil is hot and dry; the wind comes across the lazily murmuring leaves laden with a warm sickening smell drawn from the rapidly growing, broad-flung banners of the corn. The sun, nearly vertical, drops a flood of dazzling light and heat upon the

field over which the cool shadows run, only to make the heat seem the more intense.

   Julia Peterson, faint with fatigue, was toiling back and forth between the corn rows, holding the handles of the double-shovel corn plow while her little brother Otto rode the steaming horse. Her heart was full of bitterness, and her face flushed with heat, and her muscles aching with fatigue. The heat grew terrible. The corn came to her shoulders, and not a breath seemed to reach her, while the sun, nearing the noon mark, lay pitilessly upon her shoulders, protected only by a calico dress. The dust rose under her feet, and as she was wet with perspiration it soiled her till, with a woman's instinctive cleanliness, she shuddered. Her head throbbed dangerously. What matter to her that the king bird pitched jovially from the maples to catch a wandering blue bottle fly, that the robin was feeding its young, that the bobolink was singing? All these things, if she saw them, only threw her bondage to labor into greater relief. (107–8)

Garland shows geographical environment pressuring Julia Peterson into a decision that will affect the rest of her life. The narrator has already told us that Julia's parents treat her harshly and force her to work too hard. By emphasizing one sensuous quality, the heat, Garland makes us feel the hardship of her life. She has dreamed of a handsome suitor who will take her away from the farm and give her a life of ease, but the heat makes her feel that anything would be better than this misery. So when a young farmer happens along just after the incident described here and offers her a life of respect and only normal difficulty, she marries him. We infer from Garland's presentation of Julia's physical environment that it causes her to settle for less than she really wants. She is not free to choose exactly as she would choose.

QUESTIONS ABOUT TIME

Historical period. Three kinds of time occur in fiction, thus three types of questions about time are important. First, at what period in history does the action take place? Many stories occur during historical events that affect the characters and themes in major ways. Margaret Mitchell's Gone with the Wind (1936) and Tolstoy's War and Peace (1863–69) are examples. To answer this question, you may have to do background reading about the historical period. Tolstoy and Mitchell give you a great deal of historical information in their fiction, but many authors do not. In either case, you may need to supplement facts in the work with facts from outside sources.

Passage of time. Second, how long does it take for the action to occur? How many hours, days, weeks, years are involved? Authors often use the passage of time as a thematic and structuring device: The mere fact that some specific amount of time has passed help us understand characters. Years go by in Alice Walker's *The Color Purple* (1982), allowing her characters to grow and change. But because of her method of telling the stories—through letters—we are not immediately aware of how much time passes until near the end of the book. Because we read the letters one after the other, we get the illusion that time passes quickly. In fact, gaps of time occur between the letters, so that we must consciously slow down the time of the novel to understand its effect on the characters. What clues, then, indicate how much time passes? Is the passage of time related to characterization and theme? If an author seems to obscure how much time is passing, why? Does the author use time as a structuring device?

Perception of time. Third, how is the passage of time perceived? Time may seem to move very slowly or very quickly, depending on a character's state of mind. Our recognition of how a character perceives time helps us understand the character's internal conflicts and emotional states.

In *Jane Eyre* (1847) Charlotte Brontë intertwines length of time and perception of time. Jane, the narrator, describes her stays at various "houses." She devotes about one-fourth of the novel to her stays with the Reeds and at Lowood and one-fourth to her stay with the Rivers family. But she devotes over half of the novel to her stay at Thornfield, where she falls in love with Mr. Rochester. The effect of these unequal proportions is to slow down the time spent at Thornfield. This "slow" time emphasizes Jane's emotional reaction to the experiences she has there.

Brontë slows the time of specific events as well. In fact, the novel is a collection of highly charged, intensely felt moments in Jane's life that seem to last far longer than they actually do in real time. The novel opens, for example, with Jane's imprisonment in the hated "red room" of the Reed mansion. As her anger subsides, she becomes aware that the room is "chill," "silent," and "solemn." She recalls that Mr. Reed died there. In a mirror she sees her "glittering eyes of fear moving where all else was still." Daylight "forsakes" the room. She feels "oppressed, suffocated" at thoughts of Mr. Reed's death and the possibility of her own. When she sees a light on the wall, she thinks it is a ghost. She screams. When Mrs. Reed rushes to check on her, she thrusts Jane back into the room and locks the door. Jane faints from the intense stress (45–50). The length of this description corresponds to Jane's perception of time, which in turn corresponds to her fear of the room. Each detail is like the tick of a loud clock.

1. What, then, is the relationship between the length of narrated events and the amount of time in which they occur?

2. Is the author purposely slowing down or speeding up our perception of time? If so, why?

3. What mental states or internal conflicts does a character's perception of time reveal?

QUESTIONS ABOUT SOCIAL ENVIRONMENT

Social environment is the manners, mores, customs, rituals, and codes of conduct of a society. Sometimes the social environments represented in a work are of little importance. There may even be virtually no social environment. When social environments are presented in detail, however, they usually affect interpretations of the work.

1. What social environments are portrayed in the work?

2. What does the author seem to think about them? (Approving? ambivalent? disapproving?)

3. How do they affect the characters?

Sinclair Lewis spends much of his novel Babbitt (1922) detailing the flawed and constricting social environment of his fictional Midwestern city, Zenith. Some of his characters desperately want to escape this environment. But they are too weak to do so without extreme guilt or without threatening their economic and social security. Their social environment determines their behavior and entraps them. Perhaps, Lewis seems to suggest, such is the case with most people.

QUESTIONS ABOUT ATMOSPHERE

Atmosphere refers to the emotional reaction that we and—usually—the characters have to the setting of a work. Sometimes the atmosphere is difficult to define, but it is often found or felt in the sensuous quality of the setting. Our emotional reaction to the Hamlin Garland passage is probably pain, discomfort, weariness, and oppression, mainly because of his emphasis on the thermal sense, the sense of hot and cold. Fruitful questions about atmosphere are:

1. What methods does the author use to create the work's atmosphere?
2. What does the author achieve by creating this atmosphere?
3. Sometimes, authors want simply to play upon our emotions—give us chills (gothic), make us weep (romances), stir anxiety (thrillers). Garland's purpose, however, is more meaningful. He uses atmosphere to raise a philosophical point: Physical environment affects human behavior. Joseph Conrad in *Heart of Darkness* (1902) creates an atmosphere of mystery, foreboding, and imminent danger to reflect his disapproval of colonialism and his belief that "civilized" people are capable of terrible deeds.

THINKING ON PAPER ABOUT SETTING

1. Mark descriptions of physical place. Underline telling words and phrases.
2. Characterize physical locales, such as houses, rooms, and outdoor areas.
3. Explain the connection of physical place to one or more of the characters.
4. Arrange key events in chronological order. Indicate when each event occurs.
5. Mark passages where a character's emotional state affects the way the passage of time is presented to us.
6. Explain how historical circumstances and characters are important.
7. List the thoughts and actions of characters that seem to typify the social environment of the work. They go to church, obey rules of etiquette, fear scandal, gamble, throw parties, cheat in business, wander restlessly, drink heavily, value art, and so forth.
8. Mark scenes in which the narrator or characters express approval or disapproval of these patterns of behavior.
9. Explain how these patterns influence characters.
10. List traits of the atmosphere—details of plot, characterization, and setting that help establish the atmosphere.

Now It's Your Turn

Describe the setting and atmosphere of "The Cask of Amontillado" (printed in the Appendix). What purposes does the setting have?

Irony

Definition. Authors use irony pervasively to convey ideas. But irony is a diverse and often complex intellectual phenomenon difficult to define in a sentence or two. Generally, *irony* makes visible a contrast between appearance and reality. More fully and specifically, it exposes and underscores a contrast between (1) what is and what seems to be, (2) between what is and what ought to be, (3) between what is and what one wishes to be, and (4) between what is and what one expects to be. Incongruity is the method of irony; opposites come suddenly together so that the disparity is obvious to discriminating readers and hearers. There are many kinds of irony, but four types are common in literature.

Verbal irony. Most people use or hear verbal irony daily. In verbal irony, people say the opposite of what they mean. For example, if the day has been terrible, you say, "Boy, this has been a great day!" The hearer knows that this statement is ironic because of the speaker's tone of voice and facial or bodily expressions or because the hearer is familiar with the speaker's circumstances and immediately sees the discrepancy between statement and actuality. Understatement and overstatement are two forms of verbal irony. *Understatement* minimizes the nature of something. "Greg Maddox pitched a pretty good game," one says after seeing him pitch a no-hitter. Mark Twain's famous telegram is another example of understatement: "The reports of my death are greatly exaggerated." *Overstatement* exaggerates the nature of something. After standing in a long line, you say, "There were about a million people in that line!"

Why do people use verbal irony? Verbal irony is more emphatic than a point-blank statement of the truth. It achieves its effect by reminding you of the opposite reality and thus providing a scale by which to judge the present reality. Verbal irony often displays a mental agility—wit—that people find striking and, as with the Mark Twain retort, entertaining. Verbal irony in its most bitter and destructive form becomes sarcasm, in which the speaker condemns people by pretending to praise them:

> Oh, you're a real angel. You're the noble man who wouldn't dirty his pure little hands with company business. But all along, behind our backs, you were just as greedy and ruthless as the rest of us.

Situational irony.   In situational irony, the situation differs from what common sense indicates it is, will be, or ought to be. It is ironic, for example, that General George Patton should have lived through the thickest of tank battles during World War II and then, after the war, have been killed accidentally by one of his own men. It is ironic that someone we expect to be upright—a minister or judge—should be the most repulsive of scoundrels. Authors often use situational irony to expose hypocrisy and injustice. In Hawthorne's *Scarlet Letter,* the townspeople regard the minister Arthur Dimmesdale as sanctified and angelic when in fact he shamefully hides his adultery with Hester Prynne and allows her to take all the blame.

Attitudinal irony.   Situational irony results from what *most* people expect, whereas *attitudinal irony* results from what one person expects. In attitudinal irony, an individual thinks that reality is one way when, in fact, it is very different. A frequent example in literature is naïve characters—Fielding's Parson Adams, Cervantes's Don Quixote, Dickens's Mr. Micawber, Voltaire's Candide—who think that everyone is upright and that everything will turn out for the best, when in fact people they encounter treat them unfairly and events are hurtful.

Dramatic irony.   *Dramatic irony* occurs in plays when a character states or hears something that means more to the audience than to the character. An example is the play *Oedipus Rex* (429 BCE). Like all Greek tragedies, *Oedipus Rex* dramatizes a myth the audience already knows. Thus, Oedipus's boast at the beginning that he will personally punish the reprobate who killed King Laius is ironic. He does not know—but the audience knows—that he himself is the unwitting murderer of Laius. Although dramatic irony gets its name from drama, it occurs in all forms of literature. The key to dramatic irony is the reader's foreknowledge of coming events. Many works become newly interesting when we reread them because we now know what will happen while the characters do not; this dramatic irony intensifies characterization and makes us aware of tensions that we could not have known about during our initial reading.

QUESTIONS ABOUT IRONY

1. What are the ironies in the work?
2. How are the ironies important?
3. What are their implications?

An example of a work whose ironies suggest themes is Shirley Jackson's short story "The Lottery" (1948). The setting seems like everyone's nostalgic image of the ideal American small town, with its agricultural economy, central square, post office, country store, cranky old men, gossipy housewives, laconic farmers, mischievous children, settled routine, and friendly atmosphere. But the townspeople have gathered to do something horrible—commit a ritual murder. What might Jackson be hinting at with this strange juxtaposition? Do "normal" American communities conduct "lotteries" to destroy innocent people? Yes, perhaps. Not as it's done in the story but with equal arbitrariness and cruelty. If this is one of her themes, she makes it more emphatic through irony than direct comment. She shocks us into rethinking our own ways of life.

OTHER QUESTIONS

1. **Verbal irony.** If characters constantly use verbal irony, why? What do we learn about their attitudes toward the world? Does their verbal irony usually take the form of sarcasm? Are they bitter and disappointed or simply realistic?

2. **Situational irony.** Are the characters aware of the situational ironies? Should we blame the characters for creating situational ironies or not understanding them?

3. **Attitudinal irony.** What attitudes do the characters have that contradict reality? Are we supposed to admire the characters who misconstrue the world, or are we to blame them for being naïve and deluded?

4. **Dramatic irony.** What do you know about coming events or past events in the work that the characters do not know? Why does the author give us this knowledge?

THINKING ON PAPER ABOUT IRONY

1. Mark examples of verbal irony, either by the narrator or other characters. Explain how a character's verbal irony helps characterize him or her.

2. Mark episodes in which a character's beliefs and expectations are contradicted by reality. Explain what we learn about the character from these episodes.

3. List instances of situational irony; identify people, for example, whom we expect to behave in one way but who behave quite differently. Explain the importance to theme of these instances.

NOW IT'S YOUR TURN

"The Cask of Amontillado" (printed in the Appendix) is often praised for its masterful handling of irony. Explain the story's ironies and discuss their implications.

Symbolism

Definition. In the broadest sense, a symbol is something that represents something else. Words, for example, are symbols. But in literature, a *symbol* is an object that has meaning beyond itself. The object is concrete and the meanings are abstract. Fire, for example, may symbolize general destruction (as in James Baldwin's account of racial conflict in America, *The Fire Next Time* [1963]), or passion (the "flames of desire"), or hell (the "fiery furnace"). Symbols, however, are not metaphors; they are not analogies that clarify abstractions, such as the following metaphor from Shakespeare's Sonnet 116:

> [Love] is an ever-fixèd mark,
> That looks on tempests and is never shaken.

Here, the abstract concept (the referent) is "love" and the clarifying concrete object is the stable mark (buoy, lighthouse, rock) that tempests cannot budge. A symbol, in contrast, is a concrete object with no clear referent and thus no fixed meaning. Instead, it merely suggests the meaning and, in an odd way, partly *is* the meaning.

For this reason, the meaning of symbols is difficult to pin down. And the more inexhaustible their potential meanings, the richer they are.

There are two kinds of symbol: public and private. *Public symbols* are conventional, those that most people in a particular culture or community would recognize as meaning something fairly definite. Examples of public symbols are the cross, the star of David, the American eagle, flags of countries, the colors red (for "stop") and green (for "go"), and the skull and crossbones.

Private symbols are unique to an individual or to a single work. Only from clues in the work itself can we learn the symbolic value of the object. There are many examples of private symbols in literature. In F. Scott Fitzgerald's *The Great Gatsby* (1925), there is an area between the posh Long Island suburbs and New York City through which the major characters drive at various times and which Fitzgerald calls a "valley of ashes." It is a desolate, gray, sterile place, and over it all broods a partly obliterated billboard advertisement that features the enormous eyes of Doctor T. J. Eckleburg, an optometrist. Fitzgerald invests this area with symbolic meaning. He associates it with moral decay, urban blight, the oppression of the poor by the wealthy, meaninglessness, hell, and violent death. At one point he connects the eyes with failure of vision, at another with God, who sees all things. But we never know exactly what the valley of ashes represents; instead, it resonates with many possible meanings, and this resonance accounts for its powerful suggestiveness.

Questions about Symbolism

Not every work uses symbols, and not every character, incident, or object in a work has symbolic value. Some fundamental question are as follows:

1. What symbols does the work seem to have? Beware, however, of finding "symbols" where none were intended. A second question, then, is necessary to the believability of any interpretation based on symbols:

2. What makes you think that certain things in the work are symbols? (That is, how does the author signal that they are symbolic?) Once you answer this question, you can move on to a third and more interesting question:

3. What meanings does the symbol suggest?

In Hemingway's *A Farewell to Arms* (1929), for example, the following dialogue between Frederic Henry and Catherine Barkley suggests that

Hemingway intended a symbolic meaning for rain; it also suggests what the symbol represents:

> [Frederic says] "It's raining hard."
>> "And you'll always love me, won't you?" [Catherine replies] "Yes."
>> "And the rain won't make any difference?"
>> "No."
>> "That's good. Because I'm afraid of the rain."
>> "Why? . . . Tell me."
>> "All right. I'm afraid of the rain because sometimes I see me
> dead in it."
>> "No."
>> "And sometimes I see you dead in it. . . . It's all nonsense. It's
> only nonsense. I'm not afraid of the rain. I'm not afraid of the rain.
> Oh, oh, God, I wish I wasn't." She was crying. I comforted her and
> she stopped crying. But outside it kept on raining. (125–26)

Throughout the novel, Hemingway's recurrent association of rain with destruction of all kinds broadens its significance from a mere metaphor for death to other and more general qualities such as war, fate, alienation, foreboding, doom, and "reality." Because of these associations, the last sentence of the novel is more than just a description of the weather: "After a while I went out and left the hospital and walked back to the hotel in the rain" (332). The sentence seems to suggest that Frederic is stoically and bravely facing the harsh realities—including Catherine's death, the war, the arbitrariness and cruelty of fate—represented by the rain.

THINKING ON PAPER ABOUT SYMBOLISM

1. List one of the symbols in the work that you think is especially revealing about aspects of the work.
2. State why you think the object is meant as symbol.
3. List the symbol's possible meanings and how it contributes to the meanings of other parts of the work or of the work as a whole.

NOW IT'S YOUR TURN

Indicate what you think might be symbols in "The Cask of Amontillado" (printed in the Appendix), "Yours" (printed in the Appendix), or "My Last Duchess" (pages 129–30). Explain why you think the author intends them as symbols and what they seem to represent.

OTHER ELEMENTS

In this chapter we have treated the elements most obviously identified with fiction. But other elements are also sometimes important in fiction: dialogue, description, metaphor, poetic use of language, diction. We will discuss these other elements in the next two chapters.

Checklist for Interpreting Fiction

Themes (pages 40–44)

- State some of the important subjects.

- Formulate themes that emerge from these subjects.

- Mark statements by narrators and characters that might serve as themes. Assess the validity of these statements as themes.

- Use "philosophical" questions to probe thematic implications of the work.

- If there is a moral center, describe that character. Explain why this and any other character could be considered a moral center.

Point of View (pages 45–50)

- Indicate the point of view—who narrates.

- Describe the narrator's tone.

- Assess the reliability of the narrator.

- Explain who the audience—narratee(s)—of the narrative is.

Plot (pages 50–60)

- Compare arrangements of events in the plot and story.

- Outline or draw the pattern of the plot—Freytag's pattern or other patterns.

- If there are multiple plot lines, summarize each one. Indicate their connections to one another.

- Indicate the true beginning of the plot.

- Assess the appropriateness of the ending.

- Identify the major conflicts.

- Explain what the protagonists fight for and against what or whom (antagonists).

- Show how any embedded stories or frame stories illuminate the main plots.

- Indicate examples of summary narration and scenic narration. Speculate about why the author uses each.

Characterization (pages 60–68)

- Explain the traits of flat characters.

- Describe how round characters are complex.

- Indicate which characters change and why.

- Show what method or methods the author uses to render characters' thoughts.

- Summarize epiphanies characters have. Explain what causes and leads to the epiphanies.

- Mark passages where the narrator or characters make descriptive and judgmental statements about characters.

Setting (pages 68–73)

- Describe the place of the setting.

- Indicate how the place affects characters.

- Explain the time—historical period, passage of time, perception of time—of the narrative.

- Characterize the social environment and how characters respond to it.

- Describe the atmosphere. Indicate what causes it.

Irony (pages 73–76)

- Explore how irony contributes to other elements—especially characterization, tone, and themes.

Symbolism (pages 76–79)

- Describe key symbols.

- Explain why you think they are symbols and what they represent.

Works Cited

Abrams, M. H., and Geoffrey Galt Harpham *A Glossary of Literary Terms*. 9th ed. Wadsworth Cengage Learning, 2009. Print.

Austen, Jane. *Pride and Prejudice*. New York: Dodd, Mead, 1945. Print.

Booth, Wayne C. *The Rhetoric of Fiction*. Chicago: U of Chicago P, 1961. Print.

Brontë, Charlotte. *Jane Eyre*. New York: Penguin, 1966. Print.

Faulkner, William. *The Sound and the Fury*. New York: Vintage, 1987. Print.

Forster, E. M. *Aspects of the Novel*. New York: Harcourt, Brace, 1954. Print.

Freytag, Gustav. *Freytag's Technique of the Drama*. 5th ed. Trans. Elias J. MacEwan. Chicago: Scott, Foresman, 1894. Print.

Garland, Hamlin. "Among the Corn Rows." *Main-Traveled Roads*. Signet Classics. New York: New American Library, 1962. 98–121. Print.

Hemingway, Ernest. *A Farewell to Arms*. New York: Scribner's, 1957. Print.

———. "Hills Like White Elephants." *The Short Stories of Ernest Hemingway*. New York: Scribner's, 1966. 273–8. Print.

Humphrey, Robert. *Stream of Consciousness in the Modern Novel*. Berkeley: U of California P, 1954. Print.

Keen, Suzanne. *Narrative Form.* New York: Palgrave Macmillan, 2003. Print.

Murfin, Ross, and Supryia M. Ray. *The Bedford Glossary of Critical and Literary Terms.* Boston: Bedford Books, 1997. Print.

O'Connor, Flannery. *Mystery and Manners.* New York: Farrar, Straus, & Giroux, 1969. Print.

Porter, Katherine Anne. "The Jilting of Granny Weatherall." *Flowering Judas and Other Stories.* New York: Modern Library, 1935. 121–36. Print.

Pushkin, Alexander. "The Queen of Spades." *The Queen of Spades and Other Stories.* Trans. T. Keane. New York: Dover, 1994. Print.

Twain, Mark. *The Adventures of Huckleberry Finn.* Riverside Editions. Boston: Houghton Mifflin, 1958. Print.

Woolf, Virginia. *Mrs. Dalloway's Party: A Short Story Sequence.* Ed. Stella McNichol. London: Hogarth, 1973. Print.

Wright, Richard. "The Man Who Was Almost a Man." *Eight Men.* New York: Thunder's Mouth Press, 1987. Print.

4

Interpreting Drama

Drama contains many of the same elements as fiction. As with fiction, the "parts" of drama can be found in elements such as plot, characters, theme, and setting. Like fiction, drama uses irony and symbolism. And indeed, you can read a play as you would a short novel, using your imagination to fill in all the "missing" material you typically find in fiction: character description, background information, vivid action scenes. Similarly, since plays often contain poetry, you can read them just as you read any poetry. Because of the great similarity of drama to fiction and poetry, the definitions, questions, and exercises stated in the preceding chapter on fiction and in the following chapter on poetry are equally valid for drama.

In this chapter we will concentrate on the one difference between plays and other forms of literature: performance. Plays are meant to be performed rather than just read. Keeping this aspect of plays in sight can help you enjoy them more completely, imagine their full potential, and generate ideas about them. Two excellent books that focus on performance of plays are Bernard Beckerman's *Dynamics of Drama* (1979) and Martin Meisel's *How Plays Work* (2007).

THE NATURE OF DRAMA

Performance

When you just read a play, you miss the qualities that all those involved in its production could supply. You miss the set designers' vision of the physical world of the play. You miss the spectacle and suggestiveness of costumes. You miss the actors' interpretive skills and the illusion they create of real life unfolding before your eyes. You miss their energy and dexterity and their ability to imitate human types. You miss the physical and emotional *experience* of the production, including the audience, whose presence influences your own responses to the play.

An illustration of what live productions add to plays is Tom Stoppard's account of an outdoor production of Shakespeare's *The Tempest* (1611). Stoppard, the contemporary English playwright, says that he never saw this production himself but that it was so magical and inventive that he kept hearing reports of it thirty years after it was done. Especially memorable was how the "airy spirit" Ariel made his final exit:

> This production of *The Tempest* took place in the open air in the early evening, and when it became time for Ariel to leave the action of the play he turned and he ran up the stage, away from the audience. Now the stage was a lawn, and the lawn backed on to a lake. He ran across the grass and got to the edge of the lake, and he just kept running, because the director had had the foresight to put a plank walkway just underneath the surface of the water. So you have to imagine: it's become dusk, and quite a lot of the artificial lighting has come on, and back there in the gloom is this lake. And Ariel says his last words and he turns and he runs and he gets to the water and he runs and he goes splish splash, splish splash, right across the lake and into the enfolding dark, until one can only just hear his footsteps making these little splashes, and then ultimately his little figure disappeared from view. And at that moment, from the further shore, a firework rocket was ignited and just went whoosh into the sky and burst into lots of sparks. All the sparks went out one by one and Ariel had gone. This is the thing: you can't write anything as good as that. If you look it up, it says, "Exit Ariel." (200)

Reading

The richness and pleasure of performances does not mean that reading plays carefully is not worth doing. Sometimes in a performance we miss aspects of plays that people catch only when reading the play. This is especially true of plays written in poetry. When Romeo and Juliet (in Shakespeare's *Romeo and Juliet*, c. 1590)* first speak to each other, they develop a complex metaphor (a pilgrim coming to a shrine) and speak in sonnet form (1.5.95–108). It is unlikely that a playgoer would think, "Aha! That was a sonnet!" Rather, we notice such devices by reading. Even if our purpose is to produce a play, we base our production on our interpretations. Everything we read in a play, including "literary" devices like Shakespeare's sonnet, is a clue to its possible performance.

Your challenge, then, is to read plays with an eye to how they might be produced and performed. Martin Meisel says that "like a musical score, the printed play exists as a manual or a blueprint for performance." "Reading plays in the fullest sense," he continues, "means being able to read the dialogue and descriptions as a set of directions encoding, but also in a measure *enacting*, their own realization. It means bringing to bear something of a playwright's or director's understanding of how plays work on an imagined audience in the circumstances of an imagined theatrical representation" (1–2).

By reading plays in this way, you try to capture how playwrights first conceived them, and you explore how you could make them resonate with audiences today. To this end, you analyze, interpret, and make decisions about meanings.

THE ELEMENTS OF DRAMA

In the rest of this chapter, we will discuss many of the same elements as for fiction and poetry but always with potential performances in mind.

Length

One of the most pervasively influential elements of drama is length: not just the length of the printed play but the length of performance. Since the performance is physical, with the audience physically present, the performance can be only so long. Otherwise the audience will become restless and ill at ease. The longer the play, the more breaks are necessary for audiences to stretch and walk around. But

---

*Publication dates of works of literature cited in this book and dates of authors' lives can be found in the author-title index at the back of the book.

even with breaks, probably the outside time limit for a single performance is about four hours. A length of two hours or so is standard for performances today.

Audience

The presence of an audience affects how plays are written and how productions are designed. The actors, of course, pretend to be real people involved in real human relationships. But unlike real life, these fictional activities are witnessed by an audience of total strangers. It is as if the front wall of your neighbor's house were taken away and the whole neighborhood were witnessing your neighbors' lives, actions, and speech.

The playwright or producer must decide whether to exclude or include the audience as participants in the play. If the choice is to exclude the audience, the production assumes that no one is watching. The production establishes a physical and psychological distance between the performance and the audience (the performance lighted, the auditorium dark; the performance up on stage, the audience down and away from the stage), and the actors pretend the audience is not there. If the choice is to include the audience, then measures are taken to bring the audience "into" the play. The physical distance between performance and audience may be reduced (by building the stage out into the auditorium or by having the actors circulate among the audience). The actors may look at the audience, gesture to it, or talk to it as if the audience were another person. Shakespeare's drama includes these possibilities with its numerous asides and soliloquies.

QUESTIONS ABOUT PERFORMANCE AND AUDIENCE

1. To what extent does the playwright seem to want the audience involved in the action?

2. How would you perform such audience-involving devices as soliloquies and asides? To whom, for example, would you have actors make asides?

3. What advantages are there in performing a play as if the audience is **not** there?

Now It's Your Turn

For a production of Susan Glaspell's one-act play *Trifles* (printed in the Appendix), explain the extent to which you would involve the audience, how you would do it, and why.

Plot

Plot, story, and action.   As with narrative fiction, *plot* and *story* in drama have different meanings. (See the discussion of plot and story in fiction on pages 50–52.) *Plot* is the playwright's arrangement of events, which we experience as we watch or read the play. *Story* is the entire sequence of events, arranged in chronological order, of which the play is a part. A third term, useful for plays, is *action*. "Action" is what happens.

The "action" of *Oedipus Rex* (429 BCE), for example, begins with Oedipus's attempt to rid Thebes of a plague. The "plot" consists of all the actions of the play as Sophocles arranges them and as the audience witnesses them. The "story" of the play is Oedipus's entire history, arranged in chronological order, starting with his parents' attempt to kill him when he was an infant and ending with his death at Colonus. The original audiences for this play, when watching it for the first time, would have known its story but not its plot.

Some plays feature a plot that is only a small part (but usually a very important and climactic part) of a story. Other plays feature a plot that is nearly equivalent to the story. Shakespeare's *Macbeth* (1606) has almost no important past and future events; nearly all the action occurs within the play itself. Thus the plot and story of *Macbeth* are nearly equivalent. The events in *Hamlet* (c. 1601), however, occur after a murder and a marriage and, long before that, a war between Denmark and Norway, all of which affect the action of the play itself; the conclusion of the play, furthermore, suggests what the future of Denmark will be like under its new ruler, the Norwegian king Fortinbras.

Simplicity of plot.   Because the playwright has only a short time to develop plot and because the playwright's audience experiences the play in one sitting, with little immediate opportunity to review it, the playwright must keep the plot simple and clear enough for an audience to grasp during the length of the performance. This means that playwrights tend to avoid numerous subplots or intricate plot complications so as not to confuse playgoers. Playwrights typically limit the number of characters in a play. They often emphasize conflict to keep the audience involved in the action and establish discernible patterns of cause and effect.

Dialogue. Although playwrights (and directors and actors) can call for physical action without words, the action (and the conflicts implicit in the action) must be understandable to the audience. The most important and almost inevitable means for doing this is *dialogue*—characters talking to one another. Playwrights, then, strive to make every word of dialogue help move the plot forward. The near inevitability of dialogue also means that playwrights focus largely on conflicts between people rather than conflicts between people and nonhuman forces. In contrast, fiction need not represent characters' words or thoughts and so is freer to depict conflicts between people and nonhuman forces. Although Jack London's short story "To Build a Fire" (1902) renders the thoughts of the protagonist, there is no "dialogue," just the protagonist's conflict with the harsh Yukon landscape. It would be difficult for a play to duplicate this kind of conflict. Plays sometimes portray conflicts between people and nonhuman forces, but these conflicts are revealed through dialogue and usually through conflicts between the characters.

Represented action. Because the time and space for a presentation is limited, certain kinds of action—battles and sports activities, for example—cannot be represented fully or literally on the stage. These activities must be concentrated or symbolized. A duel onstage, for example, might represent an entire battle; a plantation house that gradually changes from sparkling new to ramshackle might represent the stages of a grand family's disintegration. Sometimes the playwright places activities offstage. A character might describe events that have just taken place, but the audience does not see these events. It learns about them only through the dialogue.

Expectations. Plotting in drama depends in part on establishing or playing upon audience's expectations of what will happen as the play unfolds. Both fiction and poetry, in contrast, focus more on what has already happened. The playwright, of course, predetermines the events in a play; but as we watch, we experience the illusion that the action is occurring in the present and that neither we nor the characters know what will happen next. This effect of expectation is heightened in drama because as we watch the play we have little time to reflect on what has happened; whereas, when we read a novel we can pause and think about what we have read. Playwrights often predict our expectations about certain kinds of action and certain kinds of characters and fulfill our expectations or surprise us by thwarting them. Expectations, Meisel says, "are precisely the stuff that the playwright has to work with: promoting them, teasing them, deceiving them, and finally disappointing or fulfilling them, though often in ways unexpected. What is called plot is usually a matter of anticipation and deferral, resistance and resolution within a framework of managed expectations" (18).

Structural divisions.   The *structural divisions* of plays affect plot. Playwrights usually provide structural divisions to give playgoers physical relief—a few moments to stand up, walk about, stretch, or reflect (however briefly) on what they have seen. Structural divisions also serve to allow set changes. In addition to such performance considerations, structural divisions also mark segments of the plot. *Formal structural divisions* are those specified in the play or the program—acts and scenes. *Informal structural divisions* can be smaller units within an act or scene, units not identified as such by the playwright but that nonetheless have a self-contained quality. In formal structural units, the playwright might call for the curtain to come down, the lights to go off, or the characters to leave the stage to signal the end of a unit. Shakespeare often ends his units with a couplet. In informal units, none of these things may happen; instead, the units may just flow together. Characteristic of many of them, however, is a rising action, a climax, and possibly a brief falling action. The climax of these units is sometimes a moment of revelation, either to the main characters, to other characters, or to the audience. An example is Hamlet's recognition at the climax of the play-within-a-play scene that King Claudius has murdered his father, the former king. All of the units of a play contribute to the rising action of the entire play and lead finally to its main climax.

QUESTIONS ABOUT PLOT

Plot versus story

1. What is the "plot" of the play?
2. What is the "story"?
3. If the plot is only part of the story, why does the playwright choose this part?
4. What has happened before the play begins?

5. What will happen afterward? Bernard Beckerman suggests that if the plot is only part of a larger or continuing story, the characters are more likely to seem at the mercy of forces beyond their control; whereas, if the plot and story are roughly equivalent, the characters will seem more free to choose and mold their own fate (172). The plot of *Romeo and Juliet*, for example, is only one episode—the final episode, we hope—of a generations-long, murderous, and irrational family feud. Romeo and Juliet are therefore "star-crossed" and "death-marked"; try as they will, they cannot escape the undertow of their families' history. Even Prince Escalus, the only person in the play with both power and good sense, can do nothing to avert the tragedy. Macbeth and Lady Macbeth, in contrast, choose to do evil at the beginning of the play and thus give rise to the forces that destroy them.

Simplicity

1. We said that plot in drama needs to be relatively simple and clear. In the play you are studying, is it? If not, why would the playwright want to create confusion about the important conflicts and cause-and-effect relationships? Sometimes the playwright *tries* to create such confusion. William Congreve in *The Way of the World* (1700), for example, establishes a pattern of relationships so confusing that an audience is hard pressed to figure out who has done what to whom, especially at the breakneck speed of a typical performance. He probably does this purposefully to indicate the complicated texture of Restoration upper-class society and the difficulty of finding one's way through it safely and honorably.

2. What are the main conflicts?

3. What has caused the conflicts that exist at the beginning of the play?

4. What causes the conflicts that emerge during the course of the play?

5. Who is in conflict with whom? Why?

6. Are any of the characters in conflict with forces larger than just individuals—society, for example, or fate?

7. How are the conflicts resolved?

Location of action

1. What actions occur offstage?

2. Why does the author elect to place some actions offstage and other actions onstage? In *Macbeth*, for example, Shakespeare has the murder of King Duncan (at the beginning of the play) occur offstage, but later he has the murder of Banquo and, in another scene, the murder

of Macduff's family (or part of it) occur onstage. Why, then, does he choose to put one murder offstage and other murders onstage?

3. How do the characters react to the offstage events?

4. How does the playwright present or symbolize action that occurs offstage? When Macbeth returns from killing Duncan, he carries the murder weapons, all covered with blood. His hands are covered with blood. When Lady Macbeth returns from smearing blood all over the sleeping guards, *her* hands are covered with blood. The more we see of this blood and the more they talk about it, the more grisly and physical and sticky the murder seems. Without actually describing the murder, Shakespeare uses a physical image—blood—and the characters' reaction to it to signal what the murder was like.

Audience expectations

1. What expectations does the plot call up in the audience?

2. Does the playwright fulfill those expectations? If not, how and why not? Most traditional romantic comedies, for example, offer young lovers as staple characters. We expect the lovers, after suitable complications, to find happiness together, usually signaled at the end by betrothal or marriage. But sometimes the playwright introduces potential lovers, gives us something like a light comic tone, creates comic complications, but thwarts our expectations that they will marry. Examples are Etherege's *The Man of Mode* (1676), Molière's *The Misanthrope* (1666), and Shaw's *Mrs. Warren's Profession* (1898).

   Another example is Chekhov's *The Cherry Orchard* (1904), which he called a comedy, even though it is not always played as such. In this play, the main character, Lopakhin, and the adopted daughter of the family he wants to rescue from economic disaster, seem meant for each other. There is much talk throughout the play of their marrying. Such a marriage would seem good for both of them. They seem inclined to marry. Since they are sympathetic characters, the audience wants them to marry. Yet they never do. Why does Chekhov create the expectation of their marriage and then abort it?

Formal and informal divisions

1. What are the formal structural divisions of the plays? How many are there—three acts? four? five?

2. How do the formal divisions reflect the playwright's plot structure and possible themes? Oscar Wilde's *The Importance of Being Earnest* (1895), for example, is divided into three acts. The first act takes place

in London, the second and third in the country. This division reflects the double-identity motif in the plot. The main character pretends to have two identities: a city identity and a country identity. The first two acts reflect these opposing identities. The third act, however, synthesizes the first two. Events and revelations allow the main character to blend his city and country identities into one happy whole. The structure of the play neatly reflects a "thesis, antithesis, synthesis" pattern of oppositions and resolution of oppositions.

3. What are the informal units of the play?

4. For *all* the units, what are the climaxes of each?

5. How does a unit fit into the overall plot? Is it a turning point? A turning point of *Hamlet*, for example, is the scene in which Hamlet kills Polonius. Prior to this scene, the play could potentially become a "tragi-comedy," concluding with Hamlet's marriage to Ophelia. After this scene, the play becomes a tragedy.

6. What is the climax of the play? What do you learn from it?

THINKING ON PAPER ABOUT PLOT

1. List the conflicts revealed in each major section of the play (usually acts, but sometimes scenes).

2. Summarize how one conflict is developed throughout the whole play and how it is resolved.

3. Describe one important scene in detail. Explain how the characters' actions and dialogue reveal conflict. Explain how the scene fits into the overall scheme of the whole play.

4. Describe the climax of the play. Explain what conflicts are resolved.

5. List events that occur offstage. Explain why the playwright has one or more of these occur offstage rather than onstage.

6. Summarize the situation at the beginning of the play and state what you expect to happen. Explain how the play does or does not fulfill those expectations.

NOW IT'S YOUR TURN

Discuss the plot of *Trifles* (printed in the Appendix). What are the conflicts? Are the "plot" and "story" different? What happens offstage? Although this is a one-act play, are there informal divisions in it? Where does the climax occur?

Characterization

Conflicts between characters.   Martin Meisel says that the root of conflicts in plays "lies in or between what can be thought of as the rival programs of different characters." Characters "come equipped with plots of their own—with plans, goals, desires, and interests—each character wishing to shape the action towards a particular outcome" (140). He says you can chart—or at least begin to chart—the outcome of these conflicts with a vector diagram, derived from mechanics:

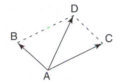

In this diagram, the line AB represents a character who "is moderately effective in exerting force in a given direction." The character represented by line AC is more effective. And the line AD is the true "path of the action," the character whose "plot" wins. This diagram, Meisel says, is too simple for most plays. Characters "adjust and improvise as matters develop, and another sort of diagram would show twists and turns, loops and tangles, generating the knot that unravels in what is aptly called the 'denouement'" (140). "As a rule," he says, "no character's path is likely to run smooth and straight" (141). But Meisel's diagram could provide a start to investigating the characters' traits and the potential effect they could have on the plot. What would happen, for example, if another character's "plot" were to win?

Stock characters.   As with plots, playwrights usually keep character portrayal simple enough for an audience to understand during the course of a single performance. Playwrights, then, often populate their plays with flat characters, especially with stereotyped (stock) characters, whose personalities and moral traits are easily caught and remembered by the audience. The playwright may even use unsubtle stratagems of dress, dialect, physical movements, and names to communicate these traits. In Restoration and eighteenth-century comedy, for example, the names signal traits of flat characters: Mrs. Loveit, Sir Fopling Flutter, Snake, Pert, Mr. Oldcastle, Lady Wishforit, Lady Sneerwell, Smirk, Handy. Playwrights also rely on static characters more heavily than dynamic characters because restricted performance times limit the opportunity to make character changes plausible.

Flat and round characters. Edward Pixley suggests that when a play is dominated by flat characters, the plot hinges mainly on external conflicts; the focus is on action. When the play includes round characters, the plot deals largely with internal conflicts; the focus is on characterization (12).

In Wilde's *The Importance of Being Earnest*, for example, all the characters are flat; the charm of the play lies not so much in character development as in the witty language, in the mild satire rippling through the dialogue, and in the plot complications resulting from the confusion of identities. In contrast, Ibsen's *Hedda Gabler* (1890) develops a complex, round character, Hedda herself; and the interest of the play lies in what she will do next and why she will do it. Hedda seems not to change during the play, but her character traits intensify and become ever more apparent to the audience. Round characters, therefore, hold the audience's attention by changing or, if they don't change, by becoming more intense. In either case, continual revelations about characters grip the audience's interest.

Playwrights sometimes use flat characters to state important ideas that could signal major themes. Molière's flat characters, for example, sometimes urge moderation on characters whose extreme irrationality gets them into trouble. Cléante is such a spokesperson in *Tartuffe* (1669). He says to his crazed brother-in-law Orgon, "You never preserve a moderate temper in anything. Right reason and yours are very different, and you are always throwing yourself out of one extreme into another" (44). Philinte advocates a similar balance in *The Misanthrope* (1666). He urges his obsessive friend Alceste (the "misanthrope" of the play) to "be a little more lenient to human nature." "Good sense," he says, "avoids all extremes and requires us to be soberly rational" (4). Moderation, "sober" rationality, and balance were ideals of Molière's intellectual environment—European Neoclassicism and Enlightenment. It's likely, then, that he uses flat characters to speak for himself.

Text and subtext. Although the playwright may depend to an extent on exterior details to reveal character traits, the playwright's most important device for character development is dialogue—what the characters say and what they say about one another. But performance time is limited; the words of the dialogue cannot describe the character fully. Playwrights, therefore, rely heavily on implication in the dialogue and on "gaps"—information left out—to indicate what characters are like and what physical things they do. Some critics mark this distinction with the terms *text* for the written words of the play and *subtext* for the implications and gaps. All literary genres make use of implication and gaps, but drama and poetry almost *must* rely on them because both genres are such compressed forms of communication.

A simple example of text and subtext is the scene near the beginning of *Hamlet* in which Hamlet, after a long absence, meets his university friends Horatio and Marcellus. The night before this meeting, Horatio and Marcellus have seen the ghost of Hamlet's father. But Hamlet doesn't know anything about the ghost; instead, he complains about his mother's marrying so soon after his father's death:

> HAMLET: Would I had met my dearest foe in heaven
> Or ever I had seen that day [the wedding day], Horatio!
> My father—methinks I see my father.
> HORATIO: Where, my lord?
> HAMLET: In my mind's eye, Horatio.
> HORATIO: I saw him once. 'A was [he was] a goodly king. (1.2. 182–8)

If you were the actor playing Horatio, how would you say the line "Where, my lord?" The "gap" here is how Horatio responds to Hamlet's statement, "My father—methinks I see my father." To fill the gap, you have to determine from the context how Horatio takes that statement (Shakespeare does not tell you how, as a novelist might), and you have to communicate his reaction to the audience by the way you say the line and by your physical demeanor. You might phrase the line as an incredulous question: "What? You see your father? But how could you, he's dead?" Or you might say it as a reflection of what you take to be Hamlet's witty mood: "I know you're joking, Hamlet. But tell me anyway. Where do you see your father?" But another possibility is that you would say it in astonishment, as if you take it literally. After all, *you* have seen the ghost of Hamlet's father just a few hours before. You probably think Hamlet has now spotted the ghost, and so you say, "Good Lord, do you see it, too? Where?" And you look fearfully around, trying to see the ghost too. When Hamlet indicates that he is only remembering his father, you calm down. At this point you might pause and make appropriate gestures to indicate your shift from fear and astonishment to calmness. The fact that you *have* made such a shift is indicated by your response to Hamlet: "Yes. Once, when the king was alive, I saw him too. He was an impressive-looking king." This last statement shows that Horatio has moved from thinking about a supernatural phenomenon (the ghost) to thinking about a natural one (Hamlet's father when he was alive).

This brief example illustrates the greatest value of understanding a play's subtext. By "reading" implications and gaps in the play, you uncover inner states of the characters—what is going on in their minds and what their hidden nature is. You also establish a correspondence between a character's inner state and what the character says and does (the character's outer state). In *Hedda Gabler*, Bernard Beckerman says, the "spoken lines only incompletely convey the underlying action. Either the depth of thought or emotion is so much greater than what is expressed or the true state is at odds with what is shown." There is, for example, a "continuous gap between Hedda's social manner and her inner frenzy" (124). Interpretation of subtext is essential for actors, who must figure out how to say the dialogue and what to do onstage. But it is important for readers, too, even though a reader may not work out intonation and physical movements in as much detail as actors do.

A character's inner life is the key to the character's nature and actions. Horatio, in the example above, is a flat character. His inner state is relatively uncomplicated. But bringing it to the surface gives the performance—whether seen by an audience or imagined by a reader—vividness. Horatio springs to life. As for round characters, the difficulty of uncovering their inner states is much greater, yet their complexity of inner state makes them fascinating. Great characters like Oedipus, Macbeth, Hamlet, and Hedda Gabler grip our imaginations just because their inner states are so mysterious. The only way we can tap into these inner states is by probing the subtext of the play.

Mask wearing.   Closely related to subtext in drama is *mask wearing*. Some plays call for actors to wear literal masks, as in the plays of Ancient Greece and *commedia dell'arte* (a form of comedy popular in Italy, c. 1600s–1800s). A few modern playwrights have experimented with real masks, such as Luigi Pirandello in *Six Characters in Search of an Author* (1921) and Eugene O'Neill in *The Great God Brown* (1926). But otherwise the "masks" in modern drama are metaphorical rather than literal.

Nearly every play employs masks as a device for developing plot and characterization. Juliet wears a "mask"—pretends to be different from how she really is—in order to fool her parents and run away with Romeo. Hamlet puts on a mask of madness to root out the murderer of his father. Hedda pretends to be the contented housewife in order to secure the wealth and social status she thinks she deserves. Macbeth and Lady Macbeth pretend to be the loyal servants and gracious hosts of King Duncan while plotting his murder. The audience may be fully aware of the mask and thus the disparity between appearance and reality, as, for example, in Juliet's case. Or the audience may at first be as unaware of the mask as are the other characters in the play, as in Hedda's case. And sometimes the mask wearers are themselves unaware or partially unaware of their masks; that is, they deceive themselves. Oedipus, for example, does not know that he is masking his true identity as murderer of the king. In all cases, both plot and characterization turn on revelation—the tearing away of the mask. At these moments of revelation, the audience and at least some of the characters see the reality behind the mask. Often the final unmasking occurs at the climax of the plot. In *Othello* the climax occurs when Iago's mask is ripped away before Othello's shocked eyes.

Costumes.   Closely related to masks are costumes. Costumes are literally masks when they hide characters' identities, as is true when some of Shakespeare's female characters—Rosalind in *As You Like It* (c. 1600) and Viola in *Twelfth Night* (1600)—disguise themselves as males. Costumes serve as part of the sets when they convey information about setting (locale, time period, social situations, characters' professional and occupational roles). But costumes can also tell us much about characters' traits, situations, and states of mine.

An example is Margaret Edson's use of costumes in *Wit* (1999). The main character, Vivian Bearing, is an austere and somewhat overbearing English professor who specializes in seventeenth-century English poetry, particularly John Donne's Holy Sonnets (c. 1610). We learn at the beginning that she has ovarian cancer and will die at the end of the play. For the most part, the action occurs in the hospital where she receives treatment. Her costume consists of hospital apparel and paraphernalia. When she first appears she "walks on the empty stage pushing her IV pole. She is fifty, tall and very thin, barefoot, and completely bald. She wears two hospital gowns—one tied in the front and one tied in the back—a baseball cap, and a hospital ID bracelet" (7). She has a "central-venous-access catheter over her left breast, so the IV tubing goes there, not into her arm" (5). This costume remains the same throughout the play, except that every time "the IV pole reappears, it has a different configuration of bottles" (5).

Vivian's costume not only communicates her physical condition and the treatment she undergoes but contrasts starkly with her status as the intellectual, haughty, and even feared college teacher. She is proud of this status, but her costume indicates not just her new physical condition but her emotional reactions to it. She is embarrassed and indignant at how the doctors and most of the staff treat her, as a thing rather than a person. The clothes represent her now "low" status, her vulnerability, her suffering, and her fear. As the disease advances, she changes. Whereas before her illness she studied Donne's Holy Sonnets for their cleverness, their "wit," now she takes their meanings personally. Edson's handling of her costume at the end suggests this change. After she dies and while the Code Blue team tries to revive her, she "steps out of the bed. She walks away from the scene, toward a little light. She is now attentive and eager, moving slowly toward the light. She takes off her cap and lets it drop. She slips off her bracelet. She loosens the ties and the top gown slides to the floor. She lets the second gown fall. The instant she is naked, and beautiful, reaching for the light—Lights out" (66). The play ends right there.

QUESTIONS ABOUT CHARACTERIZATION

1. If the characters are flat, what are their dominant traits? What is their function in the plot? How do they help establish the conflicts in the plot? What do they say that gives insight into other characters and that suggests themes?

2. If the characters are dynamic, how do they change—from what to what?

3. If they are static, do their traits intensify or become more apparent as the play moves on?

4. If the characters are round, what can you learn from the subtext of the play about their inner states?

5. What "masks" are the characters wearing? Who is hiding what from whom? When are the masks removed? What causes their removal, and what are the results?

6. What costumes would you devise for one or more of the characters? If the playwright calls for certain costumes, how well do they fit the characters and their situations?

7. If you were to act a particular character, what is your interpretation of the character and how would you manifest it? What physical devices would you use? Hedda Gabler is aristocratic, proud, and forceful; she seems strong but has an inner fragility. Her rival, Thea, is hesitant, unsophisticated, and afraid; she seems weak but has an inner strength. If you were to act these characters, how would you show—in speech, gestures, posture—these qualities?

THINKING ON PAPER ABOUT CHARACTERIZATION

1. Describe the traits, motivations, strategies, and miscalculations (if any) of a complex character. Explain what makes the character interesting or puzzling.

2. List the devices, such as dress, names, and gestures, that help establish the traits of a character.

3. Summarize how a character intensifies, changes, or comes into sharper focus for the audience.

4. Explain how you would portray one of the characters in an important scene.

5. Trace one or more of the masks characters wear throughout the play. Summarize the scene in which the mask is dropped and the effects of this revelation.

NOW IT'S YOUR TURN

Use Martin Meisel's diagram, discussed on p. 93, as a starting place to explain the "plots" of three characters in *Trifles* (printed in the Appendix). What are the "plans, goals, desires, and interests" of each character? If each character's plot could continue the way the character wants, where would it go? How would it come out? Which character's plot "wins"? How and why does it win?

Setting

Because of the limited time and space of dramatic productions, a play cannot create a "world" in the same detail and breadth a novel can. The worlds of novels like Tolstoy's *War and Peace* (1865–69) and Hugo's *Les Miserables* (1862), with their multitude of characters, scenes, physical places, and battles, are impossible to show fully in drama. Rather, such worlds can be represented only fragmentarily. The playwright must use a shorthand method of presenting the setting so that the playgoer grasps enough information about it to understand whatever relationship it might have to characterization and theme. *Setting* in drama is the same as in fiction: the social mores, values, and customs of the world in which the characters live; the physical world; and the time of the action.

Dialogue. The playwright has three main ways of communicating setting to an audience. First, we learn about setting from the characters' dialogue, dress, and behavior. In Sheridan's *School for Scandal* (1777) we know immediately that the world of this play is leisured upper-class English society. We know this from the elaborately polite and mannered way in which the characters carry themselves and from the names they so freely drop—Sir Harry Bouquet, Lord Spindle, Captain Quinze, Lady Frizzle, the Dowager Lady Dundizzy. In *Hedda Gabler* the conversations between Hedda and Judge Brack let us know that they are aristocrats and that Hedda's husband and his family are middle class. This difference in class establishes a conflict of moral and social values between Hedda and her husband.

Sets. Second, we learn about setting from the sets, created by the set designer. Sheridan doesn't tell us what the interiors for *School for Scandal* should look like. He says simply that throughout the play the setting is "London" and that in act one it is "Lady Sneerwell's house." A set designer, however, would do research on the interior design of fashionable homes in late-eighteenth-century England and produce that image on stage. The set, in short, should "say" that these people are aristocrats.

Audience's knowledge. Third, we learn about setting from the knowledge *we* bring to the performance. The playwright alludes to the nature of the setting and assumes we will fill in the details. Americans, for example, have relatively little trouble understanding the setting of Arthur Miller's *The Crucible* (1953), even though it is set in seventeenth-century New England. Audiences today may even make the connection between the Salem witch trials and the McCarthy "witch-hunts" of the 1950s that Miller assumed his original audience would make.

A problem surfaces, however, when the audience does not have the supplemental information to complete the setting of the play—audiences from other cultures or other periods. Chekhov's plays are a case in point. *The Cherry Orchard* plays against a background of Russian history that Chekhov assumes we know: the reform acts of Czar Alexander II (1855–81), including the freeing of the serfs in 1861 and the establishing of the *zemstvo* system of local self-government; Alexander's assassination by anarchists in 1881; the rigid autocracy of the next czar, Alexander III (1881–94); and the ineffectual and repressive reign of his successor, Nicholas II (1894–1917), which revived revolutionary movements in the late 1890s. *The Cherry Orchard* focuses on the passing of a decrepit aristocratic order and the rising of a vigorous middle class and financial order. For us to recognize the tensions and concerns woven into the play, it helps to know a little Russian history. Otherwise, we may be confused about why the aristocrats are so nostalgic, whimsical, and impractical in the face of imminent financial disaster. Chekhov wants us to see that their attitude is both a result and a cause of this historical change.

You can enjoy *The Cherry Orchard* without knowing this historical setting, but the play becomes richer and understandable if you do know it. Bernard Beckerman says that "dramatic action plays off the backboard of social and psychological values and customs, which, even if sketched in lightly or merely assumed, are always present" (141). As readers, we can increase our knowledge of these values and customs with a little background reading. But if you want to produce plays that are foreign to modern audiences, your challenge is to somehow make them fresh and understandable, to "find a contemporary analogue which an audience can share, yet which does not violate the central action of the work" (Beckerman, 144).

Sets as symbolic.   Playwrights and set designers can give sets symbolic value. Sets need not be symbolic. The sets in *School for Scandal* will usually be a literal suggestion of aristocratic drawing rooms and mean nothing more than that. To create the illusion of real rooms, the set designer can use physical detail lavishly—furniture, wallpaper, decorative doodads, architectural features, paintings, and clothes. But aspects of sets can take on symbolic or representational meaning. The simplest set is a bare stage, which can represent anything the playwright wants—a battlefield, a heath, a forest, a gothic cathedral. The playwright can be blatantly symbolic, assigning obvious meanings to physical objects. Thornton Wilder does this in *Our Town* (1938) when he uses stepladders to represent houses.

The playwright can also combine a realistic with a symbolic method. In *Hedda Gabler*, for example, Ibsen calls for solidly "real" things to be put in the two rooms we see of the Tesman house—an armchair, footstools, sofa, tables, French windows, and flowers in vases. But certain objects—Hedda's pistols, the portrait of General Gabler (Hedda's father), and the piano—become closely associated with her and her psychological disorders. Equally suggestive are the two rooms: one a large, elegant drawing room located in the front part of the stage and the other a smaller sitting room located in back. In act one Hedda's piano is in the drawing room, but in act two it is out of sight in the back room. In fact, as the play proceeds, the back room becomes more and more "Hedda's room" and the drawing room "Tesman's room." Even the portrait of General Gabler is in the back room. At the end of the play, Hedda retreats to the back room, pulls the curtains, frantically plays the piano, and kills herself with one of her father's pistols. It is as if the back room represents an increasingly restricted physical and emotional space for Hedda, until at last it becomes her prison and tomb.

QUESTIONS ABOUT SETTING

1. What do you learn about the setting from characters' behavior and dialogue?

2. Do you need background information to understand the play's setting?

3. What emotional feel—atmosphere—does the setting have? Is it, for example, rainy and dark or sunny and bright? Does the atmosphere change throughout the play?

4. How does the setting affect the characters?

5. What kind of sets does the play call for?

6. How does the set convey ideas, if any? Could the whole set or parts of it be symbolic?

THINKING ON PAPER ABOUT SETTING

1. For each major unit of the play, describe where and when the action occurs.

2. Give any background information that would be useful for understanding the play.

3. Describe the atmosphere of each major unit of the play and any changes in atmosphere that occur.

4. Explain the major characters attitude toward the setting.

5. Describe your design for the physical world—sets, costumes, sounds, lighting, the works—of one major unit of the play. Explain the reasons for your choices. Indicate any details of the set that are symbolic.

Now It's Your Turn

Susan Glaspell makes setting almost like another character in *Trifles* (printed in the Appendix). Discuss ways setting influences or suggests ideas about one or more of the characters. The student essay on *Trifles*, located in Chapter 13, deals with setting. Do you agree with its ideas? Can you supplement them with ideas and observations of your own?

Theme

Playwrights build themes into their plays through the development and interrelationship of all the elements of drama, most of which are the same as for fiction. Three methods of developing themes in plays, however, are particularly noteworthy: repetitions, symbols, and contrasts. All three lend themselves well to drama. Audiences pick up on them easily during performances.

Repetition.   Repetitions take many forms—gestures, phrases, stated beliefs, metaphors, symbols. Repetitions often signal ideas. Shakespeare, for example, repeats and intertwines three concepts in Hamlet: Denmark is "rotten," human beings are sinful, and the king's role is crucial to the health of the state. He characterizes Denmark by repeatedly comparing it to a garden overrun with weeds and to a diseased body, analogies borne out by Hamlet's partial madness and Ophelia's final madness and suicide. He has key characters dwell on the sinful nature of humankind. The queen says that her own soul is "sick," "as sin's true nature is" (4.5.16). The king says that his "offense is rank, it smells to heaven" because it has "the primal eldest curse" upon it (Cain's murder of Abel, 3.3.36–37). And Hamlet says that even the best people seem to have "some vicious mole of nature in them" that leads them from purity to corruption (1.4.24). (All three of these statements connect sin to sickness.) The corrupt state of Denmark, Shakespeare implies, is the result of the king's sin. For, as one character says, the king is like the hub of a wheel whose spokes connect to "ten thousand lesser things" (3.3.11–23). Whatever the king does affects everyone in the state.

Symbolism.   As we noted, *symbolism* can enrich setting. In fact, symbolism bears on both characterization and theme as well. It is often hard to separate the effect of symbolism on all three elements. In *Hedda Gabler,* for example, Ibsen contrasts Hedda and Thea's hair to symbolize their different character traits. Hedda's hair is thin and dull; Thea's is thick and luxuriant. Hedda dates her long-standing rivalry with Thea from their school days, when Hedda threatened to "burn off" Thea's hair. Hedda seems at times to want to inspire people to create, but her efforts are destructive; whereas Thea has an innate and unconscious gift for inspiring creativity. This wellspring of inspiration and fertility is symbolized by Thea's hair, which helps explain Hedda's animosity toward it. It's hard to say just what Ibsen's themes in *Hedda Gabler* are; he may simply be trying to present, not explain, Hedda's mysterious perversities. But one implication of the hair symbolism may be that creativity is a mysterious quality existing even in someone as innocent and nonintellectual as Thea and that it may not have anything to do with the intellectual sharpness and forcefulness of people like Hedda. Whatever Ibsen's themes are, they are inextricably bound up with his characterization of Hedda and Thea.

A simpler—that is, easier to interpret—example of thematic symbolism occurs in Lorraine Hansberry's *A Raisin in the Sun* (1959). Mrs. Younger, the main character, is the mother of a large extended family, but her environment—a stultifying, roach-infested, inner-city tenement—has kept her from giving the best of life to her children. The house she wants to buy in the suburbs becomes equivalent to new "earth" in which her children and grandchild can "grow," because, as she says, they are her "harvest." To emphasize the analogy between the house and a garden, Hansberry shows Mrs. Younger constantly dreaming of working in the garden at the new house, and, as a moving present, her children give her garden tools. The most visible symbol of Mrs. Younger's frustrations and aspirations is a sickly houseplant she has nurtured for years. The audience sees the plant sitting in the window. Mrs. Younger fusses over it. Her children chide her for messing with it. But she persists. The last thing she does is say goodbye to the oppressive apartment and carry the plant out the door. At the new house, it will revive in the sunshine and clean air of a better world. We can infer a theme from this symbol: People are like plants; they become healthy—mentally, morally, and physically—only in hospitable environments.

Contrast. Like symbolism, *contrast* helps develop not just theme but characterization and plot. We have already seen examples of contrast in the plays we have mentioned so far: romantic love (Romeo and Juliet) versus social constraints (the Montagues and the Capulets), Thea versus Hedda, Macbeth versus Duncan, old Russia versus new Russia, Hamlet's father versus the new king. Often, playwrights repeat situations but vary them in such ways that the differences have thematic implications. In *Macbeth,* for example, Shakespeare places nearly identical events at the beginning and end. At the beginning, Scotland has just defeated Norway. The traitorous Thane of Cawdor is executed, and Macbeth triumphantly displays the head of another rebel by putting it on a stake. As a reward for valor, the king designates Macbeth the new Thane of Cawdor. At the end of the play, another battle is fought; Macbeth is killed as a "usurper," and his head is cut off and held aloft as a sign of revenge and victory. Ironically, Macbeth has changed places with the first Thane of Cawdor in both name and nature. The circumstances of their deaths are almost identical.

A more far-reaching example of contrast is the Surface brothers in Sheridan's *School for Scandal.* Joseph Surface pretends to be good, but he is in fact selfish and destructive. Charles Surface leads a carefree and careless life; he seems to be a wastrel, but he is in fact generous and honest. Their uncle and benefactor, Sir Oliver Surface, a brusque but warmhearted man, has just returned to England after a long absence and wants to ferret out the true nature of his two potential heirs. To do this he visits each brother separately, disguised as someone else. Both scenes are so much alike that an audience cannot fail to notice the similarity; Sheridan uses the similarity to contrast the brothers. The first scene, with Charles, exposes his good qualities. The audience now knows how the scene will go and gleefully awaits the second scene, in which the despicable Joseph will unwittingly reveal his selfishness and pride. This contrast not only develops plot and character, it also suggests a theme—that the appearance of goodness is worthless without the practice of goodness.

QUESTIONS ABOUT THEME

1. What repetitions occur in the play? What ideas can you draw from these repetitions?

2. What symbols does the author seem deliberately to establish?

3. What contrasts does the playwright establish? Which ones are obvious? Which are not so obvious? In *Romeo and Juliet* we easily spot the contrast between the lovers and the parents, but other contrasts are suggestive. Romeo is different from Juliet (less mature, more impetuous) and is perhaps partly to blame for their deaths; Prince Escalus is different from the parents. The nurse's attitude toward love contrasts starkly with Juliet's. The friar's attitude toward love is different from Romeo's.

4. How is contrast related to the conflicts in the plot? Hedda and Thea are not only different from each other, they are in conflict. What values, then, do the contrasting sides of a conflict manifest?

THINKING ON PAPER ABOUT THEME

1. List the subjects of the play (the issues or problems the play seems to bring up). State themes for each of these subjects (what the play seems to be saying about these issues and problems). If the themes are unclear or contradictory or complex, explain how. See the discussion of subject and theme in Chapter 3, pages 40–44.

2. Mark speeches and sections of dialogue that help develop a particular theme. Look especially for "the big speech," which will typically be longer than most and may forcefully state a theme. Hamlet's "To be or not to be" speech is an example. Another is Figaro's long speech in Act 4 of Beaumarchais's *The Marriage of Figaro* (1775). This speech excoriates the aristocracy and, by implication, the political structure of France. It was so inflammatory that the state censors at first prevented the play from being performed. There may be more than one "big speech." Summarize them and explain how the actions of the play reflect their ideas.

3. Explain in detail how an important scene helps develop themes.

4. Trace the development of one theme throughout the play.

5. Explain the significance of motifs (words, actions, ideasand images) that recur throughout the play.

6. Describe symbols and their possible meanings in the play.

7. Explain the implications of contrasts in the play.

Now It's Your Turn

Explore how repetitions, symbols, and contrasts help develop themes in *Trifles* (printed in the Appendix).

Irony

Dramatic irony. Although plays, like other forms of literature, employ all forms of irony, one of the most important is dramatic irony. (See the discussion of irony in Chapter 3, pp. 73–76.) Dramatic irony relies entirely on the presence of an audience and on what the audience knows. *Dramatic irony* occurs when characters say or do something that playgoers know is different from the characters' beliefs and expectations. A character, for example, with high hopes and great fanfare, invests the family fortune in the stock market in 1928. We know, but the character does not, that the market will crash in 1929. Sometimes only the audience is aware of the ironic contrast between characters' statements and the truth; sometimes the audience shares this knowledge with other characters onstage.

In the two parallel scenes in *School for Scandal,* for example, summarized above, the audience knows that Sir Oliver Surface is wearing a mask to test his nephews—and, of course, Sir Oliver knows—but the nephews do not. So the audience recognizes as ironic everything the nephews do and say that works for or against their self-interest, particularly in the case of Joseph, who would treat Sir Oliver with meticulous courtesy if only he knew who he was. In another scene from this play, Lady Teazle hides behind a screen while her husband, unaware of her presence, talks about her. When he says that he doesn't want her to know that he will leave her a fortune upon his death, we know—but he does not—that Lady Teazle hears everything.

A powerful example of dramatic irony occurs in the last scenes of Shakespeare's *Othello* (1604). Before Desdemona goes to bed, she sings a song about a man who accuses his love of being promiscuous. She asks Emilia, her lady-in-waiting, if any woman could treat her husband so. Emilia says that some might for the right "price," but Desdemona says that she could never do so "for the whole world." The audience recognizes her comments as ironic, because Othello believes she is a "whore" and plans to kill her for it. Later, when Othello strangles Desdemona, he boasts that even if he is "cruel" he is at least "merciful" because he will kill her quickly without allowing her to "linger in . . . pain." But his "mercy" contrasts horribly with our knowledge of her innocence and the quality of mercy she deserves. When he defends his murder to Emilia, he says,

> Cassio did top her. Ask thy husband [Iago] else.
> O, I were damned beneath all depth in hell
> But that I did proceed upon just grounds
> To this extremity. Thy husband knew it all. (5.2. 137–40)

We know, and poor Othello is about to find out, that Iago has betrayed him and that he has in truth had no "just grounds" for the "extremity" of his deed.

QUESTIONS ABOUT IRONY

1. Like fiction and poetry, drama uses all kinds of irony. *Verbal irony* is prevalent simply because drama relies so heavily on dialogue. Sometimes the director and actors themselves must decide whether particular lines are ironic. When Thea, for example, tells Hedda about inspiring Loevborg to write his book, Hedda interjects comments such as "Poor, pretty little Thea"; "But my dear Thea! How brave of you!"; "Clever little Thea!" (284–9) Hedda surely means these statements ironically. The actress would say them with enough sarcasm to let the audience know how Hedda really feels about Thea's successes, but without allowing the slow-witted Thea to pick up on the irony.

2. What are the ironies, then, in the play you are studying? How do they relate to characterization and theme?

3. What dramatic ironies does the playwright build into the play?

4. Do the dramatic ironies—such as Othello's repeated description of Iago as "honest"—create a pattern of revelation or meaning?

THINKING ON PAPER ABOUT IRONY

1. Describe the instances of dramatic irony in the play.

2. Do the same for other ironies (verbal, attitudinal, and situational). For a discussion of these kinds of irony, see Chapter 3.

Now It's Your Turn

Identify the dramatic and other ironies in *Trifles* (located in the Appendix). Speculate about what they reveal about the characters and about possible themes of the play.

Subgenres

The best-known subgenres of drama are tragedy and comedy, but there are many others: melodrama, theater of the absurd, allegory, comedy of manners, spectacle, masque, modern drama, farce, and tragicomedy. Some, like musicals, opera, and ballet, shade into other art forms.

Tragedy.   Definitions of subgenres can lead to fruitful interpretations of individual works. The definition of *tragedy* began with the first and most famous discussion of it, Aristotle's *Poetics* (c. 342 BCE). Aristotle based his definition on an inductive examination of Greek tragedy, and he seems in particular to have had Sophocles's plays in mind. His definition focuses primarily on the effect of the play on the audience and on the nature of the tragic hero. Tragic heroes, he says, inspire "pity" and "fear" in the audience: pity because the heroes don't deserve their fate and fear because the heroes' fate could be anyone's. The audience, in other words, identifies deeply with tragic heroes. They are noble but flawed. They have one principal flaw—in Sophocles, usually the flaw of pride. This flaw Aristotle called a *hamartia*, literally a "miscalculation." Because of the heroes' flaws, they suffer emotionally and experience a reversal of fortune (*peripeteia*), moving abruptly from a high place (high social position, wealth, responsibility, purity) to a low place. Before this reversal occurs, the heroes understand for the first time their flawed state and their error-filled ways. This moment is the "recognition" and usually occurs at the climax of the play. The heroes recognize that they are responsible for their deeds and that such deeds contradict a moral order inherent in the entire cosmos. The effect of the play on the audience is to induce a *catharsis,* a feeling of emotional release and exuberance.

Comedy.   Aristotle planned to write as comprehensively on *comedy* as on tragedy, but either that part of the *Poetics* was lost, or he never got around to it. The nature of comedy is difficult to pin down,

both artistically and psychologically. Numerous critics have specu-
lated about why people laugh. Laughter is only one of the puzzling
aspects of comedy. Most critics agree on some of the characteristics
of comedy. Comedy, for example, is the depiction of the "ludicrous";
that is, a gross departure from the serious. Therefore, in order to see
something as comic, members of the audience must have a sense of
what is "serious." The comic in drama is related to what playgoers
think is serious. If the community of playgoers thinks that proper
attire for men is a business suit, tie, and polished shoes, then a gross
distortion of that dress—by a clown in a circus, for example—would
be comic.

Methods of comedy. Two methods of signaling the ludicrous are
incongruity and exaggeration. It is incongruous for a haughty, spiff-
ily dressed man, walking nose in the air, to slip and fall face first
into a mud hole or to be hit in the face with a cream pie. Further,
comedy must cause no pain to the audience. This means that the
audience cannot identify as deeply with comic figures as it does
with tragic figures and that the method of presentation—language,
acting, setting—must communicate an air of "fantasy." Through its
methods and style, the production constantly says, "This isn't true.
It's only a joke." The fantasy element in comedies helps explain why
they almost always end happily, whereas tragedies end unhappily.
Finally, the characters in comedy are more "realistic" than in tragedy. They are more like us, whereas in tragedy they are, even in their
flawed state (sometimes *because* of their flawed state), far nobler
than we are. Two excellent recent books, both by Robert Corrigan,
deal with comedy and tragedy: *Tragedy: A Study of Drama in Modern
Times* (1967) and *Comedy: Meaning and Form* (1981).

QUESTIONS ABOUT SUBGENRES

*Definitions of genres and subgenres can be useful for interpreting literature. They
help expose the parts of works of literature and thus how these parts might be
meaningful. Turn definitions of tragedy, comedy, and other subgenres into probing questions aimed at a specific work. For tragedies, ask questions like these:*

1. What is the character's major flaw? Does he or she have more than
   one flaw?

2. When does the recognition scene occur? What does the character
   recognize?

For comedies, try these:

3. What incongruities cause the comedy?
4. What do the incongruities reveal about the playwright's attitude toward the characters and setting?
5. Are there hints of satire in these incongruities?
6. How does the playwright establish the detachment necessary for us to laugh?

Try applying definitions of genres to works that do not quite fit the categories and see what you come up with. Some people regard *Hedda Gabler* as like a "tragedy" but not exactly an Aristotelian tragedy. Will any parts of Aristotle's definition apply to *Hedda Gabler?* Does Hedda have a "tragic flaw"? Is she responsible for her actions? Is she to blame for the harm she causes? Does she have a moment or moments of recognition? Is she nobler than we are? Does she experience a "reversal"? Does the audience experience pity and fear for Hedda?

Some of the most interesting questions about subgenres emerge from plays that mix subgenres. Why, for example, are there comic elements in Shakespeare's tragedies? Is *The Cherry Orchard* a comedy? a tragedy? both? Are we supposed to laugh or cry at the fate of Chekhov's ineffectual aristocrats?

THINKING ON PAPER ABOUT SUBGENRES

1. If you know the subgenre to which the play belongs (tragedy, comedy, farce, and so forth), find a good definition of the subgenre. List the characteristics of the subgenre. You can find definitions in encyclopedias and handbooks of literature.
2. Take one item from the list and explain how well it applies to the play. If Hamlet is a tragic character, for example, what might be his tragic flaw? What constitutes his reversal? When does he experience a recognition? How does the audience respond to him?

NOW IT'S YOUR TURN

Susan Glaspell wrote a short-story version of *Trifles* titled "A Jury of Her Peers." She seems to suggest that the play belongs to the "trial" subgenre. It is also a kind of detective story. What conventions of these two subgenres does the play utilize? Does Glaspell alter the subgenres any, bend them to her own purposes? Are there other subgenres to which the play might belong? In short, explore Glaspell's possible use and alteration of one or more subgenres. Compare the story with the play. Which do you like better?

Checklist for Interpreting Drama

Audience (pages 86–87)
- Consider different "locations" of the audience in relationship to the performance—up close or back away, lights up or down, on stage with the players or down away from the stage, ignored by the players or directly addressed. Explore how any of these arrangements would affect the performance of the play and the audience's response to it.

Plot (pages 87–92)
- Note the actions that occur offstage. Explain why the playwright places them offstage rather than on.

- Indicate the conflicts and how you learn about them (through dialogue, the characters' actions, and other means).

- Compare the "plot" to the "story." Determine to what extent events of the past influence actions in the play.

- Speculate about how the playwright anticipates audience expectations.

- Characterize the structure and content of formal and informal structural units. Indicate any that seem especially important.

Characterization (pages 93–99)
- Identify traits of stock characters.

- Explain what makes round characters complex.

- Indicate which characters change and which do not. Speculate about what causes the dynamic characters to change.

- Specify how subtexts influence your understanding of characters, conflicts, and themes.

- Indicate when and how characters wear masks. Show where and how the true nature of characters becomes clear. Speculate about why the characters wear masks and how their masks affect others.

Setting (pages 99–103)
- Determine how you learn about the setting—from dialogue, sets, stage directions, and other means.

- Describe the sets the playwright calls for or that you would design.

- Speculate about how the knowledge audiences bring to a performance might influence their understanding of the setting.

- If the setting or sets are symbolic, show how.

Themes (pages 103–107)
- Point out repetitions and explain their significance.

- Explore the meanings of symbols.

- Indicate telling contrasts.

Irony (pages 107–109)
- Note occurrences of dramatic irony. Explain their probable impact on the audience.

- Indicate other kinds of irony and the extent to which the playwright employs irony. Show how irony develops characters and themes.

Subgenres (pages 109-111)
- Indicate the subgenre to which the play seems to belong or to which it seems similar.

- Show how the play employs conventions of the subgenre and how it alters any of them.

- Speculate about why the playwright chose this subgenre for the play.

Works Cited

Abrams, M. H., and Geoffrey Galt Harpham. *A Glossary of Literary Terms*. Boston: Wadsworth Cengage Learning, 2009. Print.

Aristotle. *Aristotle's Poetics: A Translation and Commentary for Students of Literature*. Trans. Leon Golden. Commentary O. B. Hardison, Jr. Tallahassee: UP of Florida, 1981. Print.

Beckerman, Bernard. *Dynamics of Drama: Theory and Method of Analysis*. New York: Drama Book Specialists, 1979. Print.

Corrigan, Robert W., ed. *Tragedy: A Study of Drama in Modern Times*. New York: Harcourt, 1967. Print.

———. *Comedy: Meaning and Form*. New York: Harper, 1981. Print.

Edson, Margaret. *Wit*. New York: Dramatists Play Service, 1999. Print.

Hansberry, Lorraine. *A Raisin in the Sun*. New York: New American Library, 1987. Print.

Ibsen, Henrik. *Hedda Gabler and Other Plays*. Trans. Una Ellis-Fermor. New York: Penguin, 1988. Print.

Meisel, Martin. *How Plays Work: Reading and Performance*. New York: Oxford UP, 2007. Print.

Molière. *The Misanthrope*. Trans. Henri van Laun. Mineola, NY: Dover, 1992. Print.

———. *Tartuffe*. Trans. H. Baker and J. Miller. Mineola, NY: Dover, 2000. Print.

Pixley, Edward, George Kernodle, and Portia Kernodle. *Invitation to the Theatre*. 3rd ed. San Diego: Harcourt, 1985. Print.

Shakespeare, William. *Hamlet*. Ed. Willard Farnham. Pelican Shakespeare. Baltimore: Penguin, 1957. Print.

———. *Othello*. Ed. Gerald Eades Bentley. Pelican Shakespeare. Baltimore: Penguin, 1958. Print.

Sheridan, Richard Brinsley. *The School for Scandal. Four English Comedies*. Ed. J. M. Morrell. Harmondsworth, England: Penguin, 1950. Print.

Stoppard, Tom. "The Event and the Text." *Tom Stoppard in Conversation*. Ed. Paul Delaney. Ann Arbor: U of Michigan P, 1994. Print.

Interpreting Poetry

WHAT IS POETRY?

What is poetry? Like the question, What is literature?, there are no certain answers to this one. If you look at poems published in magazines such as the *New Yorker*, you might think, "There is no rhyme in this poem, no meter, no apparent structure. It is arranged in lines, but why couldn't I take any paragraph, arrange it in lines, and call it 'poetry'? What makes this poem—or any poem—'poetry'?"

A mystical definition.   Edward Hirsch, author of the best-selling *How to Read a Poem and Fall in Love with Poetry* (1999), claims that the defining characteristic of poetry is its spirituality. Poetry, which originated in prehistoric religious worship (86, 135), has never lost "its sense of sacred mystery" (16). The vocation of poets is thus "Orphic" (that is, mystical; associated with the miraculous gift for music manifested by Orpheus, a figure from Greek mythology). Poets enter "the mystery of a world riven with *anima,* with process, a world that awakens to the Orphic calling of the poet. The impulse [of the poet] is shamanistic" (78).

Hirsch concludes that since the essence of poetry is spiritual, it can transform us. Poetry is "the most intimate and volatile form of literary discourse" (xi). It can deepen "our capacity for personhood, our achievement of humanity" (xiii). It induces insights in which "the self is both lost and found" (243). When "I encounter and interiorize the poem, when I ingest it, dreaming it and letting it dream its way into me," then "I can feel the Orphic enchantment, the delirium and lucidity, the swoon of poetry" (261). Poetry "activates my secret world" (8).

A poem that Hirsch feels represents the mystical nature of poetry is this poem by Emily Brontë:*

THE NIGHT IS DARKENING ROUND ME

Emily Brontë

The night is darkening round me,
The wild winds coldly blow;
But a tyrant spell has bound me
And I cannot, cannot go.

The giant trees are bending
Their bare boughs weighed with snow,
And the storm is fast descending
And yet I cannot go.

Clouds beyond clouds above me,
Wastes beyond wastes below;
But nothing drear can move me;
I will not, cannot go.   1837

Brontë's poem, he says, is "spellbound," the "poetry of trance." It enacts "a sense of transfiguration and dark initiation" (66). Hirsch hails Emily Dickinson's famous definition of poetry as a fitting complement to Brontë's poem:

> If I read a book [and] it makes my whole body so cold no fire can ever warm me I know *that* is poetry. If I feel physically as if the top of my head were taken off, I know *that* is poetry. These are the only way I know. Is there any other way? (7)

Hirsch says that we should read poetry the way Dickinson does, by letting "its mysteries breathe through us" (157).

Definition by elements. Many people would disagree with Hirsch's claim for the spirituality of poetry, but most commentators posit

---

*Publication dates of works of literature cited in this book and dates of authors' lives can be found in the author-title index at the back of the book.

special qualities for poetry that are hard to define. Writing in the *New Princeton Encyclopedia of Poetry and Poetics* (1993), T. V. F. Brogan says that "a poem conveys heightened forms of perception, experience, meaning, or consciousness in heightened language." As "a heightened mode of discourse" (938), poetry exhibits "intensified speech" (939). What does he mean by "heightened" and "intensified"? Furthermore, what causes such special qualities? An answer lies in the conventions poets use to create poetry, conventions that poets have used for centuries and that are often cited as defining characteristics of poetry. Poets must learn such conventions in order to use them, to depart from them, and to invent new conventions. Even Hirsch says that poetry is a "conscious craft," not just something composed by "unconscious invention" (27).

We will explore these conventions—or elements—in this chapter. As with literature in general, traditional characteristics of a genre do not singly or collectively "define" it, but they help us recognize, read, and write it. In this chapter we arrange these conventions into four broad categories: sense (elements that convey ideas), sound (elements that underscore the musical qualities of language), structure (elements that organize), and sight (elements that affect the appearance of poems). Although the sense, sound, structure, and sight of poetry are interwoven in any poem and contribute to its meanings, we will for the sake of clarity deal with them separately.

I. SENSE IN POETRY: ELEMENTS THAT CONVEY MEANING

Getting the Facts Straight (Reading a Poem the First Time)

Understanding the words and sentences and getting the facts straight is the most basic level of meaning in works of literature. Here are some simple strategies for orienting yourself in a poem, especially when you are reading it for the first time:

1. Read the poem through once without stopping. Don't try to understand every word or phrase. Just get a general sense of the poem.

2. Reread the poem, looking up words you don't know. See *Diction* below.

3. Read the poem again. This time identify the normal word order of all the sentences. See *Syntax* below. "Normal" word order is subject-verb-object: Jane loves Joe.

4. Track down any allusions in the poem. An *allusion* is a reference to historical events and people, to mythological and biblical figures, and to works of literature. Allusions invite comparison between the work at hand and the items referred to. An example of an allusion is Matthew Arnold's reference to Sophocles in "Dover Beach" (pages 126–27). Arnold invites us to bring the weight of Sophocles's tragedies to bear on the subject matter of his poem. An allusion is a compact way of adding meaning to the work.

Diction

Diction refers to the poet's choice of words. Poets like words, sometimes unusual words. Most people, even experienced readers, have to look up such words. Don't feel ashamed that you might have to as well. Knowing the poets' understanding of the words they use is crucial to understanding the meaning of their poems.

Poets are sensitive to the subtle shades of meanings of words, to the possible double meanings of words, and to the denotative and connotative meanings of words. As we say in Chapter 2, *denotation* is the object or idea—the referent—that a word represents. The denotation of a word is its core meaning, its dictionary meaning. *Connotation* is the subjective, emotional association that a word has for one person or a group of people. See pages 17–18 for a more thorough discussion of these two concepts. Poets often choose words that contribute to the poem's meaning on both a denotative and a connotative level.

QUESTIONS ABOUT DICTION

Meanings of words. Examine the words in a poem for all their possible shades and levels of meaning. Then ask how these meanings combine to create an overall effect. Note, for example, the effect that connotation creates in William Wordsworth's "A Slumber Did My Spirit Seal."

A SLUMBER DID MY SPIRIT SEAL

William Wordsworth

A slumber did my spirit seal;
I had no human fears—
She seemed a thing that could not feel
The touch of earthly years.

No motion has she now, no force;
She neither hears nor sees;
Rolled round in earth's diurnal course,
With rocks, and stones, and trees.   1800

In order to create the stark contrast between the active, airy girl of the first stanza with the inert, dead girl of the second, Wordsworth relies partly on the connotative effect of the last line. We know the denotative meaning of "rocks, and stones, and trees," but in this context the emotional or connotative meaning is unpleasant and grating. Rocks and stones are inanimate, cold, cutting, impersonal. And although we usually think of trees as beautiful and majestic, here the association of trees with rocks and stones makes us think of tree roots, of dirt, and thus of the girl's burial. The rocks and stones and trees are not only not human, they confine and smother the girl. Another example of connotation is the word *diurnal,* which means "daily." But the Latinate *diurnal* has a slightly more formal connotation than the prosaic *daily.* The effect of the word is to make the processes of nature—death, the revolving of Earth, the existence of rocks and stones and trees—seem remote, remorseless, and inevitable.

Wordplay.   Be alert for wordplay—double meanings and puns. The speaker in Andrew Marvell's "To His Coy Mistress" (c. 1650), for example, tries to persuade a reluctant woman to make love with him. His argument is that time is running out. Unless we take opportunities when they appear, we will lose them. He concludes his speech with a pun:

Thus, though we cannot make our sun
Stand still, yet we will make him run.

That is, we cannot stop time (make the sun stop), but we can bring about new life (a child: "son"), who will "run," and thus defeat decay and death. Some poets, such as e.e. cummings, make imaginative wordplay a dominant trait of their poetry. In "anyone lived in a pretty how town," cummings uses pronouns on two levels of meaning. The words *anyone* and *noone* mean, on the one hand, what we expect them to mean ("anybody" and "nobody"); but on the other hand they refer to two people, male (anyone) and female (noone), who fall in love, marry, and die.

THINKING ON PAPER ABOUT DICTION

1. Circle all the words you do not know. Look them up in the dictionary. Write brief definitions in the margin.

2. Underline words that seem especially meaningful or well chosen. For each word, explain denotations and connotations.

3. Underline any wordplay such as double meanings and puns. Explain what the wordplay adds to the sense of the poem.

4. Underline any uses of "unusual" words—slang, profanity, archaisms, foreign language words, made-up words. Say what qualities and meanings these words add to the poem. Explore how the poem would be different without them.

5. Identify the level of diction in the poem (formal, informal, colloquial, slangy, dialect). State what the poem gains from the use of this level. Say what it would lose by changing to a different level.

6. Indicate how the choice of words contributes to the speaker's tone (attitude).

NOW IT'S YOUR TURN

Analyze Sir Walter Raleigh's diction in "The Nymph's Reply to the Shepherd" (pages 30–31). How fitting are the nuances of his words as a response to the rosy picture of love painted by Marlowe in "The Passionate Shepherd to His Love"? Assess the implication of Raleigh's allusion to Philomel, a character from Greek mythology.

Syntax

Syntax in poetry can be profoundly meaningful but also confusing.

Independent clauses. *Syntax* is sentence structure, the way words go together to make sentences. The basic unit of any English sentence is the *simple sentence* or *independent clause*. The normal word order of independent clauses is subject-verb (Jane loves) or subject-verb-object (Jane loves Joe). Poets often invert the normal word order of independent clauses. They do so to make the sentence rhyme, to fit a metrical pattern, or to emphasize an idea. An example is "A slumber did my spirit seal," the first line of the preceding Wordsworth poem. The normal word order of this sentence would be "My spirit did seal a slumber"—subject (spirit)-verb (did seal)-object (slumber). But by inverting the word order, Wordsworth gains the end-rhyme he wants, the iambic metrical pattern he wants, and an emphasis on the speaker's state of mind, "slumber."

Complex sentences. Poets also often (usually) include complex sentences—sentences containing independent and subordinate (dependent) clauses. A *subordinate clause* begins with a relative pro-noun (that, what, which, who), subordinating conjunction (because, since, although, whereas, once, wherever, etc.), or preposition (to, in, by, along, behind, with, etc.). Such a clause is always part of an independent clause; it does not stand alone. In poetry, complex sentences can be richly suggestive but confusing. The subordinate clauses may be long, there may be more than one per sentence, they may be located between subject and verb, and their normal word order—subject-verb-object—may be inverted to meet metrical and rhyme schemes.

Further causes of confusion are sentences that are so long we forget how they begin, sentences in which words are left out, and sentences marked by eccentric punctuation.

QUESTIONS ABOUT SYNTAX

Do yourself a favor. Unscramble these sentences! You really have to in order to understand the meaning of any poem. Initial questions, then, are:

1. What is the normal word order of the sentences in the poem?

2. What words have been left out?

The syntax of many poems is easy to follow. But most poems have some complexity of syntax that needs your alert attention. Arnold's "Dover Beach" (pages 126–27), for example, starts off with lucid syntax: "The sea is calm"; "The tide is full"; "the moon lies fair"; "the light gleams";

"the cliffs of England stand." But when the speaker's thoughts become more complicated (in line 7), so does the syntax: "Only, from the long line of spray/ Where the sea meets the moon-blanched land,/ Listen! <u>You</u> <u>hear the</u> grating <u>roar</u>/ Of pebbles which the waves draw back, and fling,/ At their return, up the high strand,/ <u>Begin, and cease, and then again</u> <u>begin,</u>/ With tremulous cadence slow, <u>and bring</u>/ The eternal note of sadness in" (ll. 7–14). The heart of this long sentence is the phrase "you [subject] hear [verb] the roar [object]" plus what the "roar" does. (See the underlined words in the sentence.) But to find this structure, you have to pare away the subordinate clauses from the independent clause.

3. A follow-up question is: Why does the poet diverge from normal word order or make the syntax abnormally complicated? Mary Kinzie (in *A Poet's Guide to Poetry*) says that poets' games with syntax are "thresholds of invention" that "are closely bound up with thematic suggestion. It makes as little sense to work toward complexity and tension in a poem that aims to express contentment as to compose the lines simply and uniformly in a poem of fretful brooding. Form should follow theme" (87).

4. How, then, is a poem's syntax related to its ideas?

THINKING ON PAPER ABOUT SYNTAX

1. Write out all the sentences in the poem in normal word order.

2. Fill in the "missing" words. Put them in brackets.

3. If you remember how to diagram sentences, do so for all the complex sentences. At least, indicate the relationship of the subordinate clauses to the parts of the independent clause.

4. Speculate on how the poem's ideas would be altered were the syntax "normal."

NOW IT'S YOUR TURN

Louise Bogan's "Song for a Lyre" is notable for its complicated syntax. Identify the independent clauses in her sentences. Explore the relationship of syntax and meaning in the poem.

SONG FOR A LYRE

Louise Bogan

The landscape where I lie
Again from boughs sets free
Summer; all night must fly
In wind's obscurity
The thick, green leaves that made
Heavy the August shade.

Soon, in the pictured night,
Returns—as in a dream
Left after sleep's delight—
The shallow autumn stream:
Softly awake, its sound
Poured on the chilly ground.

Soon fly the leaves in throngs;
O love, though once I lay
Far from its sound, to weep,
When night divides my sleep,
When stars, the autumn stream,
Stillness, divide my dream,
Night to your voice belongs.   1937

Characterization, Point of View, Plot, and Setting

Fiction and drama as poetry.   Poetry shares many elements with its sister genres, drama and fiction. Indeed, many works of drama and fiction are written in poetry. Plays by Sophocles, Shakespeare, and Goethe are poetry, as are epics by Homer, Dante, and Milton. Poetic narratives and dramas are similar to prose fiction and drama in their handling of characterization, point of view, plot, and setting. Thus the same questions one asks about a short story, novel, or play to probe their meanings are relevant to these poems. See the discussions of these two genres in chapters 3 (fiction) and 4 (drama).

Most poems, however, do not offer a "story" in the conventional sense. They are usually brief and apparently devoid of "action." Even so, a plot of sorts may be implied, a place and time may be important, a point of view may be operating, and characters may dramatize the key issues of the poem.

The speakers in poems. In any poem there is always one "character" of the utmost importance, the speaker or "I" of the poem. T. S. Eliot, in an essay entitled "The Three Voices of Poetry" (1954), says there are three possible speakers or voices:

> The first voice is the voice of the poet talking to himself—or to nobody. The second voice is the voice of the poet addressing an audience, whether large or small. The third is the voice of the poet when he attempts to create a dramatic character speaking in verse; when he is saying, not what he would say in his own person, but only what he can say within the limits of one imaginary character addressing another imaginary character. (96)

How can you tell the difference between these speakers? It is often easy to spot Eliot's third "voice": a speaker who is fictional, not at all equivalent to the poet. The speaker of Robert Browning's "Porphyria's Lover" (1836), for example, is a deranged killer who speaks to another character. He is clearly not Robert Browning. The "speaker" of Langston Hughes's "Vagabonds" (1947, printed on page 163) is plural, a group of people, so not Langston Hughes. But what about the speaker of Emily Brontë's poem that we read at the beginning of the chapter? Although the scene is dreamlike and thus possibly fictional, she may have had the dream and be writing about herself. The speaker of Matthew Arnold's "Dover Beach" (pages 126–27) is addressing another character, but even so this speaker may be mouthing the beliefs of the poet.

Speaker and author. The only way to know for sure if speakers are similar to poets is by means of biographical information. Consider, for example, this poem by the American poet Jane Kenyon.

IN THE NURSING HOME

Jane Kenyon

She is like a horse grazing
a hill pasture that someone makes
smaller by coming every night
to pull the fences in and in.

She has stopped running wide loops,
stopped even the tight circles.
She drops her head to feed; grass

is dust, and the creekbed's dry.
Master, come with your light
halter. Come and bring her in.   1996

Is the speaker like the poet? Probably yes. We know that she took care of her mother in her mother's final illness and wrote elsewhere about this experience. Similarly, we can be fairly sure that the speaker of Edna St. Vincent Millay's sonnet, "I, Being Born a Woman" (page 153), is like Millay. We know enough about Millay's life to make the connection. But often we don't know. Is the speaker of Shakespeare's sonnets a stand-in for Shakespeare? Lacking biographical information, we cannot be sure.

Does it matter? Yes, if you want to understand a poem in the context of the poet's philosophy or view of life. Knowing about a poet's life and beliefs can often make the meaning of poems more visible. A poet's experiences and attitudes may touch you and lead you to rich understandings of individual poems. But even when a speaker manifests beliefs and traits of the poet, you should probably think of the speaker as fictional, as a projection of the poet's imagination, as a voice not quite the same as the poet. In this sense, the speaker becomes a "character" in the poem, subject to the same questions you would pose about characters in narratives and plays.

QUESTIONS ABOUT CHARACTERIZATION, POINT OF VIEW, PLOT, AND SETTING

In analyzing poetry, your first step should be to come to grips with the "I" of the poem, the speaker. Answer questions such as these:

1. Who is speaking?

2. What characterizes the speaker?

3. To whom is he or she speaking?

4. What is the speaker's emotional state?

5. Why is he or she speaking?

6. What situation is being described?

7. What are the conflicts or tensions in this situation?

8. How is setting—social situation, physical place, and time—important to the speaker?

9. What ideas does the speaker communicate?

Matthew Arnold's "Dover Beach" provides an example of how you can use most of these questions to get at the meanings of a poem.

DOVER BEACH

Matthew Arnold

The sea is calm to-night.
The tide is full, the moon lies fair
Upon the straits; on the French coast the light
Gleams and is gone; the cliffs of England stand,
Glimmering and vast, out in the tranquil bay.   5
Come to the window, sweet is the night-air!
Only, from the long line of spray
Where the sea meets the moon-blanched land,
Listen! you hear the grating roar
Of pebbles which the waves draw back, and fling,   10
At their return, up the high strand,
Begin, and cease, and then again begin,
With tremulous cadence slow, and bring
The eternal note of sadness in.

Sophocles long ago   15
Heard it on the Aegean, and it brought
Into his mind the turbid ebb and flow
Of human misery; we
Find also in the sound a thought,
Hearing it by this distant northern sea.   20

The Sea of Faith
Was once, too, at the full, and round earth's shore
Lay like the folds of a bright girdle furled.
But now I only hear
Its melancholy, long, withdrawing roar,   25
Retreating, to the breath
Of the night-wind, down the vast edges drear
And naked shingles° of the world.

Ah, love, let us be true
To one another! for the world, which seems   30
To lie before us like a land of dreams,
So various, so beautiful, so new,
Hath really neither joy, nor love, nor light,
Nor certitude, nor peace, nor help for pain;
And we are here as on a darkling plain   35

Swept with confused alarms of struggle and flight,
Where ignorant armies clash by night.   1867
                                 °beaches covered with pebbles

Because Dover is an English port city, one of several points of
departure for the European continent, the speaker has apparently
stopped for the night on his way to Europe. As he looks out of his
hotel window, he speaks to another person in the room, his "love"
(last stanza). Arnold traces the speaker's train of thought in four
stanzas. In the first stanza, the speaker describes what he sees, and
his tone is contented, even joyous. He sees the lights on the French
coast and the high white cliffs of Dover "glimmering" in the moon-
light. He invites his companion to share the glorious view. As he
describes the sound of the surf to her, his tone alters slightly; the
sound reminds him of "the eternal note of sadness." This melan-
cholic tone deepens in the second stanza. There the speaker connects
the sea sound with a passage in a tragedy by Sophocles.

In the third stanza, the remembrance of the passage from
Sophocles leads the speaker to make a disturbing comparison. He
likens the sea to faith—apparently religious faith, both his own
and that of his age. He says that at one time the "Sea of Faith" was
full but now has withdrawn, leaving a "vast," "drear," and coarse
world. By the fourth stanza, the speaker has fallen into near despair.
He says that what merely looks beautiful—the panorama seen from
his window—is only a false image of the world, which in reality is
absurd and chaotic. He has only one hope, his companion, whom he
now urges to be true to him as he is true to her.

The speaker, in short, is an erudite, thoughtful, but deeply
troubled person. The poem takes him from momentary contented-
ness to near hopelessness. The stimulus for his train of thought is
the place of the poem—Dover Beach—and the companion to whom
he addresses his remarks. All these elements—thoughts, place, and
companion—are interrelated.

THINKING ON PAPER ABOUT CHARACTERIZATION, POINT OF VIEW, PLOT, AND SETTING

Many of the exercises one does on poetry consist of marking the poem
itself. You might photocopy the poem and even enlarge it. That way, you
can see the poem well and have plenty of space to write. If helpful, make
more than one copy of the poem. Use different copies to mark different
aspects of the poem.

1. Paraphrase the poem. This can help you understand every sentence or, at least, the major sections of the poem. The two paragraphs immediately following "Dover Beach," for example, are a paraphrase of the poem.

2. Identify the speaker of the poem. Underline the words and phrases that help characterize the speaker and bring out the speaker's concerns. Describe in detail the traits of the speaker and of any other characters in the poem.

3. Describe the situation of the poem: where the speaker is, what time of day it is, what season of the year, what historical occasion, to whom the speaker is speaking, and why. List the external and internal conflicts of the poem.

4. State the issues that concern the speaker. Explain the speaker's ideas. Note any changes in the speaker's mood or ideas as the poem moves from unit to unit. Explain what the speaker is trying to accomplish.

5. Describe the speaker's tone (angry, lyrical, hopeful, bitter, nostalgic, sarcastic, compassionate, admiring, sorrowful, amused, and so forth). Note any changes of tone.

6. If the speaker is a fictional character, estimate the poet's attitude toward the speaker and toward the issues raised by the poem. Indicate any differences between what might be the poet's attitude and the speaker's.

7. Relate the poem's title to its themes.

8. Explain any allusions in the poem.

Now It's Your Turn

Characterize the Duke of Ferrara and his deceased wife in Robert Browning's "My Last Duchess." Show how physical details, social circumstances (such as class and gender status), the duke's manner of speaking (word choice, syntax), lead you to your conclusions. The poem, based on an actual event, is set in sixteenth-century Italy. The duke negotiates to marry the young daughter of another aristocrat. Speaking to an ambassador of the girl's father, he attempts to convince the ambassador of his merits as a husband. Does he succeed? What will the ambassador tell the father? The artists the duke mentions, Frà Pandolf and Claus of Innsbruck, are fictional.

This poem has been described as a highly condensed short story or even a novel. Using the clues in the poem, can you construct a "plot" for the duke and duchess's marriage? Try a plot from the duchess's point of view, then one from the duke's.

MY LAST DUCHESS

Robert Browning

Ferrara
That's my last Duchess painted on the wall,
Looking as if she were alive. I call
That piece a wonder, now: Frà Pandolf's hands
Worked busily a day, and there she stands.
Will 't please you sit and look at her? I said   5
"Frà Pandolf" by design, for never read
Strangers like you that pictured countenance,
The depth and passion of its earnest glance,
But to myself they turned (since none puts by
The curtain I have drawn for you, but I)   10
And seemed as they would ask me, if they durst,
How such a glance came there; so, not the first
Are you to turn and ask thus. Sir, 'twas not
Her husband's presence only, called that spot
Of joy into the Duchess' cheek: perhaps   15
Frà Pandolf chanced to say "Her mantle laps
Over my lady's wrist too much," or "Paint
Must never hope to reproduce the faint
Half-flush that dies along her throat": such stuff
Was courtesy, she thought, and cause enough   20
For calling up that spot of joy. She had
A heart—how shall I say?—too soon made glad,
Too easily impressed; she liked whate'er
She looked on, and her looks went everywhere.
Sir, 'twas all one! My favor at her breast,   25
The dropping of the daylight in the West,
The bough of cherries some officious fool
Broke in the orchard for her, the white mule
She rode with round the terrace—all and each
Would draw from her alike the approving speech,   30
Or blush, at least. She thanked men—good! but thanked
Somehow—I know not how—as if she ranked
My gift of a nine-hundred-years-old name
With anybody's gift. Who'd stoop to blame
This sort of trifling? Even had you skill   35

In speech—(which I have not)—to make your will
Quite clear to such an one, and say, "Just this
Or that in you disgusts me; here you miss,
Or there exceed the mark"—and if she let
Herself be lessoned so, nor plainly set   40
Her wits to yours, forsooth, and made excuse
—E'en then would be some stooping; and I choose
Never to stoop. Oh sir, she smiled, no doubt,
Whene'er I passed her; but who passed without
Much the same smile? This grew; I gave commands;   45
Then all smiles stopped together. There she stands
As if alive. Will 't please you rise? We'll meet
The company below, then. I repeat,
The Count your master's known munificence
Is ample warrant that no just pretense   50
Of mine for dowry will be disallowed;
Though his fair daughter's self, as I avowed
At starting, is my object. Nay, we'll go
Together down, sir. Notice Neptune, though,
Taming a sea horse, thought a rarity,   55
Which Claus of Innsbruck cast in bronze for me!   1842

Imagery: Descriptive Language

Definition.   When applied to poetry, the term *imagery* has two meanings. First, imagery represents the descriptive passages of a poem. Although the word *imagery* calls to mind the visual sense, poetic imagery appeals to all the senses. Sensuous imagery is pleasurable for its own sake, but it also provides concreteness and immediacy. Imagery causes the reader to become experientially involved in the subject matter of the poem. Further, the poet often uses descriptive imagery to underscore other elements in a poem, such as tone, meaning, and characterization.

An example of descriptive imagery is the first stanza of John Keats's narrative poem "The Eve of St. Agnes" (1819):

St. Agnes' Eve—Ah, bitter chill it was!
The owl, for all his feathers, was a-cold;
The hare limped trembling through the frozen grass,
And silent was the flock in woolly fold;

Numb were the Beadsman's fingers, while he told
His rosary, and while his frosted breath,
Like pious incense from a censer old,
Seemed taking flight for heaven, without a death,
Past the sweet Virgin's picture, while his prayer he saith.

This stanza appeals to the thermal sense (the chill of the evening, the frozen grass), the sense of touch (the beadsman's numb fingers), the visual sense (the beadsman saying his rosary before the picture of the Virgin), the sense of motion (the hare trembling and limping through the grass, the beadsman's frosted breath taking flight toward heaven), and the sense of sound (the silent flock, the sound of the beadsman's monotonous prayer). The dominant sensuous appeal, however, is to the thermal sense. Keats uses every sensuous image in the stanza to make us feel how cold the night is.

Another example is the scene in Christina Rossetti's "Goblin Market" (1862) when the heroine Lizzie withstands the temptation of the evil goblins' fruit.

One may lead a horse to water,
Twenty cannot make him drink.
Tho' the goblins cuffed and caught her,
Coaxed and fought her,
Bullied and besought her,
Scratched her, pinched her black as ink,
Kicked and knocked her,
Mauled and mocked her,
Lizzie uttered not a word;
Would not open lip from lip
Lest they should cram a mouthful in:
But laughed in heart to feel the drip
Of juice that syruped all her face,
And lodged in dimples of her chin,
And streaked her neck which quaked like curd.

The dominant appeal here is to the sense of touch. Rossetti conveys the physical pain Lizzie suffers as well as the icky, sticky quality of the forbidden fruit.

Imagery: Figurative Language

Rhetorical figures of speech. Critics today use *imagery* in a second sense. They use it to mean figurative language, especially metaphor. *Figurative language* is the conscious departure from normal or conventional ways of saying things. This could mean merely a rearrangement of the normal word order of a sentence, such as "Sir Gawain the dragon slew" or "With this ring I thee wed." Such unusual rearrangements are called "rhetorical" figures of speech.

Similes. But much more common and important to poetry is a second category of figurative language: tropes. *Tropes* (literally, "turns") extend the meaning of words beyond their literal meaning. The most common form of trope is metaphor. *Metaphor* has a general and a specific meaning. Generally, it means any analogy. An *analogy* is a similarity between things that are basically different. Specifically, metaphor means a particular kind of analogy and is contrasted with the simile. A *simile* uses *like* or *as* to mark similarities; for example, "Her tears were like falling rain." The following stanza from Shakespeare's "Fair Is My Love" contains several similes (indicated by the underlinings):

> Fair is my love, but not so fair as fickle;
> Mild as a dove, but neither true nor trusty;
> Brighter than glass, and yet, as glass is, brittle;
> Softer than wax, and yet, as iron, rusty;
> A lily pale, with damask dye to grace her;
> None fairer, nor none falser to deface her.   1599

Metaphors. A metaphor also claims similarities between things that are essentially unlike, but it eliminates the comparative words (such as *like*) and thus equates the compared items. For example, "My heart was a tornado of passion" (not "My heart was like a tornado of passion"). The poem "Love Is a Sickness" by Samuel Daniel contains three metaphors—love is a sickness, love is a plant, love is a tempest—indicated here by the underlinings:

LOVE IS A SICKNESS

Samuel Daniel

> Love is a sickness full of woes,
> All remedies refusing.
> A plant that with most cutting grows,
> Most barren with best using.
>   Why so?

More we enjoy it, more it dies,
If not enjoyed it sighing cries,
           Hey ho.

Love is a torment of the mind,
   A tempest everlasting,

And Jove hath made it of a kind
   Not well, nor full, nor fasting.
           Why so?

More we enjoy it, more it dies,
If not enjoyed it sighing cries,
           Hey ho.   1623

Personification. Analogies can be directly stated or implied. The similes and metaphors in the poems by Shakespeare and Daniel are directly stated analogies; but when Daniel in the last lines of each stanza says that love "sighs," he implies a kind of analogy, *personification;* he pretends that love has the attributes of a person.

Extended metaphor. When the poet develops just one analogy throughout the whole poem, the analogy is called an *extended metaphor.* Thomas Campion's "There Is a Garden in Her Face" contains an extended metaphor comparing the features of a woman's face to those of a garden:

THERE IS A GARDEN IN HER FACE

Thomas Campion

There is a garden in her face,
Where roses and white lilies grow,
A heavenly paradise is that place,
Wherein all pleasant fruits do flow.
There cherries grow, which none may buy
Till "Cherry ripe!"° themselves do cry.

Those cherries fairly do enclose
Of orient pearl a double row;
Which when her lovely laughter shows,
They look like rosebuds filled with snow.
Yet them nor peer nor prince can buy,
Till "Cherry ripe!" themselves do cry.
Her eyes like angels watch them still;
Her brows like bended bows do stand,

Threatening with piercing frowns to kill
All that attempt with eye or hand
Those sacred cherries to come nigh,
Till "Cherry ripe!" themselves do cry. 1617
°A familiar cry of London street vendors

Another example of an extended metaphor is Jane Kenyon's "In the Nursing Home" (pages 124–25). Throughout this poem the woman is compared to a horse.

QUESTIONS ABOUT IMAGERY

Imagery is an important—some would argue the most important—characteristic of poetry. Identify the imagery of a poem.

1. What senses does the poet appeal to?

2. What analogies does he or she imply or directly state?

3. *Why* does the poet use these particular images and analogies?

Descriptive imagery in "Dover Beach." In "Dover Beach," Arnold uses both descriptive and metaphorical imagery. He emphasizes two senses: the visual and the aural. He begins with the visual—the moon, the lights of France across the water, the cliffs, the tranquil bay—and throughout the poem he associates hope and beauty with what the speaker sees. But the poet soon introduces the aural sense—the grating roar of the sea—which serves as an antithesis to the visual sense. These two senses create a tension that mirrors the conflict in the speaker's mind. The first two stanzas show the speaker merely drifting into a perception of this conflict, connecting sight with hope and sound with sadness.

Figurative language in "Dover Beach." By the third stanza, he has become intellectually alert to the full implications of the conflict. He signals this alertness with a carefully worked out analogy, his comparison of the sea with faith. In the fourth stanza, he sums up his despairing conclusion with a stunning and famous simile:

And we are here as on a darkling plain
Swept with confused alarms of struggle and flight,
Where ignorant armies clash by night.

This final analogy achieves several purposes. First, it brings the implication of the descriptive imagery to a logical conclusion. No longer can the speaker draw hope from visual beauty; in this image, he cannot see at all—it is night, the plain is dark ("darkling"). He can only hear, but the sound now is more chaotic and threatening than the mere ebb and flow of the sea. Second, the analogy provides an abrupt change of setting. Whereas before, the speaker visualized an unpeopled plain, now he imagines human beings as agents of destruction. He implies that a world without faith must be arbitrary and violent. Finally, the analogy allows the speaker to identify his own place in this new world order. Only loyalty is pure and good. So he and his companion must cling to each other and maneuver throughout the world's battlefields as best they can.

THINKING ON PAPER ABOUT DESCRIPTIVE LANGUAGE

1. Mark the descriptive images. For each image, name the sense appealed to. Characterize the dominant impression these images make.

2. Explain the relationship of descriptive images to the speaker's state of mind.

3. Describe how the descriptive images create a sense of the time of day and season of the year.

4. Note any progression in the descriptive images; for example, from day to night, hot to cold, soft to loud, one color to another color, slow to fast.

5. Explain how the descriptive images help create atmosphere and mood. Slow movements, for example, are conducive to melancholy; speed generates feelings of exuberance, excitement, and even humor.

THINKING ON PAPER ABOUT FIGURATIVE LANGUAGE

1. Mark the similes in the poem. Underline or circle the words that signal the comparisons (words such as *like, as, similar to, resembles*). Explain the implications of the analogies (that is, what they contribute to the meaning of the poem).

2. Mark the metaphors in the poem. Explain the implications of the analogies.

3. Mark any personification in the poem. Underline the words and phrases that make the personification clear.

4. Poets often use analogies to help make an abstract quality, such as "love" or "my love's beauty" or "my current predicament" or "the destructive effect of time" or "God's grandeur," concrete and knowable. They do so by comparing the abstract quality to something the reader knows well. Almost always this "something" is a physical object or reality. Name the abstract quality the poet wants to clarify and the object to which the poet compares it. List the qualities of the object. Explain how the comparison has clarified the abstraction.

5. List the senses appealed to in each analogy. Describe the dominant sensuous impression created by the analogies.

Now It's Your Turn

Explore the implications of descriptive imagery in Gwendolyn Brooks' "We Real Cool" (page 168) and of figurative language in Shakespeare's Sonnet 116 (pages 153). What are the images? What ideas do they convey?

Symbolism

Symbolism appeals to poets because symbols are highly suggestive yet succinct. As we say in Chapter 3, a *symbol* is an object—usually a physical object—that represents an abstract idea or ideas (see pages 76–77). The most powerful symbols are those that do not exactly specify the ideas they may represent.

Symbolism in Psalm 23. An example of a symbol in poetry occurs in the King James translation of Psalm 23, quoted on page 160. The poem begins with a metaphor: God is like a shepherd and I (the speaker) am like one of his sheep; just as a shepherd takes care of his sheep, so will God take care of me. But the poem shifts from metaphor to symbol with phrases such as "green pastures," "still waters," and particularly "the valley of the shadow of death." The meanings of "green pastures" (nourishment, security, ease) and "still waters" (peace, sustenance, calm, safety) are fairly easy to ascertain. But the meaning of "the valley of the shadow of death" is more difficult. It does not seem to mean just death, but a life experience—perhaps psychological or spiritual—that is somehow related to death (the "shadow" of death). We must journey through this "valley." Perhaps the indefiniteness of this phrase, combined with its ominous overtones, explains its appeal.

Symbolism in "The Sick Rose." Another example of a symbol in poetry is William Blake's "The Sick Rose":

THE SICK ROSE

William Blake

O Rose, thou art sick.
The invisible worm
That flies in the night
In the howling storm

Has found out thy bed
Of crimson joy,
And his dark secret love
Does thy life destroy.   1794

This poem might be understandable as a literal treatment of horticulture: a real rose beset by an insect that preys on roses. But Blake almost certainly means for us to see the rose, the worm, and the action of the worm as symbolic. For one thing, the poem occurs in Blake's collection of poems *Songs of Experience,* suggesting that it has to do with the ominous aspects of human life. For another, much of the poem makes little sense unless it can be taken symbolically. What can we otherwise make of the "howling storm," the bed of "crimson joy," the worm's "dark secret love"?

Blake's diction, furthermore, links to symbolic Christian literature, which he knew well. The archaic meaning of "worm" is dragon, an image of evil that harks back to the devil's appearance to Eve as a snake. In Christian romances the rose represented female beauty and purity and sometimes the Virgin Mary. Blake, then, may symbolize here the destruction of purity by evil. The poem may have sexual implications, since the worm (a phallic image) comes at "night" to the rose's "bed." More generally, the poem may show the destruction of all earthly health, innocence, and beauty by mysterious forces.

The point is that although we get the drift of Blake's meaning, we do not know precisely what the symbolic equivalents are. Yet the symbols are so sensuous and the action so dramatic that the poem mesmerizes.

QUESTIONS ABOUT SYMBOLISM

When you read poetry, keep alert for symbols. But persuade yourself—and your reader—that the objects you claim to be symbols were intended as such by the author. Remember that not every object in a poem is symbolic.

1. What are the symbols in the poem you are reading?
2. What evidence in the work suggests they are symbols?
3. What do they mean? In answer to this last question, offer thoughtful explanations for your interpretations. Stay close to meanings the author seems to have intended.

THINKING ON PAPER ABOUT SYMBOLISM

1. Circle the symbols in the poem.
2. List the possible meanings of each symbol. Explain what evidence suggests these meanings.
3. Explain what each symbol contributes to the overall meaning of the poem.

NOW IT'S YOUR TURN

Discuss the symbolism in either Ezra Pound's "Xenia" (page 162) or Robert Frost's "The Death of the Hired Man" (printed in the Appendix). What are the symbols? What makes you think they are symbols? What are their possible meanings?

II. THE SOUND OF POETRY: MUSICAL ELEMENTS

Rhythm

Rhythm is one of the most naturally pleasing elements of poetry. Edward Hirsch says that rhythm "creates a pattern of yearning and expectation, of recurrence and difference. It is related to the pulse, the heartbeat, the way we breathe. It takes us into ourselves; it takes us out of ourselves. It differentiates us; it unites us to the cosmos" (21).

Meter. All human speech has rhythm, but poetry often regularizes that rhythm into recognizable patterns. These patterns are called *meters*. Paul Fussell defines *meter* this way:

> Meter is what results when the natural rhythmical movements of colloquial speech are heightened, organized, and regulated so that pattern—which means repetition—emerges from the relative phonetic haphazard of ordinary utterance. (4–5)

Metrical patterns vary depending on the sequence in which poets arrange the accented (á) and unaccented (ă) syllables of an utterance. The unit that determines that arrangement is the foot. A *foot* is one unit of rhythm. The most common foot in English poetry is the *iamb*: an unaccented syllable followed by an accented syllable (ăá).

Here are the most used metrical feet:

iamb (iambic) ăá   ăbóve

    Bĕcaúse Ĭ coúld nŏt stóp fŏr deáth (Emily Dickinson)

trochee (trochaic) áă   lóvelў

    Cíndĕréllă, dréssed iň yéllŏw (jump-rope rhyme)

anapest (anapestic) ăăá   ŏvĕrwhélm

    Whĕn thĕy saíd, "Doĕs ĭt búzz?" hĕ rĕpliéd, "Yĕs, ĭt doés!" (Edward Lear)

dactyl (dactylic) áăă   róyăltў

    Thís ĭs tȟe forešt přimévăl (Henry Wadsworth Longfellow)

spondee (spondaic) áá   bréak, bréak

    Wé réal cóol (Gwendolyn Brooks)

    In practice, iambic and trochaic feet tend to blend together. That is, poets readily switch back and forth between the two, so that you can't always tell which foot predominates. The same is even more true of the "waltz-time" feet, anapest and dactyl. The key difference between the two sets is the number of beats: two for iambic/trochaic, three for anapestic/dactylic. An example of the iambic/trochaic blend is the third stanza of Emily Brontë's "The Night Is Darkening Round Me" (page 108).

> Clouds beyond clouds above me,
> Wastes beyond wastes below;
> But nothing drear can move me;
> I will not, cannot go.

Edward Lear mixes anapestic and dactylic feet throughout "Calico Pie." Here's the first stanza:

> Calico pie,
>   The little birds fly
> Down to the calico-tree:
> Their wings were blue,
> And they sang "Tilly-loo!"
> Till away they flew;
>   And they never came back to me!
>   They never came back,
>   They never came back,
>   They never came back to me!   1895

Measuring meter. Fussell indicates four ways in which poets "measure" meter (6). (The word *meter*, he notes, comes from the Greek word for "measure.") Least used in English is *quantitative meter*, a pattern based on duration of syllables (long sound and short sound) rather than stressed and unstressed syllables. Also little used in English is *syllabic*—the number of syllables per line. An example is the haiku, whose line lengths are based entirely on syllable count. (See pages 158 for a discussion of haiku.) Much more widespread in English is *accentual meter*—the number of stresses per line. Examples are Old English poetry, such as *Beowulf*, and Scottish border ballads. (See pages 154 for a description of ballad form.) In this pattern only stresses are counted:

> "O whére hae ye beén, Lord Rándal, my són?
> O whefe hae ye beén, my hańdsome young mán?"
> "I hae beén to the wíld woód; móther, máke my bed soón,
> For I'm weáry wi huńting, and fáin wald lie doẃn."
>   "Lord Randal," before 1600

Since ballads were meant to be sung, singers could vary stresses to fit the music or the themes of the poems.

Finally, the most utilized metrical pattern in English poetry is *accentual-syllabic,* a pattern based on the number of stresses *and* the number of syllables per line. The best known such pattern is *iambic pentameter*, which consists of five stresses (iambs) and ten syllables. Shakespeare wrote his plays and sonnets in iambic pentameter. The following are the names of accentual-syllabic line lengths:

monometer (one foot)

dimeter (two feet)

trimeter (three feet)

tetrameter (four feet)

pentameter (five feet)

hexameter (six feet)

heptameter (seven feet)

octameter (eight feet)

These iambic tetrameter lines from Andrew Marvell's "To His Coy Mistress" exemplify accentual-syllabic meter:

> Hăd wé bŭt wórld ĕnoúgh, aňd tiḿe,
> Thĭs cóyneš's, ládў, weré nŏ críme.

Each line has four iambic feet—four accented syllables, eight syllables in all.

When you begin reading a poem, it shouldn't take long to recognize its predominate metrical pattern. Usually, after you read a few lines, the pattern will become clear. Sometimes, as in *free verse* (see page 159), a poem will have no clear pattern. When it does, however, you can identify the pattern by sounding it out in your head, by reading the poem aloud, or by beating out the rhythm with your hands or feet.

Scanning. To indicate metrical patterns visually, you can scan the poem. *Scanning* is a process whereby you mark accented and unaccented syllables with symbols: a breve [ă] for unaccented (unstressed) syllables and an acute accent mark [á] for accented (stressed) syllables:

Ă blíss iň próof; aňd próved, ă vérў wóe.

This line, from Shakespeare's Sonnet 129 (which follows), is iambic pentameter, the traditional accentual-syllabic pattern of sonnets in English: five iambic feet, ten syllables.

Why scan? "To scan only to conclude that a poem is 'written in iambic pentameter,'" Paul Fussell says, "is to do nothing significant. It is only as a basis for critical perception and ultimately for critical judgment that scansion can justify itself" (28). In other words, the most valuable use for scanning is to interpret—to explore the meanings of poems. Scanning allows us to see and show not only the predominate metrical pattern but also the poet's meaningful variation from it. Poets achieve such variation by substituting feet for the regular, expected feet of the pattern. Here, for example, is the first line of Sonnet 129:

Th' ĕxpeńse/ŏf spiŕ/iˇt iň ă/ waśte/ ŏf sháme.

In the third foot of this line, Shakespeare substitutes a pyrrhic foot (two unaccented syllables: "iˇt iň") for an iambic foot. The result is that the line has four stresses, not five.

Poets rarely stick to the predominate metrical pattern of a poem. As W. K. Wimsatt and Monroe Beardsley say, "It is practically impossible to write an English line that will not in some way buck against the meter. Insofar as the line does approximate the condition of complete submission, it is most likely a tame line, a weak line" (140). Poets stray from the established meter to avoid a mechanical, sing-songy rhythm and to make the language sound more colloquial. Such is the case in "Dover Beach" and "My Last Duchess," both of which are spoken by fictional characters. Equally important, poets vary meter to emphasize ideas. By substituting feet, poets catch us by surprise and call attention to meanings.

Caesura. Another rhythmic device for emphasizing meaning is the caesura. A *caesura* is a strong pause somewhere in the line. You mark a caesura with two vertical lines: ‖. Consider the caesuras in this jump-rope rhyme:

> Cinderella, dressed in yellow,
> Went upstairs ‖ to kiss a fellow.
> Made a mistake; ‖ kissed a snake.
> How many doctors did it take?
> One, two, three, four . . .

A likely place for a caesura is in the middle of the line. If the meter of the poem is tetrameter, then a caesura in the middle neatly divides the line in half. Such is the case in lines 2 and 3 of this poem.

A caesura may also occur near the beginning of a line or near the end. Or there may be no caesuras in a line, as is probably the case in lines 1, 4, and 5 of this poem. Caesuras often emphasize meaning. Caesuras in the middle of lines can emphasize strong contrasts or close relationships between ideas. In line 3, both the caesura and the rhyme of "mistake" with "snake" link the abstraction (the mistake) with the action (kissing the snake).

Shakespeare's Sonnet 129 provides a rich example of how caesuras and metrical substitutions convey meaning.

SONNET 129

William Shakespeare

Th' expense of spirit ‖ in a waste of shame
Is lust in action; ‖ and, till action, lust
Is perjured, murderous, bloody, full of blame,
Savage, extreme, rude, cruel, not to trust;
Enjoyed no sooner ‖ but despisèd straight;   5
Past reason hunted; ‖ and no sooner had,
Past reason hated, ‖ as a swallowed bait,
On purpose laid ‖ to make the taker mad;
Mad in pursuit, ‖ and in possession so;
Had, having, and in quest to have, extreme;   10
A bliss in proof; ‖ and proved, a very woe;
Before, a joy proposed; ‖ behind, a dream.
All this the world well knows; ‖ yet none knows well
To shun the heaven ‖ that leads men to this hell.   1609

Here Shakespeare uses caesura and metrical pattern to establish a pattern of contrasts and similarities. Like most sonnets, this one has ten syllables per line and is supposed to be iambic pentameter. But for many of these lines, Shakespeare has only four accents per line, not five. This allows him to make some of his comparisons equal in weight. Line 5, for example, has a strong caesura and four accented syllables:

Enjóyed no soóner ‖ but despisèd straíght.

The effect is to contrast the two emotional states, pleasure and guilt. Since Shakespeare puts guilt last, he gives it more weight. Lines 11 and 12, however, contain caesuras and five accents each, making the two-part divisions within the lines unequal:

A bliśs in próof; ‖ and próved, a véry wóe;
Befóre, a jóy propósed; ‖ behińd, a dréam.

The "weaker" sides of the lines contain the pleasure part of the equation and emphasize the brevity and insubstantial quality of pleasure. The "strong" sides emphasize either naïve expectation or guilt.

Shakespeare's metrical substitutions also emphasize stark contrasts: Lust is like

a swallowed bait,	7
On purpose laid to make the taker mad:	8
Mád iň pŭrsuít, aňd iň pŏsséssiŏn só;	9
Hád, háving, aňd iň quést tŏ háve, ĕxtréme;	10
A bliss in proof; and proved, a very woe;	11
Before, a joy proposed; behind, a dream.	12

All these lines fit the iambic scheme except 9 and 10. Why? Shakespeare probably wanted to emphasize certain words in these two lines, particularly the first words in each. These words—"mad" and "had"—are prominent because they come first in the line, they are stressed, and they rhyme. The accents in line 10 are especially suggestive. They contrast the past ("had"), the present ("having"), the future ("quest" and "have"). They point out the psychological and moral nature of all three ("extreme").

QUESTIONS ABOUT RHYTHM

Meter has many uses in poetry. It provides a method of ordering material. It creates a hypnotic effect that rivets attention on the poem. Like the beat of music, it is enjoyable for itself. Children take naturally to the pulsing rhythms of nursery rhymes and jump-rope rhymes. But for the purposes of interpretation, the greatest value of meter is the insights it gives us to the meanings of poems.

1. Which metrical pattern does the poem use?

2. What is appealing about the pattern?

3. Where does the poem vary from the established pattern? Why?

4. How and why does the poet use pauses, especially caesuras, within each line?

THINKING ON PAPER ABOUT RHYTHM

1. Count the number of syllables for each line. Write the number at the end of the line.

2. Read the poem aloud, then mark the accented and unaccented syllables of each line.

3. Draw a vertical line between each foot in the line.

4. Identify the metrical pattern (iambic, trochaic, etc.) and the length of the lines (pentameter, hexameter, etc.).

5. Use two vertical lines to mark the caesuras in the poem. Explain how the caesuras relate to the sense of each line.

6. Underline the places where the poet departs from the established metrical pattern of the poem. Explain how these departures relate to the sense of each line.

7. Explain the appropriateness of the metrical pattern to the poem's meaning.

8. Describe how easy or difficult it is to read the poem aloud. Does its metrical pattern slow you down? Or does it allow you to read smoothly? Explain how the difficulty or ease of reading the metrical pattern relates to the poem's meaning and purpose. Line 10 of Shakespeare's Sonnet 116 (pages 153), for example, reads more slowly than the other lines:

   Within his bending sickle's compass come

   Shakespeare slows the tempo, probably to suggest the slowness of Time, personified here as a man with a scythe (sickle).

NOW IT'S YOUR TURN

Explore the implications of rhythm in Blake's "The Sick Rose" (page 137). Does it have a dominant metrical pattern? Is the pattern accentual-syllabic? What ideas do caesuras and stressed syllables bring out? Do you have alternatives—choices—for where to place stresses?

Word Sounds

Devices using word sounds.   Poets delight in the sound of language and consciously present sounds to be enjoyed for themselves. They also use them to emphasize meaning, action, and emotion, and especially to call the reader's attention to connections between words. Rhyme, for example, has the effect of linking words together. Important devices using word sounds are the following:

onomatopoeia—the use of words that sound like what they mean ("buzz," "boom," "hiss," "fizz," "pop," "glug").

alliteration—the repetition of consonant sounds at the beginning of words or at the beginning of accented syllables ("the woeful woman went wading Wednesday").

assonance—the repetition of vowel sounds followed by different consonant sounds ("O, the groans that opened to his own ears").

consonance (or *half-rhyme*)—the repetition of final consonant sounds that are preceded by different vowel sounds ("the beast climbed fast to the crest"). Consonance is the opposite of alliteration, which features initial consonant sounds.

rhyme—the repetition of accented vowels and the sounds that follow. There are subcategories of rhyme:
masculine rhyme (the rhymed words end with a stressed syllable: "man-ran," "detect-correct").
feminine rhyme (the rhymed words end with one or more unaccented syllables: "subtle-rebuttal," "deceptively-perceptively").
internal rhyme (the rhymed words are within the line).
end rhyme (the rhymed words appear at the ends of lines).
approximate rhyme (the words are close to rhyming: "book-buck," "watch-match," "man-in").

Edgar Allan Poe's "To Helen" illustrates many of these sound devices:

TO HELEN

Edgar Allan Poe

Helen, thy beauty is to me
Like those Nicean barks of yore,   masculine rhyme/
That gently, o'er a perfumed sea,   end rhyme
alliteration   The weary, way-worn wanderer bore
To his own native shore.   5

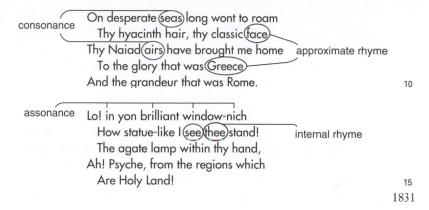

consonance

On desperate seas long wont to roam
Thy hyacinth hair, thy classic face
Thy Naiad airs have brought me home   approximate rhyme
To the glory that was Greece
And the grandeur that was Rome.   10

assonance

Lo! in yon brilliant window-nich
How statue-like I see thee stand!   internal rhyme
The agate lamp within thy hand,
Ah! Psyche, from the regions which
Are Holy Land!   15

1831

QUESTIONS ABOUT WORD SOUNDS

It's easy to lose yourself in an analysis of a poem's sound structure and forget why you are making the analysis in the first place. Instead, ask these questions:

1. What sound devices does the poet use?
2. Why does the poet use them?
3. How do they help establish the poem's tone, atmosphere, themes, setting, characterization, and emotional qualities?
4. Above all, what meanings do they suggest?

In Poe's "To Helen," for example, the alliteration in line 4 ("weary, way-worn wanderer") underscores the fatigued state of the wanderer. The consonance of "seas" and "airs" in lines 6 and 8 emphasizes the contrast between them; one is "desperate" but the other assuages despair. And the assonance in line 11 ("in yon brilliant window-nich"), with its emphasis on high, tight, "i" sounds, helps to characterize the luminosity of the place where Helen, statuelike, stands.

Be alert to relationships between ideas established by rhyme, most notably by internal rhyme and end rhyme. Rhyme is a kind of "music" that sounds pretty. But it can be used meaningfully, too. Turn back to Sonnet 129 and examine the complex sound associations Shakespeare creates there. The words sound rough, almost painful, with their harsh consonants, all of which illustrate the frustrated and frenetic emotional state Shakespeare ascribes to lust. Note the variation on "s" sounds in the first line.

Th' expense of spirit in a waste of shame

Line 3 begins a list of qualities. Shakespeare divides and associates them through assonance and alliteration: Lust

Is perjured, murderous, bloody, full of blame.

The words *perjured* and *murderous* are linked by assonance (the "er" sounds) and focus on evil deeds (falsehood, murder), leading to the second half of the line. The words bloody and blame are linked by alliteration and focus on the results of evil deeds, especially murder: blood and guilt. The linkages signaled by the poem's end rhyme are also meaningful: shame/blame, lust/not to trust, no sooner had/make the taker mad, extreme/dream, yet none knows well/leads men to this hell.

5. We can ask, then, questions like these: In the poem you are analyzing, what linkages of meaning are there to *all* the sound qualities of the words—especially to the obvious ones, such as alliteration, internal rhyme, and end rhyme?

THINKING ON PAPER ABOUT WORD SOUNDS

1. Underline instances of alliteration, assonance, and consonance in the poem. Explain the relationship between these devices and the sense of the lines where they occur.

2. Circle rhymed words. Explain similarities and contrasts the rhymed words underscore.

3. Circle words that have meaningful or attractive sound qualities, such as onomatopoetic words. Show how these words add to the poem's sense.

4. When the sounds of a poem are harsh and grating, the effect is called *cacophony*. When they are pleasing and harmonious, the effect is called *euphony*. Underline instances of cacophony or euphony. Explain how they relate to the poem's sense.

5. Describe any sound devices in the poem that catch you by surprise. Say why the poet uses such surprises.

NOW IT'S YOUR TURN

What sound devices does Robinson employ in "Richard Cory" (printed in the Appendix)? What effects do they produce? How do they help convey the poem's meanings?

III. STRUCTURE: DEVICES THAT ORGANIZE

Structure is the way the whole poem is organized and put together. Poets give structure to their poems in two overlapping ways: by organizing ideas according to a logical plan and by establishing a pattern of units. Arnold arranges "Dover Beach" in both ways, as do most poets. He divides the poem into four units, each of which has a pattern of end rhyme. And he arranges the whole poem rhetorically—that is, by ideas. Each unit elaborates a single point, and each point follows logically from the preceding one.

Lines

The most immediately visible structural device of poetry is the line. Poetry is organized in lines, prose in paragraphs. The exception is *prose poetry*, which has the verbal texture of poetry (nuanced diction, rhythmical devices, imagery, internal rhyme) but is arranged in paragraphs, not lines. The following passage from Herman Melville's *Moby-Dick* (1851, the second paragraph of Chapter 111, "The Pacific") describes the ship's passage into the mystic waters where dwells the White Whale:

> There is, one knows not what sweet mystery about this sea, whose gently awful stirrings seem to speak of some hidden soul beneath; like those fabled undulations of the Ephesian sod over the buried Evangelist St. John. And meet it is, that over these sea-pastures, wide-rolling watery prairies and Potters' Fields of all four continents, the waves should rise and fall, and ebb and flow unceasingly; for here, millions of mixed shades and shadows, drowned dreams, somnambulisms, reveries; all that we call lives and souls, lie dreaming, dreaming, still; tossing like slumberers in their beds; the ever-rolling waves but made so by their restlessness.

Melville was a sympathetic reader of Shakespeare. Although he does not say that this paragraph is "poetry," it bristles with poetic devices and could justifiably be arranged in lines that would resemble Shakespearean blank verse. As it stands, it is "prose poetry."

Poetry, however, is usually organized in lines. Poets use various criteria for choosing line lengths. The best known criterion is meter—the number of feet per line: monometer, dimeter, trimeter, etc. (See page 141 for the full list.) Pentameter (five feet per line), especially iambic pentameter, has become the most utilized line length in English poetry.

Enjambment

A decision poets face is whether to end-stop or enjamb their lines. *Enjambment* (from the French verb *enjamber,* to straddle, to encroach) is the continuance of a phrase from one line to the next so that there is no pause at the end of the line. An end-stopped line has a definite pause at the end. In Wordsworth's "A Slumber Did My Spirit Seal" (page 119), all the lines are end-stopped:

> A slumber did my spirit seal;
> I had no human fears—
> She seemed a thing that could not feel
> The touch of earthly years.

Other examples are the poems by Brontë (page 116) and Campion (pages 133–34). In contrast, most of the lines in the poems by Millay (page 153), Browning (pages 129–30), Bogan (page 123), and Arnold (pages 126–27) are enjambed. In this excerpt from Millay's sonnet, only lines 2 and 5 are end-stopped; the others are enjambed:

I, being born a woman and distressed	1
By all the needs and notions of my kind,	2
Am urged by your propinquity to find	3
Your person fair, and feel a certain zest	4
To bear your body's weight upon my breast.	5

Enjambed and end-stopped lines create different effects. Enjambed lines read more naturally, like someone speaking. Even though the poems by Millay, Browning, Bogan, and Arnold feature end-rhyme, when you read these poems aloud, the end rhyme almost disappears. You can see the end rhyme on the page, but you are less likely to hear it. Mary Kinzie says that sentences in poetry are in tension with lines; "sentence tugs against line" (68). When lines are enjambed, "the sentence takes priority over the line" (61). The "more enjambment, or run-on, there is from one line to the next, the less the lines function as individual entities" (68). But when "phrases end at the ends of lines, thus creating pauses, the *lines themselves* are emphasized as rhythmical units and as units of meaning" (68).

Blank Verse

A line form that is almost always enjambed is *blank verse:* iambic pentameter with no end rhyme. Blank verse has been made famous by Shakespeare and many other poets: Christopher Marlowe, John Milton, William Wordsworth, Alfred Tennyson, and Robert Frost, just to name a few. You can see from Frost's "The Death of the Hired Man" (printed in the Appendix) that blank verse mimics the spoken language.

The sentences run from line to line, as if the lines don't exist. Yet they do exist. Blank verse lines provide an underlying rhythmic pattern that listeners feel, even if they cannot hear where the lines end.

Stanza

A second device for structuring poetry is the *stanza*. Not all poems have stanzas. When they don't, they are *stichic*. When they do, they are *strophic*. Stanzas in a poem typically resemble one another structurally. They have the same number of lines, length of lines, metrical patterns, and rhyme schemes. They are physically separated from other stanzas (by a space inserted between each stanza) and usually present one idea (similar to a paragraph in prose), one happening, or one image. An example of a poem with stanzas is "The Daemon Lover" (pages 155–56).

Rhyme Scheme

Rhyme scheme—any pattern of end rhyme—is a traditional method of organizing stanzas. The couplet, the shortest possible stanza, rhymes aa:

Interred beneath this marble stone,	a
Lies sauntering Jack and idle Joan.	a
—Matthew Prior, "An Epitaph," 1718	

The *ballad stanza* typically rhymes abcb; that is, the second and fourth lines rhyme:

It is an ancient Mariner	a
And he stoppeth one of three.	b
—"By thy long gray beard and glittering eye,	c
Now wherefore stopp'st thou me?"	b
—Samuel Taylor Coleridge, *The Rime of the Ancient Mariner*, 1798	

Ottava rima has eight lines (thus *ottava*, "eight") and rhymes abababcc:

'Tis sweet to win, no matter how, one's laurels,	a
By blood or ink; 'tis sweet to put an end	b
To strife; 'tis sometimes sweet to have our quarrels,	a
Particularly with a tiresome friend:	b
Sweet is old wine in bottles, ale in barrels;	a

Dear is the helpless creature we defend   b
Against the world; and dear the schoolboy spot   c
We ne'er forget, though there we are forgot.   c
—George Gordon, Lord Byron, *Don Juan*, 1818–24

The *Spenserian stanza* (invented by Edmond Spenser for *The Faerie Queen*, 1590-96) has nine lines and rhymes ababbcbcc. An example is the stanza from John Keats's "The Eve of St. Agnes," printed on pages 130–31.

Fixed and Nonce Forms

These are but a few of the many shapes stanzas can take. Poets can, of course, create any rhyme scheme or stanza form they choose. But they often work instead within the confines of already established poetic structures. These are called *fixed forms*. Stanzas that conform to no traditional limits, such as those in "Dover Beach," are called *nonce forms*. Fixed forms provide ready-made structural units by which a poet can arrange ideas. But they also challenge poets to mold unwieldy material into an unyielding structure. The result is a tension between material and form that is pleasing to both poet and reader.

To illustrate how poems can be structured, we will look at four well-known poetic forms: the sonnet, the ballad, the haiku, and free verse.

The Sonnet

The *sonnet* is the most famous fixed form in English. All sonnets consist of fourteen lines of iambic pentameter. The two best known kinds of sonnets are named for their most famous practitioners. A *Shakespearean sonnet* rhymes abab/cdcd/efef/gg and has a structural division of three *quatrains* (each containing four lines) and a *couplet*. A *Petrarchan sonnet* rhymes abbaabba in the octave (the first eight lines) and cdecde in the sestet (the last six lines). Poets often vary the pattern of end rhyme in sonnets, especially in Petrarchan sonnets. Each kind of sonnet has a *turn*, a point in the poem at which the poet shifts from one meaning or mood to another. The turn in the Shakespearean sonnet occurs between lines 12 and 13 (just before the couplet). The turn in the Petrarchan sonnet occurs between the octave and the sestet. In both forms, the part of the poem before the turn delineates a problem or tension; the part after the turn offers some resolution to or comment on the problem and releases the tension.

SONNET 116

William Shakespeare

Let me not to the marriage of true minds	a	
Admit impediments. Love is not love	b	
Which alters when it alteration finds,	a	
Or bends with the remover to remove:	b	4
Oh, no! it is an ever-fixèd mark,	c	
That looks on tempests and is never shaken;	d	
It is the star to every wandering bark,	c	
Whose worth's unknown, although his height be taken,	d	8
Love's not Time's fool, though rosey lips and cheeks	e	
Within his bending sickle's compass come;	f	
Love alters not with his brief hours and weeks,	e	
But bears it out even to the edge of doom.	f	12
If this be error and upon me proved,	g	
I never writ, nor no man ever loved.	g	14

three quatrains (brackets lines 1–12)
turn →
couplet (brackets lines 13–14)

1609

Shakespeare molds the ideas and images of this poem to fit its form. He states the theme—that love remains constant no matter what—in the first quatrain. In the second, he says that cataclysmic events cannot destroy love. In the third, he says that time cannot destroy love. Finally, in the couplet, he affirms the truth of his theme.

I, BEING BORN A WOMAN

Edna St. Vincent Millay

I, being born a woman and distressed	a	
By all the needs and notions of my kind,	b	
Am urged by your propinquity to find	b	
Your person fair, and feel a certain zest	a	
To bear your body's weight upon my breast:	a	
So subtly is the fume of life designed,	b	
To clarify the pulse and cloud the mind,	b	
And leave me once again undone, possessed.	a	8
Think not for this, however, the poor treason	c	
Of my stout blood against my staggering brain,	d	
I shall remember you with love, or season	c	
My scorn with pity,—let me make it plain:	d	
I find this frenzy insufficient reason	c	
For conversation when we meet again.	d	14

octave (brackets lines 1–8)
turn →
Sestet (brackets lines 9–14)

1923

Millay uses the structure of the Petrarchan sonnet to shape her ideas. The turn occurs between the octave and the sestet. In the octave she tells her lover why she succumbed to his charms. In the sestet, she dismisses him. The ideas in the sestet overthrow those in the octave. Although the last two lines do not rhyme, they are similar to the couplet in a Shakespearean sonnet. They drive home the decisive and climactic point of the poem.

The Ballad

M. H. Abrams defines a *ballad* as "a song, transmitted orally, which tells a story" (21). He distinguishes between folk ballads, which are anonymous and sung aloud, and literary ballads, which are written for publication by a known author. *Literary ballads*, like John Keats's "La Belle Dame Sans Merci" (1819) and Samuel Taylor Coleridge's *The Rime of the Ancient Mariner* (1798), imitate many of the characteristics of folk ballads. Among these characteristics is the *ballad stanza*, a quatrain that typically has four stresses in lines one and three and three stresses in lines two and four. The rhyme scheme of the ballad stanza is abcb:

He turned him right and round abóut,	a
And the téar blinded his ée:	b
"I wad néver hae tródden on Irish gróund,	c
If it hád not béen for thée."	b

Other characteristics of ballads include the following: They feature intense conflicts and thus are highly emotional, even melodramatic. Their narratives are so condensed and spare that they leave out whole swatches of the story. Ballads are impersonal; that is, the narrator stands back from the story, taking no sides, making no comments. They often feature a dialogue between two people. These dialogues sometimes proceed by *incremental repetition,* in which lines and even whole stanzas are repeated but with subtle variations that advance the plot. Mary Kinzie claims that the third line of each stanza is the most important because it emphasizes ideas and actions or marks a change (420).

All of these characteristics are subject to alteration. Singers may change them, depending on the ideas or events they want to stress, or the tune they use. Known authors, like Keats and Coleridge, pick and choose the characteristics that suit their purposes. A substantial tradition of folk ballads in English emerged in the Middle Ages along the border of Scotland and England—the Scottish border ballads. When these began to be collected and written down in the eighteenth century, they exerted an enormous influence on English poetry, especially on the Romantic poets. An example of a Scottish border ballad is "The Daemon Lover."

THE DAEMON LOVER

"O where have you been, my long, long love,
    This long seven years and mair?"
"O I'm come to seek my former vows
    Ye granted me before."

"O hold your tongue of your former vows,
    For they will breed sad strife;
O hold your tongue of your former vows
    For I am become a wife."

He turned him right and round about,
    And the tear blinded his ee:
"I wad never hae trodden on Irish ground,
    If it had not been for thee.

"I might hae had a king's daughter,
    Far, far beyond the sea;
I might have had a king's daughter,
    Had it not been for love o thee."

"If ye might have had a king's daughter,
    Yer sel ye had to blame;
Ye might have taken the king's daughter,
    For ye kend that I was nane.

"If I was to leave my husband dear,
    And my two babes also,
O what have you to take me to,
    If with you I should go?"

"I hae seven ships upon the sea—
    And the eighth brought me to land—
With four-and-twenty bold mariners,
    And music on every hand."

> She has taken up her two little babes,
>> Kissd them baith cheek and chin:
> "O fair ye weel, my ain two babes,
>> For I'll never see you again."
>
> She set her foot upon the ship,
>> No mariners could she behold;
> But the sails were o the taffetie,
>> And the masts o beaten gold.
>
> She had not sailed a league, a league,
>> A league but barely three,
> When dismal grew his countenance,
>> And drumlie grew his ee.
>
> They had not saild a league, a league,
>> A league but barely three,
> Until she espied his cloven foot,
>> And she wept right bitterlie.
>
> "O what hills are yon, yon pleasant hills,
>> That the sun shines sweetly on?"
> "O yon are the hills of heaven," he said,
>> "Where you will never win."
>
> "O whaten a mountain is yon," she said,
>> "All so dreary wi frost and snow?"
> "O yon is the mountain of hell," he cried,
>> "Where you and I will go."
>
> He strack the tap-mast wi his hand,
>> The fore-masts wi his knee,
> And he brake that gallant ship in twain,
>> And sank her in the sea.   before 1600

As with most folk ballads, "The Daemon Lover" exists in numerous versions.

Common Meter

Common meter is the adaptation of the ballad stanza for hymns. Like the ballad stanza, common meter stanzas have four lines, alternating lines of tetrameter and trimeter, and a rhyme scheme of abcb or abab. A well-known eighteenth-century author of such hymns was Isaac Watts:

> Our God, our Help in Ages past,
> Our Hope for Years to come,
> Our Shelter from the Stormy Blast,
> And our eternal Home.   1707

Emily Dickinson was one of many poets who drew inspiration from the forms and subject matter of hymns. She grew up hearing Watts's hymns and wrote nearly all her poems in common meter. An example is this poem, which exhibits other characteristics of ballads as well:

BECAUSE I COULD NOT STOP FOR DEATH

Emily Dickinson

Because I could not stop for Death—
He kindly stopped for me—
The Carriage held but just Ourselves—
And Immortality.

We slowly drove—He knew no haste
And I had put away
My labor and my leisure too,
For His Civility—

We passed the School, where Children strove
At Recess—in the Ring—
We passed the Fields of Gazing Grain—
We passed the Setting Sun—

Or rather—He passed Us—
The Dews drew quivering and chill—
For only Gossamer, my Gown—
My Tippet—only Tulle—

We paused before a House that seemed
A Swelling of the Ground—
The Roof was scarcely visible—
The Cornice—in the Ground—

Since then—'tis Centuries—and yet
Feels shorter than the Day
I first surmised the Horses Heads
Were toward Eternity—   c. 1863

The Haiku

Like the sonnet, the *haiku* is an imported form of poetry—the sonnet
from Italy, the haiku from Japan. Harold Henderson indicates four
"rules" that govern and help define the haiku: (1) It has three lines,
with five syllables in the first, seven in the second, and five in the
third—a total of seventeen syllables. Since the Japanese language
has almost no stresses, haiku meter is syllabic. (2) It makes some
reference to nature, especially to the season of the year. (3) It refers
to a specific event. (4) The event takes place in the present (14). The
following haiku manifests all of these characteristics:

> Children play outside
> while their parents watch and talk:
> summer shadows fall.

In practice, these rules are flexible, both in English and Japanese.
Translators of Japanese haiku often cannot maintain the syllable count,
because Japanese syllables are sounded differently from English.
Haiku has other characteristics. Its diction is simple. It rarely
includes end rhyme. William Howard Cohen says that it presents
a "pure image" stripped of extraneous details that suggests rather
than directly states meanings. Haiku is charged with emotion (21)
and, in keeping with the Zen Buddhist concept of *satori* (sudden
realization of one's unity with nature), can "startle us awake to a
world in which clarity, mystery, and wonder merge to make the everyday life around us seem as if we have just looked at it for the
first time" (28). To achieve this power, haiku will juxtapose seemingly unrelated things to reveal their hidden unity (25). Mary Kinzie
claims that a turn occurs "after the fifth syllable or the twelfth" that
indicates "a separation between the small and local on one hand,
the cosmic, or spiritual, on the other" (327). In the haiku above, for
example, the third line "comments" on the other two.
Here are translations of haiku by three of Japan's most
renowned writers of haiku: Matsuo Basho (1644–1694), Taniguchi
Buson (1715–1783), and Kobayashi Issa (1763–1827).

How to say goodbye!
so like a bee who would stay
all day in one flower.
    [composed on leaving the house of a friend]

                                    —Basho, c. 1680

Under the blossoming pear
a moonlit woman
reading a faded letter.

                                    —Buson, c. 1765

The old, plump bullfrog
held his ground and stared at me—
what a sour face!

                                    —Issa, c. 1800

Free Verse

The "freedom" of free verse. In some ways *free verse*—poetry without meter—has the look and feel of metrical poetry. It is arranged in lines, it often has units that look like stanzas (lines grouped together and set apart from other groupings by spaces), and it has the verbal texture of poetry: alliteration, internal rhyme, occasional end rhyme, nuanced diction, rhythmic phrasing). But it is "free" in that it obeys no set metrical patterns.

    The first practitioner of free verse in modern times was Walt Whitman (beginning with the 1855 edition of *Leaves of Grass*). Many readers, when they saw Whitman's poetry for the first time, wondered if it was really poetry. They asked why any "prose" writings could not be arranged into lines of varying lengths and be called poetry. Since Whitman's time, so many poets have written in free verse that it has became the predominate form of modern poetry.

    Biblical free verse. Free verse is not really "free." In his book-length treatment of free verse, Charles Hartman says that free verse, like any other poetry, "depends on conventions. Eliminating those of meter merely throws the poet back on those that define verse and govern language in general" (27). There are two broad categories of free verse, each with distinctive conventions. The first is *biblical free verse,* so called because of its antecedents in ancient Hebrew poetry—books from the Hebrew Bible (Old Testament) such as the

Psalms, the Song of Solomon, Ecclesiastes, Isaiah, and Jeremiah. The King James translation of the Bible (1611) provided models for Whitman and other authors of free verse.
Here is a well-known example.

PSALM 23

The Lord is my shepherd; I shall not want.
He maketh me to lie down in green pastures; he leadeth me beside the still waters.
He restoreth my soul; he leadeth me in the paths of righteousness for his name's sake.
Yea, though I walk through the valley of the shadow of death, I will fear no evil, for thou art with me; thy rod and thy staff they comfort me.
Thou preparest a table before me in the presence of mine enemies; thou anointest my head with oil; my cup runneth over.
Surely goodness and mercy shall follow me all the days of my life, and I will dwell in the house of the Lord forever.

c. 800 BCE

Characteristics. Characteristics of biblical free verse include the following: (1) Lines are typically stopped, not enjambed. (2) Lines are often quite long. (3) Rhythms are established by repetitions of phrases that have the same syntactical structure: "He maketh me," "he leadeth me," "he restoreth my soul," "he leadeth me" (Psalm 23). When such phrasal repetitions occur at the beginning of lines, they are called *anaphora*. An example is the first section of Whitman's "Out of the Cradle Endlessly Rocking" (1859):

Out of the cradle endlessly rocking,
Out of the mockingbird's throat, the musical shuttle,
Out of the Ninth-month midnight . . .

Whitman's "Cavalry Crossing a Ford" (page 21) features two anaphoric phrases:

Behold the silvery river . . .
Behold the brown-faced men . . .

(4) Biblical free verse, like other poetry, includes word sounds—assonance, alliteration, internal rhyme, onomatopoeia,

consonance—that make music and highlight ideas. (5) Catalogues (long lists of things) abound:

> The pure contralto sings . . .
> The carpenter dresses his plank . . .
> The married and unmarried children ride home . . .
> The pilot seizes the king-pin . . .
> The mate stands braced in the whaleboat . . .
> The duck-shooter walks by . . .
> The deacons are ordained . . .
> The spinning-girl retreats and advances . . .
> The farmer stops by the bars . . .
> The lunatic is carried at last to the asylum . . .
> —Whitman, "Song of Myself," ll. 257–266, 1855

Mary Kinzie says that biblical free verse has a characteristic subject matter and tone: "the sublime setting, the landscape cosmic and majestic, the wonders persisting in time, the emotions elevated and rapturous (or their opposite—desperate and extreme)." It swells with "visionary authority and the massive breath the poet must take to utter it" (338).

Imagist free verse. The second kind of free verse is less oracular, less meant to be spoken aloud. It was created by the Modernist poets of the early twentieth century—Ezra Pound, Amy Lowell, D. H. Lawrence, Carl Sandburg—and continues to hold sway over poetry written in English. Kinzie calls it "imagist free verse." Other names for it are "meditative" or "private" free verse (Paul Fussell) and "conversational" free verse (M. H. Abrams). *Imagist free verse*, Kinzie says, is biblical free verse "condensed into its minim" (340). Its lines are shorter. The poems themselves are shorter. It emphasizes "sharply drawn visual detail," as advocated by the Imagist movement of the early twentieth century (423). It deemphasizes direct statement of ideas. Lines are enjambed, making the sentences seem more colloquial. Rhythms are more subtle and much less pronounced. Donald Wesling and Eniko Bolloba claim that "more explicitly than the metrical poetry of the period from Chaucer to Tennyson, from Pushkin to Tsvetaeva, free verse claims and thematizes a proximity to lived experience" (427). That is, free verse replicates the activities, concerns, and language of ordinary people.

An example that blends biblical and imagist free verse is this early poem by Ezra Pound:

XENIA

Ezra Pound

And
Unto thine eyes my heart
Sendeth old dreams of the spring-time,
Yea of wood-ways my rime
Found thee and flowers in and of all streams
That sang low burthen, and of roses,
That lost their dew-bowed petals for the dreams
We scattered o'er them passing by.   1909

Here Pound employs the archaic diction and even the syntactical rhythms of the Hebrew Bible, but his lines are so enjambed that they disappear in an out-loud reading. Perhaps because of this, the syntax becomes increasingly obscure toward the end of the poem. We have to reread, even study the poem, in order to puzzle out how the sentence fits together.

A simpler example is a poem by Amy Lowell. Like Pound, Lowell was influenced by Japanese and Chinese poetry. This poem is set in Japan and has the spare quality of a haiku. As in haiku, the poem presents an evocative image without comment about its meaning.

ROAD TO THE YOSHIWARA

Amy Lowell

Coming to you along the Nihon Embankment,
Suddenly the road was darkened
By a flock of wild geese
Crossing the moon.   1919

A third example is a poem by Langston Hughes—unusual in its inclusion of end rhyme. This poem invokes the experience and language of ordinary people.

VAGABONDS

Langston Hughes

We are the desperate
Who do not care,
The hungry
Who have nowhere
To eat,
No place to sleep,
The tearless
Who cannot
Weep.   1947

QUESTIONS ABOUT STRUCTURE

Definitions of poetic forms appear in handbooks and encyclopedias of literature, such as *The New Princeton Encyclopedia of Poetry and Poetics* and *A Glossary of Literary Terms* (M. H. Abrams and Geoffrey Harpham). You can use these definitions as tools to analyze poems—to identify their formal qualities and explore how they convey meanings. Some questions to pose about a poem's structure are these:

1. What devices does the poet use to give the poem structure—rhyme scheme, stanzas, double spaces, indentations, repetition of words and images, varying line lengths, rhetorical organization?
2. How do these devices help communicate the poem's meaning?

An example of the relationship between structure and meaning is the final stanza of "Dover Beach." Here Arnold uses end rhyme to emphasize opposing worldviews:

Ah, love, let us be true	a
To one another! for the world, which seems	b
To lie before us like a land of dreams,	b
So various, so beautiful, so new,	a___
Hath really neither joy, nor love, nor light,	c
Nor certitude, nor peace, nor help for pain;	d
And we are here as on a darkling plain	d
Swept with confused alarms of struggle and flight,	c
Where ignorant armies clash by night.	c

The rhyme scheme of the first four lines is almost the same as the next five lines; the only difference is the addition of the fifth line. This similarity divides the stanza in half, and the difference in rhymes corresponds to the difference of the ideas in the two halves (the new, beautiful world versus the war-torn, chaotic, threatening world). The extra line in the second half gives the gloomier view more weight.

THINKING ON PAPER ABOUT STRUCTURE

1. Write a sonnet.
2. Write a ballad.
3. Write a haiku.
4. Write a free verse poem.
5. Mark the rhyme scheme of an existing poem.
6. Mark each division or unit of the poem. For a sonnet, for example, indicate divisions between quatrains, couplets, octaves, and sestets. Show structuring devices, like end rhyme.
7. Summarize the meaning of each division of the poem.
8. State relationships between ideas and end rhyme.
9. Account for the different lengths of lines. Why, for example, does Pound make the first line of "Xenia" (page 162) just one word? Why does Hughes make the lines of "Vagabonds" (page 163) increasingly short?
10. Describe the imagery of each unit. Show differences of imagery from unit to unit.

The Villanelle

A *villanelle* is a fixed form that originally came from Italy and France. It has nineteen lines and six stanzas. Each stanza except the last has three lines; the last has four. The first and third lines establish the rhyme scheme: aba, aba, aba, aba, aba, abaa. The first line is repeated at the end of stanzas two and four, the third line at the end of stanzas three and five. These two lines form a couplet at the end of the poem.

NOW IT'S YOUR TURN

Elizabeth Bishop's "One Art" is a villanelle. Show how she uses the villanelle conventions in this poem to convey ideas. What are her ideas? Why would she choose the villanelle to develop them?

ONE ART

Elizabeth Bishop

The art of losing isn't hard to master;
so many things seem filled with the intent
to be lost that their loss is no disaster.

Lose something every day. Accept the fluster
of lost door keys, the hour badly spent.
The art of losing isn't hard to master.

Then practice losing farther, losing faster:
places, and names, and where it was you meant
to travel. None of these will bring disaster.

I lost my mother's watch. And look! my last, or
next-to-last, of three loved houses went.
The art of losing isn't hard to master.

I lost two cities, lovely ones. And, vaster,
some realms I owned, two rivers, a continent.
I miss them, but it wasn't a disaster.

—Even losing you (the joking voice, a gesture
I love) I shan't have lied. It's evident
the art of losing's not too hard to master
though it may look like (*Write* it!) like disaster.   1976

IV. SIGHT: THE VISUAL QUALITIES OF POETRY

Until the invention of writing, all poetry was oral. But once it was written down, it became visual as well. This was especially true after the invention of the printing press by Johannes Gutenberg in 1450. With the advent of mass printing, poets could assume that large numbers of people would see their poetry. Readers could then see rhyme schemes, punctuation, spelling, stanza sizes, line lengths, the visual shape of the poem.

The visibility of poetry allowed poets to take new liberties with their compositions. They could enjamb lines, knowing that even if people couldn't hear where the lines stopped, they could see where. They could insert approximate or visual rhymes, assuming that even if people couldn't hear them, they could spot the similarities between words. They could block off poems into irregular stanzas, knowing that people could see these units separated by spaces.

Visual Poetry

The printing of poetry led to a kind of poetry called *visual poetry* or *pattern poetry*. Eleanor Berry defines *visual poetry* as "poetry composed for the eye as well, or more than, for the ear" (1364). Visual poetry, Dick Higgins says, fulfills the "human wish to combine the visual and literary impulses, to tie together the experience of those two areas into an aesthetic whole" (3).

A famous example of visual poetry is this poem by George Herbert. To see its shape—the angel's wings—you have to turn the page sideways.

EASTER WINGS

George Herbert

Lord, who createdst man in wealth and store,°   °*abundance*
　　Though foolishly he lost the same,
　　　　Decaying more and more
　　　　　　Till he became
　　　　　　　Most poor:
　　　　　　　With thee
　　　　　　O let　me　rise
　　　　As　larks,　harmoniously,
　　And　sing　this　day　thy　victories:
Then shall the fall° further the flight in me.　°*Adam and Eve's sin*

　　My　tender　age in sorrow did begin:
　　　And still with sicknesses and shame
　　　　　Thou didst so punish sin,
　　　　　　That I became
　　　　　　　Most thin.
　　　　　　　With thee
　　　　　　Let me combine,
　　　　And feel this day thy victory;
　　For,　if　I　imp°　my　wing　on　thine,　　　°*graft*
　Affliction　shall　advance　the　flight　in　me.

　　　　　　　　　　　　　　　　　c. 1630

Typical of visual poetry, the words of Herbert's poem conform to a recognizable shape. The shape, in turn, contributes to the poem's meaning. Higgins, in his history of visual poetry, points out the numerous traditional shapes of visual poetry, including love knots, crosses, animals, pyramids, labyrinths, stars, chalices, hearts, musical instruments, roses, trees.

Modern Poetry

Pattern poetry has a limited appeal because there are only so many shapes words will fit into and because it sometimes seems more like a trick than a meaningful device. But for much poetry, especially that written since 1900, the visibility of poetry is crucial. Modernist free verse, with its enjambed lines and conversational style, depends on our ability to see the lines. We can't hear where they end; we have to see. The poet e. e. cummings, for example, built visual elements into his poetry with verve and ingenuity. Unless we can see his quirky punctuation and arrangement of words on the page, it's hard to make sense of his poems. Even his name (all lower case) partakes of the visual nature of his poetry.

Examples. The following poem by cummings comes close to being entirely visual. He didn't give it a title. The one we use here is the first line of the poem.

l(a
_____

e. e. cummings

l(a

le
af
fa

ll

s)
one
l

iness   1958

Can this poem be read out loud? Perhaps with two readers?

A less radical example of the ingenuity with which Modernist poets include visual elements is "We Real Cool" by Gwendolyn Brooks:

WE REAL COOL

The Pool Players.
Seven at the Golden Shovel.

We real cool. We
Left school. We

Lurk late. We
Strike straight. We

Sing sin. We
Thin gin. We

Jazz June. We
Die soon.   1960

Except for one thing, this poem looks fairly traditional. It has four stanzas. Each stanza is a couplet, rhyming aa. The unusual thing—noticeable only because we see it—is where she places each "we." Syntactically—as subjects of the sentences—they should go at the beginning of the lines. Instead, except for the first one, they appear at the ends.

QUESTIONS ABOUT THE VISUAL ELEMENTS OF POETRY

1. What effect does the look of a given poem have on you?

2. What can you see in a poem that is missing from its sound?

3. How do the visual elements of a poem enhance its sound qualities?

4. How crucial to understanding the implications of a poem are its visual features?

THINKING ON PAPER ABOUT THE VISUAL ELEMENTS OF POETRY

1. Write a pattern poem.

2. Have someone read out loud a poem you have never read or heard. Then read the poem. Write out your reactions to both experi-

ences. What was missing from each experience? Was one experience better—more meaningful, more fun, more interesting—than the other?

3. Mark the visual qualities of a poem. Explain how they contribute to the poem's meaning.

Now It's Your Turn

Show how the visual qualities of "We Real Cool" and the cummings's poem contribute to their possible meanings. More broadly, speculate about why you think these poets arrange the appearance of these poems the way they do.

Checklist for Interpreting Poetry

Sense in Poems (pages 117–138)

- Look up words you don't know.

- Locate the normal word order (subject-verb-object) of all sentences.

- Inform yourself about all allusions.

- Characterize the person or persons speaking—the "I" of the poem.

- Construct the story of the poem—what has happened in the past, what is going on now, what is likely to happen in the future.

- Establish the temporal, social, and physical context of the poem.

- Note all descriptive images and the senses to which they appeal.

- Account for tropes and all analogies—metaphors, similes, personifications.

- Explore the implications of symbols.

Sound in Poems (pages 138–148)

- Establish the predominate metrical pattern or lack of one. Where helpful, scan key passages.

- Mark important caesuras.

- Note sound devices, such as alliteration, assonance, and end rhyme.

- Think about how a poem's sound devices contribute to the pleasure of reading or hearing it.

- Speculate about the connection between any of a poem's sound devices and its possible meanings.

Structure of Poems (pages 148–165)

- Track the organization (arrangement, logical development) of ideas.

- Note the method of organizing lines—meter and rhyme for metrical poetry; ideas and sound devices for free verse.

- Account for variations in line length.

- Discern the effect of end-stopped and enjambed lines.

- Note how stanzas are organized—rhyme scheme, fixed forms, ideas.

- If the poem is a fixed form, learn about its structural conventions.

- Show how the poem adheres to or abandons any of these conventions.

- For a free verse poem, indicate devices that give it structure.

Sight of Poems (pages 165–169)

- Think how the look of the poem—its appearance on the page—affects you.

- Explore the connection between the poem's appearance and its possible meanings.

Works Cited

Abrams, M. H. *A Glossary of Literary Terms.* 7th ed. Fort Worth, TX: Harcourt Brace College Publishers, 1999. Print.

Berry, Eleanor. "Visual Poetry." *The New Princeton Encyclopedia of Poetry and Poetics.* Ed. Alex Preminger and T. V. F. Brogan. Princeton, NJ: Princeton UP, 1993. Print.

Brogan, T. V. F. "Poetry." *The New Princeton Encyclopedia of Poetry and Poetics.* Ed. Alex Preminger and T. V. F. Brogan. Princeton, NJ: Princeton UP, 1993. Print.

Cohen, William Howard. *To Walk in Seasons: An Introduction to Haiku.* Rutland, VT: Charles E. Tuttle, 1972. Print.

Eliot, T. S. "The Three Voices of Poetry." *On Poetry and Poets.* New York: Octagon Books, 1975. 96–112. Print.

Fussell, Paul. *Poetic Meter and Poetic Form.* Rev. ed. New York: Random House, 1979. Print.

Hartman, Charles O. *Free Verse: An Essay on Prosody.* Princeton, NJ: Princeton UP, 1980. Print.

Henderson, Harold G. *Haiku in English.* Rutland, VT: Charles E. Tuttle, 1967. Print.

Higgins, Dick. *Pattern Poetry: Guide to an Unknown Literature.* Albany: State U of New York P, 1987. Print.

Hirsch, Edward. *How to Read a Poem and Fall in Love with Poetry.* San Diego: Harcourt, 1999. Print.

Kinzie, Mary. *A Poet's Guide to Poetry.* Chicago: U of Chicago P, 1999. Print.

Wesling, Donald, and Eniko Bolloba´s. "Free Verse." *The New Princeton Encyclopedia of Poetry and Poetics.* Ed. Alex Preminger and T. V. F. Brogan. Princeton, NJ: Princeton UP, 1993. Print.

Wimsatt, W. K., and Monroe C. Beardsley. *Hateful Contraries: Studies in Literature and Criticism.* Louisville: U of Kentucky P, 1965. Print.

6

Specialized Approaches to Interpreting Literature

LITERARY CRITICISM

When people interpret works of literature, they practice "literary criticism"; that is, they study works in order to discover their meanings. So far in this book we have described a strategy for doing this—analyzing the works themselves. For the most part, you can use this strategy without having to seek information outside the works. But as fundamental and necessary as analyzing works is, reading outside the works greatly expands the possibility of finding meanings within them. This chapter describes places you can look, both inside and outside works of literature, that invite you to do this.

SITES OF MEANING

Where are these places? An expanded version of the author/work/reader pattern, introduced in Chapter 1, suggests some possibilities.

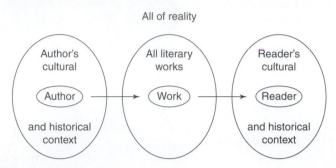

All of reality

This diagram highlights four general "sites" that relate to a work's meaning. The first centers on the author, who begins the process of creation and communication. It includes the circumstances of the author's life (biography); the author's values, intentions, and methods of composition (the author as artist); and the events, patterns of life, and beliefs of the author's time (historical and cultural environment).

The second centers on the work. It encompasses the elements of the work (its form), the language of the work (its linguistic makeup), and the work's relationship to other works and literary practices (its intertextuality).

The third centers on the reader. It includes the individual reader: his or her reading skills, knowledge, and psychology. Included also are groups of readers, such as those who first read the work as well as those who read the work now. And, as with authors, it focuses on the influence of cultural environment on readers.

The final place is all of reality. This includes the work's connection to the universe outside it, its "truth." But, also, just as the work is surrounded by all of reality, so too are authors and readers, all of whom have their own understanding of "reality."

LITERARY THEORY

How can you mine these sites of meaning? Perhaps the best way to begin is with *literary theory*. All literary criticism, including your own, is undergirded by a theory or theories about how and why to interpret literature. You may be unaware that you "have" a literary theory, but you do. All interpreters of literature do. You might, then, ask questions like these: What is your literary theory? Where did you get it? What theories are out there for you to choose from? Which one or ones are best for you? Before 1900, almost no one raised such questions. But since the 1920s and especially since the 1960s, literary theory has become an almost unavoidable companion to literary criticism. This chapter has a dual purpose. It offers suggestions about how you can use these four areas to search out meanings in works of literature. It also reports briefly on influential literary theories that illuminate these four areas. At the end of each section, you will find "Applications," a discussion that suggests practical ways you might use these theories in your own reading and writing.

Literary Theory Before 1900

Before the twentieth century, there was little systematic attempt to interpret works of literature, to probe their meanings. There was, in short, almost no *literary criticism*. Gerald Graff, in *Professing Literature* (1987), a history of literary studies in higher education, says that before then there was a widespread "assumption that great literature was essentially self-interpreting and needed no elaborate interpretation" (20). Instead, students studied classical works such as *The Aeneid* and *The Odyssey* to learn Latin and Greek grammar. They used bits and pieces of literature in English, such as Mark Antony's funeral speech in Shakespeare's *Julius Caesar*, for training in oratory (28, 41). Otherwise, people could not believe that "the literature in one's own language needed to be taught in formal classes instead of being enjoyed as part of the normal experience of the community" (19).

Even so, prior to the twentieth century, *literary theory*—the investigation of the nature and value of literature—had had a long and distinguished history, beginning with Plato and Aristotle and continuing into modern times with such figures as Sir Philip Sidney, John Dryden, Samuel Johnson, William Wordsworth, Samuel Taylor Coleridge, and Matthew Arnold. These theorists explored what literature is and praised or condemned works that failed to meet whatever standards they deemed essential. In *The Republic,* to cite one extreme example, Plato condemned *all* literature because he claimed that it falsely represents reality and that it stirs up the passions—lust, desire, pain, anger—rather than nurtures the intellect. At the end of the nineteenth century, however, universities began to include courses in modern literature, and teachers and writers began to give attention to interpreting literature.

Literary Theory in the Twentieth Century

Accompanying this shift in attitude was a renewed interest in literary theory. In *Literary Theory: A Very Short Introduction* (1999), Jonathan Culler defines literary theory generally as "the systematic account of the nature of literature and of the methods for analyzing it" (1). Through the first half of the twentieth century, a handful of new theories influenced the interpretation and teaching of literature. The most important of these was Anglo-American criticism ("practical criticism" in Great Britain, and New Criticism in the United States), whose methodology was effective and accessible. But with the discovery of French structuralism in the 1960s, new literary theories swamped the old ones and elicited an enormous body of writings.

Resources for Theory

This near-obsessive interest in literary interpretation and theory is cause for wonder. "One of the most dismaying features of theory today," Culler says, "is that it is endless. It is not something that you could learn so as to 'know theory.' It is an unbounded corpus of writings which is always being augmented as the young and the restless, in critiques of the guiding conceptions of their elders, promote the contributions to theory of new thinkers and rediscover the work of older, neglected ones" (15).

If you want to find out more about literary theory and read some of it yourself, Culler's book is an excellent place to begin. Rather than describe theoretical approaches in detail, Culler addresses the issues that theory since 1960 has taken up. A readable and engaging book that does survey literary theory is Peter Barry's *Beginning Theory: An Introduction to Literary and Cultural Theory* (2nd ed., 2002). He writes for undergraduates and a general audience and is especially helpful in suggesting what to read and how theoretical approaches can be used for interpretation. Equally well written and instructive is his introduction to literary studies *English in Practice: In Pursuit of English Studies* (2003). Richard Harland's *Literary Theory from Plato to Barthes: An Introductory History* (1999) fills in the story of literary criticism and theory up to the 1960s. There are numerous collections of writings by theorists themselves. One such is David Lodge and Nigel Wood's *Modern Criticism and Theory: A Reader* (2nd edition, 2000). M. H. Abrams and Geoffrey Galt Harpham's *A Glossary of Literary Terms* (9th, ed., 2009) provides succinct and up-to-date overviews of literary theories and definitions of theoretical terms.

One of the best ways to understand literary theories is to see how critics apply them to individual works of literature. The "Case Studies in Contemporary Criticism" is a series published by Bedford/St. Martin's Press (now Palgrave Macmillan) that gives full texts of works such as *Dracula, Frankenstein, Hamlet, The Rime of the Ancient Mariner*, and *Wuthering Heights* plus interpretations that represent theoretical approaches. Ann B. Dobie's *Theory into Practice: An Introduction to Literary Criticism* (2nd edition, 2009) gives brief introductions of theories followed by instructions for using them. Donald Keesey's *Context for Criticism* (4th edition, 2002) is organized somewhat like this chapter and includes writings by theorists as well as interpretive essays.

THE WORK

We turn now to the four sites of meaning listed above. Interpreters of literature typically deal with more than one of these sites. They may, for example, focus largely on the work itself, but may also draw upon information about an author's life or about philosophical concepts of reality. M. H. Abrams, who in *The Mirror and the Lamp* (1953) originated this concept of sites of meaning, says that literary criticism almost always touches on more than one of these sites, but most criticism exhibits "a discernible orientation toward one only" (6). Even though these sites are interrelated and can't really be separated, we will take them up one at a time. For several reasons, we start with the work. First, interpreting just the work has been our focus so far. Second, the most influential literary theories—Anglo-American criticism, structuralism, and poststructuralism—have risen out of concern with the work. These three theories have provided the basis for nearly all the theory and criticism that have come after them. Starting with the work, then, allows us to arrange our report on the development of literary criticism and theory into a rough chronological order.

Anglo-American Criticism

The English origins of Anglo-American criticism. A product of the rise of Modernism, Anglo-American criticism provided the twentieth century's first set of theories and practices for interpreting literature. The practitioners of Anglo-American criticism were often themselves writers of literature, like T. S. Eliot, John Crowe Ransom, Allan Tate, and Robert Penn Warren. Perhaps the most important theorist of this movement was the Englishman I. A. Richards. In a series of theoretical books, including *Principles of Literary Criticism* (1924), *Science and Poetry* (1926), and *Practical Criticism* (1929), he laid down a set of beliefs that became the basis for critical practices in both countries. The language of literature, he claimed, is different from and more expressive of human emotions than scientific language. The more a work's complexities can be synthesized into a unified whole, the better it is. The "truth" or "meaning" of a work cannot be paraphrased; the work *is* the meaning. Interpretation of works should be "scientific" in that it examines works carefully and supports claims with details from them (Harland 169–172).

Underlying Anglo-American criticism are assumptions that Peter Barry associates with "liberal humanism," a value system that Matthew Arnold espoused in the nineteenth century. According to this system, human nature is unchanging and individuality transcends "the forces of society, experience, and language" (Barry18–19). Good literature "is of timeless significance" and "speaks to what is constant in human nature" (17). The purpose of literature is "the enhancement of life and the propagation of humane values" (19). Like many Modernist authors, these critics felt that literary criticism has a similar function to religious faith, which they felt had fallen away in the face of science. For Richards, K. M. Newton says, "interpretation of poetic texts was as important in the modern era as the interpretation of religious texts had been in the past" (12). Since great works of literature are timeless and express universal truths, they deserve the same reverence and attention as religious icons. The critic's function, then, is like the priest's, to "interpret the text, to mediate between it and the reader" (Barry, *Beginning*, 20). Perhaps the best known English critics who advocated such a priestly role were F. R. Leavis and his wife Q. D. Leavis. He edited and they both contributed to the influential journal *Scrutiny*.

New Criticism. New Criticism was the American version of Anglo-American criticism. Its theorists and practitioners were critics such as John Crowe Ransom, W. K. Wimsatt, Allen Tate, Cleanth Brooks, and Robert Penn Warren. Through best-selling textbooks, Brooks and Warren made the methods of Anglo-American criticism standard in American undergraduate and graduate education.

The term *New Criticism* comes from the title of a book published by John Crowe Ransom in 1941, *The New Criticism*. Ransom surveyed the work of recent ("new") critics and thereby made clear some of his own critical principles. Other critics who agreed with Ransom came to be called the New Critics. The New Critics broke dramatically with the nineteenth-century emphasis on historical and biographical background. They held that understanding and appreciating a work of literature need have little or no connection with the author's intended meanings, with the author's life, or with the social and historical circumstances that may have influenced the author. Everything the reader needs to understand and appreciate a work is contained within the work itself.

Irony and unity.   The New Critics saw their method as "scientific." The work is a self-contained phenomenon made up of "physical" qualities—language and literary conventions. These qualities can be studied in the same way a geologist studies a rock formation or a physicist the fragmentation of light particles. But some New Critics, like Cleanth Brooks, claimed that because of the metaphorical nature of literature, ideas in literature cannot be paraphrased, cannot be separated from the work's form. One can state what a work is "about" or summarize a work's themes, but a work's meaning is far more complex than such statements alone. Brooks argued that a work's complexity lies in its "irony"—its inclusion of "discordant" elements that clash and cause tension within the poem. Meaningful poetry "does not leave out what is apparently hostile to its dominant tone, and which, because it is able to fuse the irrelevant and discordant, has come to terms with itself and is invulnerable to irony." By "invulnerable to irony" he means "the stability of a context in which the internal pressures balance and mutually support each other" (732). Such a hard won stability and balance gives poems unity: The "poem is like a little drama. The total effect proceeds from all elements in the drama, and in a good poem, as in a good drama, there is no wasted motion and there are no superfluous parts" (730).

Evaluation of works.   The New Critics used their theories to judge the quality of works of literature. Because they favored complex yet unified works, they downgraded works that seemed simple or those that lacked unity. They preferred "difficult" works that contained apparently illogical and troubling material. They approved of works that stayed away from social and historical subject matter and that dealt instead with private, personal, and emotional experience.

Influence of New Criticism. As a method for teaching and interpretation, New Criticism was highly appealing. The New Critics believed that the language of great works of literature was accessible to modern readers. They were confident that well-trained interpreters could analyze, understand, and evaluate works of literature. Since to them great literature was one of civilization's proudest achievements, they imbued literary criticism with a noble, even priestly quality. Their method of analyzing literature—using literary elements to reveal artistry and meaning—was easy to understand and even "democratic"; anyone could appreciate great literature and learn to interpret it. Finally, their method excused interpreters from having to master biographical and historical background. They believed that all that was needed was a careful and thorough scrutiny of the works themselves.

Resources for Anglo-American Criticism. Two influential New Critical essays are "The Intentional Fallacy" and "The Affective Fallacy," both by W. K. Wimsatt and Monroe Beardsley, contained in Wimsatt's *The Verbal Icon* (1954). A stimulating work of New Criticism is Cleanth Brooks's *The Well Wrought Urn* (1947). See especially Chapter 1 ("The Language of Paradox") and Chapter 11 ("The Heresy of Paraphrase"). The works mentioned above—by I. A. Richards, F. R. Leavis's *The Great Tradition* (1948), and William Empson's *Seven Types of Ambiguity* (1930)—are stellar examples of the English half of Anglo-American criticism.

Structuralism

A new approach. By the 1950s and 1960s, especially in the United States, New Critical textbooks, like Brooks and Warren's *Understanding Poetry* (1938) and *Understanding Fiction* (1943), pervaded the classrooms. New Critical interpretations of literature filled the scholarly journals. College students who took introductory courses in literature were asked to learn the characteristics of fiction, drama, and poetry and tease out their implications from works—usually short stories and poems—published in anthologies. But at the peak of this dominance, a new generation of graduate students and teachers discovered structuralism, which had existed since the 1930s in Europe but whose theorists' works were not translated into English until the 1950s and 1960s. Although structuralism shared some of the methods of New Criticism—notably an emphasis on close reading and attention to the particularities of the text—it was diametrically opposed to it in fundamental ways and took the teaching and interpretation of literature in new directions.

Saussure's theories of language. Like New Criticism, *structuralism* denied the value of historical, social, and biographical information, and concentrated on identifiable elements in works of literature. Unlike New Criticism, its theory and methodology were grounded in the social sciences, most notably psychology, anthropology, and linguistics. There were several versions of "structuralism" promulgated in the twentieth century, but by far the most influential originated from the work of the Swiss linguist Ferdinand de Saussure (1857–1913). Early in the twentieth century, Saussure taught three innovative courses in linguistics. Because he left no notes on the content of these courses, his students pooled their notes and published a reconstruction of the courses called *Course in General Linguistics* (1916). This work is the basis of Saussure's fame and provides the theoretical underpinning of both structuralism and poststructuralism.

Saussure's key points about the nature of language broke new ground for studying literature. First, a language is a complete, self-contained system and deserves to be studied as such. Before Saussure, linguists investigated the history of languages (how languages evolved and changed through time) and the differences among languages; for this kind of study, Saussure coined the word *diachronic* (literally "through time"). Saussure argued that, instead of the history of a language, linguists should also study how it functions in the present, how its parts interrelate to make up a whole system of communication. This kind of study Saussure called *synchronic* ("at the same time"). Second, Saussure claimed that a language is a system of signs. He defined a *sign* as consisting of two things—a *signified* and *signifier*. The concept of an object—"tree"— is the signified. The word sound for the concept—*tree*—is the signifier. Third, Saussure held that the basic structure of language rests on differences between the sounds of words. The difference between the initial consonants of *path* and *math* gives both words meaning. The structure of language rests on binary oppositions like this one—sets of two words that have meaningful differences of sound.

Fourth, Saussure said that the connection between the sounds of a language system and the concepts they represent is completely arbitrary. Any sound, it does not matter which one, could represent the concept of a given thing. The sound for the concept "tree" varies from language to language, yet users of each language know that the sound represents (signifies) "tree." Fifth, any given language is self-contained. The signs that make up a language have no meaning outside the system of that language. Finally, Saussure distinguished between the whole system, which he called *langue* (French for "language"), and one person's use of the system, which he called *parole* (French for "word" or "speech"). *Langue* consists of everything that makes the system work, such as binary oppositions, words, syntax, and inflections. *Parole* consists of these same elements but with variations from user to user. Each speaker of a language uses the same system but does so in a slightly different way.

Structuralist literary theory. In the 1930s and 1940s, literary theorists in Europe began applying Saussure's ideas and methods to the study of literature. This application followed two different but merging paths: focus on literature and focus on culture. The study of not just literature but all sign systems in a culture, including literature, is called *semiotics*.

Unlike Anglo-American criticism, structuralism, Richard Harland says, "had no interest in promoting a particular literary movement, nor in promoting the importance of literature in general, nor in discovering what makes one individual piece of writing work better than another. Such evaluative concerns come naturally to the writer-critic, but not to the social scientist" (219–20). Nor, according to Martin Barry, are structuralists interested in interpreting individual texts. In "the structuralist approach to literature there is a movement away from interpretation of the individual literary work and a parallel drive towards understanding the larger, abstract structures which contain them" (40). Another break with Anglo-American criticism was that structuralists made no distinction between "great" literature and popular literature, like science fiction, ghost stories, detective, spy, and thriller novels. All were fair game for structuralist studies.

The "abstract structure" that mattered most to Saussurian structuralists was language. They attempted to show that literature is a form of language or that it functions like language. The individual work of literature, they claimed, is similar to *parole,* and literary genres or literature in general is similar to *langue.* "Genres," Harland says, "are viewed as social codes governing individual texts in the same way that *langue* as a social code governs individual acts of *parole"* (222). The structuralist study of literature, then, is intertextual, in that it examines many works to discover the principles that govern them all.

An example of this kind of study is Vladimir Propp's *The Morphology of the Folktale* (first published in Russian in 1928; translated into English in 1958). Propp reports on his analysis of one hundred Russian folk tales and the conclusions he drew about the structural elements that bind them together. He identified thirty-one "functions" that appear in these tales. Some of the functions are as follows:

1. A family member (the hero) leaves home (24).

2. The hero is forbidden to do something (25).

3. The hero violates the taboo (26).

8. The villain injures one or more members of the hero's family (29).

9. The hero learns of a misfortune and leaves to address it (33).

14. The hero gains a magical agent (such as an apple, horse, hen, dog, tree) (40–41).

16. The hero and villain fight each other (47).

18. The hero defeats the villain (48).

20. The hero returns (50).

31. The hero marries and becomes king (57).

Although no single tale has all thirty-one functions, Propp says that they always occur in the order he gives. The tales, which seem on the surface to be very different, are in fact unified by a common structure. The functions, furthermore, group together into seven "spheres of action" (72–73):

1. Villain

2. Donor

3. Helper

4. Princess and her father

5. Dispatcher

6. Hero

7. False hero

From these thirty-one functions and seven spheres of action, Propp claims that we can generate any folk tale from his group of 100 tales (72–75). The goal of structuralist studies like Propp's is to uncover the structures that govern even larger groupings and perhaps even literature itself. It's fairly easy to see these same structural elements in numerous other stories, especially stories that feature traditional heroes. Think, for example, of popular stories like the Harry Potter novels or the Star Wars movies. Propp's approach, furthermore, is enlightening about individual works. It hints, Barry says, "at the way simple archetypes from much more basic narrative material can provide the shadowy deep foundations of complex realist fictions—the way, for instance, the Cinderella archetype (a tale found in some form in cultures worldwide) lies beneath novels like *Mansfield Park* and *Jane Eyre*" (230–31).

Semiotics. Structuralists who study entire cultures attempt to understand a culture's sign systems. The study of signs is called *semiotics*. The most prominent practitioner of this kind of criticism is the French anthropologist Claude Lévi-Strauss (b.1908). Lévi-Strauss claims that a culture is bound together by systems of signs and that these systems are like language. He uses Saussurian linguistics as a way of describing the "grammar" of these systems. All aspects of a culture—technology, religion, tools, industry, food, ornaments, rituals—form sign systems. The people of the culture are unaware of these systems, so the structural anthropologist's task is to bring them to light. Lévi-Strauss is perhaps best known for his study of myth. He examines multiple versions of individual myths in order to isolate their essential structural units. Although Lévi-Strauss applies his theories to the study of tribal cultures, other critics, like the Frenchman Roland Barthes (1915–80), use Lévi-Strauss's approach to "psychoanalyze" modern society. They look for the unconscious sign systems that underlie all aspects of Western culture, including food, furniture, cars, buildings, clothing fashions, business, advertising, and popular entertainment. For Barthes, Richard Harland says, the "whole human world is revealed as a text, to be read under symbolic techniques of the kind originally developed for literary texts" (236).

Resources for structuralism. Two readable, book-length overviews of structuralism are Robert Scholes's *Structuralism in Literature: An Introduction* (1974) and Terence Hawkes's *Structuralism and Semiotics* (1977). Tzvetan Todorov's "The Grammar of Narrative" in *The Poetics of Prose* (1977) equates narrative structure to sentence structure. Umberto Eco's *The Role of the Reader: Explorations in the Semiotics of Texts* (1979) includes essays on the structure of narratives about Superman and James Bond. Eco has also written a "semiotic" detective novel, *The Name of the Rose* (1983).

Archetypal Criticism: Another Kind of Structuralism

Archetypes.   Another approach to the structures of literature is archetypal criticism. Northrop Frye (1912–91), a preeminent advocate of archetypal criticism, defines *archetype* as "the recurring use of certain images or image clusters" in literature (*Critical Path*, 23). More broadly, archetypes can be defined as any repeated pattern in literature, whether of plot, character, themes, settings, or images. *Archetypal criticism* attempts to identify archetypes in works of literature and explain their meanings. Archetypal criticism was prominent in the 1950s through the 1970s, especially in North America. Frye, a Canadian, wrote perhaps the most influential book of archetypal criticism, *Anatomy of Criticism* (1957).

Advocates of archetypal criticism claim that archetypes impose a "structure" on works of literature. An example is the hero archetype. As outlined by Joseph Campbell in *The Hero with a Thousand Faces* (1949), the hero's career has a "structure" consisting of three main parts. In the first, the "Departure," heroes receive a "call to adventure." By a seeming accident, someone or something invites the hero into "an unsuspected world," into "a relationship with forces that are not rightly understood" (51). Often heroes receive supernatural aid from a "protective figure" who helps them in their adventures (69). In the second part of the hero's story, the "Initiation," heroes cross a dangerous "threshold" into a strange, fluid, dreamlike world where they undergo a succession of trials (77, 97). The climax of these trials is the hero's victory over all opposition. Sometimes this victory is accompanied by a mystical vision that exposes the life-creating energy of all existence (40–41). The third part of the hero's story is the "Return." Because of their victory, heroes now have a boon to bestow upon those left behind (30). The trip home can be arduous, but once back they have a choice: they can withhold or bestow the boon. They also face the problem of integrating their transcendent experiences with the "banalities and noisy obscenities" of their old world (218).

The hero is one of numerous archetypal characters. Others include such figures as the scapegoat, the outcast, the earth goddess, the fatal woman, the rebel, the cruel stepmother, the "spiritual" person, the tyrannical father, the star-crossed lovers. These characters often find themselves in archetypal situations such as the quest, the journey to the underworld, the ascent to heaven, the search for the father, the initiation, the fall from innocence, death and rebirth, and the seemingly impossible task. The more archetypal a work, the more it seems dominated by polarities, such as good versus evil, light versus darkness, water versus desert, heights versus depths.

Sources of archetypes. What is the source of archetypes? Where do they come from? Some critics say that archetypes are merely structural elements in literature. They do not come from anywhere except literature itself. This claim would seem to support the Saussurian structuralist's claim that all patterns in literature come from language. Other critics, like Northrop Frye, agree that this might be so, but suggest also that archetypes exist in real life and are incorporated into literature as part of its meaning. In his best-known work, *Anatomy of Criticism* (1957), Frye attempts to show that all of literature is bound together by a structure of archetypes, which arise from human experiences, wishes, and needs.

Robert Scholes provides an example of such a "natural" structure: the love story. "In fiction, as in life," he says, "the coming together of two human beings in the sexual embrace of love represents the reconciliation of all opposites, the peaceful resolution of all disputes, the melting of all swords into plowshares. In such an embrace, the cyclical dominates the temporal, the lovers are united with all lovers, and we partake of the universal. Marriage is a sacrament of structuralism. It is also precisely the point at which structural ideas and fictional structure are brought into the closest correspondence. From ancient fiction to modern, the structural pattern of courtship and marriage, separation and union, has been one of the most persistent and popular. It has proved capable of the highest development and the most basic appeal. Love stories and allegories of love have gone hand in hand since the 'Song of Songs' and even before that" (197–98).

Another possible source of archetypes is the human psyche. The Swiss psychologist Carl Jung (1875–1961) argued that archetypes exist in the human "collective unconscious." Jung accepted Freud's concept of the unconscious mind, but, whereas Freud held that each person's unconscious is unique, Jung argued that a part of the unconscious is linked by historical associations and communal "memories" to the unconscious minds of all people. To represent this phenomenon, he coined the phrase "collective unconscious." The collective unconscious is deeper and more primitive than the individual unconscious and is the same for all people. Archetypes populate the collective unconscious. An archetype is a "primordial image," a "figure—be it a demon, a human being, or a process— that constantly recurs in the course of history and appears wherever creative fantasy is freely expressed" (quoted in Harland 194). These archetypes manifest themselves in dreams, myths, symbols, ritual, and literature.

Still another source of archetypes is culture. Richard Slotkin, in his mammoth three-volume investigation of the influence of the frontier on American culture—*Regeneration Through Violence* (1973), *The Fatal Environment* (1985), and *Gunfighter Nation* (1992)—claims that numerous archetypes that influence American culture arose from the frontier experience. The most important of these, he says, is regeneration through violence, the concept that as a nation and as individuals, Americans must undergo violence in order to gain psychic wholeness and take possession of their rightful heritage. The "artifacts" of American culture—novels, films, legends, paintings, comic books, television shows—bear witness to this archetype's influence on American life. The title of Slotkin's third volume— *Gunfighter Nation*—sums up his belief about how this archetype continues to shape the American consciousness.

Literary criticism.   What meanings do archetypes impart to works of literature? The task of the archetypal critic, Frye says, is to help readers see the "structures" of what they read by identifying literature's "organizing patterns of convention, genre and archetype" (*Critical Path* 24). Like any other structural element, archetypes are potential but not inevitable places of meaning. But those critics who see archetypes as linked to real life—to universal human experience, the human psyche, or culture—claim that archetypes import powerful ideas to works of literature, ideas that resonate subliminally and emotionally with readers. An example is Robert Scholes's paean to the love story, quoted above. Scholes not only describes how the love story provides structure to narratives, but he extols its meaningfulness.

Because many literary structures, like the love story, touch something deep within people, archetypal criticism is sometimes called *myth criticism*. Alan Watts defines *myth* as "as a complex of stories—some no doubt fact, and some fantasy—which, for various reasons, human beings regard as demonstrations of the inner meaning of the universe and of human life" (7). "A mythology," Slotkin says, "is a complex of narratives that dramatizes the world vision and historical sense of a people or culture, reducing centuries of experience into a constellation of compelling metaphors (*Regeneration* 6). Myths, in other words, can come from sacred narratives, like the Bible and the Hindu scriptures, but they can also emerge from national or cultural sources. They can be fictional or quasi-historical, like the King Arthur stories. What they have in common is that large groups of people find them meaningful, perhaps even profound.

Poststructuralism

Poststructuralism evolved from Saussure's theories of language. It became the most influential and eye-opening application of structuralism to the interpretation of literature. It accepts Saussure's analysis of language and uses his methodology to examine the language of literary works, but it concerns itself with the relationship between language and meaning. Poststructuralism, in fact, offers a radical theory of reading that altogether rejects the certainty of meaning. The philosopher-critic who invented poststructuralism is the Frenchman Jacques Derrida (1930–2004).

Structuralism and poststructuralism. The basis of Derrida's radical skepticism is Saussure's distinction between signifier and signified. Before Saussure, theorists of language maintained that words represent concrete objects. The word *tree* represents the object "tree." But Saussure questioned the pervasiveness of such one-to-one correspondences. Words, he said, refer not to objects but to "concepts," which are expressed by other words. It seems possible, then, that language, or at least parts of language, may not refer to anything in the sensuously apprehensible world. Saussure said that language is a self-contained system and that to function it does not need to reflect reality, it needs only to reflect itself. Signs gain meaning from other signs in the system, not necessarily from the real world. This possible separation between language and the world outside language (the "real" world) suggests that language molds human thought. Language, Terence Hawks says, possibly "constitutes the characteristic structure of human reality" (28).

    Derrida concludes from Saussure's theories that there is a "gap" between signifier and signified. This gap blurs the meaning of the signifier so that we cannot know exactly what it refers to. Derrida coined the term *différance* to represent this ambiguity of language. The French verb *différer* means "to differ" and "to defer." Saussure based his concept of the structure of language on sound differences—binary oppositions—between words. The French term is *différence*. Derrida, however, seizes upon the other meaning of *différer* to show that certainty of meaning, certainty of connection between signified and signifier, is constantly deferred. His coinage is *différance*.

These two words, différence and différance, sound the same in French, which points to another of Derrida's concepts. Saussure emphasized the sound of language in his concept of its structure. Derrida, however, believes that the presence of people speaking a language creates the false illusion that secure connections exist between signified and signifier. This emphasis on the sound of language Derrida calls phonocentrism. Only in writing can the endless displacement of meaning, the "undecideability" and "free play" of meaning, be exposed. Derrida thus favors writing as a more revealing representation of language.

Implications of poststructuralism. Derrida's claim that meaning is constantly deferred in language has broad implications. He rejects, as Terence Hawkes says, the belief "that, in spite of our always fragmentary experience, somewhere there must exist a redeeming and justifying *wholeness,* which we can objectify in ourselves as the notion of Man, and beyond ourselves as the notion of Reality. This yearning underwrites and guarantees the belief that *necessary* connections exist between signifier and signified, and that these are ultimately locked in a 'meaningful,' wholly unbreakable, real-world-generating union" (146). Derrida holds that because language is our only means of knowing anything and because language is ambiguous, no such comforting notions exist. For Derrida, says Peter Barry, "we enter a universe of radical uncertainty, since we can have no access to any fixed landmark which is beyond linguistic processing, and hence we have no certain standard by which to measure anything" (61).

Poststructuralism and literary criticism. Literary critics who utilize Derrida's ideas see literature as like language, a "text" that consists of an infinite chain of postponed connection between signified and signifier. A work of literature is a self-contained system that exists independently from the real world. This system is intertextual in that literary texts are based solely on other texts. "There is nothing outside the text," Derrida says. As we read, we absorb this system with our consciousness, which Derrida maintains is itself made up of language. Reading is the confrontation of one language system (our consciousness) with another (the text). Recovering meaning from texts, then, is impossible because interpretations of a text never point to the real world but only to more language. Our interaction with the text makes us *think* we are moving toward meaning, but we never get there.

The purpose of poststructuralist criticism is to expose the indeterminacy of meaning in texts. Derrida calls his critical method *deconstruction*. To "deconstruct" a work, the critic analyzes the text—especially its language—to show that whatever connection may seem to exist between the text and the real world is an illusion created by the author's clever manipulation of language. Whatever the author may have intended the work to mean or whatever a reader may think it means is always undercut by the ambiguity of the work's language. The gap between signifier and signified is symptomatic of a "space" of emptiness, of nothingness, of nonmeaning that lies at the heart of every text. The critic attempts to demonstrate that the presence of this space makes the text an "abyss" of limitless and contradictory meanings.

Peter Barry sums up the practice of deconstructionist critics this way: The deconstructionist "practices what has been called textual harassment or oppositional reading, reading with the aim of unmasking internal contradictions or inconsistencies in the text, aiming to show the disunity which underlies its apparent unity. The aim of the 'New Critics' of the previous generation, by contrast, had been precisely the opposite of this, to show the unity beneath apparent disunity. In pursuance of its aims, the deconstructive process will often fix on a detail of the text which looks incidental—the presence of a particular metaphor, for instance—and then use it as the key to the whole text, so that everything is read through it" (72). The deconstructionist, J. Hillis Miller says, seeks to find "the element in the system studied which is alogical, the thread in the text in question which will unravel it all, or the loose stone which will pull down the whole building" (quoted in Newton 84).

The appeal of deconstruction. Deconstruction may seem disquieting for those who want to understand the meaning of literature. Without question, nihilism pervades Derrida's theory of language and literature. But when deconstruction became known in the United States and Great Britain in the 1970s, it seemed like a breath of fresh air to those who felt excluded by New Criticism.

The New Critics' certainty about interpreting literature led them to downgrade many works and authors. Many of the New Critics— Brooks, Warren, Ransom, Tate—were from the American South and espoused conservative political and social values. But the next generation of critics came of age in the 1960s, a time of radical rethinking of social and political practices. They embraced deconstruction as a means of expanding the literary canon to include previously "marginalized" groups of authors, especially women and persons of color, as well as genres the New Critics denigrated or ignored. Semiotics further made interpreting popular culture, not just "high" culture, appealing.

Resources for poststructuralism. The accounts of poststructuralism in Peter Barry's *Beginning Theory* (2002) and K. M. Newton's *Interpreting the Text* (1990) are cogent and practical. An accessible, book-length study is Christopher Norris's *Deconstruction: Theory and Practice* (2002). The seminal text on deconstruction is Derrida's *Of Grammatology* (1976).

Suggestions for Applying Literary Theory and Criticism about the Work

How might you use these theoretical approaches—Anglo-American criticism, structuralism, and poststructuralism—in your own writings? The following are some suggestions for each one.

Anglo-American Criticism. The interpretive method advocated by Anglo-American Criticism—close reading of individual works— has been enormously influential. It is still a much-used, even assumed approach in undergraduate literature courses, especially introductory courses. It is, furthermore, the approach described in the first five chapters of this book. This approach assumes that readers, after learning something about how literature works, how it is put together, can interpret works without having to know much if anything about historical background or authors' biographies. Close reading, in other words, is a practice you probably already know how to do and may have done a great deal.

You probably, however, have not been asked to do what the New Critics did—use close reading to uncover the thematic and structural unity of works of literature. But you might like to try this. John Ellis is a strong advocate of this goal. Take a look at his prescription for the best interpretation of a work, printed at the beginning of Chapter 1. Use this as a guide for interpreting a work. Can you come up with an interpretation that is "the most satisfying" because it is "the most inclusive"?

Structuralism. Structuralism, whether language-based or archetypal, is intertextual. Unlike Anglo-American criticism and deconstruction, which focus on one work at a time, structuralism looks at many works to discern the characteristics they have in common. One kind of structure they uncover or focus on is genre. We discuss genres in Chapter 2 (the intertextuality of literature) and Chapter 3 (subgenres of drama). And Part I of this book divides literature into three very broad genres—fiction, drama, and poetry.

Whether or not you accept the idea that genres are a kind of "grammar" for the "language" of literature, they are interesting and fun. Can you spot a new genre and describe the traits that make up its structure? Can you explain why a popular genre is appealing? (Why do you like or not like it? Why is it popular?) Can you identify the features of a work that place it within a genre? How does an author bend the "rules" of a genre to make or begin to make a new genre? Can you trace the evolution of a genre, showing how it changes? What are the features of a historical genre, like the Elizabethan revenge tragedy? Why is Shakespeare's *Hamlet* a much better revenge tragedy than the first one, Thomas Kyd's *The Spanish Tragedy* (1586)? How do other plays in this tradition—like Christopher Marlowe's *The Jew of Malta* (1592) and John Webster's *The Duchess of Malfi* (1612–13)—conform or not conform to the genre? Are there recent works that seem like revenge tragedies?

Archetypes, another structural device, sometimes help define genres. The hero story, for example, seems necessary to the adventure, romance, and epic genres. But archetypes also cross generic boundaries. Perhaps because they come from cultural or psychological sources rather than linguistic structures, they can appear in different genres. Examples are archetypes like the femme fatale, the quest for the father, the descent into hell, the earth goddess, and death and rebirth. Another example is the coming-of-age archetype, which you can find in tragedy (*Romeo and Juliet*), fiction (L. M. Montgomery's *Anne of Green Gables* [1908]), comedy (Bernard Shaw's *Mrs. Warren's Profession* [1898]), and poetry (John Keats's "The Eve of St. Agnes" [1819]). What are some archetypes that are especially interesting to you? How does this or some other archetype make a work meaningful or appealing?

Poststructuralism. Deconstruction, the interpretive method of poststructuralism, uses the same strategy as Anglo-American criticism—close reading and careful attention to language—but to a different end. Whereas Anglo-American criticism aims to show harmony and unity in works of literature, deconstruction tries to expose the disharmony and contradictions in them. This purpose rests on the belief that language, the medium of literature, is an untrustworthy bearer of meaning.

Deconstruction points to several interpretive strategies you can try. One strategy is to focus on the language of a work. Look especially for incoherence within the language, especially language that seems on the surface to be clear but under the surface is unclear or contradicts the surface meaning. Poststructuralists maintain that one reason language is contradictory is that it is metaphoric. Nearly every word is or was a metaphor. Choose, then, a work—or a key passage from a long work—and examine its language. Pay close attention to the interplay of metaphors. Works with verbal density lend themselves to this strategy (works, for example, by Shakespeare, John Donne, Herman Melville, James Joyce, and Emily Dickinson). But even works whose language seems "simple," like Hemingway's short stories, might respond well to this strategy.

Another strategy is to uncover possible contradictions within the whole work. Deconstructionists like to discuss works that are inherently complex, that are in a sense already deconstructed, rather than those that are simple and straightforward. Nonetheless, they remind us that many works include meanings that are contradicted by subcurrents within the text. You might, then, look for elements that establish such contradictions. An example is Hawthorne's *The Scarlet Letter* (1850), which dramatizes warring philosophies. Most important are those represented by Arthur Dimmesdale and his lover Hester Prynne. Hawthorne seems to favor Arthur's values (town, law, intellect, "civilization," punishment) over Hester's (forest, freedom, intuition, tolerance, escape). The deconstructionists are interested in contradictions that are much less obvious than this one, but it at least illustrates the possibility of contradictory meanings within works.

Such contradictions make works interesting. They remind us that our interpretations are always incomplete and imperfect, that works of literature are never fully and finally interpreted. Any interpretation will be "partial," says Peter Barry, because "it will not be able to take account of every element in the poem [the work]" and because "it will be the product of a personal predisposition or prejudice of which we ourselves must remain unaware" (*English* 56).

THE AUTHOR

Although not the only determiners of meaning in a literary work, authors are the most important. They choose the genres and conventions of their works. They craft their works to embody ideas. As readers, we are drawn to certain works because we like the way authors write—their style, values, and artistic techniques. Most theoretical approaches to literature manifest at least some interest in the author. Three that focus largely on either the author or the author's period are historical criticism, biographical criticism, and new historicism.

Historical and Biographical Criticism

Historical criticism. *Historical* and *biographical criticism* are closely related and received their theoretical impetus from nineteenth-century ideas about science. Historical critics believed they could illuminate works of literature by studying what gave birth to them: the intellectual and cultural environment from which they came; their sources and antecedents; and authors' lives, intentions, and language. They believed that their approach was "scientific" because they were dealing with objective reality—historically verifiable facts—and were using a scientific method for collecting such facts.

Two French philosophers influenced historical and biographical criticism: Auguste Comte (1798–1857) and especially Hippolyte Taine (1828–93). Taine, in his *History of English Literature* (1863), held that all art is an expression of the environment and time in which the artist lived. Historical critics concentrated on authors they assumed were "great," not worrying much about why or what the works meant. A major emphasis of historical criticism was the historical periods and intellectual movements to which works belonged. Critics studied the conventions and ideas that characterized movements, such as blank verse during the Renaissance and an emphasis on free will during the Romantic period. They placed works within evolving traditions (the novel, Christian literature, allegory, political fiction, the epic) and compared them to the literature of other countries.

In higher education today, a prevalent manifestation of historical criticism is the literature survey course, which links literature to authors' lives, historical periods, and intellectual movements. Literary histories, such as the *Columbia Literary History of the United*

States (1988) and *The Literary History of England* (1967), owe their methodology and format to historical criticism. Although the meaning of individual works of literature was not explicit in such venerable historical studies as E. M. W. Tillyard's *The Elizabethan World Picture* (1943), M. I. Finley's *The World of Odysseus* (1978), and A. O. Lovejoy's *The Great Chain of Being* (1936), meaning was implicit. These historical critics assumed that the ideas associated with a particular age were manifested in the works of the age.

Biographical criticism. Samuel Johnson (1709–84) was the first great biographical critic. His *Lives of the Poets* (1779, 1781) provided truthful accounts of authors' lives and astute assessments of their literary achievements. Biographical criticism became increasingly popular during the nineteenth and twentieth centuries and is still very much practiced. The assumption lying behind all literary biography is that the facts of authors' lives suggest meanings in their works. Some well-known examples are Leon Edel's *Henry James: A Life* (1985), Richard Ellman's *James Joyce* (1982), Edgar Johnson's *Charles Dickens: His Tragedy and Triumph* (1977), Richard B. Sewall's *Life of Emily Dickinson* (1980), R. W. B. Lewis's *Edith Wharton: A Biography* (1985), Juliet Barker's *The Brontës* (1994), and Arthur Mizener's *The Far Side of Paradise: A Biography of F. Scott Fitzgerald* (1965).

Goals of historical and biographical criticism. The purpose of historical and biographical criticism is well summed up by Douglass Bush, himself the author of outstanding historical criticism: "Since the great mass of great literature belongs to the past, adequate criticism must grow out of historical knowledge, cultural and linguistic, as well as out of intuitive insight. Every work must be understood on its own terms as the product of a particular mind in a particular setting, and that mind and setting must be re-created through all the resources that learning and the historical imagination can muster—not excluding the author's intention, if that is known. The very pastness of a work . . . is part of its meaning for us and must be realized to the best of our power" (8). If we do not pay attention to authors and their historical context, Bush says, we run the risk of anachronistic misreadings and misunderstandings. We may be limited in our ability to "re-create the outward and inward conditions in which a work of art was engendered, but unless we try, we cannot distinguish between its local and temporal and its universal and timeless elements, indeed we may not be able to understand some works at all" (8).

Some theorists have gone so far as to claim that interpretations are valid *only* if they are based on authors' intentions. E. D. Hirsch in *Validity in Interpretation* (1967) says that to "banish the original author as the determiner of meaning," as the New Critics did, is "to reject the only compelling normative principle that could lend validity to an interpretation" (5). Without "a genuinely stable norm [the author's intentions] we cannot even in principle make a valid choice between two differing interpretations, and we are left with the consequence that a text means nothing in particular at all" (251). We have a "chaotic democracy of 'readings'" in which "one interpretation is as valid as another, so long as it is 'sensitive' or 'plausible'" (4–5). The purpose of the critic, then, must be to reconstruct "the author's aims and attitudes in order to evolve guides and norms for construing the meaning of his text" (224). "The text," Hirsch says, "is the safest source of clues to the author's outlook" (241), but critics must also examine biographical and historical evidence to determine "the cultural and personal attitudes the author might be expected to bring to bear in specifying his verbal meanings" (240).

Some would say that Hirsch's views are unnecessarily exclusive. But historical and biographical information often does point to meanings in works of literature and, more basically, clarifies puzzling information, especially in works from cultures that are foreign to us. An example is *The Princess of Clèves* (1678) by Marie-Madeleine de Lafayette (1634–93). On the one hand, Madame de Lafayette tells a story about a love triangle. The princess, at a young age, marries a man she respects but does not love. Another man falls in love with her. She falls in love with him. What will they do? This novel is often cited as the first psychological novel, so we learn much about the inner lives of these three characters as they work out their relationships.

On the other hand, although this story could take place at almost any historical period, the author goes to much trouble to place it within a densely-packed historical situation, the final two years of Henry II's reign (1547–49). Woven around this story are a bewildering number of characters, court factions, and family relationships. Almost all of these "extra" characters are historical: the king, his wife (Catherine de Medici), the heir to the throne (Francis II), his wife (Mary Queen of Scots), the king's mistress, plus numerous court officials and military people.

Why does she do this? What meaning(s) might she have had in mind by focusing so intently on this period in French history? She probably assumed that her readers would know something about the people and events of 125 years before the publication of her novel. They probably would have known, for example, that just after Henry II's death, the worst civil war in French history broke out (between Catholics and Protestants) and that all the historical characters in the novel were players in that war. But most readers today, especially non-French readers, are unlikely to have this knowledge. In order to answer these questions, we have to educate ourselves about the novel's setting. Instructive, also, might be information about the author. She was, for example, an aristocrat (a countess). She was a careful observer of Louis XIV's court (through her friendship with his sister-in-law). She was allied with people who opposed the king's policies and who had, years before, tried to overthrow the king. She was sympathetic to a form of Catholicism (Jansenism) that was similar to Calvinist Protestantism and that the king had banned. She was a writer, a suspect career for women. She very much had a mind of her own. Given what we learn about her circle of friends and about her, might we conclude that her novel, though set in an earlier period, is really be about the France of her own day. Is she using it to criticize present-day court life and the king's policies? More broadly, is she saying something about our control or lack of control over events, both personal (the princess's love story) and historical (the French civil war)? These aren't rhetorical questions. The answers might be yes or no. But knowing about the historical setting and author's life at least gives us the knowledge to ask them. Such questions could lead us toward what E. D. Hirsch deems so important: a window into the author's intended meanings.

Authors, furthermore, write within intellectual and aesthetic traditions, such as the Middle Ages, the Renaissance, the Enlightenment, Romanticism, Realism, Modernism, and now Postmodernism. Each of these traditions is a network of practices and products based on ideas that differ from tradition to tradition. Authors aren't slaves to their own traditions; they often rebel against them or don't fit neatly within them. But learning about these traditions makes us aware of ideas that are likely to appear in authors' works.

Intellectual and aesthetic traditions also connect literary works to other art forms—to music, architecture, clothing, painting, sculpture, furniture—many of which share ideas and methods. The literary works of European Neoclassicism (c. 1680–1800) have much in common with the operas of Mozart, the paintings of Fragonard, Hogarth, and Reynolds, the architecture of Robert Adam and Thomas Jefferson, and the symphonies of Haydn. Those of the Romantic period (c. 1789–1850) are siblings of the music of Beethoven and Chopin, the neo-gothic architecture of Pugin, the operas of Verdi and Wagner, and the paintings of Turner, Friedrich, and Goya. An individual work, in other words, shares a cultural tradition that is larger and richer than just the work alone.

New Historicist Criticism

New versus "old" historicism. New historicism emerged in the 1970s and 1980s as a "new" way to use history to interpret literature. It shares "old" historicism's belief that the historical culture from which a work comes helps us understand the work. It differs drastically in its beliefs about the nature of literature and the purpose of literary studies. Its sympathy for disadvantaged—"marginalized" people—adds a political slant lacking in older historicism. The term *new historicism* applies to the American version of "cultural studies." The British version, cultural materialism, is more overtly Marxist than new historicism. Both are influenced by Marxist literary theory, by the French historian Michel Foucault (1926–84), and by poststructuralist theories of language.

Culture. New historicism is undergirded by several related concepts: culture, text, and discourse. The first term, *culture*, is the most important. In an anthropological sense, "culture" is the total way of life of a particular society—its language, economy, art, religion, and attachment to a location. For new historicists, culture is also a collection of codes that everyone in a society shares and that allows them to communicate, create artifacts, and act. These codes include not just language but every element of a culture—literature, dress, food, rituals, and games. Literature doesn't transcend culture but is embedded in it.

Text. As a web of sign systems, culture is thus "textual." A *text*, traditionally defined, is a written document that employs a symbolic system (words, mathematical symbols, images, musical notation). The structuralists expand "text" to mean any system of codes. The poststructuralists go further by claiming that because everything we know is filtered through "language," *everything* is text. "There is nothing outside the text," Derrida says. New historicists accept the structuralist concept of text but many reject the poststructuralist concept that people cannot see the texts that surround them.

Yes, they say, cultures consist of "texts," and "discourses," but people can analyze them and expose their weaknesses.

Discourse. By *discourse*, structuralists mean any system of signs, whether verbal or nonverbal. "Discourse," then, is analogous to language (Saussure's *langue*) and "text" to specific uses of language (*parole*). Foucault claims that groups of people, such as doctors, lawyers, priests, and athletes, create their own discourses. Each discourse has its own unique "discursive practice"—word choice, sentence structure, bodily movements, prejudices, rhetorical forms, and "rules" about where and when to use the discourse. Foucault claims that discourses are "political": People with power—social, economic, political, or artistic—use discourse to manipulate other people and maintain their own power.

Literary criticism. How do new historicists apply these concepts to the study of literature? First, they believe that literature must be studied within a cultural context. Old-style historicists see historical facts mainly as a means to clarify ideas, allusions, language, and details in literature. New historicists believe that literature *is* history, is "enmeshed" in history. They draw upon many disciplines—anthropology, sociology, law, psychology, history—to show what role literature has played in history, from the author's time to the present.

Second, new historicists focus on literature as cultural text. They study the relationship between literature and other texts, including nonliterary and popular texts. They identify the codes that constitute literary discourse and ascertain how people use such discourse to communicate with one another and to comment on society.

Third, new historicists scrutinize the relationship of literature to the power structures of society. They want to show how literature serves, opposes, and changes the wishes of the power elites.

Finally, many new historicists see literary criticism itself as an "intervention" in society. By marking what literature shows about the misuses of power, they aspire to diminish the injustices of race, class, and gender. New historicism, Peter Barry says, "is resolutely antiestablishment, always implicitly on the side of liberal ideas of personal freedom and accepting and celebrating all forms of difference and 'deviance.' At the same time, though, it seems simultaneously to despair of the survival of these in the face of the power of the repressive state, which it constantly reveals as able to penetrate and taint the most intimate areas of personal life" (175).

The typical method of new historicism, Barry says, is "based on the *parallel* reading of literary and non-literary texts, usually of the same historical period. That is to say, new historicism refuses (at least ostensibly) to 'privilege' the literary text: instead of a literary 'foreground' and a historical 'background' it envisages and practices a mode of study in which literary and non-literary texts are given equal weight and constantly inform or interrogate each other" (172).

Examples. Some examples should help make clear the goals and methods of new historicist criticism. Paul Brown, in his essay "'This Thing of Darkness I Acknowledge Mine': *The Tempest* and the Discourse of Colonialism" (1985), uses a letter by John Rolfe to expose the nature and evils of colonialism in Shakespeare's *The Tempest*, performed for the first time at James I's "expansionist" court in 1611. Rolfe's letter, written to the governor of Virginia in 1614, requests the governor's blessing to marry Pocahontas, the abducted daughter of the Indian chief Powhatan. Brown "reads" the two texts together to show what colonialism was and how it operates in the play. Brown wants, also, to expose the evils of colonialism not just in Shakespeare's day but our own. In this way, his article is an "intervention." If we follow Brown's guidance, every time we read or see the play, we should think of how we can or should end colonialist oppressions.

A second example, Jonathan Arac's "The Politics of *The Scarlet Letter*" (1986), is less "oppositional" than Brown's. Arac's method is to read Hawthorne's *The Scarlet Letter* (1850) along side his *Life of Franklin Pierce* (1852) to explore what, if anything, the novel reveals about Hawthorne's attitude toward slavery, the most divisive political issue of his day. Hawthorne, Arac points out, was one of America's most politically active authors. "The Custom House," the preface to *The Scarlet Letter,* chronicles his political appointment as surveyor of customs at Salem and his dismissal when the Democrats lost power in 1850. Hawthorne wrote the biography of Pierce, a college friend, to support Pierce's successful bid for the presidency in 1852. Arac argues that, just as the biography reveals that Pierce planned to take no action about slavery, so Hawthorne manifests a similar attitude in the novel.

A third example is Edward Said's essay "Jane Austen and Empire" (1989). Said is perhaps the best known and most influential practitioner of "postcolonial" criticism, an off-shoot of new historicism. Said's purpose in this well-known essay is to expose and condemn attitudes that "devalue other worlds and, perhaps more significantly . . . do not prevent or inhibit or provide a resistance to horrendously unattractive imperialist practices" (293). He focuses on an "absence" in Jane Austen's *Mansfield Park* (1814), the true nature of the plantation in Antigua (in the British West Indies) that provides the Bertram family with the bulk of its wealth. We learn near the beginning of the novel that the plantation is poorly run. For much of the first half of the novel, Sir Thomas Bertram visits the plantation to set it in order, which he successfully does. When he returns to England, he must now bring his own household into order. Said links these two actions and, more generally, he points out characters' yearnings, notably the desire for more "space," similar to the ones that spurred English imperialism. Most disturbing is the nature of Sir Thomas's plantation: "Sir Thomas's property in the Caribbean would have had to be a sugar plantation maintained by slave labor (not abolished until the 1830s): these are not dead historical facts but, as Austen certainly knew, the results of evident historical processes" (301). The novel thus represents "a broad expanse of domestic imperialist culture without which the subsequent acquisition of territory would not have been possible" (307). For a vivid rendition of Said's interpretation, see the movie *Mansfield Park* (1999), directed by Patricia Rozema.

Resources for new historicist criticism. Excellent brief accounts of new historicism and cultural materialism are in Peter Barry's *Beginning Theory: An Introduction to Literary and Cultural Theory* (2nd ed., 2002) and K. M. Newton's *Interpreting the Text: A Critical Introduction to the Theory and Practice of Literary Interpretation* (1990). Longer studies include Jerome McGann's *Historical Studies and Literary Criticism* (1985) and Harold Veeser's *The New Historicism* (1989). Some of the best-known new historicist criticism has focused on Renaissance literature, such as the essays in *Political Shakespeare: New Essays in Cultural Materialism* (1985), edited by Jonathan Dollimore and Alan Sinfield, and Stephen Greenblatt's *Renaissance Self-Fashioning from More to Shakespeare* (1980). *Ideology and Classic American Literature* (1986) is a collection of essays by different authors. Sacvan Bercovitch's *The Office of the Scarlet Letter* (1991) focuses on just one work.

Edward Said is perhaps the best-known exponent of postcolonial criticism. As an exiled Palestinian, he was personally involved in international political struggles. He argues in *Orientalism* (1978) that Western culture has fabricated a distorted and unfair discourse about the East, manifested in countless works of literature and popular culture. *Orientalism* expands beyond literature to cover all of Western culture. Another post-colonial author is the Nigerian Chinua Achebe, who eloquently attacks the racism in Joseph Conrad's *Heart of Darkness* in "An Image of Africa: Racism in Conrad's *Heart of Darkness*." His novels, beginning with *Things Fall Apart* (1958), offer an alternative presentation of colonial expansion in Africa. Other exponents of postcolonialism are Gayatri Spivak and Homi Bhabha. Many of Foucault's works are excerpted in *The Foucault Reader* (1985). David R. Shumway's *Michel Foucault* (1989) and Lois McNay's *Foucault: A Critical Introduction* (1994) are succinct overviews.

Suggestions for Applying Literary Theory and Criticism about the Author

Historical and biographical criticism. To use historical and biographical criticism yourself, you need to search out information about the author, the author's time, and the settings of the work. Your goals would be, first, to eliminate or reduce puzzlement about the work and second, to make educated guesses about the author's intended meanings. Often such searches begin because of confusion about some aspect of the work. An example is Madame de Lafayette's *The Princess of Clèves*, discussed above. We ask, Why does she include so much historical information in the novel? We answer—at least, try to answer—by doing historical research. We want to reduce our confusion about the setting and we want to know what she meant by it. Another example is the sample research essay in Chapter 11 about Mary Shelley's novel *Frankenstein*. After researching Mary Shelley's life, the author concludes that Shelley's own education was similar to the monster's and that she uses the monster's education to develop themes that were personal to her.

New historicist criticism. You can, of course, use the methods of new historicism to develop its typical "oppositional" attitudes toward Western civilization or, more generally, toward any abuses of power. But you can employ new historicist methods without predetermined conclusions in mind.

Try, for example, the strategy of interpreting a historical "text" alongside a work of literature. The text should be from the author's time period and should be relevant to key characters, issues, or events in the work. A study of Hawthorne's *The Scarlet Letter* (1850) might compare Hester's feminist beliefs, ambitions, and actions with documents from the Seneca Falls Convention (1848), the first public political gathering in the United States dealing with women's rights. It's likely that Hawthorne would have known details about the convention. Do speeches and declarations, such as the "Seneca Falls Declaration of Sentiments" and "Resolutions" shed light on Hester or themes of the novel?

THE READER

So far in this chapter we have looked at the first two parts of our diagram, author→work→reader. In this section, we examine how readers influence the interpretation of literature. You can get a sense of this approach by thinking of your own experiences as a reader. You may, for example, find that you dislike a work that you once really liked. Or you discover that someone else's perception of a work is very different from yours. Or you belong to a group—women, teenagers, college students, parents, Latinos, Muslims, Christians—that interprets literature differently from other groups. Most of the theoretical approaches we have already discussed—Anglo-American, structuralist, poststructuralist, biographical/historical—assume that any well-trained reader can learn how to interpret works of literature, that interpretations are based on objective material in the works, and that people can agree on the meanings in works. Reader-based criticism, known today as *reader-response criticism*, holds that as the "receivers" of works of literature, readers complete them and actually contribute to their meanings. Reader-response critics are more interested in mapping the process of reading than in interpreting individual works.

European Reader-Response Criticism

Phenomenology. Reader-response criticism emerged, in part, from the philosophical movement called *phenomenology*. The founder of this movement was the German philosopher Edmund Husserl (1859–1938). He defined phenomenology as the study of the essential structures of consciousness. Husserl's works, especially *Ideas* (1913), dealt with how human consciousness processes information—phenomena—that can enter the consciousness, whether from exterior sources (sense data) or interior sources (memory, intuition, feelings). Husserl rejects a rationalist approach to understanding consciousness. He advocates that people set aside ("bracket") all presuppositions and intellectual concepts in order to experience objects of consciousness "naively." In Husserl's phenomenology, Richard Harland says, "real-world" data are "projected from the mind of the perceiver—through the guidance and channelling of perceptual sense-data" (204). The consciousness, in other words, helps create what it perceives.

Two members of a circle of scholars at the University of Konstanz in southern Germany applied Husserl's phenomenology to the study of literature: Wolfgang Iser (1926–2007) and Hans-Robert Jauss (1921–97). Their concepts of the reader's relationship to literature took different paths.

Ingarden and Iser. Iser was influenced by one of Husserl's students, the Polish philosopher Roman Ingarden (1893–1970). Ingarden's most influential work was *The Literary Work of Art* (1931). In it he holds that information about objects in works of literature is incomplete. This is especially true of fictional characters. No matter how much information novelists give about them, details are missing. A character might be described as short and stocky, but we don't know how short or how stocky. The hero might be "handsome" and the heroine "beautiful," but we don't know how so. All works of literature are thus "indeterminate." Readers respond to this indeterminacy by adding missing information, an imaginative process Ingarden called "concretisation." Each reader's version of a literary work, therefore, is different. One person's image of a "beautiful" heroine is different from other people's.

Iser, whose most influential books were published in the 1970s, expanded on Ingarden's concept of missing information. Iser claimed that works, especially works of fiction, have "gaps" that constantly interrupt the smooth flow of a work and thwart readers' expectations. Whereas Ingarden held that the artistic unity of a work leads readers to a pleasant conception of it, Iser claimed that a work's indeterminacy catches readers off guard and forces them to new, perhaps painful, understandings. For Iser, K. M. Newton says, such understandings could be liberating: reading literature is "a dynamic process in which the norms and codes that govern the reader's thinking and perception may be called into question by having to confront textual gaps and blanks, thus making it possible for reading to be liberating" (139).

Gadamer and Jauss. The other member of the Konstanz circle, Hans-Robert Jauss, was influenced by the German philosopher Hans-Georg Gadamer (1900–2002). Gadamer, whose most important book was *Truth and Method* (1960), followed the Existentialist philosophy of his teacher Martin Heidegger (1889–1976) in arguing that our view of anything, including literature, is limited by our own historical period and by our "existential" interests. To appreciate and interpret a work of literature, we must be able to connect it to ourselves. When we read we should be aware of our own prejudices and at the same time open our minds to new ideas.

Jauss, whose major work appeared in the 1970s and 1980s, continues this line of thought by holding that all audiences for a work, from the first audience to the present, create and interpret it differently. The work, therefore, is never the same from audience to audience. Readers are shaped by the values and attitudes of the audiences to which they belong. Like Iser, Jauss claims that literature can liberate readers by challenging their assumptions. Each reader, each audience, has a "horizon of expectations" that the best works call into question. Jauss urges us to learn about the mindset of past audiences, especially the first audience, and to blend those expectations with our own.

American Reader-Response Theory

Rosenblatt. Reader-response theory has had its greatest impact in the United States, especially on the teaching of literature. Louise Rosenblatt (1904–2005), through books like *Literature as Exploration* (1938) and *The Reader, the Text, the Poem* (1994), has had a strong impact on the teaching of literature. She holds that reading is a "transaction" between reader and work. As readers read, they interact with the work and bring it to life. And since each reader's background, beliefs, physical state, moods, and circumstances are different, each reading is unique.

Fish. Another American theorist, Stanley Fish (b. 1938), follows Jauss in emphasizing the importance of audiences of readers. In his best known book, *Is There a Text in This Class?* (1980), he states that a reader's understanding of what "literature" is and what works of literature mean is formed by "interpretive communities"— groups to which readers belong. These groups could be small (a circle of friends) or large (a region or cultural entity like "Western civilization"). Fish rejects the idea that a text has a core of mean-ing that everyone in any age would accept. Rather, shared under-standings of a text's meaning come from the beliefs of a community of readers, not from the text. Each reader's preconceptions actually "create" the text. If, for example, a reader believes that a miscella-neous collection of words is a religious poem, the reader will per-ceive it as a religious poem. If a reader believes that the work fits a particular theory, the reader will find facts in the work to support that theory. The theory, in a sense, "creates" the facts.

Holland.   The most relativistic American reader-response theorist is Norman Holland (b. 1927), who bases his approach to literature on psychoanalysis. Critics like Iser and Rosenblatt hold that readers' interpretations cannot be entirely subjective. They must be grounded in objective materials in the works. Holland, in contrast, writing in books like *The Dynamics of Literary Response* (1968) and *Five Readers Reading* (1975), says that there is no separation between reader and work. Interpretations emerge from the psychological makeup of each reader and are thus different, even wildly different. The most valuable result of reading literature, furthermore, is that it allows readers to recreate their identities. Holland seems to believe that the reading process is almost intuitive. Readers' psyches respond subconsciously to aspects of works. As readers read, they automati-cally throw out hypotheses about what a work means. If the work "responds" favorably, the reader's psyche accepts the hypothesis as correct.

Resources for reader-response criticism.   Because of the influence and provocative nature of reader-response criticism, writings about it abound. Susan R. Suleiman and Inge Crosman's *The Reader in the Text: Essays on Audience and Interpretation* (1980) and Jane Tomkins's *Reader-Response Criticism* (1980) are collections of readings by vari-ous theorists. General overviews are Robert C. Holub's *Reception Theory: A Critical Introduction* (1984) and Elizabeth Freund's *The Return of the Reader: Reader-Response Criticism* (1987).

Suggestions for Applying Literary Theory and Criticism about the Reader

Reader-based criticism invites us to study how individual readers and groups of readers respond to works of literature.

Yourself as reader.   A good place to start is with yourself. Anything about how you read and what you read is fair game. What do you like to read? Why? Can you create a psychology of your reading—what your reading tells you about who you are and about your inner life? If you don't like to read, why not?

Try this experiment. When you read a work for the first time, make notes about how you respond to it. Pay attention to your changing responses to it—what's confusing, what's interesting, what puts you off, what topics and themes seem to emerge, what surprises you as you read. When you have finished, summarize your experience with the work and where you think you have ended up with it. Do you like it? Do you think you understand its topics and themes? Would you recommend it to others?

The student essay in Chapter 13 on George Eliot's novel *Adam Bede* follows Gadamer's recommendation that readers should connect a work to their own experiences. Try this strategy yourself. You might choose two works, one that seems remote from your experience and one that you strongly identify with. Compare your reactions to each.

Many reader-response critics agree that works of literature have "gaps"—missing information. By filling in the gaps with their imaginations, readers become cocreators with authors. Test this theory out by noting how and to what extent you do this. Modernist authors often deliberately leave gaps in their works and thus invite readers' collaboration. Examine the stories by Hemingway and Robison, printed in the Appendix, for such purposeful gaps. Which gaps do you think the authors left intentionally? How do you think they expected readers to fill them?

Compare your interpretations of a work to other people's. Do a brief survey. How similar or different are the interpretations or, for that matter, the readers' grasp of details in the work? Do you think the readers, including yourself, could ever agree on a common interpretation? If the interpretations are different, can you explain why?

Some reader-response theorists value works because they have the power to change readers, to broaden their "horizons of expectations." If this has happened to you or to someone you know, describe the experience. What was it in the work that brought about the change? What in yourself made you receptive to such a change?

Groups as readers.   Some reader-response theorists are interested not just in individual readers but groups of readers. Following

Jauss's belief that information about original audiences holds clues about authors' intended meanings, find out as much as you can about the original audience of a work. Compare the expectations, interpretations, and receptions of that audience to another audience, either from the past or one from today (say, the members of a reading group or a university class).

A similar project is to examine why the original audience rejected or disapproved of or failed to understand a work we revere today. A famous example is Herman Melville's *Moby-Dick* (1851), which was a disaster in the marketplace. Another is Kate Chopin's *The Awakening* (1899). In contrast to the original audience, why do we admire this book?

What group—interpretive community—do you belong to? What works or kinds of works appeal to your group? Why? Are your reading tastes the same as the group's, or do you rebel against them?

Examine a group's fascination with a book or author or genre. What explains, for example, the enormous popularity of the Twilight vampire books or the Harry Potter books?

Interview people who belong to a group. Ask them about their reading interests. If you see similarities among the people you interview, describe the similarities and speculate about why this group has these same interests.

ALL OF REALITY

We are all part of the universe outside literary works, the multifarious and infinite "all of reality." One of the pleasures of reading literature is noticing its connection to reality. When people praise a work because it is "so true to life," they express that pleasure. There are at least two ways that works of literature reflect reality. First, works can mirror the details of something. This "something" can be almost anything: a historical event, a psychological condition, a situation (Saturday nights in a hospital emergency room, playing baseball, engaging in battle), a period of human life (teen age, old age), the tribulations and joys of parenthood, a crisis (illness, bankruptcy, divorce). Second, works of literature can reflect theories about what reality is. These theories can be our own about, say, human behavior or proper moral practices. Or they can be carefully worked out systems, as in religions, philosophies, and scientific theories. There is, of course, much disagreement about the "truth" of any one theory of reality.

Literary theorists vary in their belief that works of literature can show reality, or, for that matter, that people can know "reality." Theorists who come out of the liberal humanist tradition, like Anglo-American critics and traditional historical critics, were strongly confident that authors can exhibit and readers can spot "reality" in literature. Poststructuralists, however, such as the deconstructionists and Lacanian psychoanalysts, are so skeptical about "truth" that, for them, all knowledge seems uncertain and relative.

Most theoretical approaches make at least minimal claims about the nature of reality and urge readers to rely on those claims to interpret literature. But some approaches make their understanding of truth the sole or major basis for reading literature. No matter what the author may have intended, they examine works of literature for signs of their own understanding of reality. We will briefly describe three such approaches to interpreting literature that have claimed much attention in the last fifty years. They are psychological criticism, Marxist criticism, and feminist and gender criticism.

Psychological Criticism

Freud's influence. *Psychological criticism* applies modern psychological theories to authors and their works. Because the psychoanalytic theories of Sigmund Freud (1856–1939) dominated the discipline of psychology during the first half of the twentieth century, psychological critics found his ideas especially fruitful for interpreting literature. Although not all of Freud's ideas relate to literature, three were pertinent to early Freudian literary critics: the dominance of the unconscious over the conscious mind, the expression of the unconscious mind through symbols (most notably within dreams), and the primacy of sexuality as a motivating force in human behavior. These three ideas are related. Freud believed that sexual drives reside in the unconscious, that the conscious mind represses them, and that unconscious symbols usually represent this repressed sexual energy. Later in his career Freud divided the psyche into three interrelated parts: the *id* (unconscious but irrepressible sexual and other desires), the *superego* (social and moral values constituted as one's "conscience"), and the *ego* (the negotiator between the id and superego). Put more simply, the id is the unconscious, the superego is the conscience, and the ego is the consciousness.

Freud's concept of dreams was especially appealing to writers and critics of literature. Dreams contained repressed memories and urges that were manifested but also disguised in several ways. "Condensation" omitted parts of the repressed material and fused the rest into one entity, such as a character or image. "Displacement" was the substitution of one object for another that was more acceptable to the unconscious. "Symbolism" was the representation of one thing by another. "Thus, characters, motivation, and events," Peter Barry says, "are represented in dreams in a very 'literary' way, involving the translation . . . of abstract ideas or feelings into concrete images. Dreams, just like literature, do not usually make explicit statements. Both tend to communicate obliquely or indirectly, avoiding direct or open statement, and representing meanings through concrete embodiments of time, place, or person" (98). Literary criticism, then, is similar to psychoanalysis. Both try to uncover hidden meanings as manifested by indirect means of communication.

One approach early Freudian critics took was to regard works of literature as symbolic of authors' unconscious minds. Freudian critics created psychological portraits of authors. An example of such *psychobiography* is Marie Bonaparte's *The Life and Works of Edgar Allan Poe: A Psychoanalytic Interpretation* (1949). Later examples are Leon Edel's massive (five-volume) *Henry James* (1953–72) and Justin Kaplan's *Mark Twain and His World* (1974). Early Freudian critics also used psychoanalytic principles to analyze literary characters. They looked upon characters as having motivations, conflicts, desires, and inclinations similar to those of real people. They sought psychological clues to the makeup of literary characters, especially the unconscious symbolic expressions found in dreams and repeated patterns of behavior. In Eugene O'Neill's *Long Day's Journey into Night* (1956), for example, the drug-addicted Mary Tyrone constantly raises her hands to her hair. This physical tic unconsciously expresses her repressed anxiety about her wrecked youth, health, and innocence. Psychological critics were also drawn to works that are themselves dreamlike, such as Lewis Carroll's *Alice's Adventures in Wonderland* (1865), or that contain accounts of characters' dreams.

Authors themselves often imported psychological ideas into their works. Eugene O'Neill (1888–1953), D. H. Lawrence (1885–1930), Tennessee Williams (1911–83), and many others were well-read in Freudian psychology. Some writers employed structural devices based on psychological theories. Examples are the *stream of consciousness* technique, which conforms to William James's ideas about the workings of the conscious mind, and the surrealistic technique, which conforms to Freud's ideas about the undisciplined unconscious. Examples of stream-of-consciousness narration are

James Joyce's *Portrait of the Artist as a Young Man* (1915) and *Ulysses* (1922), William Faulkner's *The Sound and the Fury* (1929), T. S. Eliot's "The Love Song of J. Alfred Prufrock" (1917), Virginia Woolf's *To the Lighthouse* (1927), and Eugene O'Neill's *Strange Interlude* (1928). Examples of surrealism are James Joyce's *Finnegans Wake* (1939) and the fiction of Franz Kafka (1883–1924).

Recent criticism.   Recent psychological critics continue to find Freud's theories a rich source of ideas about literature, but whereas earlier critics focused on authors and characters, recent critics have turned their attention to readers and literary texts. The critic Norman Holland, for example, (discussed above in this chapter under the Reader) argues that readers' psyches respond subconsciously to certain aspects of works of literature. The reader in effect "makes" the text, so that the text is different for every reader.

Like Holland, the psychologist Carl G. Jung (1875–1961) and his followers focus on readers. As we say above in this chapter under the Author, Jung expanded Freud's concept of the unconscious to include all people. The unconscious is no longer just individual but "collective." The collective unconscious contains "racial memories" and primordial images and patterns that he called "archetypes." Everyone recognizes these archetypes when they appear in myths, rituals, paintings, and works of literature. In contrast to Holland, who claims that each person's response to literature is unique, Jung says that everyone's response is the same. The critic's purpose, then, is to show what the archetypes are and thus explain why people respond not just to "great" works of literature but also to popular works and genres.

Most influential on recent literary criticism has been the work of the French psychologist Jacques Lacan (1901–1981). Lacan combined Freud's theories of the unconscious with Saussurian linguistics. He held that the human psyche is structured like language. Our conscious and unconscious minds are born into language, a system of signifiers. From infancy to adulthood, we grow toward what we think is a secure and coherent identity. But at the heart of the psyche is an unbridgeable gap between signifier and signified. As a result, our psyche is never fully coherent, our identity never stable. For Lacan, Peter Berry says, "words and meanings have a life of their own and constantly override and obscure the supposed simplicities and clarity of external reality. If signifiers relate only to one another, then language is detached from external reality, and becomes an independent realm" (111). The same is true of literary characters.

Since "Lacan deconstructs the idea of the subject [person] as a stable amalgam of consciousness, we can hardly accept novelistic characters as people but must hold them in abeyance, as it were, and see them as assemblages of signifiers clustering round a proper name" (Barry 113).

Lacan's best known application of his theories to literature is a long essay on Edgar Allan Poe's "The Purloined Letter." Lacan claims that the missing letter, which the detective Dupin has been commissioned to find, is equivalent to the signifier. But because it is missing it is a "symbol only of an absence" (Lacan, 38). It stands for the "lack" or emptiness that lies within all of us. As in this essay, Lacanian critics probe the language of the work to discover contradictory subtexts and elusive language. They look for the emptiness and unstable identity that Lacan says exists in all people.

Resources for psychological criticism. An overview of Freud's theories is Pamela Thurschwell's *Sigmund Freud* (2000). A well-known work of early psychological criticism is Ernest Jones's *Hamlet and Oedipus* (1949), in which Jones, a British psychiatrist and colleague of Freud's, elaborates on Freud's hypothesis that Hamlet's inability to take decisive action stems from Oedipal conflicts. Laurence Olivier incorporated this interpretation in his film *Hamlet* (1948). Collections of readings are *Psychoanalytic Literary Criticism* (ed. Maud Ellmann, 1994) and *Literature and Psychoanalysis* (ed. Edith Kurzweil and William Phillips, 1983). *The Purloined Poe*, edited by John Muller and William Richardson (1988), features psychoanalytic readings of Poe's story "The Purloined Letter," including Lacan's. A feminist application of Lacan's theories is Jane Gallop's *Reading Lacan* (1985). An introduction to Lacan is Madan Sarup's *Jacques Lacan* (1992).

Marxist Criticism

Basic Concepts of Marxism. *Marxism* is an economic and cultural theory based on the writings of German philosophers Karl Marx (1818–83) and Friedrich Engels (1820–95). Its goal is to bring about a society in which the entire economic system, including property, is owned by all the people, not just a few, and in which distinctions between classes no longer exist. When Marx and Engels wrote, the dominant economic system in Europe was industrial capitalism, which they felt was grossly unfair and destructive to the working class. Because capitalists exploited them, workers were in a state of perpetual alienation. The ruling class controlled the underclasses by political and military means, but also, more subtly, through ideology. Marx and Engels defined *ideology* as the beliefs that pervade and underlie a culture and that support the status quo. In a famous metaphor, Marx described the structure of society as consisting of a *base* (the economic system) and a *superstructure* (cultural products such as films, works of art, consumer goods, and literature, all of which disseminate and reinforce ideology). The economic system causes the superstructure. Resistance to oppressive systems will come about by means of a struggle between the ruling class (the *bourgeoisie*) and the alienated and dissatisfied workers (the *proletariat*).

Early Marxist critics.   Fully developed *Marxist criticism* appeared early in the twentieth century, especially in the 1930s during the Great Depression. This "socialist" criticism applauded literature that depicted—was reflective of—the difficulties of the poor and downtrodden, especially when they struggled against oppressive capitalist bosses. Examples of literature with such strong "proletarian" elements are works by Carl Sandburg, Émile Zola, Maxim Gorky, Charles Dickens, Richard Wright, John Steinbeck, Theodore Dreiser, and John Dos Passos. Some of the first Marxist critics tried to show that works of literature were "caused" by economic conditions. They also approved of a socialist solution to the problems of the oppressed and judged the quality of works on the basis of their Marxist orientation. In the mid-1930s the Soviet Union even passed laws insisting that all literature published in the Soviet Union must adopt a stance known as "socialist realism." This heavy-handed application of Marxist principles to literature has come to be known as "vulgar Marxism."

More subtle is the literary theory and criticism of the Hungarian Marxist critic György Lukács (1885–1971). Although he argues that literature should reflect the real world, he does not mean that it should be a mirror image of society by, for example, giving detailed descriptions of its physical contents or its patterns of behavior. Rather, literature can reveal the contradictions within the dominant ideology and thus reflect the economic tensions in society as indicated by Marx. Ironically, for Lukács, works that mirror the real world may be less real than works that emphasize themes (ideas) over description. Lukács believed that literature that distorts reality may better represent the "truth" about society. The economic struggles caused by capitalism, for example, may better be shown by character types one would never meet in real life. Lukács, therefore, prefers the novels of Balzac to those of Flaubert because, even though Balzac's plots and characters are less plausible than Flaubert's, Balzac reveals the economic pitfalls of capitalism as Marx saw them.

Recent critics. Since World War II, a new generation of critics has infused Marxist criticism with renewed vigor. Perhaps the most influential has been the French theorist Louis Althusser (1918–1990). Writing in the 1960s and 1970s, Althusser claimed that ideology is implicit rather than explicit within a culture and thus not consciously recognized by people. People think they are choosing what they believe when in fact, without their knowing it, their beliefs are controlled by ideology. Literature, furthermore, does not merely mimic ideology, but because it is richly complex ("overdetermined"), it escapes ideology and thus provides a vantage point to critique it. The French theorist Pierre Macherey (b. 1938) further elaborated on Althusser's concept of ideology. Any ideology, he said, has "gaps" and "silences" wherein lie "contradictions" that manifest the flaws in an ideology. These contradictions are repressed in much the same way Freud's superego represses the things it doesn't want to admit or know about. Works of literature contain these contradictions, but they are hidden. Marxist criticism, then, attempts to bring them to the surface.

Nearly all recent Marxist critics—such as the Englishman Terry Eagleton (b. 1943) and the American Frederic Jameson (b 1934)—have tried to do just this. They typically conceive of ideology and literature in psychoanalytic or poststructuralist terms. Marx's base is equivalent to Saussure's *langue* and ideology to his *parole*. Or ideology is like the Freudian unconscious. The purpose of the critic is to mine the subterranean depths of literature to expose the repressed and hidden fault-lines of a culture's ideology. The ultimate purpose of this criticism is always political. In Marxist criticism, says K. M. Newton, politics and art are "inseparable" (107). Criticism for a Marxist "can be a worthwhile activity only if it is directed by the aim of emancipating humanity by means of a socialist transformation" (119).

Resources for Marxist criticism. Granville Hicks's *The Great Tradition: An Interpretation of American Literature Since the Civil War* (1935) is a still-readable example of early Marxist criticism. For György Lukács, see his *Studies in European Realism* (1950). Collections of writings include *Marxism and Art: Essays Classic and Contemporary* (ed. Maynard Solomon, 1979) and *Marxist Literary Theory: A Reader* (eds. Terry Eagleton and Drew Milne, 1996). Overviews are Terry Eagleton's *Marxism and Literary Criticism* (1976) and Philip Goldstein's *The Politics of Literary Theory: An Introduction to Marxist Criticism* (1990). A focus on an individual author is Jean Howard and Scott Shershow's *Marxist Shakespeares* (2000).

Feminist and Gender Criticism

Influence of feminist criticism.   Feminist and gender criticism have much in common with reader-response and new historicist criticism, especially with critics who, like Stanley Fish, believe that interpretations of literature are influenced by communities of readers. We include it here under "All of Reality" because it bases its interpretations on ideas about the nature of females and female experience. With the rise of feminism in the 1950s and 1960s, feminist critics claimed that, over the years, men had controlled the most influential interpretive communities. Men decided which conventions made up "literature" and judged the quality of works. Men wrote the literary histories and drew up the lists of "great" works— the literary canon. Because works by and about women were largely omitted from the canon, female authors were ignored, and female characters misconstrued.

Since the 1960s, feminist literary critics have successfully challenged these circumstances. Far more women now teach, interpret, evaluate, and theorize about literature than ever before. Previously neglected works such as Zora Neale Hurston's *Their Eyes Were Watching God* (1937), Kate Chopin's *The Awakening* (1899), Charlotte Perkins Gilman's "The Yellow Wallpaper" (1892), and Rebecca Harding Davis's *Life in the Iron-Mills* (1861) are now widely read. Certain literary genres practiced by women, such as diaries, journals, and letters, have gained more respect. Numerous anthologies, literary histories, and interpretive studies explore women's contributions to literature. Recently, however, a new movement, "gender studies," has evolved out of feminist studies in order to address broader issues; notably, the nature of both femininity and masculinity, the differences within each sex, and the literary treatment of men and homosexuals. Gender studies "complicate" feminist studies because, although they share many interests, they are not exactly the same. Both, however, are political in that they argue for the fair representation and treatment of persons of all "genders."

First stage. A survey of the history of feminist and gender criticism helps spotlight their concerns. The first stage of feminist criticism began with two influential books: Simone de Beauvoir's *The Second Sex* (1949) and Kate Millet's *Sexual Politics* (1970). Both authors criticized the distorted representation of women by well-known male authors. Their work laid the foundation for the most prevalent approach of this stage, the "images of women" approach. Following de Beauvoir and Millet, feminist critics called attention to the unjust, distorted, and limited representation ("images") of females in works of literature, especially works authored by males. They celebrated realistic representations of women and brought to light neglected works by and about women. They sought to expose the "politics" of self-interest that led people to create stereotypical and false images of women.

Second stage. In the second stage of feminist criticism, beginning in the early 1970s, critics shifted away from works by males to concentrate on works by females. Elaine Showalter, a prominent critic from this period, called this approach "gynocriticism." Especially influential was the work of French critics such as Luce Irigaray, Julia Kristeva, and Hélène Cixous. Their criticism, called *écriture féminine* (female writing), argued for an "essential" (biological, genetic, psychological) difference between men and women that causes women to think and write differently from men. Gynocritics urged women to become familiar with female authors and to discover their own female "language," a language that supposedly enters the subconscious before the "patriarchal" language of the dominant culture. They tried to delineate a female poetics, a use of literary conventions and genres that seems typically "female." Some critics based feminist poetics on the possible connection between writing and the female body. Because women's bodies have more fluids than men's, they argued, women's writing is more "fluid." It is less structured, less unified, more inclusive of many points of view, less given to neat endings, and more open to fantasy than writing by men. It rejects or undermines the "marriage plot" and the "happy ending," in which a strong female protagonist "capitulates" to a male by marrying him. Female poetics seeks to understand why female authors tend to favor certain genres (lyric poetry, novel, short story, tale, letters, diaries, memoirs) over others (epic, martial romance, drama, satire), favored by males.

Third stage. The third stage of feminist criticism rebelled against the "essentialist" assumptions of gynocriticism and is closely allied with new historicism in its focus on the cultural creation of identity. Gayle Rubin, in two influential essays—"The Traffic in Women" (1975) and "Thinking Sex" (1984)—distinguishes between "sex" and "gender." Whereas *sex* is the biological difference between males and females, *gender* is the cultural difference. Culture determines the traits and behavior that set masculinity apart from femininity and rules on "normal" and "natural" gender distinctions. Western culture, for example, has seen women as passive rather than active, irrational rather than rational, subjective rather than objective, at home rather than at "work," spiritual rather than material, and impractical rather than practical. It has ruled that certain kinds of behavior are "abnormal" and "unnatural" for females to practice, such as pursuing careers, doing construction work, being pastors or priests, wearing "male" clothes, or being assertive. Such gender distinctions, feminist critics claim, are arbitrary and almost always give women less power, status, and respect than men. In one sense, the feminist focus on gender is deterministic: Many women are "trapped" by the gender traits assigned to them by culture. In another sense, however, it offers hope. Culture, unlike biology, can be changed—through education, social action, and politics.

Gender criticism.   All three of these "stages" of feminist criticism have overlapped and coexisted. They continue to be practiced. But the focus on gender in the third stage led not only to a new stage of feminist criticism, it also helped to establish the broader movement of gender criticism. Until the mid-1980s, many feminist critics assumed that all women were the same in their biological nature, their gender traits, their shared history of oppression, and their aspirations. Most feminist critics, furthermore, wrote from the perspective of an elite group of people: women who were Western, politically liberal, middle class, and highly educated. Beginning around 1985, some feminist critics challenged these assumptions and this perspective. Feminist critics, they said, should look at the many ways in which women differ from one another. Factors other than gender, they said, give females identity. These factors include such things as race, ethnic background, and socioeconomic circumstances. Critics began studying the literary representation of women in minority cultures, in non-Western cultures, at various economic levels, and in different work situations. They began examining ways females themselves marginalize or "erase" other females. Perhaps most important, they began to pay attention to sex and gender differences among women, especially between heterosexuals and homosexuals.

Foucault.   Gender criticism, perhaps because it is so new, remains a nebulous, difficult-to-define approach to the study of literature. It covers almost anything having to do with "gender," including feminist criticism, theories of cultural influence, and crimes such as sexual abuse. One of the most important aspects of gender criticism is its exploration of the literary treatment of homosexuality. As with new historicism, the theorist who most influences gender studies is Michel Foucault. The first volume of his three-volume study *The History of Sexuality* (1976) states his basic ideas about sexuality. The Western concept of "sexuality," Foucault maintains, is not a universal category but was invented in the late nineteenth century. Sexuality in the modern West is not innate or biological but is instead a matrix of concepts created by society. Society, in other words, "constructs" sexuality. These concepts constitute an "ideology" that benefits people in power, most notably bourgeois capitalists. Like all ideologies, this one is manifested in discourses such as religion, science, politics, medicine, and literature.

Some gender critics disagree with Foucault's heavy emphasis on cultural determinism. They believe that sexual identity, including homosexuality, results from biological rather than cultural causes. Gay criticism (which deals with men) and lesbian criticism (which focuses on females) at first espoused homosexuality as no less "natural" and "normal" than heterosexuality. Gay and lesbian "pride" meant coming out of the closet, accepting a common identity, and joining the struggle against homophobia. Gay and lesbian critics studied the works and lives of authors who were admitted homosexuals and bisexuals or who seemed to have suppressed homosexual tendencies. They sought to expose the politics of gender in society and literature—how certain groups manipulate concepts of gender for their own benefit.

Queer theory.   But *queer theory*, a new and still evolving branch of gay and lesbian criticism, calls into question the "essentialist" concepts of gender held by earlier gay and lesbian critics. As Annamarie Jagose (in *Queer Theory: An Introduction*) says, instead of holding that homosexuality, or any sexuality, is the same for everyone, queer theory embraces the post-structuralist notion that all meanings, including sexual identity, are unstable: "within poststructuralism, the very notion of identity as a coherent and abiding sense of self is perceived as a cultural fantasy rather than a demonstrable fact" (82). Foucault's belief that sexuality is "not an essentially personal attribute but an available cultural category" (79) has greatly influenced queer theory. But perhaps even more influential is Judith Butler's argument (in *Gender Trouble*) that sexuality is "performative," or based on behaviors we learn from culture. "Performing" these behaviors constructs our sexual identity. The main goals of queer theory seem to be to describe such "performances" and to challenge the validity of all "normal" identities, not just sexual but racial, ethnic, and national (99).

Resources for feminist and gender criticism. Perhaps the best place to begin reading feminist criticism is with an anthology of essays such as *The New Feminist Criticism: Essays on Women, Literature, and Theory* (1985), edited by Elaine Showalter. Ellen Moers's *Literary Women* (1976); Sandra Gilbert and Susan Gubar's *The Madwoman in the Attic: The Woman Writer and the Nineteenth-Century Literary Imagination* (1979); and Kate Millett's *Sexual Politics* (1970), mentioned above, are among the best examples of "images of women" criticism. Virginia Woolf's *A Room of One's Own* (1929) and Hélène Cixous's "The Laugh of the Medusa" (1976) are examples of gynocriticism. Gayle Rubin's essays, mentioned above, and Elaine Showalter's edited collection, *Speaking of Gender* (1989), represent the shift of interest toward gender. Two texts that deal with the broadening of feminist criticism are Barbara Smith's "Toward a Black Feminist Criticism" (1975) and *Wild Women in the Whirlwind: Afra-American Culture and the Contemporary Literary Renaissance*, edited by Joanne Braxton and Andree Nicola McLaughlin (1989). *The Gay and Lesbian Literary Heritage* (rev. ed. 2002), edited by Claude J. Summers, is a one-volume encyclopedia featuring articles on authors, terms, and theoretical approaches. *The Gay and Lesbian Studies Reader,* edited by Henry Abelove (1993), is an anthology of essays. Eve Kosofsky Sedgwick's *Between Men: English Literature and Male Homosocial Desire* (1985) deals with heterosexuality and homosexuality in literature before the twentieth century. Judith Butler's *Gender Trouble: Feminism and Popular Culture* (1990) develops her concept of sexual identity as "performative." For works by and about Michel Foucault, see the discussion of new historicism.

Suggestions for Applying Literary Theory and Criticism about All of Reality

To uncover a work's connection to "reality," you have to know about the "reality" in the work. You can do so in at least two ways. First, you can draw upon your own experiences and knowledge. You have experiences that are unique to you. You also share experiences with others—families, organizations, sports teams, classmates. You have specialized skills that many others don't have. By the time you are in high school and college, you have had so much interaction with other people that you know a lot about how people typically behave and about what works in human relationships. All of this knowledge can help you discover the "reality" in works of literature.

Second, you can do research. Research involves not just reading, but it can involve "field" work, like interviewing people, learning by doing (sailing, construction work, travel, managing money), attending events, and being alert to the significance of what's going around you.

An example of a work that at least attempts to reflect reality is Mark Haddon's novel *The Curious Incident of the Dog in the Night-Time* (2003). The narrator of this novel is Christopher John Francis Boone, age 15. He is autistic, and the novel exhibits his fears, likes, language, ways of relating to people, ambitions, entertainments, moral principles, and abilities. It also depicts the challenges that others face in caring for him. How accurately does the novel reflect the nature of this illness, the experiences of those who have it, and the challenges faced by caregivers? To answer that question, you would have to know about autism, either from research or personal experience or both. And you would have to read the novel with care in order to gather evidence for your conclusions.

A less clear-cut example is Frances Hodgson Burnett's novel *The Secret Garden* (1910). Burnett was enamored of the Christian Science religion and, it has been said, incorporated some of its principles in *The Secret Garden*. Is this true? Can you find examples of Christian Science in the novel? As above, you would have to do research and read the novel carefully. Unlike Haddon's novel, however, which is clearly about something in the real world, Burnett's novel doesn't announce a "Christian Science" topic.

Indeed, most works of literature are not so clearly intentional about the "reality" they reflect as Haddon's. And even his novel isn't about just autism. When we explore the realities in works of literature, we are at least partly on our own. We may find the suggestions of other people—friends, teachers, critics—helpful, but finally we base our conclusions on what we know and on our careful examination of the works themselves.

As for the three "reality-based" theories outlined above—psychoanalytic, Marxist, and feminist/gender—like any theories about reality, they can be thought-provoking even if you don't accept some of their premises. Freud's theories, for example, have been strongly contested by recent developments in psychology. Yet they brilliantly point to the complexity and mysteriousness of the human psyche. The heart, D. H. Lawrence said, is a dark forest, not a well-manicured garden. Freud's ideas get us started toward understanding the unpredictable and often stunningly wrong choices fictional characters make, as well as the subtle yet powerful forces that tie characters, especially in families, together. Similarly, Marxist criticism, even if you aren't a "Marxist," points to the literary depiction of poverty and financial entrapment. And feminist/gender criticism casts light on the struggle for dignity and fulfillment by women and homosexuals. Theories like these establish bridges between works of literature and the world outside them. They invite our empathy and, in some cases, encourage our active involvement in that world.

Works Cited

Abrams, M. H. *The Mirror and the Lamp: Romantic Theory and the Critical Tradition*. New York: Norton, 1958. Print.

Arac, Jonathan. "The Politics of *The Scarlet Letter*." *Ideology and Classic American Literature*. Ed. Sacvan Bercovitch and Myra Jehlen. Cambridge: Cambridge UP, 1986. 247–266. Print.

Barry, Peter. *Beginning Theory: An Introduction to Literary and Cultural Theory*. Manchester, England: Manchester UP, 2002. Print.

Brooks, Cleanth. "Irony as a Principle of Structure." *Literary Opinion in America*. Ed. Morton Zabel. Vol. II. Gloucester, MA: Peter Smith, 1968. 729–41. Print.

Brown, Paul. "'This Thing of Darkness I Acknowledge Mine': *The Tempest* and the Discourse of Colonialism." *Political Shakespeare: New Essays in Cultural Materialism*. Ed. Jonathan Dollimore and Alan Sinfield. Ithaca: Cornell UP, 1985. 48–71. Print.

Bush, Douglass. "Literary History and Literary Criticism." *Literary History and Literary Criticism*, Ed. Leon Edel. New York: New York UP, 1965. Print.

Campbell, Joseph. *The Hero with a Thousand Faces*. New York: World, 1949. Print.

Culler, Jonathan. *Literary Theory: A Very Short Introduction*. New York: Oxford UP, 1999. Print.

Frye, Northrop. *The Critical Path*. Bloomington: Indiana UP, 1971. Print.

Graff, Gerald. *Professing Literature: An Institutional History.* Chicago: U of Chicago P, 1987. Print.

Harland, Richard. *Literary Theory from Plato to Barthes: An Introductory History.* New York: St. Martin's Press, 1999. Print.

Hawkes, Terence. *Structuralism and Semiotics.* Berkeley: U of California P, 1977. Print.

Hirsch, E. D. *Validity in Interpretation.* New Haven: Yale UP, 1967. Print.

Jagose, Annamarie. *Queer Theory: An Introduction.* New York: New York UP, 1996. Print.

Lacan, Jacques. "Seminar on 'The Purloined Letter.'" *The Purloined Poe: Lacan, Derrida, and Psychoanalytic Reading.* Ed. John P. Muller and William J. Richardson. Baltimore: Johns Hopkins UP, 1988. Print.

Newton, K. M. *Interpreting the Text: A Critical Introduction to the Theory and Practice of Literary Interpretation.* New York: St. Martin's Press, 1990. Print.

Propp, Vladimir. *Morphology of the Folktale.* Ed. Svatava Pirkova-Jakobson. Trans. Lawrence Scott. Philadelphia: American Folklore Society, 1958. Print.

Said, Edward W. "Jane Austen and Empire." *Theory into Practice: A Reader in Modern Literary Criticism.* Ed. K. M. Newton. New York: St. Martin's Press, 1992. 291–309. Print.

Scholes, Robert. *Structuralism in Literature: An Introduction.* New Haven: Yale UP, 1974. Print.

Slotkin, Richard. *Regeneration Through Violence.* Hanover, MA: Wesleyan UP, 1973. Print.

Watts, Alan. *Myth and Ritual in Christianity.* New York: Vanguard, 1954. Print.

PART TWO

Writing about Literature

7

Writing about Literature

WHY WRITE ABOUT LITERATURE?

The answer to this question rests upon two considerations: your purpose and your audience. You may be so enthusiastic about a work that you e-mail friends to read it. You may be so confused by a work that you write down your thoughts just to clarify them. You may be so excited about your insights that you write people to share them. You may care so much about a work that you write a carefully thought-out interpretation of it. Your audiences for such writings vary, but the one thing they have in common is that they want to understand at least something about the works you write about. Your purpose is to help them do so.

HOW CAN YOU WRITE ABOUT LITERATURE?

The Essay

Writing about literature can take many forms, such as informal jottings, meant only for yourself; effusions of praise or condemnation; and even book-length studies of complex interpretive problems.

The kind of writing we emphasize in this book is the essay. An *essay* has the following characteristics:

1. Relative brevity—from about two to fifty pages.

2. Formality. It does not have to be stuffy and stilted, but it follows certain forms that have become conventional, thus its "formality." It adheres, for example, to rules of usage—punctuation, spelling, syntax, diction—characteristic of mainstream publications (newspapers, magazines, and books). It has a thesis that unifies the whole essay. It follows an organizational pattern that emphasizes intellectual coherence.

3. A "serious" audience, persons who care about the subject and will take time to consider what the author has to say.

4. Persuasiveness. Its purpose is to persuade readers that the author's ideas are worthy of consideration.

5. Give-and-take between author and readers. It often responds to others who have written or spoken on the topic and assumes that its readers can talk back.

6. Argumentation. Although in common usage *argument* means a heated exchange between angry people, for writing it means reasoned discussion. Essays are "argumentative." They develop a line of thought (a logically related series of claims), support a thesis and related claims with evidence, and organize claims and evidence coherently and logically.

The essay is a versatile and elastic genre, applicable not just to literature but to all kinds of subject matter and circumstances. Take, for example, the crime scene we mentioned in Chapter 1. You, the detective, have examined the scene, sifted through the evidence, and decided who is guilty. Now you have to tell people your conclusions. Your "telling" could, of course, be aloud, but if you are like most police detectives, you will have to write it out as an essay. It may be called something else—a report, say—but it will have the characteristics of an essay: a thesis (so-and-so did the deed) and an orderly presentation of claims and evidence that support the thesis (*because* of what I learned at the crime scene and elsewhere, I conclude that so-and-so is guilty). Your audience will be those who must rely on the essay to render justice: other police officers, the district attorney, the defending attorney, the judge, the jury.

Or consider another scenario. For a year, you have worked amazingly well in a new job, but your immediate supervisor threatens to fire you. To keep your job, you write a letter to your supervisor's boss. Although this letter will not be called an essay, it really is. It will argue a thesis—that you have done outstanding work and should retain your job. You will defend your thesis with claims about your successes and with specific evidence to support your claims. The outcome, we can hope, is that your supervisor will be fired, not you.

The Essay as Communication

In both of these examples, we can see a pattern of communication similar to that introduced in Chapter 1: author-work-reader. The same pattern applies to writing about literature, only this time, you are the author. The complete pattern looks like this:

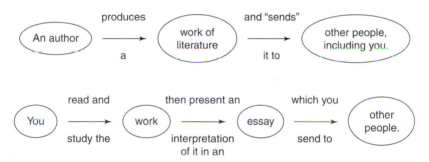

The purpose of your essay is to explain your interpretation to readers and persuade them that your interpretation is worthy of serious consideration. As a reader you were the receiver of an author's work of literature. Now you turn that situation around. You become an author *about* that same work of literature.

THE WRITING PROCESS

When we write essays, we typically think and write in stages. Writers rarely follow this process rigidly—first one step, then another, then another. Rather, they go back and forth among stages and do many tasks simultaneously. But as they write, they follow the general outline of a process. Understanding this process—the writing process—helps us plan the task of writing. It also helps reduce "writer's anxiety," the dreadful feeling that we must come up with an essay all at once, produce it out of thin air. Like building a house, writing goes in small steps. Knowing what the usual process is helps us relax and take steps one at a time. Even when we have to go back to earlier steps, as most writers do, we can feel sure we are moving toward completion. The writing process consists of four main sets of activities.

- **First Stage: Inventing**

  1. Studying the subject. The "subject" of essays about literature is the work of literature.

  2. Identifying your audience (its needs and interests).

  3. Recognizing any limitations placed on your essay (length, time in which you have to write it, specifics of an assignment).

  4. Generating topics. (See Chapter 8.)

- **Second Stage: Drafting**

  1. Determining a thesis and supporting claims.

  2. Gathering facts from the work and, if helpful, from secondary sources to support claims.

  3. Creating a plan of organization for a first draft.

  4. Writing the first draft.

- **Third Stage: Revising**

  1. Reading your draft critically. If possible, getting others to read and comment on it.

  2. Rethinking the topic, plan of organization, and line of reasoning.

  3. Gathering more support for claims.

  4. Writing further drafts.

- **Fourth Stage: Editing**

  1. Producing a final draft in the format expected by your audience.

  2. "Publishing" the essay (by turning it in to your professor, by sending it to a circle of readers, by submitting it to a real publication such as a magazine or newspaper).

The next chapter, Chapter 8, takes up the first stage of the writing process: inventing.

8

Choosing Topics

The most challenging question of the invention stage of the writing process is, "What can I write about?" For writers about literature, the answers are as varying as the people who write. People respond so differently to works of literature that it is hard to predict what they—and you—might choose to write about. For each of us, the most fruitful question for raising topics is probably, "What connections within the work or to the world outside the work do I find?" Answer that for yourself and then write about one of those meanings. This chapter offers a number of more specific suggestions about how to search for topics and how to state them so that they are interesting and easy to discuss.

PRELIMINARY STEPS

Be an Active Reader

We discussed this topic in Chapter 1 and throughout the first half of the book. Read actively rather than passively. Rather than just absorb works of literature, think about them as you read. Ask questions like the following:

- What don't I understand?
- Why is the author using this convention over other conventions?
- What ideas do the characters espouse?
- Can I detect the author's bias in favor of certain ideas?
- What interests me about the work?
- What do I dislike? What do I like?
- What experiences in my own life does the work reflect?

If it helps to skim parts of a work—even the whole work—and then reread, so as to get the whole picture, then do that. Consider the "places" to look for meaning we surveyed in Part One. Choose one or more of them to concentrate on as you read. Rather than let the work control you, use strategies of investigation and analysis to control it. You might object that such an "intellectual" approach to reading literature takes the fun out of it. Yes, there are times when we want to relax and not think much about what we are reading. But analyzing and interpreting works of literature is pleasurable, too. In the long run, it is the most satisfying way to read literature.

Identify Your Audience

Writing as dialogue.   A handy way to think about audiences for essays, no matter what the subject matter, is to imagine yourself in conversation with a friend. This person likes you and is interested in your ideas. You are having coffee with her at an outdoor café. You say, "The other day I was reading this strange story by Edgar Allan Poe, 'The Cask of Amontillado.' What puzzles me is that the narrator, Montresor, is not telling the story to us but to somebody else, someone in the story. But we never learn who it is. I think, though, that I can make a good guess." Your friend asks, "Who do you think it is?" You tell her. She then asks, "Why do you think so?" You explain, giving reasons and details from the story. She may disagree with some of your claims, maybe all of them. You respond to her challenges until you both come to agreement or get tired of the topic. Throughout your conversation with her, you tailor your comments for her—explaining what you think she needs to know, using language she can understand, anticipating questions she might ask.

Different friends would elicit different approaches from you. If your friend were eighty years old, you might speak to her differently than if she were twelve.

Such a dialogue between people who care about the topic and who respect one another is the basis of all essays. It is what makes them meaningful, productive, and enjoyable. When you write essays, your readers will not be right there in front of you, ready to speak back about every nuance of your argument. But readers will respond to your surrogate, the words on the page. Inwardly, they will ask the same questions they would ask if you were there with them.

Write, then, as if your readers are in a conversation with you and are eager to learn your ideas. Determine who they might be—their values, level of knowledge, facility with language, and so on, and adjust your writing for them accordingly. Sometimes, readers may not be friendly toward you. They might be skeptical about your subject, your ideas, or even your ability. If so, anticipate their questions. Ask yourself questions like these: To whom are you writing? What do they want from you? What information and explanation do they need from you in order to understand you? What effect do you want to have on them?

Professors as audience.   When you write for courses, however, identifying your audience becomes tricky. In such a case, isn't your professor your audience? Yes, of course. You want him or her to think well of your essay and to give it a high grade. It behooves you to learn the professor's criteria for judging essays. Most professors want a well-crafted essay—such qualities as a clear statement of thesis, logical and coherent organization, fluent and correct prose, convincingly supported claims, thorough development of the topic. So far, so good. But professors often have a second audience in mind when they evaluate your essays—not just themselves but a *general audience*, one that is larger than the professor, one that includes the professor.

A general audience.   Who belongs to this audience? Two groups who do *not* belong are (1) experts on your subject and (2) people incapable of grasping your reasoning (children, for example). You could write for both of these audiences, but if you wrote for an audience of experts, you would have to be an expert yourself and have something to tell them that they do not already know. Most students do not have enough time to master subjects that thoroughly.

This, by the way, is another reason for not writing solely for your instructor. The instructor is an "expert" who, fortunately, rarely expects students to meet the needs of an audience of experts. On the other hand, if you wrote for the mentally immature, your essay would be too simpleminded for college courses.

Rather, a general audience consists of persons who are intelligent, who have read or can read the work you want to discuss, and who want to understand it better. It consists of individuals who are your equals, who form a community of which you are a part, to whom you can talk with equal authority. They share your interests and eagerly await your comments. If it will help, visualize people you know—classmates, friends, relatives, students at other campuses—as belonging to this audience. As with our conversation-over-coffee scenario, imagine yourself in a dialogue with them, saying things that would interest them, responding to their questions and comments. Project an image of yourself as the conscientious searcher for truth. Let your audience know that you are doing everything possible, within the limits of your time and ability, to answer the questions you have raised.

One reason professors may prefer you to write for a general audience is that you are more likely to include the facts and reasoning needed by *both* a general audience and your professors to understand and be convinced by you. When writing solely for professors, students often think, "The professor already knows this, so I won't include it." The professor usually *does* want you to include it. Professors cannot read your mind. In order to think well of your work, they need to see how you arrived at the claims you make. Professors know, furthermore, that writing for a general audience is the kind of writing you are most likely to do once you leave college. Your writing in the "real world" will usually be for groups of people, not just one person. Writing college essays for a general audience gives you practice in this kind of writing.

Yourself as audience. A third audience to write for is yourself. Writing essays is one way of satisfying your own intellectual needs and desires. Writing is not simply the product of thinking; it is a *way* of thinking. Some theorists argue that only when you write your ideas can you be sure you have thought them through carefully. The process of writing essays, for example, underscores the need to use sound logic, to include all the steps in your reasoning, to state ideas precisely so your arguments will withstand scrutiny. It is easy *not* to do these things when you are just thinking to yourself or speaking to other people. Francis Bacon's maxim sums this point up well: "Reading maketh a full man, conference a ready man, and writing an exact man."

Perhaps the most important aspect of writing is its ability to draw forth your ideas. One kind of essay about literature is the essay examination (discussed in Chapter 12). While writing essay examinations, students often discover ideas they never knew they had. In this situation, writing joins your knowledge of the literature with the instructor's questions about it to give birth to new ideas. Essays about literature, then, can be journeys of self-discovery that lead you to new intellectual vistas. In this sense, you are part of your audience. You share your readers' curiosity and their desire to have puzzling questions answered. You write to convince them. You write also to discover and clarify your own ideas and to convince yourself of their validity.

Raise Questions about the Work

Related to the identity and needs of your audience is the nature of your topic. Your audience wants to understand the work and wants to know your interpretations of it. But what will you interpret— everything in the work or just some part of it? Since essays are relatively short, rarely can you interpret everything in a work. Instead, limit yourself to some part of it. But which part?

The answer: Write about a specific problem of interpretation. The "problem" should be a question about how the work holds together, how it "works." Your question could focus on the motivation of characters, the effect of physical surroundings on characters, the arrangement of events in the plot, the sound devices in a poem, a theme in the work—anything that demands interpretation. Your essay should identify that question and provide an answer to it. The topics of interpretive essays always refer to questions. You might announce your topic as "Hamlet's Indecision" or "Macbeth's Hunger for Power," but the audience knows that behind topics like these lie questions: Why does Hamlet hesitate to act? What propels Macbeth to seek power? The purpose of taking up such topics is to answer the questions that give rise to them. When you state your topic, you do not have to phrase it as a question, yet good topics always imply questions of interpretation.

Narrow Your Topic

Topic as thought-provoking. What makes a topic good? One way to judge the quality of an essay topic is to ask yourself how easily your audience could answer the question that lies behind it. A useful criterion is that a topic is "good" if your readers could readily *not* answer the question after reading the work once. They could not answer it convincingly, either for themselves or for others, without reviewing and studying the work. The topic, in short, must be genuinely thought provoking.

Topic as interesting. A second consideration is the meaningfulness of your topic. As the author, you should care about the topic, and your audience should be interested in it. To assess your audience's interest, imagine yourself as part of your audience. What would you want to know if you were reading your own essay? One of the *least* interesting questions is: What happens? True, the events and details are sometimes hard to understand and need clarification, but usually readers can understand a work's details after reading it one time. You do not need to provide information your audience already knows.

Topic as focused. A third way to assess the quality of a topic is to ask if it is focused narrowly enough for the confines of your essay. Most of the essays you write for college literature classes will run from three to ten printed pages (900 to 3,000 words). Your topic is good if you can deal with it thoroughly within those limits. For example, "Comedy in *Romeo and Juliet*" would probably be too broad for an essay topic; "The Nurse as Comic Figure" would be more specific and manageable. "Love in *Romeo and Juliet*" would be too broad; "Juliet's Mature Love versus Romeo's Adolescent Love" would be better. "Values in *Romeo and Juliet*"—too broad; "Shakespeare's Attitude toward Suicide"—better. "Juliet as Character"—too broad; "Juliet's Change from Child to Young Woman"—better.

Charlotte Brontë's novel *Jane Eyre* (1847) provides an example of an essay topic that meets these three criteria. Brontë grew up absorbing the superstitions of the English north country. These superstitions included beliefs in fairies, elves, and demons. We do not have to read far into *Jane Eyre* before encountering references to them. Jane, the narrator and main character, says that as a child she looked in vain for elves "under mushrooms and beneath the ground-ivy" and concluded that "they were all gone out of England to some savage country where the woods were wilder and thicker, and the population more scant" (53). After her first encounter with Mr. Rochester, he accuses her of being a fairy who "bewitched" his horse and caused it to fall. Her reply is that the fairies "all forsook England a hundred years ago" (153–54). Throughout her relationship, he calls her "elf," "fairy," "dream," "changeling," "sprite" (272, 302). After she returns at the end of the novel, he reverts to his epithets, once again calling her "fairy," "ghost," "changeling," "fairyborn and humanbred" (457–63).

If you were to spot this fairy lore motif in *Jane Eyre* you might think, "Aha, why not write an essay on that?" You could title the essay "Charlotte Brontë's Use of Fairy Lore in *Jane Eyre*." The question underlying the topic would be: What significance does this lore have in the novel? The purpose of the essay would be (1) to raise this question, (2) to show that the fairy lore actually does exist in the novel, and (3) to provide an answer to the question. This answer would be the *thesis* of the essay. The topic is meaningful because fairy lore is prominent in the work and is consistently associated with the main character; the topic promises to lead to an interpretation of the novel. Furthermore, the topic is complex enough so that most readers could not convincingly answer its implicit question without rereading and studying the novel. And the topic is specific enough to be dealt with thoroughly in an essay of about six or so double-spaced pages. The topic, in short, is "good."

For some individuals, finding a good topic is easy and automatic. One person might happen to notice the references to fairies in *Jane Eyre,* and think, "Hey, that would be interesting to write about." For others, however, discovering good topics is difficult and frustrating, capable of inducing writer's block. You or any writer can experience both situations. One work suggests all kinds of topics; another leaves you at a total loss. When you're stumped, try a search strategy.

SEARCH STRATEGIES

A *search strategy* is a procedure for locating and examining important aspects of a work. It is a *heuristic*—a self-teaching device that helps you think about the work. As you examine the work, you become aware of areas you can raise questions about, questions that may lead to good topics. The following are brief descriptions of some well-known search strategies.

Focus on the Work's Conventions (Its Formal Qualities)

The *conventions* (elements) of a work—such things as characterization, setting, plot, poetic style—make up its form and are "places" to locate meaning in works of literature. (See Part One of this book for a thorough discussion of these conventions.) In your search for a topic, you don't need to examine *every* component of a work, but focus on various ones until you hit on ideas that interest you. Systematically examining conventions in a work, in other words, is a process of discovery, like shining a flashlight on different parts of a darkened room. You could even turn conventions of a work into essay topics: "Setting in Austen's *Pride and Prejudice*," "Meter and Rhyme in Shakespeare's Sonnet 116," "Characterization in O'Neill's *The Hairy Ape*," "Irony in Poe's 'The Cask of Amontillado.'" Your purpose would be to show how the author uses these conventions and how they are important to the overall scheme of the work. See, for example, the essay in Chapter 13 on the poem "Richard Cory."

Use *Topoi* (Traditional Patterns of Thinking)

Generations of communicators have recognized that certain ways of thinking—patterns of thought—are helpful tools for examining subjects and developing ideas about them. In his *Rhetoric* (c. 322 BCE) Aristotle called these patterns *topoi*, which means "places." Aristotle seems to have meant that these patterns are "places" to look when you need to find ideas. Several of the traditional patterns are especially useful—at times inevitable—for coming up with ideas about literature and for explaining it. The following are descriptions of well-known *topoi*.

Definition.   Definition is unavoidable in arguments because your claims often contain terms that must be defined. Quite often, these terms are not controversial or ambiguous and therefore need no formal definitions. However, when you have controversial terms, you must define them, and you must define all such terms so that readers know what you mean by them.

Apart from the necessity of defining terms, definition can be useful in two other ways. First, your claims may rest upon the definition of a word within the work. Second, you may want to focus your whole essay on a definition. You might, for example, show that "imagination" is Isabel Archer's most admirable trait in Henry James's novel *The Portrait of a Lady* (1881). Your essay would attempt to explain what James means by the term. Or you might argue that Jane Austen in *Pride and Prejudice* distinguishes between "good pride" and "bad pride." Again, you would discuss the novel in order to define these terms. Finally, you might claim that Emily Brontë uses "gothic" elements in *Wuthering Heights*. You would need to find a reliable definition of *gothic* to make your case convincing, and to apply all parts of the definition to the work, showing which ones fit and which do not. A handbook of literary terms, such as M. H. Abrams and Geoffrey Galt Harpham's *A Glossary of Literary Terms* (2009), offers succinct definitions of concepts and terms related to literature.

Structure. Focus on structure helps identify an object's parts and how they contribute to the coherence and meaning of the whole. A structure has a definite pattern of organization. Works of literature always have a structure, sometimes more than one. Some works conform to established structures like the sonnet form; other works conform to newly invented structures. Your purpose would be to identify the structure and explain its relationship to other elements such as theme and characterization. You might, for example, claim that the passage of the seasons provides the structure of William Wordsworth's poem "The Ruined Cottage," or that the rhyme scheme of his "I Wandered Lonely as a Cloud," emphasizes the narrator's shift from feeling isolated to feeling connected to nature. The less obvious the structure or its effect on the work, the more revealing your essay would be. You might even argue that the work has several structures—an obvious structure and a less-obvious structure.

Process. *Process* is the order in which things occur. An example is a recipe, which indicates the materials for a dish and the order in which to put it together. Because literature often represents events occurring in time, it lends itself to process analysis: Characters change from weak to strong, societies from coherent to incoherent, settings from beautiful to ugly. Something may even change in opposite ways. A character, for example, may grow physically weaker but morally stronger.

When describing a process, avoid just retelling the plot. Instead, indicate clear *steps* in the process. Present them in the order in which they occur in time. Each step would be a unit—probably a paragraph—of your paper. You would state what the step is and describe it.

Cause and effect.   Examining cause and effect helps you investigate the causes and effects of events. When you investigate *causes*, you deal with happenings in the past. Why does Goodman Brown go into the forest? Why does Hedda Gabler act the way she does? What causes Pip to change? Two kinds of causes usually figure in works of literature, the immediate or surface cause and the remote or deep cause. In Theodore Dreiser's *An American Tragedy* (1925) the immediate cause of Roberta Alden's death is that she is pregnant. Clyde Griffiths kills her because he wants her out of the way so he can marry the beautiful and wealthy Sondra Finchley. The remote cause, however, is all those forces—childhood experiences, parental models, heredity, financial situation, cultural values, religious background, and accident—that have molded Clyde and that make the reasons he kills Roberta complex.

When you investigate *effects*, you can deal with things in either the past or the future. In William Faulkner's fiction, you could examine the effect of slavery on Southern society and on his characters. These effects are part of the historical past in his work. You could also predict what the South, given how Faulkner depicts it, will be like in the future.

Because literature often deals with the actions of complex characters and societies, analyzing cause and effect is a fruitful source of essay topics. We constantly wonder why characters do what they do and what effects their actions have had or will have. Just as in real life, cause and effect in literature can be subtle. Your task is to discover and communicate those subtleties.

Comparison.   *Comparison* means indicating both similarities and differences between two or more things. One use of comparison is to establish the value of something. You might argue that one of Shakespeare's comedies is not as good as the others because of qualities the others have. Another use of comparison is to explain your insights about aspects of a work. A comparison of the two sets of lovers in Tolstoy's *Anna Karenina* (1875–78), for example, helps us understand his distinction between sacred love and profane love. Comparing the themes of one work to another is also revealing. Sir Walter Raleigh's poem "The Nymph's Reply to the Shepherd" is a response to Christopher Marlowe's poem "The Passionate

Shepherd to His Love." (See Chapter 2, pages 30–31, for the texts of these poems.) Raleigh not only disagrees in general with the premise of Marlowe's poem, he also makes nearly every line of the poem respond to the parallel line in Marlowe's poem. A line-by-line comparison of the two poems brings Raleigh's themes to light.

Comparison is revealing also when the author of a work contains allusions. An *allusion* refers to something else—another work, a historical event, a myth, or an author. Allusions always invite us to compare the work at hand to the thing alluded to. Philip Pullman's His Dark Materials fantasy trilogy (*The Golden Compass* [1995], *The Subtle Knife* [1997], and *The Amber Spyglass* [2000]) is a recasting of John Milton's *Paradise Lost* (1667). Pullman opens *The Golden Compass* with an epigraph (quotation) from *Paradise Lost* and refers to the epic often throughout the series, especially in the final book. Why does he do this? What parallels does he have in mind between his and Milton's work? Is his retelling of Milton's epic successful? A comparison of the two works would strive to answer these questions.

Respond to Comments by Critics

Comments by literary critics are often a fruitful source of topics. Critics write about individual works, about an author's entire work, about the nature of literature itself, about a work's connection to society. Your purpose would be to make a critic's whole approach or an isolated comment by a critic the starting point of your essay. Chapter 6 outlines several well-known critical approaches to literature, but consider for the moment how you might use the following observation made by Terry Eagleton in *Literary Theory: An Introduction* (1983):

> Watching his grandson playing in his pram one day, Freud observed him throwing a toy out of the pram and exclaiming *fort!* (gone away), then hauling it in again on a string to the cry of *da!* (here). This, the famous *fort-da* game, Freud interpreted in *Beyond the Pleasure Principle* (1920) as the infant's symbolic mastery of its mother's absence; but it can also be read as the first glimmerings of narrative. *Fort da* is perhaps the shortest story we can imagine: an object is lost, and then recovered. But even the most complex narratives can be read as variants on this model: the pattern of classical narrative is that an original settlement is disrupted and ultimately restored. (185)

Here, Eagleton states an aspect of narratives that most people have probably not thought about: that there is a lost-and-found pattern and variations on it in many narratives. Examples abound: Homer's *Odyssey* (c. 800 BCE), Milton's *Paradise Lost* (1667), Melville's *Moby-Dick* (1851), Coleridge's *Rime of the Ancient Mariner* (1798), Keats's "La Belle Dame sans Merci" (1819), Shakespeare's *King Lear* (1605-06), Jane Austen's *Pride and Prejudice* (1813). You could make Eagleton's comment the basis for an essay. You would try to explain how the pattern or a variation on it operates in your work. You would begin by explaining Eagleton's idea, giving proper credit to him. (For when and how to give credit in your essays, see Chapter 11.) Then you would answer questions such as the following: What has been lost? How was it lost? How are the protagonists trying to recover it? Do they succeed? What qualities allow them to succeed or cause them to fail?

Eagleton's comment covers many works of literature, but critics also write extensively about individual works. You could use a critic's idea about a specific work as a starting point for an essay. Your essay could support or disagree with it. For an explanation of how to find critical interpretations of individual works, see the treatment of sources in Chapter 11, pages 301–303. The student essay in Chapter 13 about E. A. Robinson's "Richard Cory" responds to a critic's comments about the poem and offers an alternative view of it.

When you think of literary criticism, you may think only of published works, but do not forget your instructor and the other students in your class. Your instructor is a critic who "publishes" comments in class, aloud to you, and students often give interesting responses to the instructor and to one another. All of these comments can provide excellent starting points for essays.

Draw from Your Own Knowledge

Specialized knowledge.   People at all levels of achievement know a great deal and are learning all the time. If you are a student, you are most likely taking courses in a wide range of disciplines. All of this knowledge interconnects. You can bring it to bear on works of literature. Subject areas such as psychology, sociology, philosophy, design, art history, history of science, religious studies, cultural history, political history, even landscape gardening illuminate literature. Ibsen's Hedda Gabler (in the play *Hedda Gabler* [1890]) is a deeply troubled person. Can you find in your psychology textbooks theories that would help explain her problems? Ernest Hemingway said in an early version of "Big Two-Hearted River" that he wanted to write the way Paul Cézanne painted. Can you explain Hemingway's themes and methods by comparing his writing to Cézanne's pictures and his theories of art? In the poem "Heritage" (1925) Countee Cullen conveys an ambivalent attitude toward Africa. How does the American understanding (or misunderstanding) of Africa when he wrote the poem explain his frustration? Anton Chekhov wrote plays at the turn of the twentieth century. What was happening in Russia then that his plays reflect?

Personal experience. Another kind of knowledge writers often overlook is their own experience. Most students have expertise outside the academic world—through work, travel, family, and other activities. This expertise can illuminate works of literature. Have you done some sailing? If so, explain the complex maneuvers the young captain makes at the end of Joseph Conrad's "The Secret Sharer" (1909) and suggest what this knowledge tells us about the captain. (Is he taking a foolish, irresponsible risk?) Speaking of Conrad, have you been to the Congo River, the setting of *Heart of Darkness* (1902)? If so, are vestiges of the colonialism he condemns still there? What can you tell us about the landscape and atmosphere that would help us better understand this puzzling novel? Have you seen any bullfights? If so, help us understand the symbolic meaning of bullfighting in Hemingway's fiction. Have you been the victim of prejudice? If so, provide insights into the dynamics of bigotry dramatized in Bernard Malamud's *The Assistant* (1957) or Richard Wright's *Black Boy* (1945).

TALKING AND WRITING STRATEGIES

Talking and writing are themselves ways of generating ideas. When you talk with someone—even to yourself—about a work, or when you write about it, you often come up with ideas you never knew you had. This is why the writing process often involves going back and forth among stages. As you write a first draft, you discover ideas that lead you to rethink your topic and major claims.

Talk Out Loud

Imagine yourself talking to a friend about a work you want to write about. Or, better, find a real person to talk to. Talk out loud. Keep your partner in mind. You really want to explain this work to her. Say anything you want about the work—what you like and dislike, what interests you or does not interest you. Make claims about the work— what it means, what motivates the characters, what the setting is like. Support your claims with evidence. Ask your listener to respond. Does she agree or disagree? Listen to her counterclaims and reasons. Summarize the work for her. Ask if she understands and agrees with your summary. As you exchange ideas—or imagine that you are exchanging ideas—focus on themes of the work. What points does the writer seem to be making? By talking out loud, you get your mind working and push yourself toward interpretations of your own.

Make Outlines

Outline the work. The outline need not be formal (complete sentences, Roman and Arabic numerals, and so forth). Rather, it can be a list or a series of statements that indicate key aspects of the work. Write down the outline, so you can remember everything you put in it. Focus the outline on the whole work or one element of the work.

Possibilities for organizing outlines abound. An outline can follow the spatial order of the work; that is, the order events appear in the work. It can follow a chronological organization, the order in which the events occur in time. Or it can be arranged according to journalist's questions: who, what, when, where, why, how. The first four questions get the facts straight. The last two start you thinking about relationships among the facts. Who are the important characters in the work? What are they like? What has happened before the work begins? During what period is the action set? Where does the action occur? Why does the action happen? The journalist's questions often lead to other questions and finally to a careful consideration of the work.

Freewrite

Begin writing about a work or some aspect of it. Keep writing for five or ten minutes. If you can't think of anything new to say, repeat the last sentence over and over until something new occurs to you. While doing this forget about sentence structure and correct usage. Freewriting generates thought, even if you repeat ideas or write nonsense. Freewriting may provide you a topic and a rough outline for a full-blown essay.

Brainstorm

Brainstorm—think and write without restraint—about a work of literature. Let your mind flow where it will, but maintain focus on the work or some aspect of the work. Brainstorming requires pen and paper—lots of paper. As ideas come to you, jot them down. Make a game of this—creative play. Don't worry about spelling, complete sentences, and orderly arrangements of ideas. Include even crazy ideas. Channel thought with questions like these: Which works do I like best? (Jot down the possibilities.) What interests me most about the work? (Jot these down.) What do I dislike? (Jot these down.) Why do I like or dislike these things? (Jot down your reasons.) What do I want to write about? (Jot these down.) If characters interest you, brainstorm about them. If you tire of characters, shift to something else.

When you stop brainstorming, sort out, make connections, arrange your jottings into groups, and eliminate the unusable. Try different arrangements and relationships. Try even the strangest, most unlikely connections. If you have a list of ten items, group them. If you see connections between some but not others, keep the ones that connect and cross out the others. Then brainstorm about the qualities that link the remaining items. These could be the basis for your essay.

Create Graphic Organizers

If you have a visual imagination, try graphic organizers to generate and arrange ideas and information. There are hundreds of these already existing. Check out options by searching for "graphic organizers" on the Web or perusing David Hyerle's *Visual Tools for Constructing Knowledge* (1996). Or make up your own. The bubble graphic below was generated by the student whose notes, journal, and essay on *The Odyssey* immediately follow.

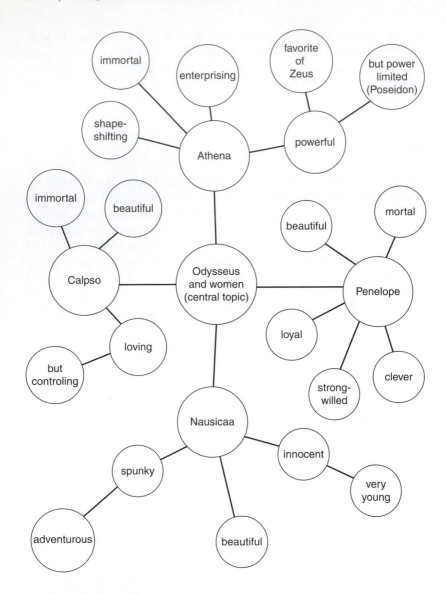

Make Notes

Notes are bits of writing you do for yourself. Write them wherever is most convenient and helpful: in the margins of books you own, on slips of paper, in a notebook. Since they are for yourself only, you need not worry about spelling, punctuation, or even coherence.

Notes are almost always short and pithy. Jotting down notes *as* you read stimulates interaction between you and the text. Writing notes *after* you read helps you think about the whole work, raise questions, state interpretations, and call attention to intriguing passages and details. The following are notes made by a student after she read Homer's *Odyssey*:

Notes on the *Odyssey*

Why does Odysseus want to leave Calypso's island? He's got such a good deal there.

If he loves Penelope, why does he sleep with Calypso? And Circe? Is this being "faithful"? I wonder what Penelope will think when he "confesses" (if he ever does). Could she do the same thing—sleep around—and get away with it? Double standard.

Athene: Obsessed with tying up loose ends. Although a goddess, power limited. Poseidon. Are they rivals?

Nausicaa: my favorite. "There slept a girl who in form and feature was like the immortal goddesses" (86). The "handsome girl" who, like Leto's daughter, is "the loveliest amid a whole bevy of beauties" (89). Innocent but spunky.

Zeus is patron of "strangers and foreigners in distress" (92). Why doesn't Zeus just zap the suitors?

Odysseus: A Greek Woody Allen (always worrying and down on himself).

At the end, Odysseus's treatment of the servant girls: horrible. Bloody and excessive. Sexist?

Keep a Journal

Journals are more coherent, more polished, and more developed than notes. You may be the sole audience for your own journals, but sometimes they are for others as well. The journals of authors like

Ralph Waldo Emerson, Henry James, and F. Scott Fitzgerald provide fascinating insights into their lives and works. Like these authors, writers often use journals not only to try out lines of thought, but also to get other peoples' reactions to them. The root word for journal—*jour,* French for "day"—suggests that they are more systematic and regular than notes. Write in your journal, if not daily, then regularly. Take more time developing your ideas than for notes. The journal below is by the same student who wrote the previous notes on the *Odyssey*. Notice how her journal entry is more developed than her notes and less developed than her essay (which immediately follows the journal entry).

Journal Entry on the *Odyssey*

Two things bother me about the *Odyssey*. One is the way Homer presents women. Women are almost always more limited in what they can do than men and are treated as inferiors by the male characters. As a female I resent this attitude. I will admit that females in the *Odyssey* are stronger—more admirable and influential—than in some of the other things we have read this semester. If Athene weren't always helping Telemachus and Odysseus, where would they be? But Athene's femaleness seems unimportant. She isn't human, for one thing. And for another, when she takes human form, she almost always appears as a male. Penelope is admirable, I suppose, for being so loyal and patient, but she has to stay home and do domestic duties (for twenty years!) while her husband gets to roam the world, have adventures, and sleep with beautiful goddesses. What would the men of Ithaca have thought had Penelope had similar adventures? Probably lynched her. Finally, at the end, I think that Odysseus's treatment of the disloyal female servants is excessive. They are sentenced without a trial. Who knows, they might have been coerced by the piglike suitors. They don't deserve to die, especially in such a gruesome way. What threat to Odysseus and Ithaca could they be if left alive?

The other thing is Odysseus's attitude toward Ogygia, Calypso's island. I keep wondering why he wants to leave. Ogygia seems like paradise. Odysseus says he loves Penelope and wants to return to her, but is that the real reason? Ogygia strikes me as being similar to Eden in the Bible. It even has four rivers, just like Eden. In the Bible, Adam and Eve are kicked out of Eden as punishment for eating the apple. Yet, in the *Odyssey*, Odysseus *wants* to leave. Why? I think I would want to stay. Look at what he's got. He has a beautiful woman who loves him and takes care of him. He could have immortality. (Calypso promises to make him immortal if he will stay.) Ogygia is beautiful. All my life I have thought that losing paradise, as Adam and Eve did, would be terrible. Why would someone wish to lose it? As a person (character), Odysseus seems very restless. Maybe that's the reason. Once he returns home, you wonder if he will stay for long.

SAMPLE ESSAY ABOUT LITERATURE

The following essay is by the student whose notes and journal are immediately above. It is a response to her reading of the *Odyssey*. Notice how the essay evolves out of her informal writing. In her notes she comments briefly on the "paradise" theme. She returns to it for more extended comment in her journal. She decides, finally, to focus an entire essay on this one theme. You can see from her notes and journal entry that she could have also written on other topics—the nature of the gods, Nausicaa, Athene, and gender equity. But she chose instead to write on this one.

Michelle Henderson

Professor Elliott

English 251–03

2 October 20—

Paradise Rejected in Homer's *Odyssey*

For centuries, people have considered the biblical Garden of Eden a model for "paradise." Surprisingly, a work of literature nearly as ancient as the Bible, Homer's *Odyssey*, contains a place so similar to Eden that it, too, qualifies as a paradise. This place is Calypso's island, Ogygia. Yet as alike as Eden and Ogygia are, the mortals who dwell there react to them very differently. Adam and Eve want to remain in Eden, but because of their disobedience they are expelled. In contrast, Odysseus chooses to leave Ogygia. This choice is puzzling. Why would he want to leave paradise?

Ogygia is similar to Eden in at least four ways. First, it looks and feels the same. The Genesis account says that God caused trees to "spring from the ground," trees that were "pleasant to look at and good for food" (2:9). A river flows "from Eden to water the garden" and branches into four "streams," called Pishon, Gihon, Tigris, and Euphrates (2:10–14). Eden is a "garden," a pleasant place where all forms of vegetation and animal life exist together in harmony (2:19–25). Homer's description of Calypso's Ogygia is almost the same, complete with the four springs:

> Round her cave there was a thick wood of alder, poplar, and sweet smelling cypress trees, wherein all kinds of great birds had built their nests—owls, hawks, and chattering

sea-crows that occupy their business in the waters. A vine loaded with grapes was trained and grew luxuriantly about the mouth of the cave; there were also four running rills of water in channels cut pretty close together, and turned hither and thither so as to irrigate the beds of violets and luscious herbage over which they flowed. Even a god could not help being charmed with such a lovely spot . . . (73–74).

Ogygia, furthermore, is fragrant: "There was a large fire burning on the hearth, and one could smell from far the fragrant reek of burning cedar and sandal wood" (73).

Ogygia is like Eden in a second way: its inhabitants live in comfort and without pain. Adam, Eve, and Odysseus hardly have to lift a finger to get the necessities of life. Although God puts Adam "in the garden of Eden to till it and care for it" (2:15), Adam doesn't work. "Work" is what he has to do after he is cast out of the garden: "You shall gain your bread by the sweat of your brow until you return to the ground" (3:17). Adam and Eve are free from pain in Eden. Only after they eat the apple does God give them pain. He tells Eve that he "will increase your labor and your groaning, and in labor you shall bear children" (3:16). He says that Adam will have to overcome the "thorns and thistles" of the earth (3:17). As for Odysseus, Calypso seems to provide all the food he could want: "Calypso set meat and drink before him of the food that mortals eat; but her maids brought ambrosia and nectar for herself, and they laid their hands on the good things that were before them" (77). We get the impression that, just as she provides food for Odysseus, she can protect him from pain. "Good luck go with you," she tells him, "but if you could only

Henderson 3

know how much suffering is in store for you before you get back to your own country, you would stay where you are, keep house along with me, and let me make you immortal . . ." (77).

Third, like Eden, Ogygia provides loving companionship. After creating Adam, God worries that Adam will be lonely, so God first creates the animals and then Eve to keep him company. Adam and Eve are the first married couple, becoming "one flesh" (2:18–25). Odysseus, of course, yearns to be with his wife, Penelope, but he has a loving companion in Calypso and seems to enjoy her company: "Presently the sun set and it became dark, whereon the pair retired into the inner part of the cave and went to bed" (78).

Finally, in Ogygia as in Eden, there is no death. God tells Adam and Eve that if they eat of the tree of knowledge they will die (2:16–18). And, sure enough, after they eat the apple God tells them, "Dust you are, to dust you shall return" (3:19). We can infer, then, that before they eat the apple, they have eternal life. Odysseus is mortal, but he, too, has the promise of immortality. Calypso tells Hermes, "I got fond of him and cherished him, and had set my heart on making him immortal, so that he should never grow old all his days" (75).

In sum, Adam, Eve, and Odysseus possess the benefits of paradise: a beautiful environment, an easy and painless life, loving companionship, and eternal life.

Yet Odysseus rejects this paradise. Why?

The answer Odysseus gives is that he loves Penelope and wants to be with her. His actions support this statement. When we first see him, he is "on the sea-shore as usual, looking out upon the barren ocean with tears in his eyes, groaning and breaking his heart for sorrow" (74). Odysseus admits that Calypso is far more beautiful than Penelope. He tells Calypso, "I am quite aware that my wife Penelope is nothing like so tall or so beautiful as yourself. She is only a woman, whereas you are an immortal. Nevertheless, I want to get home, and can think of nothing else" (77). At the end of the *Odyssey*, after many hardships, he does just that. The climax of the story occurs when Odysseus and Penelope at last retire to bed to consummate their long-awaited reunion.

A less obvious explanation for Odysseus's rejection of paradise, however, springs from his nature. He is incredibly creative and energetic and thrives on meeting challenges and devising stratagems. Early in the epic (52–53) Helen of Troy recounts the story of Odysseus's most famous stratagem, the Trojan Horse. Odysseus later tells with loving detail how he crafted his marriage bed:

> [The bed] is a marvelous curiosity which I made with my very own hands. There was a young olive growing within the precincts of the house, in full vigor, and about as thick as a bearing-post. I built my room round this with strong walls of stone and a roof to cover them, and I made the doors strong and well-fitting. Then I cut off the top boughs of the olive tree and left the stump standing. This I dressed roughly from the root upwards and then worked with carpenter's tools well and skillfully, straightening my work by drawing a line on the wood, and making it into a bed-prop. I then bored a hole down the middle, and made it the center-post of my bed, at which I worked till I had finished it, inlaying it with gold and silver; after this I stretched a hide of crimson leather from one side of it to the other. (354–55)

Homer gives a similarly detailed and admiring account of how
Odysseus constructs the raft on which he escapes from Ogygia
(78–79).

Odysseus, in short, is a craftsman, a maker, a builder. He
crafts the stratagem of the Trojan Horse. He crafts his escape
from Polyphemus, the Cyclops (135). He crafts his way past Scylla
and Charybdis (188–89). He crafts his artful speech to Nausicaa
that wins her help (90–91). He tells the story of his adventures,
Alcinous says, "as though you were a practiced bard" (172).
Finally, he crafts the defeat of the suitors. He loves stratagems
so much that he invents them for the sheer pleasure of it. After
telling Athene one of his elaborate falsehoods, she says,

> He must be indeed a shifty lying fellow who could surpass
> you in all manner of craft even though you had a god for
> your antagonist. Dare-devil that you are, full of guile, un-
> wearying in deceit, can you not drop your tricks and your
> instinctive falsehood, even now that you are in your own
> country again? (205)

The answer—unstated—is no. Odysseus loves his craftiness
too much to stop. How satisfied would he be in a place like
Ogygia? He would hate it. Ogygia, like the Garden of Eden,
provides everything one could possibly want. That's the trouble
with it. There are no challenges, no obstacles to overcome. People
whose love for overcoming obstacles is "instinctive" would be
so bored and so restless they would go crazy. That is the real
reason Odysseus chooses to leave Ogygia. He loves Penelope. But
he loves, also, the very things we usually think of as bad—the
difficulty and pain of life. Athene tells Zeus at the beginning that
Odysseus "is tired of life" (2). Odysseus would rather die than live
forever in the static eternity of "paradise."

Henderson 6

Works Cited

Homer. *The Odyssey*. Trans. Samuel Butler. New York: E. P. Dutton,

1925. Print.

The New English Bible. New York: Oxford UP, 1971. Print.

Note: Normally, the Works Cited list would appear on a separate page, but we print it here, right after the essay, to save space.

Comments on the Essay

This essay represents the interpretive and argumentative nature of essays about literature. The author begins by raising a question: Why does Odysseus leave Ogygia? This is her *topic*. She follows the question with claims about the nature of paradise and about Odysseus's motivation for leaving. She supports her claims with evidence. In her conclusion (final paragraph), she answers her question. This answer is her *thesis*. The essay deals with a serious issue that would interest thoughtful readers of the *Odyssey*. She shows them that the paradise theme is *meaningful* because of the light it sheds on Odysseus's values and motivations.

Checklist for Choosing Topics

- Be an active reader.
- Write for a general audience (not just your professor).
- Identify questions that underlie your topics.
- Choose topics that are
  - thought-provoking
  - interesting
  - focused enough to develop thoroughly in an essay.

- Use search strategies to generate topics:
  - analysis of the work's conventions
  - *topoi*
  - comments by critics
  - your knowledge
  - talking out loud
  - outlining
  - freewriting
  - brainstorming
  - create graphic organizers
- Make notes on the work.
- Keep a journal.

Works Cited

Brontë, Charlotte. *Jane Eyre.* New York: Penguin, 1966. Print.

Eagleton, Terry. *Literary Theory: An Introduction.* Minneapolis: U of Minnesota P, 1983. Print.

Drafting the Essay

This chapter deals with the second stage of the writing process, drafting the essay. By the time you reach this stage, you should have chosen a topic and thought about what you want to say about it. Now your task is to draft the essay. How do you do this? To help you answer this question, we discuss the basic aspects of the interpretive essay and offer some guidelines for writing a first draft.

THE ARGUMENTATIVE NATURE OF INTERPRETIVE ESSAYS

Qualities of essays. Essays about literature are "arguments." You may think of an *argument* as a verbal fight between people. But in rhetoric, it is a form of persuasive discourse that employs logic to explain and defend ideas. Although writings about literature can be solely informational (just give information) or expressive (just state opinions), essays are argumentative. An *argumentative essay* has three main qualities. First, its goal is to persuade people of the validity of its ideas. Second, it has a *thesis,* an overall claim. Third, it supports its thesis with evidence (facts, reasoning, and, when necessary, testimony).

Essays as arguments. The argumentative nature of essays about literature arises from the relationship between the work and its reader. Good literature is complex. It communicates on many levels of meaning and by many methods. A single work may exist as a system of sounds, symbols, ideas, images, analogies, actions, psychological portrayals, moods, or grammatical structures—all of which are separate entities, yet all of which interrelate. Furthermore, literature also invites readers to participate in creating the work. A work is not complete until it is read. The author leaves *gaps in the work* for readers to fill with their imagination. The completed work—the work that is read—is something more than the words on the page. It is a collaboration between text and reader. As a result, perceptions of a work vary from age to age, reader to reader, even reading to reading. This variability of perception occurs because no single reading, however careful, can take in all the elements of most works, or synthesize them into all their structural relationships, or include all the vantage points from which even one reader might experience a work.

Consequently, no single view of a work, whether your own or someone else's, can be the all-encompassing or final view. Cultures change, people change and, as a result, perception changes. It is a common experience for children to enjoy works—*Huckleberry Finn, Gulliver's Travels,* "Rip Van Winkle," *Alice in Wonderland*—and as adults to enjoy them again, but for different reasons and with new understandings of them. This does not mean that all interpretations of a work are equally valid. Interpretations of literature are subject to the same rules of human thought—accurate observation, sound reasoning, systematic procedure, thoroughness of treatment—as any other interpretive discourse. But no single interpretation can encompass the whole work.

Because literature is complex and can be perceived variously, essays about literature are arguments. You, the writer of the essay, cannot take for granted that your interpretation of the work is the same as your reader's. Your reader may have missed the very facts in the work you have found most compelling or most "obvious." Your reader may have a totally different understanding of the work than you do. If you want your reader to grasp your interpretation or accept it as valid, you must explain and persuade. You must write an argument.

THE STRUCTURE OF ESSAYS
ABOUT LITERATURE

Argumentative essays have two interrelated structures: an *argumentative structure* based on logic and a *rhetorical structure* based on persuasion. Because argumentation is a means of persuasion, the argumentative structure is really part of the rhetorical structure. But the two structures are not exactly the same, so we will talk about them separately.

The Argumentative Structure

Inductive reasoning. The argumentative structure of an essay consists of two kinds of reasoning: inductive and deductive. *Inductive reasoning* is the "scientific method." It consists of observing specific instances of something and drawing conclusions about them. You notice, for example, that in Act One of *Hamlet*, Hamlet is melancholy all the time. Then in Act Two, he is melancholy most of the time. In Act Three, he is melancholy four times. In Act Four, just two times. And in Act Five, none of the time. Having observed these instances of Hamlet's behavior, you can conclude that Hamlet starts out as a melancholy fellow but that his melancholia decreases throughout the play.

Inductive reasoning is essential for interpreting literature, but in itself it can seem like a dead end. So what if Hamlet is melancholy? To get beyond the "so what?" question, you need a second kind of reasoning, deduction. What if, for example, you want to claim that Hamlet's melancholia is the cause of something or, that by Act Five, it reaches crisis proportions? *Deductive reasoning* allows you to support such claims, to *do* something with your inductive conclusions.

Deductive reasoning. Syllogisms are the basis of deductive reasoning. A *syllogism* is a unit of reasoning that consists of two claims that support a third claim. The two supporting claims are called *premises*, and the third claim is called a *conclusion*. The *major premise* states a general concept. The *minor premise* is a specific instance of that concept. The *conclusion* connects the specific instance to the general concept:

MAJOR PREMISE: All complex characters are fascinating.
MINOR PREMISE: Anna Karenina is a complex character.
CONCLUSION: Therefore, Anna Karenina is fascinating.

Although in formal logic all three parts of a syllogism are stated, in argumentative essays parts of syllogisms are usually left unstated. The above syllogism would probably be stated something like this: "Anna Karenina is fascinating because she is so complex." Here, the major premise has been left out and is present only as an assumption.

Such incompletely stated syllogisms are called *enthymemes*. Authors use enthymemes when they believe the unstated premises would seem obvious or readily acceptable to their readers. But just because an author uses enthymemes does not mean that the syllogisms are absent. You can recover all the parts of such syllogisms in order to test their validity.

The deductive reasoning of an essay consists of a series of syllogisms that support a thesis. Consider, for example, the deductive reasoning of the student essay on the *Odyssey* in the previous chapter (pages 248–253). The student's thesis is that although Ogygia might seem like paradise to most people, Odysseus leaves it because to him it is not. She supports this thesis with two sets of syllogisms. In the first set she reasons why Ogygia seems like a paradise:

- MAJOR PREMISE: Many people believe that all places like Eden are paradises.

  MINOR PREMISE: Ogygia is like Eden.

  CONCLUSION: Therefore, many people would believe that Ogygia is a paradise.

In the second set of syllogisms, she reasons why Odysseus fails to find Ogygia a paradise.

- MAJOR PREMISE: All people who constantly scheme and love to overcome challenges are creative.

  MINOR PREMISE: Odysseus constantly schemes and loves to overcome challenges.

  CONCLUSION: Therefore, Odysseus is creative.

- MAJOR PREMISE: All creative people would hate living in a place that demands no creativity.

  MINOR PREMISE: Odysseus is a creative person.

  CONCLUSION: Therefore, Odysseus would hate living in a place that demands no creativity.

- MAJOR PREMISE: All places that anyone would hate are not paradise.

  MINOR PREMISE: Places that demand no creativity, like Ogygia and Eden, are places that some people (namely, Odysseus) would hate.

  CONCLUSION: Therefore, Ogygia is not, for Odysseus, a paradise.

These two sets of syllogisms—the syllogism about the nature of paradise and the ones about Odysseus—form the deductive framework of this student's essay. If you read her essay carefully, you will see that she leaves parts of her syllogisms unstated. She uses enthymemes. Such incompleteness is typical of essays. The point, however, is that the deductive reasoning of all essays consists of a chain of syllogisms, whether fully stated or not, that lead to and support a thesis.

But what about the inductive reasoning in her essay? We see inductive reasoning in two crucial places: (1) her claim that Ogygia is like Eden and (2) her claim that Odysseus is a craftsman. She arrived at these claims by noticing numerous related facts about Ogygia and about Odysseus's behavior. Now, in her essay, she supports her claims with some of these facts. But had she done no more than this, we might be tempted to ask, "So what?" So what if Ogygia is like Eden? So what if Odysseus is crafty? She anticipates our "so what?" questions with deductive reasoning that leads to her thesis: Someone as enterprising and clever as Odysseus would hate living in a static place like Eden and Ogygia, even though many people think of them as "paradise." She thus joins inductive reasoning and deductive reasoning to establish the argumentative structure of her essay.

The Rhetorical Structure

Rhetoric defined. *Rhetoric*, simply put, is the art of persuasion. It consists of all the devices writers use to make their claims attractive and convincing. For essays, the most important rhetorical device is argumentation—the reasoning that supports your thesis. Reasoning, however, is not the only rhetorical device you can use in an essay. Other rhetorical choices include how you organize the essay, where you put your thesis, what parts of your syllogisms you leave unstated, and which parts you emphasize and support with evidence from the text. All these choices help create the rhetorical structure of the essay.

How to organize your essay. The organization of any essay depends in part on the line of reasoning you develop, and this will vary from topic to topic. But the general structure of an argumentative essay is fairly standard and almost always contains the following units:

1. **Title.** The *title* should tell enough about the topic of the essay to capture the interest of readers and let them know the focus of the essay. The topic is what the essay is about. For the sake of clarity, include the author's name and the title of the work you will discuss: "The Jungle as Symbol in Joseph Conrad's *Heart of Darkness*."

2. **Introduction.** The *introduction* should state the topic of the essay and should be interesting enough to make the reader want to keep

on reading. You can state your thesis here, or you can choose to state it later. Keep introductions short—one to three paragraphs.

3. **Body.** The *body* is the place where you develop your line of reasoning. It consists of a series of paragraphs that contain claims (usually one claim per paragraph) along with supporting evidence. The body should contain as many paragraphs as necessary to make your argument convincing.

4. **Conclusion.** The *conclusion* signals that the essay has come to an end. It should remind the reader of the problem posed at the beginning of the essay (the topic) and briefly summarize the solutions. It should state or restate the thesis. The conclusion should be brief, a paragraph or so.

The following graphic represents this structure:

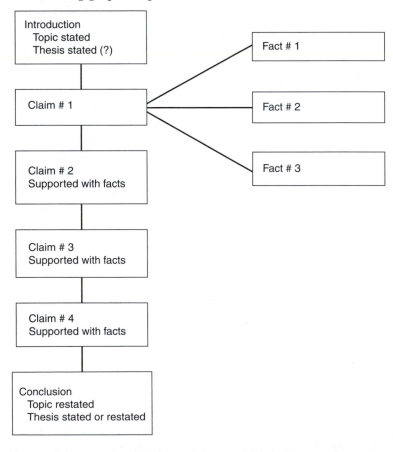

The student essay on the *Odyssey* illustrates these structural principles. The title—"Paradise Rejected in Homer's *Odyssey*"—gives enough information about the topic for readers to know, and be intrigued by, the focus of the essay. The introduction (the first paragraph) presents the topic as a problem to be solved: Why does Odysseus leave "paradise"? The body of the essay consists of a series of paragraphs spelling out the chain of syllogisms that make up the author's reasoning. The conclusion—the last paragraph—answers the question raised in the beginning.

Where to put the thesis. You have three choices: You can put it in the introduction, you can put it in the conclusion, or you can leave it unstated but implicit. You have to decide which is rhetorically most effective for your topic. If you state the thesis at the beginning, readers have the comfort of knowing what to look for as they read the rest of the essay. If you withhold it until the end, you create a sense of suspense that climaxes with the revelation of thesis. If you leave the thesis implicit, you allow readers to infer it and thus to participate in its discovery.

The author of the essay on the *Odyssey* puts her thesis at the end of the essay rather than at the beginning. Her rhetorical strategy is to open the essay with an intriguing question, then lead us toward an answer—her thesis—at the end.

Which premises to support with evidence from the text. Your syllogisms, and ultimately your thesis, are believable only if your audience accepts the premises of the syllogisms. You do not have time to support all your premises with evidence, and you do not really need to. Your audience will accept most of them as true, but you will have to support some of them to make your argument believable. Which ones? This, too, is a question about rhetorical strategy. You have to decide which premises your audience will accept as true and which ones they will want supported with evidence. For essays about literature, "evidence" consists of anything inside or outside the text that bears on your topic.

The author of the student essay on the *Odyssey* leaves many of her premises and conclusions unstated. The ones she emphasizes and supports with evidence are (1) that Eden and Ogygia are similar and (2) that Odysseus is creative. Is she right to have supported these claims and not some others? Only she and her readers can answer that question for sure. Some readers might say no, that she needs to support other claims as well. Others may say yes, that these are the key claims needing support. Arguing effectively depends on your ability to choose for the benefit of your audience which claims to state and support. Where you present them—and how—becomes part of the rhetorical structure of your essay.

GUIDELINES FOR WRITING FIRST DRAFTS

You are now about to begin writing. The following are suggestions about what to think about and do as you write.

Keep in Mind the Needs of Your Audience

As you write the drafts of your essay, calculate the needs of your audience. You will write better essays if you write for an audience that includes not just your instructor but anyone who enjoys literature and has ideas about it. Your goal is to convince them that your ideas have merit. Imagine yourself in conversation with your audience. In order to follow your line of thought, they will want to know certain things. Anticipate and supply their needs, just as you would if you were talking with them in person.

One of their needs is for clarity. They deserve a full and clear explanation of the points you are making. Your readers—including your instructor—cannot read your mind. Assume that they have already read the work or can read it. You need only to summarize and paraphrase those parts of the work that illustrate your points. But if you do not spell out your ideas, your readers may miss them altogether. In being fully clear, you may feel that you are being childishly obvious, but it is better to be obvious than risk having readers miss your points.

Your readers also need to be convinced. Assume that they want to learn from you, but do not expect them to surrender their views of the work just because you tell them to. Think of them as constantly asking, Why should we believe what you say? Your task is to explain and show them why.

Avoid Extreme Subjectivity (Overuse of "I")

Should you use "I" in essays about literature? Some teachers insist that students not use "I." One reason is that teachers want students to avoid stating their opinions without supporting them with facts and reasoning. We are used to asserting opinions in casual conversation: "The Harry Potter books are wonderful!" But the essay form demands proof and reasoning. Another reason is that if you fill your essays with phrases like "I feel," "I think," "I believe," "It seems to me," your essay, no matter how thorough and well reasoned, will sound overly opinionated. Notice how the author of the essay on the *Odyssey* uses "I" frequently in her notes and journal but eliminates it entirely from her essay.

Having said this, however, essays about literature are inevitably "subjective." Yes, you have to pay careful attention to details in the text. These are the basis for all your claims about it. Yes, you have to use sound logic to support claims. Yes, you have to be objective—willing to entertain understandings of a work other than your own. But nearly all works of literature are open to interpretation. That is why we write about them. Your interpretations are likely to be different from other people's. For this reason, it is standard practice for critics to use "I" when writing interpretations of literature, even in the most scholarly writing. Many essays, in fact, would sound stilted and strange if their authors did not use "I." An example is the student essay on George Eliot's *Adam Bede*, printed in Chapter 13. The author compares her own experiences to those of a character in the novel. Even in essays that do not, like this one, take a reader-response approach to literature, the inclusion of an occasional "I believe" makes rhetorical sense. It emphasizes where the author departs from others' opinions: "Many critics see Hetty as selfish and thoughtless, but I see her more sympathetically."

Two suggestions, then, pertain to the use of "I" in your essays. First, use "I" helpfully but sparingly. Second, find out your teacher's preference about the use of "I" and write accordingly.

Draw Up a Rough Outline

Many people find rough outlines indispensable for drafting essays. A rough outline consists of the main points you want to make, including the thesis. If the author of the essay about the *Odyssey* had made a rough outline, it would look something like this:

Introduction

Raise this question: Why does Odysseus leave Ogygia, which seems like paradise?

Body

Claim #1: Ogygia is a paradise.

Support this claim by comparing Ogygia to Eden (my standard for what paradise is). Give facts from the two texts.

Claim #2: Odysseus leaves Ogygia because he wants to be with Penelope and because he is too creative to be happy there.

Support these claims with facts from the Odyssey.

Conclusion

Claim #2 is the answer to my question and therefore my thesis. I will make it my conclusion as well.

Rough outlines are just that—*rough*. They include only the main points of your draft, not all the nuances. Their usefulness is to give you a general sense of your line of thought and rhetorical strategy and to help you make sure that all claims relate to your topic. When you start writing, you may discover new ideas or run into dead ends. If so, redo your rough outline and go on from there.

Begin Writing

Don't bog down. If you have trouble with the introduction (as many people do), move on to the body of the paper. Work on stating your claims clearly and supporting the key ones with evidence. Tackle the claims that seem easiest to support first. Once you get a draft written, it is easier to rearrange claims, to fill in gaps, and to decide for sure what your thesis is.

Use Sound Deductive Reasoning

The deductive logic of your essay is made up of the syllogisms and chains of syllogisms that constitute your reasoning. If one or more of your syllogisms is invalid, the whole of your argument is undermined. Logic is a complex topic we do not have the space to discuss thoroughly here. But a general rule is to avoid *non sequiturs.* The Latin term *non sequitur* means, "It does not follow." A *non sequitur* results from the improper—that is, illogical—statement of a syllogism. For example, the conclusion of the following syllogism "does not follow" from the premises:

MAJOR PREMISE: All complex characters are fascinating.
MINOR PREMISE: Anna Karenina is fascinating.
CONCLUSION: Therefore, Anna Karenina is complex.

You can test syllogisms with a graphic that uses circles.

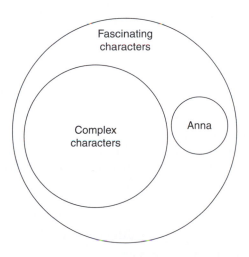

Just because Anna is fascinating does not mean she is complex. She may be fascinating for many other reasons. The correct statement of this syllogism is as follows:

MAJOR PREMISE: All complex characters are fascinating.
MINOR PREMISE: Anna Karenina is a complex character.
CONCLUSION: Therefore, Anna is fascinating.

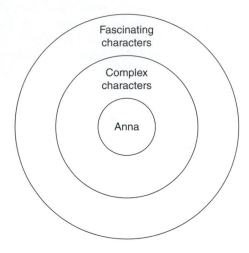

When you plan and write your essay, test the validity of your syllogisms. After you finish the first draft, go back over it to make sure your syllogisms are valid. For practice, identify some of the key syllogisms in one of the essays in Chapter 13 or in an argumentative essay in a newspaper or news magazine. Write down the syllogisms and see if they are properly stated.

Support Key Claims with Facts

The believability of your argument rests not only on the validity of your reasoning but on the truth of your premises. The logic of your syllogisms may be perfectly valid, but if readers do not accept your premises as true, they will reject your conclusions, including your thesis:

MAJOR PREMISE: All healthy people eat spinach.
MINOR PREMISE: Hugo is a healthy person.
CONCLUSION: Hugo eats spinach.

This syllogism is stated correctly, but the major premise is highly questionable. Look again at the correctly stated syllogism about Anna Karenina above. Is it true that "all complex characters are fascinating"? If not, the conclusion that Anna is fascinating is dubious.

Establish the truth of premises by supporting them with facts. Anything in the work is a *fact*. Facts can be quotations, words, incidents, details of setting, descriptions of characters, conflicts within the plot, word sounds, punctuation—anything in the work. Facts need not be just quotations; they can be your summaries of scenes and events.

Notice, for example, how the author of the essay on the *Odyssey* combines summary and quotation to support her claim that Odysseus is a craftsman:

> Odysseus is a craftsman, a maker, a builder. He crafts the stratagem of the Trojan Horse. He crafts his escape from Polyphemus, the Cyclops (135). He crafts his way past Scylla and Charybdis (188–89). He crafts his artful speech to Nausicaa that wins her help (90–91). He tells the story of his adventures, Alcinous says, "as though you were a practiced bard" (172). Finally, he crafts the defeat of the suitors. He loves stratagems so much that he invents them for the sheer pleasure of it. After telling Athene one of his elaborate lies, she says,
>
>> He must be indeed a shifty lying fellow who could surpass you in all manner of craft even though you had a god for your antagonist. Dare-devil that you are, full of guile, unwearying in deceit, can you not drop your tricks and your instinctive falsehood, even now that you are in your own country again? (205)

The only "long" quotation in this paragraph is the one at the end. Otherwise, the paragraph consists of the author's summary of relevant facts as well as brief quotations she weaves into her own sentences. She also gives page references, so readers can check her facts or get a sense of their context. Page references have a rhetorical function as well. They say, in effect, "Reader, I know what I'm talking about. If you don't believe me, go check my references."

Use Sound Inductive Reasoning

When you reason inductively, you draw conclusions from facts in the work. Instances of Hamlet's melancholia, for example, lead you to conclude that he is melancholy. When you include inductive reasoning in an essay, you usually reverse this order. You state a claim (the conclusion of your inductive reasoning). Then you present facts that led you to it.

To make your inductive reasoning convincing, follow three rules of evidence. First, give enough facts to support your claims. You need not cite every relevant fact, just enough so readers can see the reasonableness of your claim. Second, report facts that are representative of all the facts, not just isolated, atypical facts (the one and only time that Hamlet is melancholy). Third, account for facts that contradict your thesis. If there are incidents in which Hamlet is not melancholy, explain why these do not nullify your claim that he is melancholy. Often, when you explain away negative examples of your claims, you make your overall argument more subtle and convincing. Hamlet's occasional gaiety, you might argue, does not contradict his melancholia; rather, it is a cover for it, a mask he wears.

Define Key Terms

Learn the meaning of important words in primary sources. Look up words in a good dictionary when you have any doubts about their meaning. Doing so is especially necessary for poetry and earlier authors such as Shakespeare and Chaucer. For definitions of terms, the two most authoritative dictionaries are *The Oxford English Dictionary* (1989); and *Webster's Third New International Dictionary of the English Language* (1966). *The Oxford English Dictionary (OED)* is based on "historical principles"; it describes and gives examples of a word's use over the years. If you want to know what a word meant to Shakespeare or Chaucer, look it up in the *OED*. The *Merriam-Webster's Third International* is a "descriptive" dictionary; it describes how the word is used and spelled today. The college edition of the

Merriam, abridged from the *Third New International,* is adequate for nearly all your needs, as are most hardcover "desk" dictionaries on the market. As of this writing, you can search *The American Heritage Dictionary* (3rd edition, 1996) online at *Bartleby.com.* Also, your library may subscribe to the online version of the *OED.* A Web site that includes *Webster's New World College Dictionary* (4th ed., 1999) and other materials related to languages is yourdictionary.com. For definitions of specialized literary terms, such as *gothic* and *naturalism,* see M. H. Abrams and Geoffrey Harpham's *A Glossary of Literary Terms* (2009).

Organize Evidence According to a Coherent Plan

Evidence consists of everything you offer in support of your claims and thesis. It includes both your reasoning and whatever facts you use to buttress your reasoning. The most important "coherent plan" for presenting evidence is your line of thought, the chain of enthymemes that lead to your thesis. These will vary from topic to topic. You will have to work out a different plan of reasoning for each essay.

Nonetheless, there are several ways of presenting facts from literature that make evidence easy to follow.

1. *Spatial organization* presents the facts as they appear in the work, from beginning to end.

2. *Chronological organization* takes up the facts in the order in which they occur in time. Often, spatial order is the same as chronological but not always. Many works employ devices such as stream of consciousness and flashbacks that make spatial sequence different from chronological. Detective fiction, for example, depends on a gradual revelation of past events. Not until you finish reading a detective novel can you know the chronological order of events. One advantage of either organization is that you give the reader the sense that you are covering all the important details of the work.

3. *Organization by ascending order of importance* moves from the least important facts or claims to the most important. The advantage of this method is that it gives your essay suspense by ushering readers toward a climax. Organizing from the least controversial claims to the most controversial is a variation on this plan.

The paragraph about Odysseus's craftsmanship (page 267) combines two of these plans of organization. The author arranges her facts *chronologically* by starting with the Trojan Horse and ending with the defeat of the suitors. Had she arranged them spatially—as they appear in the text—they would be out of chronological sequence. She also arranges her facts in *ascending order of importance*. She ends with Odysseus's most important stratagem, the defeat of the suitors, and with his most surprising trait, his love of stratagems. This plan provides an orderly review of Odysseus's career, makes her facts easy to follow, and gives her presentation a measure of suspense.

Make Comparisons Complete and Easy to Follow

When you make extended comparisons, organize them so they are easy to follow.

- Cover the *same aspects* of all the things compared. If you talk about metaphor, symbolism, and imagery in one work, you need to talk about these same things in the other work.
- Also, discuss items *in the same order.* If you talk about metaphor, symbolism, and imagery in one work, keep this same order when you discuss the other work: metaphor first, symbolism second, imagery last. The outline for such a comparison would look like this:

Work #1
   Metaphor
   Symbolism
   Imagery

Work #2
   Metaphor
   Symbolism
   Imagery

    For comparisons of more than two things or for long, complex comparisons, another method of organization may be easier for readers to follow:

Metaphor
   Work #1
   Work #2
   Work #3

Symbolism
    Work #1
    Work #2
    Work #3

Imagery
    Work #1
    Work #2
    Work #3

The student essay on the *Odyssey* uses this second plan of comparison:

Claim: Eden and Ogygia are similar.
    Reason #1: Their physical features are similar.
        A. Eden has certain physical features (described).
        B. Ogygia's physical features (described) are almost exactly the same.
    Reason #2: Their inhabitants live comfortable and pain-free lives.
        A. Eden
        B. Ogygia
    Reason #3: The inhabitants have companionship.
        A. Eden
        B. Ogygia
    Reason #4: Both places are free from death.
        A. Eden
        B. Ogygia

There are other ways to organize comparisons. You could, for example, discuss all the similarities together, then all the differences. The general rule is to make the comparison thorough and orderly, so readers can see all the lines of similarity and difference. Doing this usually requires ample revisions of your outlines and drafts. The next chapter, Chapter 10, deals with the revision and editing stages of the writing process. It concludes with two drafts of a comparison essay, and shows how revision can improve the arrangement of extended comparisons.

Checklist for Drafting the Essay

- Plan the rhetorical structure of your essay.

- Make a rough outline of the essay.

- Compose a title that signals the focus of the essay.

- Decide where you will state your thesis.

- Write an introduction that explains the problem(s) you plan to solve.

- Lay out the organization of the body of the essay.

- Write out your key syllogisms. State them so they make logical sense.

- Decide which premises you will support with evidence.

- Make sure your premises follow convincingly from the evidence.

- Define important terms.

- Organize comparisons so they are easy to follow.

- Write a conclusion that announces how the problem is solved.

Works Cited

Abrams, M.H., and Geoffrey Harpham. *A Glossary of Literary Terms.* 9th ed. Boston: Wadsworth Cengage Learning, 2009. Print.

The American Heritage Dictionary. 4th ed. Boston: Houghton Mifflin, 2000. *Bartleby.com.* Web. 25 June 2009.

Gove, Philip Babcock, ed. *Webster's Third New International Dictionary of the English Language.* Unabridged. Springfield: Merriam, 1966. Print.

Simpson, J.A., and E.S.C. Weiner. *Oxford English Dictionary.* 2nd ed. 20 vols. Oxford: Oxford UP, 1989. Print.

Webster's New World College Dictionary. 4th ed. Foster City, CA: IDG Books, 2001. *yourDictionary.com.* Web. 1 June 2009.

10

Revising and Editing

REVISE THROUGHOUT THE WRITING PROCESS

The third stage of the writing process is revision. The word *revision* means "to see again." Revision takes place throughout the writing process. You constantly see your work anew, and act upon that fresh understanding by rewriting. Assume that you will make several drafts of the essay, from scribbled lists to finished product—say, three to five drafts. Give yourself time—a week or so—to write the essay. You may be able to manage an "all-nighter" every now and then, but few people can do so consistently. Work hard for a while, put your essay aside, let the ideas percolate, then come back to the essay fresh.

REVISE FOR THE FINAL DRAFT

Some people could go on revising forever, but most need to move efficiently toward a final draft. The final draft differs from the earlier drafts because readers expect it to conform to "formal" rules that govern a particular format. To help yourself prepare the final draft, think about what the members of your audience expect from it. They want, of course, the qualities of a good argument we have discussed: interesting topic, sound logic, thorough discussion of the works, easy-to-follow organization. But readers want also to feel that your writing is worth reading, that you are competent to talk about your topic, and that you can teach them something. Rhetoricians call this personal quality ethos. *Ethos* is the image that writers project of themselves. You cannot help projecting a "self" when you write. Create, then, a compelling, trustworthy ethos.

The content and organization of the essay are the most important indicators of ethos. By reasoning well and supporting claims with evidence, you make readers feel that you are conscientious and that your essay is intellectually sound. Other aspects of the final draft also help create a persuasive ethos. They are prose style, rules of usage, and physical format (the appearance of the essay). We treat these aspects in this chapter.

WRITE A CLEAR AND READABLE PROSE STYLE

Style is the way writers put words together in units of thought—sentences—and the way they link sentences to make larger units—paragraphs, essays, books. Closely related to style is tone. *Tone* is a writer's attitude toward the material and the readers. You convey tone through style.

Adjust your style and tone to fit the occasion and audience. Sometimes the occasion and audience call for informal and humorous writing, such as for speeches made at parties or essays written for satirical magazines. At other times, they call for gravity and formality, such as for newspaper editorials and letters of application. The occasion and audience for essays about literature almost always require a measure of formality. Assume that your audience is intelligent, literate, and serious. They take the trouble to read your essay because they want to learn. They might welcome some levity, some lightheartedness, but they mostly want you to get down to business and not waste their time. They want to learn from you economically, to get through your essay with pleasure but as effortlessly as possible.

Your style for this audience should meet these needs. Make your style clear, interesting, and readable: vary sentence structure, avoid the passive voice, emphasize active and concrete verbs, eliminate wordiness and unnecessary repetition, use words with precision, and base syntax on the natural rhythms of spoken English. Give your tone seriousness of purpose but avoid stiff formality: Stay away from incomprehensible words and long complex sentences. Because essays about literature involve personal judgment, use "I" to distinguish your ideas from those of others and to stress the individuality of your views. But use "I" sparingly, so you do not give the impression of being subjective and egotistical.

A well-known guide to writing graceful and clear prose is *The Elements of Style* (1918) by William Strunk, Jr., available on the Web at *Bartleby.com.*

HAVE OTHER PEOPLE READ AND RESPOND TO YOUR DRAFT

In one sense, writing is an isolated, individualized task. We have to do it alone. In another sense, however, it can be collaborative. Other people's reactions to your writing can help you to improve. After all, your writing is *for* an audience. So, before you draw up a final draft, you might get someone else to read your essay. Ask them to answer such questions as these: Can you follow my line of thought? Do you agree with my reasoning? Can I support my claims more convincingly? Is my writing clear and fluent? Should I use different strategies of persuasion? Will my audience understand me? You may disagree with the answers you get, but even "wrong" answers can help you see "right" strategies. Your goal is to get fresh perceptions of your essay so you can make your final draft as good as it can be.

EDIT THE FINAL DRAFT

The final draft of your essay is the one you will "publish." Publishing can mean printing the essay in a journal, newspaper, magazine, or book, or sending it to a Web site. It can also mean distributing it yourself to a group of people. For university courses, it means turning in the essay to the professor or to the rest of the class. The "published" draft of the essay should follow a certain format. What should that format be? The format described in the following sections is typical of the writing done in a university setting and is based on the guidelines in the *MLA Handbook for Writers of Research Papers* (7th ed., 2009).

Rules of Usage

Usage refers to the way English is applied in most published writing: in newspapers, magazines, books, advertisements, brochures, financial reports, and scholarly journals. Although some rules of usage are arbitrary and seem to serve no purpose other than convention, most serve important purposes. First, they aid clarity. Punctuation, for example, represents parts of the sentence—pauses and inflections—that words do not. Marks of punctuation can be as important as the words. Misplace a comma, and you can change the meaning of a sentence. A hilarious treatment of punctuation gone astray is Lynne Truss's *Eats, Shoots & Leaves: The Zero Tolerance Approach to Punctuation* (2004). Second, rules of usage help communicate your ethos. They are a form of etiquette; educated people are expected to follow them. By doing so, you communicate an image of competence and respect for your readers.

If you are unfamiliar with basic rules of usage, they are not difficult to learn. Study and practice using them, and you will learn them quickly. Get a handbook of usage, such as *Hodge's Harbrace Handbook* (9th ed., 2009), and refer to it when you write. An online resource is *Guide to Grammar and Writing*.

Although all rules of usage are important for your writing, in this book we concentrate on rules common to essays about literature. These include rules that govern documentary procedure, which we discuss in Chapter 11, as well as those that apply to such things as quotations, punctuation, capitalization, underlining, and the physical format of papers. In the following sections, we describe basic rules of usage. For a more thorough treatment of such rules, see the *MLA Handbook for Writers of Research Papers* (2009). See, also, the sample essays in Chapters 8, 11, 13, and at the end of this chapter for examples of how these rules are used in practice.

Citations of Sources

Give credit for the sources you draw upon. These include primary sources (the works of literature you discuss) and secondary sources (works by critics and historians that bear upon the primary sources). You give credit in two ways: by means of **parenthetical citations** within your text and a **Works Cited list** located at the end of the essay. Guidelines for both are in Chapter 11. The sample essays throughout the book, including the one at the end of this chapter, illustrate both kinds of citation.

Quotations

Quotations serve two key purposes in essays about literature: They help illustrate and support claims, and they reproduce the language of the source.

1. **Identify quotations in your text.**
   a. For primary sources, identify the author, the work, and the context of quotations.

   Incomplete Information

   Example: The woman tells her lover that the world "isn't ours anymore."

   Complete Information

   Example: Near the climax of the lovers' conversation in Hemingway's "Hills Like White Elephants," the woman tells the man that the world "isn't ours anymore."

   Readers need to know *where* in the text quotations occur. Otherwise, the quotation could seem meaningless.

   b. Identify quotations from secondary sources by giving the author's name or claim to authority.

   Name Missing

   Example: "A fully articulated pastoral idea of America did not emerge until the end of the eighteenth century."

   Name Included

   Example: Leo Marx claims that a "fully articulated pastoral idea of America did not emerge until the end of the eighteenth century."

   Claim to Authority Included (Instead of Name)

   Example: A prominent American critic says that a "fully articulated pastoral idea of America did not emerge until the end of the eighteenth century."

   There are several reasons for introducing quotations: First, giving the critic's name or claim to authority clearly distinguishes your ideas from the other writer's. Quotation marks can of course help make this distinction, but introducing the quote by author makes the distinction emphatic. Second, when readers see quotation marks, they are naturally curious about who said the quoted passage. As they read your essay, they want also to note the different approaches of the critics you cite. Third, by giving the author's name, you distinguish between secondary and primary sources, a distinction that may not be clear from the quotation alone. Finally, it is a matter of courtesy to give credit in your text to the words and ideas of other people. You are, in a way, thanking them for their help.

2. **Introduce quotations with your words and with correct punctuation.**

Although quotation marks provide visual evidence of a quotation, you need to indicate who speaks and, if relevant, the nature and context of the speech. You do this in your own words and with proper punctuation.

a. When you introduce a quotation with a complete sentence, end the sentence with a colon.

> *Example:* The sheriff has nothing but scorn for Mrs. Peters and
>
> Mrs. Hale's interest in the "trifles" of women's work: "Well, can
>
> you beat the women! Held for murder and worrying about her
>
> preserves."

b. When you introduce a quotation with an incomplete sentence, end the phrase with a comma. Such phrases are usually "tags" that indicate who speaks: "he says," "she states," "they shout out," etc.

> *Example:* The monster tells Victor, "I was benevolent and good; misery
>
> made me a fiend."
>
> *Example:* As Sterrenburg states, "The Monster proves a very philosophi-
>
> cal rebel."

If you put the tag inside the quotation, separate it from the quotation with commas.

> *Example:* "I am malicious," he says, "because I am miserable."

c. When you blend quotations into your own sentences, so that the quotations are part of the grammatical structure of your sentences, you don't need to separate the quotation from your words with commas or colons.

Example: She realizes that "he has come home to die."

Example:

His physical weakness

> hurt my heart the way he lay
>
> And rolled his old head on that sharp-edged chair-back.

Note that even though the second example is an indented quotation, it is nonetheless a grammatical part of the author's sentence and thus needs no comma or colon.

3. **Integrate quotations into your own sentences.**

Example: Because of this increasing darkness, Brown cannot be quite sure of what he does or hears. The devil's walking stick, for example, seems to turn into a snake, but this may be "an ocular deception, assisted by the uncertain light" (76). He thinks he hears the voices of Deacon Gookin and the minister, but "owing doubtless to the depth of the gloom of that particular spot, neither the travellers nor their steeds were visible."

Once you introduce your source, you may want to integrate short quotations—words or phrases—into your own sentences, as in the above example. The quotations become part of your own thoughts rather than thoughts separate from yours. This technique allows you to summarize a source concisely and yet retain some of the language and authenticity of the source. If you use this method, you should obey several rules.

a. As much as possible, make the tenses in the quotation correspond to the tenses of your sentences.

Awkward

Example: While the legislators cringe at the sudden darkness, "all eyes were turned to Abraham Davenport." [*Cringe* is present tense; *turned* is past tense.]

Better

Example: While the legislators cringe at the sudden darkness, "all eyes [turn] to Abraham Davenport."

Example: While the legislators cringe at the sudden darkness, "all eyes" turn to Abraham Davenport.

b. Be sure that sentences are complete.

Incomplete

Example: Yeats asks if "before the indifferent beak." [Incomplete sentence; makes no sense.]

Complete

Example: Yeats asks if Leda "put on [the swan's] knowledge" before his "indifferent beak could let her drop."

c. Clarify pronouns that have no clear antecedents.

Unclear

Example: Captain Wentworth says, "It had been my doing—solely mine. She would not have been obstinate if I had not been weak." [The antecedent of "she" is unclear.]

Clear

Example: Captain Wentworth says, "It had been my doing—solely mine. [Louisa] would not have been obstinate if I had not been weak."

d. Be sure that subject and verb agree.

Disagreement

Example: Wilfred Owen says that the only prayer said for those who die in battle is war's noise, which "patter out their hasty orisons." [Subject: *noise*; verb: *patter*. The subject is singular, the verb plural.]

Agreement

Example: Wilfred Owen says that the only prayer said for those who die in battle is the "rapid rattle" of guns, which "patter out their hasty orisons." [Subject: guns; verb: patter. Both subject and verb are now plural.]

When you integrate a quotation into your sentence, make it a grammatical part of the sentence. The entire sentence, including the quotation, must conform to the standard rules of usage. See item 5 below for methods of altering (interpolating) quotations.

4. **Quote accurately.** Copy exactly what the author has written.

5. **Make editorial changes in quotations clearly and correctly.** You may legitimately change the quotation in two ways:
   a. By using *ellipses*. An ellipsis (three spaced periods) indicates omitted material—a few words, a sentence, or several sentences. Writers often leave out sections of quotations for the sake of brevity or clarity. To indicate omitted material in the middle of a sentence, use three periods. Put spaces before each period and after the last one. Here, for example, is a quoted sentence with omitted material *within* the sentence.

   Example: As one critic says, "Oedipus is guilty for two reasons: because of the deeds he actually committed . . . and because of his desire to commit them."

   To indicate omitted material from the *end* of a sentence, follow this sequence: space after the last word, then three spaced periods, then the end punctuation mark (period, question mark, exclamation point), and finally the quotation mark.

   Example: In certain moods, Wordsworth confessed, he "was often unable to believe that material things can live for-ever . . . ."

   If your *parenthetical reference* comes at the end of a quotation with omitted material, put a space after the last word, then the three spaced periods, then the quotation mark, then the parenthetical reference, then the end punctuation mark.

   Example: In certain moods, Wordsworth confessed, he "was often unable to believe that material things can live for-ever . . ." (175).

   You can also use ellipses to indicate the omission of whole sentences, a paragraph, or several paragraphs. The following example omits part of a long paragraph.

   Example: Ruskin gives two reasons for his belief that to demand perfection of art is to misunderstand it: "The first is that no great man ever stops working till he has reached his point of failure. . . . The second reason is

that imperfection is in some sort essential to all that we know of life."

In this example the period goes immediately after the final word of the sentence ("failure"), then a space, then the three spaced periods.

There is no need to place ellipses at the *beginning* of quotations:

Example: Even the commonest people, the duke says, would elicit from

her "the approving speech,/Or blush, at least."

b. By using *brackets*. Brackets indicate editorial changes that *you*, not the author, make to clarify the quotation or to make it fit the grammatical structure of your sentence. Use brackets for *your* changes, not parentheses. Otherwise, your reader will construe them as part of the original quote.

Unclear

Example: Alceste says that "sins which cause the blood to freeze/Look

innocent beside (Célimène's) treacheries."

Clear

Example: Alceste says that "sins which cause the blood to freeze/Look

innocent beside [Célimène's] treacheries."

Example: Flaubert says that "she [has] an excess of energy."

6. **Punctuate quotations correctly.**
   a. Use *double quotation* marks (" ") for quotations. For quotations within quotations, use double quotation marks for the main quotation and single quotation marks (the apostrophe mark) for the inner quote.

   Example: After his interview with Hester, Dimmesdale sinks into self-

   doubt: "'Have I then sold myself,' thought the minister, 'to the fiend

   whom, if men say true, this yellow-starched and velveted old hag has

   chosen for her prince and master!'"

   b. Put *periods* and *commas* that directly follow quotations inside quotation marks.

After performing her "duties to God," as she called them, she was ready for her "duty to people."

c. Put *colons* and *semicolons* outside of quotation marks, unless they are part of the original text being quoted.

Example: She had the "exquisite pleasure of art"; her husband had only envy and hatred.

d. Put *other marks of punctuation* (question marks, dashes, exclamation points) inside quotation marks when they are part of the quoted material, outside when they are not.

Example: One critic asked, "Could the Pearl Poet really be the author of *Sir Gawain and the Green Knight?*"

Example: But can it be, as one critic claims, that "the Pearl Poet really [is] the author of *Sir Gawain and the Green Knight*"?

e. *When quoting one line of poetry or less,* you can make the quotation part of your sentence. Use a slash mark, with a space before and after it, to indicate line divisions.

Example: Hopkins describes God's grandeur as gathering "to a greatness, like the ooze of oil/crushed" (3–4).

7. **Indent long quotations from poems.** Quotations of poetry are "long" if they are more than three lines. Introductions to indented material are often complete sentences. End such introductions with a *colon.* Indent the quotation one inch from the left margin. Do not enclose indented quotations with quotation marks or divide lines with slash marks.

Example: The duke is chagrined that his own name and presence were not the sole sources of her joy:

> She had
> A heart—how shall I say?—too soon made glad,
> Too easily impressed; she liked whate'er
> She looked on, and her looks went everywhere.

> Sir, 'twas all one! My favour at her breast,
>
> The dropping of the daylight in the West,
>
> The bough of cherries some officious fool
>
> Broke in the orchard for her, the white mule
>
> She rode with round the terrace—all and each
>
> Would draw from her alike the approving speech,
>
> Or blush, at least.

a. *As in the first line of this example,* position the words of an indented poem exactly where they appear in the line.

b. Some people prefer to indent even a short selection from poems in order to avoid using slash marks.

Example:

Hopkins describes God's grandeur as gathering

> to a greatness, like the ooze of oil

Crushed.

c. *If a line of poetry extends past the right margin,* continue it on the next line. Indent the continued line 1/4 inch.

Example:

> They take a serpentine course, their arms flash in the sun—
>
> hark to the musical clank,

This example is from Whitman's "Cavalry Crossing a Ford" (printed in Chapter 2). Many of his long lines turn over to a second line.

8. **Indent long quotations from prose.** A long quotation of prose is more than four lines. As with indented quotations from poetry, your introduction to the indented material is likely to be a complete sentence. If so, end it with a colon. Indent the quotation one inch from the left margin. Do not enclose indented quotations with quotation marks. If you are quoting a whole paragraph, do not indent the first line. Instead, place it flush to the left margin of the quotation.

Example: Hugh Kenner sums up his discussion of *Waiting for Godot* with this suggestion about its meaning:

> So. They are waiting. And they will wait for the duration of the second act as well. We have all waited, perhaps not by a tree

at evening or on a country road, but waited. The details are immaterial.

If you quote more than one paragraph, indent the first line of each as you normally would.

> *Example:* Kenner completes his suggestions about the play's meaning with these thoughts:
>
>> They are waiting "for Godot." Each of us has had his Godot, if only someone from whom, for several days, we have expected a letter.
>>
>> The substance of the play, in short, is as common a human experience as you can find. This seems hardly worth saying, except that it is so seldom said. To read critics, or to listen to discussion, we might well suppose that the substance of the play was some elusive idea or other, and not a very well expressed idea since there is so much disagreement about what it is.

9. **Punctuate quotations from drama correctly.** Indent exchanges between two or more characters. Place the quotation one inch from the left margin. Print the first speaker's name in capital letters, followed by a period, then by a space, and then by the speech. Indent subsequent lines of the speech an additional 1/4 inch. Follow this pattern throughout the quoted passage.

> *Example:* Almost from the beginning of *Waiting for Godot*, Vladimir and Estragon make constant references to events in the Bible:
>
>> VLADIMIR. Two thieves, crucified at the same time as our Saviour. One—
>>
>> ESTRAGON. Our what?
>>
>> VLADIMIR. Our Saviour. Two thieves. One is supposed to have been saved and the other . . . (*he searches for the contrary of saved*) . . . damned.

Other Rules of Usage Related to Essays about Literature

Essays about literature obey the same rules of usage as other essays. Several rules deserve special mention.

1. **Tense.** Describe fictional events, whether in drama, poetry, or prose fiction, in the present tense. For examples of this practice, see the student essays in this and other chapters. The concept behind this convention is that, even though actions in most works of fiction are narrated in the past tense, they are—for us, as readers—always present, always taking place now.

2. **Authors' names.** When you mention an author the first time, use the full name (Charles Dickens). For subsequent references, use the last name (Dickens).

3. **Words used as words.** Italicize words used as words or called attention to as words.

    Example: In England the word *honor* is spelled with a *u: honour.*

4. **Titles**
    a. Capitalize the first letter of the title, plus the first letter of all words except articles, short prepositions, conjunctions, and the preposition *to* in infinitives ("First to Go").

    Example: "How I Won the World but Lost My Soul to the Devil's Wiles"

    Capitalize the first letter after a colon. In the following example, the colon indicates the subtitle of the book.

    Example: Exile's Return: A Narrative of Ideas

    b. Use quotation marks for titles of works published within larger works. Examples are short stories; short poems; songs; chapter titles; articles in journals, magazines, and newspapers; and unpublished works such as dissertations and master's theses.

    Example: "A Good Man Is Hard to Find"

    c. Italicize the titles of works published independently, such as books, plays, long poems published as books, periodicals, pamphlets, novels, movies, compact discs, works of art, works of music, and radio and television programs. An exception is sacred writings such as the Bible, books of the Bible (Genesis, Isaiah, Proverbs, Luke), the Koran, and the Talmud.

    When the title of a poem is the same as the first line of the poem, print the first line exactly as it is in the text.

Example: Emily Dickinson's poem "I like to see it lap the Miles—" is a riddle for a train.

d. Do not italicize or put in quotation marks the titles of your own essays.

e. Many instructors prefer that your essay titles include full names of authors and works.

Incomplete

Example: The Four Stages of Knowledge in *Huck Finn*

Complete

Example: The Four Stages of Knowledge in Mark Twain's *The Adventures of Huckleberry Finn*

f. Unless your instructor objects, in the text of your essay you may use shortened titles for works you frequently cite: "Prufrock" for "The Love Song of J. Alfred Prufrock" or *Huck Finn* for *The Adventures of Huckleberry Finn*.

5. **Foreign language terms**
   a. Italicize foreign words used in an English text, such as *sans doute, et tu Brute, amor vincit omnia.*

   Example: She objected to her son-in-law's behavior because it was not *comme il faut.*

   Reproduce all marks and accents as they appear in the original language: *étude, à propos, même, übermensch, año, leçon.*

   b. Some foreign words, like *cliché, laissez-faire,* and *genre,* have been naturalized—that is, incorporated into English usage—and need not be italicized. Use your dictionary to determine whether the word or phrase needs italicizing. Foreign words in dictionaries are either italicized or placed at the back of the book in a separate section.

   Example: Adam Smith advocated a laissez-faire economic policy.

   c. Do not italicize quotations that are entirely in another language.

   Example: Louis XIV once said, "L'état, c'est moi."

PHYSICAL FORMAT

As with rules of usage, the appearance of your essay also affects your argument. Readers want an essay that is easy to read, pleasant to hold, and attractive to view. The more care you take with the appearance of the essay, the more competent your readers will think you are. Although your instructor may have specific preferences, the following are standard guidelines.

1. **Typewritten and handwritten essays.** Most instructors prefer that you print all your essays. Some may allow you to handwrite college essays. Before you do, however, check with your instructor. Whether you handwrite, type, or print your essay, use only one side of each sheet of paper. For *handwritten* essays, use black or blue ink. (Pencil smears and rubs off). Use lined paper. Write on every other line. Write legibly.

2. **Paper.** Use standard-size paper (8½ by 11 inches or as close to this size as possible), not legal-pad size or notepad size. Use a sturdy weight of paper. Avoid paper that has been ripped out of a spiral-bound notebook.

3. **Spacing.** Double-space everything, including indented quotations and works cited entries.

4. **Pagination.** Number *all* pages, beginning with the first page. Number pages consecutively, including pages for endnotes and Works Cited. Put the page numbers in the upper right-hand corner of each page, 1/2 inch from the top. To avoid having pages misplaced, put your last name before each page number, with a space between the two. Example:

Caraway 16

5. **Margins.** For printed essays, leave one-inch margins at the top, bottom, and sides. This gives the page a "frame" and a place for corrections and comments. For handwritten essays, leave margins at the top, bottom, and left side.

6. **First page.** One inch from the top of the first page, flush with the left margin, put your name, the instructor's name, the course title, and the date, each on a separate line. Double-space between the lines. After the last line (the date), double-space again and center your title. If your title has more than one

line, double-space between lines. Double-space between the title and the first line of text. Indent the first line and the first line of subsequent paragraphs 1/2 inch from the left margin. Do not underline your own title or put it in quotation marks.

Title pages for college essays—even research essays—are unnecessary. But if your instructor expects a title page, check with him or her for its content and form. For examples of first pages, see the sample essay at the end of this chapter and those in the last chapter of this book.

7. **Corrections.** For printed versions of your essays, make corrections on the computer and print the corrected page or pages. If your corrections are few and far between, your instructor may allow you to handwrite them in. For handwritten essays, draw a horizontal line through unwanted words and write the correct words just *above* the line. Separate run-together words with vertical lines (for example, made/a/mistake). To delete words, phrases, and clauses, draw a single horizontal line through them. Add words, phrases, and clauses by writing them in above the line. Use a caret (∧) below the line to show where inserted material should go.

8. **Putting the essay pages together.** Avoid covers or binders. Join the pages of your essay with a paperclip, unless your instructor specifies some other method.

9. **Copies.** Make a photocopy of your essay or backup a copy on a disc. If your instructor loses your essay, you can immediately present him or her with a copy. If your instructor keeps your essay indefinitely, you will have a copy for your files.

10. **To fold or not to fold.** Leave your essay unfolded unless your instructor specifies otherwise.

SAMPLE ESSAY IN TWO DRAFTS

The following student essay gives a brief idea of how the revising process works. Nearly all writers, no matter how experienced, go through several drafts of an essay before they produce the final draft. Printed here are an early draft of the essay and, after considerable revision, a final draft. Robert Frost's poem, "The Death of the Hired Man," first appeared in *North of Boston* in 1914. The full text of the poem is printed in the Appendix.

Early Draft

Jennifer Hargrove

Professor Bell

English 105–13

14 April 20--

A Comparison of Mary and Warren in Robert Frost's

"The Death of the Hired Man"

Robert Frost in "The Death of the Hired Man" (1914)
presents two different views of how to respond to human need.
Into the home of Mary and Warren comes the derelict hired hand,
Silas. Mary and Warren disagree over how to treat him.

Mary tells Warren to "Be kind" (line 7) to Silas. Warren,
however, is upset with Silas for having run out on him the year
before, when he needed him most. "There's no depending on
[him]," Warren says (17). Mary shushes Warren so Silas will not
hear him, but Warren does not care if Silas hears or not: "I want
him to: he'll have to soon or late" (32).

In my opinion, Mary understands Silas much better than
Warren. She is also much more sympathetic than Warren. Her
sympathy is like that extended to all people by the Virgin Mary.
This may be why Frost chose Mary's name, to underscore this
quality. She reminds Warren, for example, of Silas's longstanding
argument with the college student Harold Wilson. Warren
agrees that Silas is proud of his one accomplishment, building a
load of hay:

> He bundles every forkful in its place,
> And tags and numbers it for future reference,
> So he can find and easily dislodge it
> In the unloading. (89–92)

Hargrove 2

Mary then tells Warren that Silas has come home to die: "You needn't be afraid he'll leave you this time" (112).

One of the things that most upsets Warren is that Silas comes to them rather than going to Silas's brother for help:

> Why didn't he go there? His brother's rich
> A somebody—director in the bank. (128–129)

But Mary explains that probably there is some misunderstanding between Silas and his brother. Also, she says that Silas is "just the kind that kinsfolk can't abide" (141). He may be "worthless," she argues, but he "won't be made ashamed/To please his brother" (144–145).

The climax of the poem comes when Warren seems to agree reluctantly with Mary that Silas should stay. She tells him to go inside and check on him. He quietly returns and catches up her hand. When she asks him what happened, he replies, simply, "Dead."

In sum, Warren has many qualities that Mary does not have. He is quick to blame, cynical, and even a little stingy. But most of all he lacks the sympathy, the kindness, and the understanding that Mary has. She seems also to be more imaginative than he. Finally, though, her kindness wins him over to her side. Even though Silas dies, Warren seems ready to do what Mary wants.

Comments on the Early Draft

This draft was one of several the author wrote before she produced the final draft. You can see in the first few paragraphs that she is moving toward a concept of how Mary and Warren are different.

In the final paragraph she even states some specific ways in which they are different. You can see, also, how the details and quotations she gives between the beginning and end of the essay *might* be relevant to her claims about difference. But notice how almost all the paragraphs in the body of the paper lack topic ideas (topic sentences). Notice also how she never connects any of the poem's details to specific claims. As a result, although the paper begins and ends promisingly, it is more like a summary of the poem than an argument in support of a thesis.

To make the paper better, the author needs to do several things. In the introduction, she needs to clarify and emphasize her thesis. If she put the thesis at the end of the introduction rather than at the beginning, she could better show how all the sentences in the introduction relate to the thesis. In the body of the paper, she needs to state her claims about how Mary and Warren are different and support each with evidence from the text. Each claim could be the topic sentence of a paragraph, followed by supporting evidence. In the conclusion, she needs to restate her thesis, summarize her reasoning, and offer some generalizing idea that pulls the entire essay together.

Final Draft

Hargrove 1

Jennifer Hargrove

Professor Bell

English 105–13

14 April 20--

A Comparison of Mary and Warren in Robert Frost's

"The Death of the Hired Man"

When Silas, the unreliable hired hand, returns to the farm owned by Mary and Warren in Robert Frost's "The Death of the Hired Man" (1914), Mary and Warren immediately disagree about what to do with him. Warren wants to send him packing.

Mary wants to keep him on and care for him. In recounting

their disagreement about how to treat Silas, the poem reveals

fundamental differences between them.

The most obvious difference is that Mary is compassionate

and Warren is not. The poem continually reveals Mary's pity for the

sick and troubled Silas. She tells Warren that she discovered him

> Huddled against the barn-door fast asleep,
> A miserable sight, and frightening, too—.
> (lines 35–36)

His physical weakness

> hurt my heart the way he lay
> And rolled his old head on that sharp-edged chair-
> back. (147–48)

She says that his prospects are bleak:

> Poor Silas, so concerned for other folk,
> And nothing to look backward to with pride, And
> nothing to look forward to with hope.
> So now and never any different. (99–102)

Mary's pity leads her to certain moral conclusions. She feels

that they should not just take Silas in, but should try to protect his

pride as well. "Be kind," she tells Warren (7). Warren, in contrast,

resists hints that he has not done right by Silas. Mary's gentle

request to be kind elicits an almost angry response: "When was I

ever anything but kind to him?" (11). He is impatient with Silas's

shortcomings and unforgivingly judgmental:

> "I told him so last haying, didn't I?
> 'If he left then,' I said, 'that ended it.'" (13–14)

Hargrove 3

Not caring if Silas hears, he loudly expresses his bitterness (32).
He dismisses Silas's plans to "ditch the meadow" as the foolish
promises of an insincere old man (44–46).

Underlying their disagreement about how to treat Silas
are more fundamental differences. One is that they value people
differently. Warren values people for their usefulness and wants
to cast them off when they are no longer useful:

> What good is he [Silas]? Who else will harbor him
> At his age for the little he can do?
> What help he is there's no depending on. (15–17)

Even one of Warren's few positive comments about Silas concerns
a useful skill, Silas's ability to load hay: "Silas does that well" (92).
Warren believes, then, that one should be kind to people only if
they are useful.

Mary's compassion for Silas reveals a different view of
people. She sees them as good in themselves. She admits that Silas
may be "worthless" (145) as a hired hand:

> You'll be surprised at him—how much he's broken.
> His working days are done; I'm sure of it. (152–53)

But she insists that their farm is his "home," and it is their
responsibility to receive him. Warren's definition of home is in
keeping with his attitude toward people:

> "Home is the place where, when you have to
>   go there,
> They have to take you in." (118–19)

At "home," in other words, people take care of you out of duty, not love. Mary's counter definition is in keeping with her belief that people are valuable in themselves:

> I should have called it
> Something you somehow haven't to deserve.
> (119–20)

People at home give you tenderness no matter what you've done.

Another difference between them is that Mary is imaginative and Warren is not. Frost suggests this quality in the opening line of the poem: "Mary sat musing on the lamp-flame at the table." The word *muse* means "to ponder or meditate," "to consider reflectively." The word is associated with the Muses of Greek mythology, "each of whom presided over a different art or science." Because of this association, the noun *muse* means "the spirit or power regarded as inspiring and watching over poets, musicians, and artists; a source of inspiration" (*American Heritage Dictionary*). Frost's use of the term presents Mary as something of a poet. Her imagination allows her to "understand" Silas. She guesses why he says he wants to ditch the meadow, even though he probably knows he cannot:

> Surely you wouldn't grudge the poor old man
> Some humble way to save his self-respect. (49–50)

She recognizes why Silas remains troubled by his arguments with the college boy Harold Wilson:

> I sympathize. I know just how it feels
> To think of the right thing to say too late. (75–76)

She realizes that "he has come home to die" (111). Warren,

in contrast, lacks the imagination to see past his own practical

needs. This limited vision causes him to be unsympathetic to

people who hinder them. When Warren asks why Silas's brother

(a "somebody—director in the bank," [129]) cannot take care

of Silas, Mary has to tell him that the banker brother may not

want to take Silas in. When Warren wonders why, Mary uses her

imagination to guess what the trouble may be:

> He don't know why he isn't quite as good
> As anyone. He won't be made ashamed
> To please his brother, worthless though he is.
> (143–45)

Their different imaginative capacities lead them to different

moral conclusions. Warren wants to get as much as he gives.

Mary's ability to put herself in the place of troubled people leads

her to want to help them.

A final difference between them is that Mary is allied to

nature and Warren is not. Frost connects Mary to nature twice.

Just before Mary and Warren exchange definitions of *home*, Frost

describes nature in metaphoric terms:

> Part of a moon was falling down the west,
> Dragging the whole sky with it to the hills.
> Its light poured softly in her lap. (103–05)

Mary's sympathetic response to this fanciful and beautiful quality

in nature fortifies her compassionate impulses:

> She saw
> And spread her apron to it. She put out her hand
> Among the harp-like morning-glory strings,

Hargrove 6

Taut with the dew from the garden bed eaves,
As if she played unheard the tenderness
That wrought on him beside her in the night.
(105–10)

At the end, Mary sends Warren to check on Silas and again urges

him to be kind. While she waits, she says, she will

see if that small sailing cloud
Will hit or miss the moon. (160–61)

Frost blends her in with nature: The cloud

hit the moon.
Then there were three there, making a dim row,
The moon, the little silver cloud, and she. (161–63)

Mary's sympathy with nature, like her view of people and her

imagination, also leads to moral conclusions:

Of course he's nothing to us, any more
Than was the hound that came a stranger to us
Out of the woods, worn out upon the trail. (115–17)

They should care for Silas for the same reason they cared for the

stray dog: Both are living creatures. Frost does not say anything

about Warren's attitude toward nature, but Warren's not

responding suggests that he lacks Mary's poetic love for nature.

He is a farmer who has reduced nature to its economic value, just

as he has done with people.

We might wonder why, if Warren and Mary are so

different, they ever got married. But as it turns out, Warren is

Hargrove 7

not so different from Mary as he seems. Who knows, he may have married Mary just for her imaginative and compassionate qualities. By the end of their conversation he comes around to her view. He is now sympathetic to Silas and takes his side against the status-minded brother: "*I* can't think Si ever hurt anyone" (146). He even asserts that maybe Silas's working days are not over after all (154). When he brings news of Silas's death, he does so as Mary would have done, with solemnity and tenderness.

Works Cited

The American Heritage Dictionary of the English Language. New College Edition. New York: Houghton, 1981. Print.

Frost, Robert. "The Death of the Hired Man." *North of Boston*. New York: Henry Holt, 1914. 14–23. Print.

Comments on the Final Draft

The final draft is much better than the early draft. The author opens with just enough information to give readers their bearings and get quickly to her thesis. In the body of the paper, each of the paragraphs has an unmistakable topic sentence. Each of the topic ideas is supported with reasoning and facts from the poem. The last paragraph closes the essay with a summary of the differences between Mary and Warren and an explanation of how, at the end of the poem, they achieve harmony.

Notice how the final draft is more complex in its interpretation of the poem than the early draft. The rewriting process often brings about this enhancement. Good argumentative essays have a necessary structure: thesis clearly stated, claims supporting the thesis, evidence supporting claims, conclusion tying everything together. If there is a problem with an essay's structure—as there was in the early draft of this essay—it usually reflects problems with reasoning and organization. Most writers struggle just to get ideas on the page. Their early drafts typically have gaps and inconsistencies. But as writers rethink and rewrite, they force themselves to pay attention to the necessary structures of the essay. By doing so, they make their ideas, reasoning, and organization better.

Checklist for Revising and Editing

- Regard your final draft as a "publication" that requires the same care and orderliness as real publications.
- Write clear and readable prose.
- Follow helpful and expected rules of usage for
  - Quotations
  - Tense
  - Names
  - Underlinings
  - Words used as words
  - Titles
  - Foreign language terms.
- Format your paper neatly and correctly.

Works Cited

Darling, Charles. *Guide to Grammar and Writing*. Capital Community College Foundation. 2004. Web. 6 June 2009.

Glenn, Cheryl, and Lortetta Gray. *Hodges' Harbrace Handbook*, 17th ed. Boston: Cengage, 2009. Print.

MLA Handbook for Writers of Research Papers, 7th ed. New York: Modern Language Association of America, 2009. Print.

Strunk, William, Jr. *The Elements of Style*. Ithaca, NY: W. P. Humphrey, 1918. *Bartleby.com*. 1999. Web. 19 June 2009.

Truss, Lynne. *Eats, Shoots & Leaves: The Zero Tolerance Approach to Punctuation*. New York: Gotham, 2004. Print.

11

Documentation
and Research

Documentation, or "giving credit," means identifying the sources you consult when you prepare your essays. Two kinds of sources are relevant to writing about literature: primary sources and secondary sources.

PRIMARY SOURCES

The *MLA Handbook for Writers of Research Papers* (2009) defines *primary research* as "the study of a subject through firsthand investigation." *Primary sources* include such things as "statistical data, historical documents, and works of literature" (3). For all practical purposes, the primary sources for undergraduate research essays will be the works of literature themselves. If your essay is about *Hamlet*, then *Hamlet* is your primary source. If you are writing about all of Shakespeare's sonnets, then all of these comprise your primary source. Primary sources are crucial for essays about literature. After all, they are what your essays are about, what you want to interpret. Your most important facts, the ones that support your claims, will come from primary sources.

SECONDARY SOURCES

Facts. The *MLA Handbook* defines *secondary research* as "the examination of studies that other researchers have made of a subject." Examples of *secondary sources* are "articles and books about political issues, historical events, scientific debates, or literary works" (3). For many of your essays, primary sources are the only ones you will need. But if you want to include facts from outside the work or commentary from people outside the work, then you need to use secondary sources. Facts from secondary sources include such things as information about the author's life, the period in which the author lived, the author's philosophy, literary history, other authors, the original audience, the work's influence, and similarities to other works. Secondary sources are valuable for what they teach us about the work. They give information that helps us form our own opinions. When we study Hawthorne's fiction, our perception of his themes sharpens when we learn that he was ashamed of his Puritan ancestors' dire deeds. When we learn that Jane Austen used an actual calendar to plot the events of *Pride and Prejudice,* we appreciate the care with which she crafted her fiction. When we read critics who compare Shakespeare's sources to his plays, we see his genius for deepening characterization and philosophical themes.

Employ secondary sources, then, to learn as much as you can about a work. Use reliable secondary sources—accurate histories and biographies. When you include facts from secondary sources, cite them and your sources for them. Keep in mind, though, that secondary sources must be backed up by facts from primary sources. When you quote or summarize critics, make it a practice to buttress their claims with your own analysis of the works themselves.

Testimony. In addition to facts, secondary sources also contain *testimony,* interpretation by critics. You can find testimony in such places as lectures, television programs, comments by teachers, introductions to individual works, head notes in anthologies, opinion columns on Web sites, articles in professional journals, chapters in books, and book-length studies.

Although testimony is no substitute for your own skillful argumentation, it can add to the persuasive power of your essays. If you show that certain literary critics agree with your interpretation, readers may more readily accept your claims. Furthermore, testimony indicates that your argument is part of an ongoing debate about the work. Testimony signals that you are aware of the debate and, therefore, of the different solutions already proposed to your problem. By explaining other solutions, you can highlight the one that seems most reasonable or offer new solutions of your own.

Use testimony, then, as a complement to your reasoning and facts. If critics make especially good points or give persuasive analyses, summarize their ideas and include apt or telling quotations from their writings. Think of critics as witnesses on your behalf or points of departure for your own ideas.

RESEARCH PAPERS AND THE USE OF SECONDARY SOURCES

Research paper as interpretation. Because most people associate the use of secondary sources with "research" and "research papers," it is appropriate here to address just what research papers are. Although research papers about literature sometimes deliver information for its own sake, they usually are interpretive. They use information to develop interpretations of one or more works of literature. The writer searches through secondary sources to find facts and opinions that lead to an interpretation. Some research papers begin with summaries of different interpretations before settling on one. Others use only a few secondary sources, either to support and illustrate the author's own ideas or as springboards for alternative interpretations. The sample essay on E. A. Robinson's "Richard Cory" in Chapter 13, for example, takes issue with one critic's opinion in order to present another view.

Research paper as an essay. Interpretive research papers are essays. Here, the terms *research paper* and *research essay* are synonymous. Like all essays, research essays present opinions about a subject. They synthesize *your* discoveries about a topic and *your* evaluation of those discoveries. The reader should hear *your* voice speaking throughout the paper and should be constantly aware of *your* intelligence and consciousness. Research essays are not mere anthologies of facts or other people's ideas. They have the same qualities of all essays: a unifying idea expressed directly and emphatically in a thesis, an introduction and a conclusion, and paragraphs that relate to the essay's thesis and that follow a logical plan. The sample essay at the end of this chapter exemplifies these traits.

HOW TO FIND INFORMATION
AND OPINIONS ABOUT LITERATURE

How do you find information and opinion about literature? Where do you start? In the next four sections, we present a plan for learning about and gaining access to secondary sources. Since most secondary sources are located in libraries, we base this plan on three major places typical of university libraries: the stacks, the reference area, and the periodicals area. We conclude with a fourth "place," one that exists outside libraries, the Internet.

I. Library Catalogs and Stacks

Your research needs will vary from writing project to writing project. Some projects will require minimal research, others more elaborate research. Let's say, however, that you want to write an essay about one work, "Porphyria's Lover," a well-known poem by Robert Browning. Your instructor asks only that you use the primary source (the poem), but you want to read some secondary sources to get yourself thinking about the poem. Go to the *online catalog* of your college library, find where the author's works are located in the *stacks*—the shelves where books are stored—and browse among the books in that section. Most college libraries have many books about well-known authors. For Browning, choose several books. Look up "Porphyria's Lover" in the indexes, and read what each book has to say about the work. This should not take long, a few minutes per book.

By doing such exploratory reading, you familiarize yourself with critics' ideas about the work. Sometimes, no matter how carefully you read a work, you may be at a loss for what it means. Doing introductory reading in secondary sources can clue you in to issues critics have been debating about the work. In your own writing, you can join the discussion by seizing upon one of these issues as your topic. If it turns out you want to incorporate some of this material in your essay, then you need to read the sources carefully, take notes, and give credit for the sources you use.

II. Library Reference Area

What if you need more resources than those in the stacks, or what if your teacher asks you to do a full-fledged research paper? You can supplement material you find in the stacks with what you turn up in a second place in the library, the *reference area*. The reference area is especially helpful when books are missing from the stacks (lost or checked out) or when your library's collection on an author is small.

A. Background Information

The reference area of a college library typically includes several kinds of materials. First, it contains books with background information, such as encyclopedias, literary histories, brief biographies, books that survey critical reactions to authors, handbooks of literary terms, surveys of contemporary authors, and guides to works by ethnic minorities. Consider beginning your writing project with one of these. They can tell you when and what your author wrote, the author's cultural context, and how critics have interpreted and evaluated the author's work. Some recently published examples are as follows:

American Women Writers: A Critical Reference Guide. Ed. Taryn

Benbow-Pfalzgraf. 2nd ed. 4 vols. Detroit: St. James, 2000. Print.

American Writers: A Collection of Literary Biographies. Ed. Leonard Unger et al.

Multivolumes. New York: Scribner's, 1974–present. Print.

Benson, Eugene, and William Toye. *The Oxford Companion to Canadian*

Literature. 2nd ed. New York: Oxford UP, 1997. Print.

British Writers. Ed. Ian Scott-Kilvert et al. Multivolumes. New York: Scribner's,

1979–present. Print.

Dictionary of Literary Biography. Multivolumes. Detroit: Gale, 1978–present.

Print.

Encyclopedia of Latin American Literature. Ed. Verity Smith. Chicago: Fitzroy

Dearborn, 1997. Print.

European Writers. Ed. George Stade. Multivolumes. New York: Scribner's,

1983–present. Print.

The Greenwood Encyclopedia of African American Literature. Ed. Hans Ostrom

and J. David Macey, Jr. 5 vols. Westport, CT: Greenwood, 2005. Print.

The Johns Hopkins Guide to Literary Theory and Criticism. Ed. Michael Groden,

Martin Kreiswirth, and Imre Szeman. 2nd ed. Baltimore: Johns Hopkins UP,

2005. Print.

The Oxford Encyclopedia of American Literature. Ed. Jay Parini. 4 vols.

New York: Oxford UP, 2004. Print.

The Oxford Encyclopedia of British Literature. Ed. David Scott Kastan. 5 vols.

New York: Oxford UP, 2006. Print.

The Oxford Encyclopedia of Children's Literature. Ed. Jack Zipes et al. 4 vols.

New York: Oxford UP, 2006. Print.

World Authors. The Wilson Authors Series. New York: Wilson, 1996–present.

Print.

B. Information about Primary Sources

Another kind of resource in the reference area is books that give specific and specialized information about primary sources. These include concordances and indexes to standard authors, such as Tennyson, Milton, and Shakespeare, as well as books dealing with specialized qualities of works, such as author's use of allusions, Greek mythology, or the Bible. An example:

Webber, Elizabeth, and Mike Feinsilber. *Merriam-Webster's Dictionary of*

Allusions. Springfield, MA: Merriam, 1999. Print.

C. Bibliographies

Finally, reference areas house bibliographies. With these, you can make your research systematic and thorough. There are many kinds of bibliographies for the study of language and literature, but for the sake of simplicity we divide them here into five categories.

1. General Reference

Baker, Nancy L., and Nancy Huling. *A Research Guide for Undergraduate*

Students: English and American Literature. 6th ed. New York: MLA,

2006. Print.

Book Review Digest. New York: Wilson, 1905–present. Print. Also available

online.

Book Review Index. Detroit: Gale, 1965–69, 1972–present. Print. Also available online.

The Essay and General Literature Index. New York: Wilson, 1931–present. Print. Also available online.

Harner, James L. *Literary Research Guide: An Annotated Listing of Sources in English Literary Studies.* 5th ed. New York: MLA, 2008. Print.

Humanities Index. New York: Wilson, 1975–present. Print. Also available online as *Humanities International Index.*

MLA International Bibliography of Books and Articles on the Modern Languages and Literatures. New York: MLA, 1922–present. Print. Also available online.

Readers' Guide to Periodical Literature: An Author and Subject Index. New York: Wilson, 1901–present. Print. Also available online.

MLA International Bibliography. An excellent place to begin your quest for secondary sources on an author or work is the *MLA International Bibliography (MLAIB).* The *MLAIB* is the most comprehensive bibliography of books and articles on authors and their works. The *MLAIB* is published annually and covers nearly everything published each year on modern languages, literature, folklore, and linguistics. Since 1981 the bibliography has been published in five parts: Part 1 (British Isles, British Commonwealth, English Caribbean, and American Literatures); Part 2 (European, Asian, African, and South American); Part 3 (Linguistics); Part 4 (General Literature and Related Topics); and Part 5 (Folklore). Most libraries will have all five parts bound together in a single volume. A very helpful feature of the bibliography since 1981 is a subject index for each of the five parts. You can use these subject indexes to locate works about topics and authors. For the *MLAIB* before 1981, you have to look up an author by country and period and look up topics under a limited number of headings. The online version of the *MLAIB,* available by subscription, covers editions from 1926 to the present and is much easier to search than the print version.

Other resources. Harner's *Literary Research Guide* is a selective but comprehensive guide to reference works for the study of literature in English. It covers just about every area of the study of literature, with chapters on, among other things, research methods, libraries, manuscript collections, databases, biographical sources, genres, national literatures in English (English, Irish, American, and so forth), and foreign language literature. Harner is most valuable for accessing *areas* of study rather than specific authors. If, for example, you are interested in the English Renaissance, find the section on the Renaissance and locate the reference works—encyclopedias and bibliographies—that lead you to the information you need. The book's index is very helpful for locating topics.

Baker and Huling's *A Research Guide for Undergraduate Students* is an excellent brief introduction to research methods in English and American literature. The authors, both librarians, provide a guide to the basic tools of the library. They discuss, among other things, research strategies and how to use bibliographies, library catalogs, and computer databases.

The *Humanities Index* (the online version is called *Humanities International Index*) lists articles about all the humanities (including literature) in nearly 300 periodicals. It is organized alphabetically by topic and author and is issued four times a year.

The *Essay and General Literature Index* lists essays that appear in books. Library catalogs and many bibliographies do not do this. Someone, for example, might have written an essay on Robert Browning's "Porphyria's Lover" for an anthology of essays titled *Psychotics in Literature*. If you were doing a paper on this poem, you might overlook this essay because it is "hidden" by the title of the book. The *Essay and General Literature Index*, however, would have it. This bibliography comes out twice a year and is easy to use. Authors and topics are listed alphabetically.

The *Readers' Guide to Periodical Literature*, the *Book Review Digest*, and the *Book Review Index* list articles and reviews in newspapers and popular journals.

2. Genres

Drama

American Drama Criticism: Interpretations 1890–1977. Comp. Floyd Eugene
   Eddleman. 2nd ed. Hamden, CT: Shoe String, 1979. Supplements 1984–96.
   Print.

The Columbia Encyclopedia of Modern Drama. Ed. Gabrielle H. Cody and Evert
Sprinchorn. 2 vols. New York: Columbia UP, 2007. Print.

*Dramatic Criticism Index: A Bibliography of Commentaries on Playwrights from
Ibsen to the Avant-Garde.* Comp. Paul F. Breed and Florence M. Sniderman.
Detroit: Gale, 1972. Print.

European Drama Criticism: 1900 to 1975. Comp. Helen H. Palmer. Hamden, CT:
Shoe String, 1977. Print.

A Guide to Critical Reviews: Part I: American Drama, 1909–1982. Comp.
James Salem. 3rd ed. Metuchen, NJ: Scarecrow, 1984. *Part II: The Musical,
1909–1989*, 3rd ed. (1991). *Part III: Foreign Drama, 1909–1977*, 2nd ed. (1979).
Part IV: *Screenplays from The Jazz Singer to Dr. Strangelove* (1971). *Part IV:
Screenplays 1963–1980* (1982). Print.

Fiction

Beene, Lynndianne. *Guide to British Prose Fiction Explication: Nineteenth and
Twentieth Centuries.* New York: G. K. Hall, 1997. Print.

*The Contemporary Novel: A Checklist of Critical Literature on the English
Language Novel since 1945.* Comp. Irving Adelman. 2nd ed. Lanham, MD:
Scarecrow, 1997. Print.

The Continental Novel: A Checklist of Criticism in English 1900–1966. Comp.
E. I. Kearney and L. S. Fitzgerald. Metuchen, NJ: Scarecrow, 1968. Print.

The Continental Novel: A Checklist of Criticism in English 1967–1980. Comp.
E. I. Kearney and L. S. Fitzgerald. Metuchen, NJ: Scarecrow, 1983. Print.

English Novel Explication: Criticism to 1972. Comp. Helen H. Palmer and Anne
Jane Dysen Hamden, CT: Shoe String, 1973. Supplements 1976–2000. Print.

*Twentieth-Century Short Story Explication: Interpretations 1900–1975, of Short
Fiction since 1800.* Comp. Warren S. Walker. 3rd ed. Hamden, CT: Shoe String,
1977. Supplements 1980–98. Print.

Poetry

Martinez, Nancy C., Joseph G. R. Martinez, and Erland Anderson. *Guide to
British Poetry Explication.* 4 vols. New York: G. K. Hall, 1991. Print.

Poetry Explication: A Checklist of Interpretation since 1925 of British and

American Poems Past and Present. Comp. Joseph Kuntz and Nancy Martinez.

3rd ed. Boston, MA: G. K. Hall 1980. Print.

Ruppert, James, and John R. Leo. *Guide to American Poetry Explication.* 4 vols.

Boston, MA: G. K. Hall, 1989. Print.

If the *MLAIB* seems too daunting, try more selective bibliographies, like those that focus on genres of literature—drama, novel, poetry, short story. These bibliographies provide lists of books and essays about authors and works that the editors deem important. The disadvantage of theses bibliographies is that, because they are selective, they may leave out works on the very topics you want to research. To use these bibliographies, look up the author and the work in the appropriate bibliography; there you will find a list of critical essays on the work you are studying. These bibliographies undergo constant revision, so check for supplements that bring them up to date. You can bring them up to date yourself with the *MLAIB*. The works listed above are only a few of the ones available. Your library may carry these or others like them.

3. Regions and Nations

The Cambridge Bibliography of English Literature. Ed. Joanne Shattock. 3rd ed.

Vol. 4 (1800–1900). New York: Cambridge UP, 1999. Print. (This is the first

available volume of a new edition of *The New Cambridge Bibliography of*

English Literature, listed below.)

The New Cambridge Bibliography of English Literature. Ed. George Wilson.

5 vols. Cambridge: Cambridge UP, 1969–77. Print.

Literary History of the United States. Ed. Robert E. Spiller et al. 4th ed. rev. Vol.

2. New York: Macmillan, 1974. Print. (Vol. 1 is the literary history; Vol. 2 is the

bibliography.)

Fenwick, M. J. *Writers of the Caribbean and Central America: A Bibliography.*

2 vols. New York: Garland, 1992. Print.

Gwinup, Thomas, and Fidelia Dickinson. *Greek and Roman Authors: A Checklist*

of Criticism. Metuchen, NJ: Scarecrow, 1982. Print.

Jenkins, Frew W. *Classical Studies: A Guide to the Reference Literature*. 2nd ed.

   Westport, CT: Libraries Unlimited, 2006. Print.

Pendergast, Sara, and Tom Pendergast. *Reference Guide to World Literature*.

   3rd ed. 2 vols. Farmington Hills, MI: St. James, 2003. Print.

Latin American Writers. Ed. Carlos A. Sole. 3 vols. New York: Scribner's, 1989.

Like the bibliographies on genres, these bibliographies provide *selected* lists of sources on regional literatures and on specific authors within regions. The *Literary History of the United States, The New Cambridge Bibliography of English Literature,* and the emerging *Cambridge Bibliography of English Literature* are especially helpful in pointing to important studies done on American and English literature up to their dates of publication.

4. Authors

Weiner, Alan R, and Spencer Means. *Literary Criticism Index*. 2nd ed. Metuchen,

   NJ: Scarecrow, 1994. Print.

Literary Criticism Index is a bibliography of bibliographies. It is organized alphabetically by authors, and keys their works to specific bibliographies. If, for example, you wanted to know where to find critical studies of Browning's "Porphyria's Lover," you would look for the title of the poem under "Browning, Robert." The entry would tell you which bibliographies contain lists of works on the poem.

   For the most thorough bibliographies of works by and about authors, seek out **bibliographies devoted solely to individual authors**. In contrast to the bibliographies listed above, these bibliographies usually contain *complete* listings of works by and about an author. These listings are complete—up to the publication date of the bibliography. For anything after that date, consult the *MLAIB*.

5. Computer Databases Available through Purchase or Subscription

Computer databases can save you enormous amounts of time. Using a bibliography database, for example, is the same as going through hard-bound print bibliographies, only the computer does it for you and much faster. Computer databases are available on compact disc (CD-ROM and DVD-ROM), magnetic tape, diskette, and the Internet. Most college and university libraries subscribe to various databases. Ask your librarian or check the library's online catalog to see which databases are available to you and how to search them.

The following is a brief list of databases helpful for students of English. Some are nothing but bibliographies (or "indexes," a comparable term). Some are bibliographies that also provide abstracts or full-text versions of articles from books, journals, and newspapers.

MLA International Bibliography
Covers books, articles from nearly 4,000 scholarly journals, dissertations. Excludes book reviews. Of all the databases, this is probably the best place to begin a research project about literature. *MLA* stands for the Modern Language Association.

ABELL (Annual Bibliography of English Language and Literature)
Bibliography covering books, scholarly articles, book reviews, collections of essays, and dissertations. Produced by the Modern Humanities Association, the British counterpart to the MLA.

World Shakespeare Bibliography (1962–six months ago)
Annotated listings of books, journal articles, dissertations, book reviews, theatrical productions, other materials related to Shakespeare.

Academic Search Premier (1984–present)
Interdisciplinary bibliography of over 7,900 journals. Provides full-text of over 4,500 journals.

Academic One File (Info Trac) (1980–present)
Indexes and abstracts of over 10,000 general periodicals and scholarly journals.

JSTOR
Full-texts of scholarly journals, some of which focus on literature. Covers the beginning of a journal's publications to within three to five years of the present.

ProQuest Research Library **(1971–present)**
Indexes and abstracts of several thousand general periodicals and scholarly journals.

Project Muse **(early 1990s–present)**
Full-text images of over 250 scholarly journals.

Times (of London) **1785–1985**
Full-text articles.

New York Times **(1851–three years ago)**
Full-text articles.

One more database is worthy of mention here: the **online catalog of your library**. Many online catalogs have the capacity to perform sophisticated and thorough searches of authors and topics. Your library's online catalog may be limited to only the material in that library, but it may be all you need. Many online catalogs link to catalogs of nearby libraries.

III. Library Periodicals Area

Now that you have drawn up a list of resources for your project—by consulting bibliographies and databases—your next step is to locate these resources in the library. Does your library own them or provide access to them? To find out, use your library's online catalog to see which books the library owns. Then locate them in the stacks. For computer databases and Internet resources, use either the computers on campus (in the library or labs) or your own computer. For journal articles, look up the title of the journal in the online catalog or in a "serials holding catalog." Either should tell you whether the library subscribes to the journal you want and, if so, where it is located. Recent issues of journals are usually stored in the *periodicals area* of the library, and back issues are kept in the stacks. To save space, some libraries also store past issues of journals on microfilm. If you have difficulty finding the journal articles you need, ask the librarian in the periodicals area for help.

This discussion of how to find information is basic. If you want more thorough guidance on a particular project, see Nancy L. Baker and Nancy Huling's *A Research Guide for Undergraduate*

Students: English and American Literature, listed above under "General Reference." Perhaps the most valuable resource for doing research is the reference librarian. Reference librarians are experts on locating sources of information and opinion. They are usually eager to help and can save you time.

IV. Information and Opinion on the Web

The Internet is an enormous, constantly changing, continuously growing collection of documents. It is an "ocean" that we have to "navigate." This ocean is so vast and changes so fast that almost anything published about it is dated as soon as it is released. What follows, then, are a few observations about how to use the Internet for conducting research about literature. Once you get the hang of using the Internet, you can catch up with new developments on your own.

More than anything, the emergence of the World Wide Web in 1993 has made the Internet easier to search than ever before. Most Web documents are hypertexts. *Hypertext* is a document containing *links* (also known as *hyperlinks* or *embedded links*), highlighted phrases that take you to other portions of the document or other hypertexts. Click on a link, and you are whisked to another place within the document or to a completely new Web site. That site will have links of its own, which take you to other sites, which in turn connect to new sites—many of which may link back to your original site. You can see why the World Wide Web is called a "web."

Because of the Web's ease of use, it has just about subsumed everything else on the Internet. You can search the Web by means of an *Internet search engine* such as Yahoo!, Windows Live, and Google. The search engine will typically have a box, located near the beginning of the document, that allows you to search by typing in *keywords.* Type in any terms or combination of terms you want: an author's name ("William Shakespeare"), a literary movement ("English Romanticism"), a geographical or national region ("Canadian literature"). The search engine will find documents related to your keywords, tell you how many documents it has found, and arrange them in descending order of relevance: the most relevant documents first, the least relevant last. Some are more detailed and comprehensive than others. A useful feature of most Web browsers is the *Favorites* option, located at the top of the screen. If you find a site you want to keep for future reference, click Favorites to store the Web address, also known as the Uniform Resource Locator (URL). When you want to get to that site quickly, open your Favorites file and go directly to the addresses stored there. Favorites saves you from having to retrace steps to get back to sites you want.

You can also go directly to any site on the Web if you know its address (URL). Look for a box at the top of the screen that contains the address of the site where you are. The address for the search engine Yahoo, for example, is http://www.yahoo.com. The "http" stands for Hypertext Transfer Protocol, the program that establishes a common language between computers and accommodates the transmission of all documents on the Web. Click on the address, delete all or part of it, type in a new address, and press Enter. The browser takes you to the site of the new address.

General databases

Three free databases are especially helpful for starting literary research on the Internet.

- *Voice of the Shuttle: Electronic Resources for the Humanities,* maintained by Alan Liu and the English Department at the University of California, Santa Barbara
- *Intute.* The "Arts and Humanities" section maintained by the University of Oxford and Manchester Metropolitan University (UK)
- *The Internet Public Library,* hosted by the Drexel University College of Information Science and Technology

These three sites are "gateway" sites—entries to areas of study. They are excellent places to begin searches on the Web. *Voice of the Shuttle* focuses on all the humanities and includes sections such as "General Humanities Resources," "Literature (in English)," "Literatures (Other than English)," "Literary Theory," "Minority Studies," and "Philosophy." It also provides links to listservs and news groups devoted to literary studies. *Intute* is similar to *Voice of the* Shuttle but more broadly focused, dividing into "Science and Technology," "Arts and Humanities," "Social Sciences," and "Health and Life Sciences." Under "Arts and Humanities" are sections such as "Humanities General," "English," "Gender Studies," and "Comparative Literature." *The Internet Public Library* provides access to all areas of knowledge.

The following is a very select list of more narrowly focused sites. Unless otherwise noted, they are all free:

Dictionaries and Encyclopedias
Dictionary of Symbolism
Encyclopedia Britannica
Britannica Online. Available by subscription.

Literary Reference Center
Numerous encyclopedias, including the *New Princeton Encyclopedia of Poetry and Poetics.* Available by subscription.
Oxford English Dictionary
   OED Online. Available by subscription.
Oxford Reference
Access to over 100 dictionaries and reference works published by Oxford UP. Available by subscription.

Literary criticism of authors and works
Online Literary Criticism Collection

Author sites
Jane Austen Information Page
Mr. William Shakespeare and the Internet
Absolute Shakespeare
The William Blake Archive

Multiauthor sites
American Studies Crossroads Project
Latina/o Literature and Literature of the Americas
The Literary Encyclopedia
The Literary Gothic
Literary Reference Center
Full-text articles of literary criticism, author biographies, interviews with authors, book reviews, plot summaries, and definitions of literary terms. Available by subscription.
Literature Resource Center
Full-text biographical and critical materials published by Gale (*Contemporary Authors, Dictionary of Literary Biography, Contemporary Literary Criticism,* etc.). Available by subscription.

The ORB: On-line Reference Book for Medieval Studies

Postcolonial Studies

Romantic Circles [the Romantic movement]

Scribner Writers Series
Full-text essays on more than 2,000 authors and genres from the Scribner print series on authors and literature. Available by subscription.

Storytellers: Native American Authors Online

The Victorian Web

Electronic texts
Bartleby.com

Chadwyck-Healey
Full-text collections of poetry, such as *20th Century African-American Poetry, 20th Century American Poetry, 20th Century English Poetry.* Available by subscription.

Early American Imprints
Full-texts for books and other materials 1639–1800 (Series I) and 1801–1819 (Series II). Available by subscription.

Early English Books Online
Full-texts for books published in the British Isles, North America, and British territories 1701–1800. Available by subscription.

The Online Books Page

Project Gutenberg

Women Writers Online
Full-texts of over 230 works by English and American women 1500–1830. Available by subscription.

Grammar, style, documentary guidelines
The Elements of Style (by William Strunk, Jr., available from Bartleby.com)

Guide to Grammar and Writing

Poetic techniques
Poetry: Meter, Form, and Rhythm

Online journals
Domestic Goddesses: AKA "Scribbling Women"
The home page of this journal says that it is a "moderated E-journal devoted to women writers, beginning in the 19th century, who wrote 'domestic fiction.'"

Other Voices: The ejournal of Cultural Criticism
Renaissance Forum

Newsletters, discussion groups, and electronic mail
Interpersonal communication by means of newsletters, discussion groups, and e-mail is a wonderful opportunity for people doing research. You can exchange opinions, share information, and keep up with trends. *Voice of the Shuttle*, mentioned above, includes a directory of literary discussion lists. Bear in mind that newsletters and discussion lists are most valuable for researchers who have *long-term* projects. They are less helpful for people who need to get research papers done quickly, say within a semester. It is a breach of "Netiquette" (etiquette for using the Internet) for someone to send out a message on a discussion list saying something like, "I have a paper due in three weeks on *Beowulf.* Can anyone out there help me think of a topic?"

EVALUATING THE QUALITY OF INTERNET SITES

How do you know if a Web site is reliable? In contrast to scholarly books and journals, which are published by reputable publishers with high standards of acceptance, Web sites can be created by anyone with a Web address. To evaluate their quality, ask questions like the following:

1. **Who is the developer of the site?** How trustworthy is this person? Is the developer or "owner" a scholar, well-versed in the subject? Or is the developer an enthusiastic amateur who has limited knowledge and yet spews forth lots of opinions? Does the developer give his or her name (something other than "Webmaster")? Can you get in touch with the developer?

2. **How authoritative is the site?** Who publishes the site? Does it originate from a school (university, college, high school) or from a single individual? How commercial is it? Does it seem more interested in selling you things than in presenting information and interpretation?

3. **Is the site well maintained?** Has the site been updated recently? How thorough, thoughtful, and careful is the site? Does the

developer seem active in maintaining the site? Are the links current? (How many dead links are there?) Does the information on the site seem dated?

4. **How knowledgeable are the authors who write for the site?** Do the writers document their information and opinions? Do they refer to just a few sources? Do they seem well-read in their subject, familiar with groundbreaking and essential treatments of their subject? How detailed is the treatment of the subject? Is the information accurate?

5. **For e-texts, how reliable are they?** Are e-texts well-edited? Are they accurate? Is the source of the text given? How trustworthy is the source?

In general, Web sites are best when they meet the following criteria:

- The developers are scholars in the field.
- The developers are accountable. They tell you who they are and how to get in touch with them.
- They constantly and thoughtfully maintain the site, keeping information and links current.
- The site is noncommercial and is associated with a school or press. Be wary of .com sites. More trustworthy are nonprofit domains: .edu, .gov, .org, and .net.
- Information and interpretation is well documented and gives evidence of sound knowledge of the subject.
- E-texts are edited recently by scholars.

GIVING CREDIT TO SOURCES

Why Should You Give Credit?

First, give credit so readers can find and read the same material you read. They may also want to check the reliability of your sources or your ability to use them fairly and accurately. Giving credit, to put it positively, is good rhetoric. The more careful and honest you are in giving credit, the stronger your argument will be. Second, give credit to distinguish your ideas from those of others. The purpose of the essay, after all, is to express *your* ideas, to argue *your* position. You may use facts, ideas, and words from other sources to clarify and support your ideas, but readers are interested, finally, in knowing what *you* think. That is why they are reading your paper. By giving credit, you show them exactly where your ideas begin and where other writers' ideas leave off.

Finally, give credit to be ethical. Honor policies stress this reason heavily. Although the ethical principle is obvious, it is not always simple. The usual definition of *plagiarism* is "the presentation of someone else's ideas, work, or facts as your own." The moral judgment that follows is, "Plagiarism is stealing and therefore wrong." These judgments are apt when applied to blatant plagiarism, cases in which someone copies the work of someone else and claims it as his or her own. Most cases of student plagiarism, however, are not so intentional. The issue of plagiarism is clouded with some uncertainties. Everything you know comes from a "source." When is what you know "yours" and not someone else's? Another uncertainty is that when you summarize someone else's ideas, you will probably use some of that writer's words. How many and what kind of words can you use without plagiarizing? A third uncertainty is the nature of facts. Some facts, even when they appear in a source, do not need documentation. But which ones? Because of uncertainties like these, most students who "plagiarize" do so unintentionally. The following are principles and guidelines that anyone using sources in essays about literature should follow. They can help you use sources meaningfully, clearly, and ethically.

When Should You Give Credit?

For primary sources. Whenever you make specific reference to an incident or words in a work and whenever you quote from a work, you need to cite the source (give credit) from which you obtained the information. This is as true for primary as for secondary sources. You must do this for several reasons. Works of literature, especially famous ones, often go through many editions. Readers need to know which edition you used so they can find the parts of the work you discuss. You document your primary source, then, for their convenience. Another reason is that the edition you use may affect the validity of your argument. If the edition is unscholarly and contains misprints or omissions, your interpretations will be suspect.

A well-known example is Emily Dickinson's poetry. After her death in 1886, Thomas Wentworth Higginson and Mabel Loomis Todd edited Dickinson's poetry for publication. They published it (or some of it) in four volumes throughout the 1890s. But instead of printing it as Dickinson had written it, they "regularized" it for the tastes of nineteenth-century readers. They changed the meter to make it more conventional, changed words to make them rhyme, normalized punctuation, and altered metaphors that seemed illogical. Not until Thomas H. Johnson published a new edition of Dickinson's poems in 1955 did we have versions of her poetry as she had written it. If you write an essay about her poetry, your readers will want to know that you used Johnson's edition (or reprints therefrom). By giving full information about the editions you use, you enhance the reliability of your essay.

Often the nature of college courses allows you to omit complete citations for primary sources. If you write about a work assigned for a course, page numbers may be the only documentation you need. Check with your professor to be sure this practice is acceptable. If so, follow each quotation or reference with appropriate page numbers in parentheses, placing your final mark of punctuation after the closing parenthesis.

Quotation

> Lawrence says that when she is with her children she feels "the center of her heart go hard" (125).

A specific reference but not a quotation

> When she returns home from the party, she finds Paul riding the rocking horse. Lawrence contrasts her elegant, icy dress to Paul's frenzied and exhausted state (134–35).

More formal usage requires a complete citation for the edition you are using. Complete citations—located on a Works Cited page—are necessary when you use a book that is not a basic text in your course.

For facts that are not common knowledge. "Common knowledge" facts are those the average well-read person would likely know: very basic facts about history (that Woodrow Wilson was president of the United States during World War I, that the United

States entered the war several years after it began), birth and death dates, occupations, publication dates, basic biographical facts about famous people (that Ernest Hemingway began his writing career as a newspaper reporter, that he entered World War I as an ambulance driver, that in 1929 he published a famous novel, *A Farewell to Arms*, based on his wartime experiences, that just before the outbreak of World War II he published a novel, *For Whom the Bell Tolls*, about the Spanish Civil War). Facts that are not common knowledge (what Hemingway's parents thought of his newspaper career, where he saw action during the war, how he was wounded, the identity of the nurse he fell in love with while recuperating, what he actually said to people about the war) come from secondary sources and must be cited. Also, controversial facts need to be documented. If you claim that Theodore Roosevelt was a secret Marxist, or had an affair with the anarchist Emma Goldman, or conspired to assassinate President McKinley, you must give sources for such outlandish assertions; otherwise readers will write you off as a crank.

For all direct quotes. This kind of documentation is crucial, whether you quote from primary or secondary sources.

For summaries or paraphrases of someone else's ideas. Even when you do not quote directly from the work, you must provide documentation when you repeat someone else's ideas. This includes ideas held by other writers, by your instructor, or even by other students. It also includes ideas you arrive at on your own and then find expressed in print.

For ideas not "assimilated" by you. Once you have absorbed someone's ideas, thought about them over a time, added ideas of your own or of others, you can assume that these ideas are now "yours." If, however, your memory is so good that these ideas remain in your mind exactly as they were when you read and heard them, then you must give credit to the original author.

A final word. The dividing line between facts that are common knowledge and those that are not is sometimes frustratingly vague. So too is the line between ideas assimilated by you and those that are not. *When in doubt about where that line is, give credit.* Doing so takes a little extra time and trouble, but the trouble and time are worth it to protect yourself against charges of plagiarism and to provide curious readers with enough information to check your facts.

Where Should You Give Credit?

By introducing your source in your text. When you use the ideas and specialized or controversial facts of another person, introduce them *in your own text*, not just in parenthetical references. To do this, use introductory phrases like the following:

> As Jane Tompkins says, "The ground for complaint . . ."
>
> One critic has called attention to "the absurdity of Huck's shore experience."
>
> Annette Kolodny suggests . . .
>
> Tuchman's second point is . . .
>
> Judith Butler sees queer theory as . . .

All of these introduce paraphrases, summaries, and short quotations. The following example introduces an indented or blocked quotation (that is, a long quotation moved right ten spaces [one inch] from the established left margin).

> Friedman's definition of plot focuses on the changes the protagonist undergoes:
>> The end of plot, then, is to represent some completed process of change in the protagonist.

Acknowledgments for facts are also necessary when the facts are very specialized or controversial. For example, details about F. Scott Fitzgerald's love life in Hollywood during his last years can come from only a few people. You must mention such people *in your text* when you use them:

> Sheilah Graham claims that . . .
>
> Budd Schulberg saw that Fitzgerald was . . .
>
> Nathanael West said that at the party Fitzgerald concentrated his attention on . . .

Note, however, that facts available from many sources do not have to be introduced in your text. Details about English history, for example, are available in many textbooks and are not associated with any one person or group. You do, however, need to provide parenthetical references for such information and to cite your sources in the Works Cited list.

> Anarchism was such a compelling theory at the turn of the century that six heads of state—of France, Austria, Italy, the United States, and two of Spain—were executed by anarchists (Tuchman 72).

In parenthetical citations.   See "Guidelines for Parenthetical Citations" in the next section.

In a Works Cited list.   Together, the parenthetical citations and Works Cited list give readers complete information about your sources and how you use them. In parenthetical citations, give enough information so readers can find the sources in the Works Cited list. The Works Cited list enables readers to check out the sources themselves.

CORRECT DOCUMENTARY FORM

Documentary form varies from discipline to discipline. For people writing about literature, the authoritative guide to documentary form is the *MLA Handbook for Writers of Research Papers.* (*MLA* stands for Modern Language Association, the preeminent scholarly organization in the United States devoted to the study of modern languages and literature.) In 1984 the MLA created a new documentary format, one that resembles the formats of the social and natural sciences. The guidelines in this chapter are from the seventh edition of the *MLA Handbook* (2009). If you purchase the book, you can gain access to the book's Web site by means of an access code located at the back of the book. The site provides the full text of the book, materials not in the book (sample research papers), and a search option. The sample papers are accompanied with explanations of such procedures as choosing topics, evaluating sources, and using correct documentary formats.

Guidelines for Parenthetical Citations

Purpose. Parenthetical citations are markings, placed in parentheses, that point to exact locations in the primary and secondary sources you draw upon for your paper. These markings can be page numbers (for prose), line numbers (for poetry), act, scene, and line numbers (for verse drama), and chapter and verses (for religious texts).

Your goals in making parenthetical citations are twofold. First, you show readers where they can locate, in the sources themselves, any quotations, facts, and ideas that you incorporate in your paper. If, for example, you provide a page number for a quotation, readers should be able to go to that page in the source and find the section you quoted.

Second, you give enough information for readers to locate the source in the Works Cited list at the end of your paper. For guidelines about setting up a Works Cited list, see the next section of this chapter.

Placement. For **material that's not indented,** place the parenthetical citation immediately after the material that needs referencing. Usually this is at the end of a sentence or paragraph, but sometimes it can be within a sentence as well. Put the reference before the closing punctuation of the phrase or sentence (comma, period, semicolon, colon, question mark, exclamation point).

Examples:

- James Joyce, as Arnold Kettle notes, was consistent about employing his artistic principles (301), but that does not mean his works are all the same.
- John H. Arnold points out that although Herodotus seems strikingly modern to us, his histories cannot be fully trusted (17).
- The Major's wife cried out, "No, Ekeby shall belong to the cavaliers so that it may be their ruin!" (293).

For **indented material** (quotations), place the citation one space over from the closing punctuation. Note that indented quotations require no quotation marks and should be set back one inch from the left margin. Place the parenthetical reference *after* the closing punctuation mark.

Examples:

Near the climax of the story, Wells has Nunez recognize the pleasing qualities of life in the Country of the Blind:

> They led a simple, laborious life, these people, with all the elements of virtue and happiness, as these things can be

> understood by men. They toiled, but not oppressively; they had food and clothing sufficient for their needs; they had days and seasons of rest; they made much of music and singing, and there was love among them, and little children. (15)

Primary sources.

Prose. When referring to primary sources, use page numbers for prose works.

> In Shirley Jackson's "The Lottery" the people are at first reluctant to participate in the lottery. The men standing around waiting are subdued: "Their jokes were quiet and they smiled rather than laughed" (219). The children, when called, come "reluctantly, having to be called four or five times" (220). Once the black box is brought out, the villagers keep "their distance" (221).

Verse drama. For plays written in poetry, use Arabic numbers to indicate act, scene, and line numbers.

> In *Hamlet* the queen bids farewell to Ophelia by saying, "I hoped thou shouldst have been my Hamlet's wife" (5.1.211).

Here the reference is to act five, scene one, line 211. You may also use Roman numerals instead of Arabic numbers to cite acts and scenes.

> In *Hamlet* the queen bids farewell to Ophelia by saying, "I hoped thou shouldst have been my Hamlet's wife" (V.i.211).

Poetry. For poems, especially long ones (more than about ten lines), cite line numbers. As in the following example, place "line" or "lines" before the number(s) in your first reference. That way, your reader will know you are referring to lines rather than page numbers. After the first reference, give just the numbers.

> In commenting on our growing distance from heaven, Wordsworth says in "Intimations of Immortality,"
> > Heaven lies about us in our infancy!
> > Shades of the prison-house begin to close
> > Upon the growing Boy. (lines 66–68)

The Bible.   Refer to the Bible by indicating chapter and verse numbers. Use Arabic numbers:

> When Solomon became old, his many wives "turned away his heart after other gods." He worshiped the goddess Ashtoreth and "did evil in the sight of the Lord" (1 Kings 11.4–6).

More than one page.   Use hyphens between line or page numbers to indicate material that lies within a continuous sequence of lines or pages.

> (231–33).

Use commas between line or page numbers to indicate interruptions in sequence.

> (200, 219).

Multivolume works.   If your reference is to a work with more than one volume, indicate in your parenthetical reference the volume to which you refer. Separate volume and page numbers with a colon. Insert a space between the colon and the page number.

> Even on the point of death, Clarissa writes to her father asking his forgiveness. She begs him "on her knees" to forgive her for "all her faults and follies," especially "that fatal error which threw her out of [his] protection" (4: 359).

Here the reference is to the fourth volume, page 359. If you use only one volume from a multivolume work, you need not give the volume number in the parenthetical reference. Instead, include the volume number in the Works Cited listing.

Secondary sources.

Single author books.   For most parenthetical references, especially for books, it is usually enough to give the author's last name and the page number(s) of the reference. Place the reference at the end of the sentence before the period.

> Long historical poems, such as *The Battle of Maldon*, provide "the soundest evidence we have" for recreating the Europe of 1,000 years ago (Reston 5).

An alternative way of giving the same information is to mention the author's name in your text. In this case, only the page number need appear in the parenthetical reference.

> James Reston, Jr. says that poetic depictions of historical events, such as *The Battle of Maldon,* provide "the soundest evidence we have" for recreating the Europe of 1,000 years ago (5).

In both instances, the author's name points to the work in the Works Cited list, and the page number points to the citation in the work itself. The above citation is to the following work in the Works Cited list:

> Reston, James, Jr. *The Last Apocalypse: Europe at the Year 1000 AD.* New York: Anchor Books, 1998.

Two or three authors. When referring to a work by two or three authors, give all their names in the text or in the reference.

Examples:
- One work makes the useful distinction between "representational" and "illustrative" narrative (Scholes and Kellogg 84).
- Scholes and Kellogg make the useful distinction between "representational" and "illustrative" narrative (84).

More than three authors. When referring to a work by more than three authors, give all their names or, more simply, give the first name and "et al." (the abbreviation for Latin *et alii,* "and others").

> The trickster has been a traditional folk hero not just of American "Yankee" narrative but of American Indian and African-American narrative as well (Spiller et al. 729).

Several works by the same author. If you use several works by the same author, give the author's last name, a portion of the title, and the page number.

> Reston claims that Olaf Trygvesson's conversion to Christianity in 994 AD diminished Viking hostility in southern England (*Last Apocalypse* 18).

When you use more than one work by the same author, you can refer to the work in the text or in a parenthetical reference.

Examples:

- Lawrence describes the two mothers differently. Elizabeth Bates is "a tall woman of imperious mien, handsome, with definite black eyebrows" ("Odour of Chrysanthemums" 248), whereas Paul's mother is simply "a woman who was beautiful" ("The Rocking-Horse Winner" 271).
- Lawrence describes the two mothers differently. Elizabeth Bates in "Odour of Chrysanthemums" is "a tall woman of imperious mien, handsome, with definite black eyebrows" (248), whereas Paul's mother in "The Rocking-Horse Winner" is simply "a woman who was beautiful" (271).

Authors with the same last name. If you have several authors with the same last name, give initials or the whole name to distinguish among them:

> (J. Reston 58–60)

Titles without authors. If the author of a work is anonymous, give the complete title or the first few words of the title, plus the page number. (Anonymous works are alphabetized by title in the Works Cited list.)

> Unlike the pilgrims, the Puritans remained members of the Anglican Church. But like the Pilgrims, they adhered to a Calvinistic theology ("Early American Literature" 2).

If you use the title in your text, give only the page number(s) in the reference.

> As indicated in "Early American Literature," unlike the pilgrims, the Puritans remained members of the Anglican Church. But like the Pilgrims, they adhered to a Calvinistic theology (2).

Whole works. When you refer to an entire work (not some part of it), you may omit a parenthetical reference to it if you identify the author or, if anonymous, the title of the work in your text:

> E. M. W. Tillyard devotes a short book to explaining how the Elizabethans saw the structure of the cosmos.

If readers are interested in Tillyard's book, they can find it listed under his name in the Works Cited list.

More than one work. Refer to more than one work in a single parenthetical reference by separating the works with semicolons.

> At least two critics have seen the similarity between Voltaire's character Candide and the young Benjamin Franklin in the *Autobiography* (Orkney 13; Scott 151–52).

If, however, you want to refer to more than two or three works, use a footnote or endnote instead of a parenthetical reference. (See the discussion of footnotes and endnotes below.)

Works quoted in other works. If you find a quotation in a book or article but cannot find the original source for the quotation, rather than abandon the quotation, cite the place where you found it. Use "qtd. in" ("quoted in").

> When Dreiser was a magazine editor, he would write on rejection slips, "We like realism, but it must be tinged with sufficient idealism to make it all a truly uplifting character" (qtd. in Fiedler 46).

Sources with no page numbers. Some works, like many on the Web, may have no page numbers. If so, give other information—if available—to mark the location of references. Use abbreviations, like sec. (for section), par. and pars. (for paragraph and paragraphs), and ch. (for chapter). Indicate paragraph numbers only if they are marked in the text. Don't try to count them yourself. The goal is to give your reader some idea of where your reference is. Do the best you can. You can even say things like "near the beginning," "about half way through," "several paragraphs from the end."

> Diane Elam worries that because a university education is becoming more of "a vocational exercise," the value of reading literature "is no longer a self-evident proposition in market-driven universities" (par. 4).

If you refer to more than one paragraph, use the abbreviation "pars.": (pars. 15–18). You could refer also to screens, if they are numbered: (screens 8–9).

Magazines and newspapers. Like sources on the Web, magazine and newspaper articles may have unusual page indicators. As always, give enough information so readers can find your references. The following example is from a newspaper article:

Kunitz said that one of the advantages of being so old is that "I encountered a good portion of the best poets of the twentieth century" (C5).

Guidelines for Using Endnotes and Footnotes

You can place explanatory notes either at the foot of pages (footnotes) or on separate sheets at the end of the paper (endnotes). Unless your instructor tells you otherwise, place all notes at the end.

Citing several sources (more than two or three) all at once.
Text

> A host of critics agree that Swift does not share Gulliver's condemnation of human beings at the end of Gulliver's Travels.[1]

Note

> 1. Abrams 23–28; Converse 55–70; Portnoy 150–65; Clore and Barchester 300–05; Kellerman 83; Soles 15–20.

Comments or information relating to something in your text.
These comments or facts are not necessary to your line of thought, but you may want to include them because you think your readers would find them useful and interesting.

Text

> Irving adopts the stance of the ironic narrator in his comic masterpiece "The Legend of Sleepy Hollow."[2]

Note

> 2. The ironic narrator was a common fictional device in eighteenth-century English fiction and was most notably present in novels by one of Irving's favorite authors, Henry Fielding.

Setting up a footnote or endnote

- In the text of your essay where you want the reference to appear, place a number raised slightly above the line (*superscript;* note the examples above).
- Place a corresponding number before the note (see the examples above), then a period, then a space, then the note.

- Number the notes sequentially throughout the paper. In other words, do not restart your numbering (with "1") when you come to a new page. Rather, go from "1" to the final number all the way through the paper.
- Place your notes at the end of the paper (endnotes). You can also place them at the bottom of the page (footnotes), but it's much easier to format endnotes than footnotes.
- Place endnotes on a separate page or pages and position them between the text of your essay and the Works Cited page. Center the title "Notes" one inch from the top of the page. Double-space.
- Indent the first line of each note. The rest of the note goes all the way to the left margin. Double-space within and between endnotes. For a "real life" example of the use of endnotes, see the sample paper at the end of this chapter.
- Place footnotes at the bottom of the page, four lines below the text (two double spaces). Use the same format as for endnotes, only single space them. If you have more than one footnote on a page, put a double space between them.

Guidelines and Form for the Works Cited List: General Rules

The Works Cited list, placed at the end of the paper, contains citations for all the resources—primary and secondary—to which you refer in the body of your paper. The *MLA Handbook* recommends that you prepare your Works Cited list before you write your paper. Otherwise, you won't know what to put in your parenthetical references (129). Be sure that every source you referred to is included in the Works Cited list. If you are confused about what information to put in your entries, keep in mind your main purpose for documenting any sources—to give enough information so readers can find these same sources and verify their content and reliability. Follow the guidelines below. Use the sample entries as models for each guideline or category.

1. **Put the Works Cited list at the end of your paper, on sheets separate from your text.** Center the title, "Works Cited." Double-space. Begin the list of entries, double-spacing between and within them. Continue the page numbers of the essay. If the last page of the essay is 10, the page number for the Works Cited list would be 11.

2. **Arrange entries alphabetically by author.** If the author is anonymous, list the entry alphabetically by its title. For the purpose of alphabetizing, ignore *A, An,* and *The* at the beginning of titles.

3. **Do not number entries.** Since the entries are listed alphabetically, numbers are unnecessary.

4. **In each entry, put the author's last name first.** The author's last name appears first because the list is in alphabetical order. If more than one author appears in an entry, put the last name first for the first author: Rochester, Henry. Put the names of the other authors in regular order: Rochester, Henry, Roch Small, and Leonard Handy.

5. **Put the first line flush with the left margin.** Indent any subsequent (turnover) lines of the entry one-half inch from the left-hand margin. This format is called a "hanging indentation."

6. **Include without exception every source—primary or secondary—cited in your paper.**

7. **Divide your entries into three main sections:**

   - author's name (last name first)
   - the title of the article or book
   - information about publication

   Sometimes more sections are necessary—information about editors, volume numbers, or reprinted editions. But these three divisions are essential for all entries. Punctuate citations as indicated in the sample entries below.

8. **Missing information.** Don't panic. Provide as much information as you can.

Sample Entries for Nonperiodical Print Materials

"Nonperiodical" materials include books, pamphlets, brochures, and other publications that appear either one time only (a first edition) or later in revised form (second edition, third edition, revised edition). "Periodical" materials, like newspapers, magazines, and scholarly journals appear regularly (daily, weekly, monthly, quarterly, annually). Perhaps the most cited publication in research essays is the first one below, the book.

Book with one author

You can usually find the date of publication of books on the copyright page (the opposite side of the title page) or, for some books published outside the United States, at the back of the book. If there is more than one date, choose the most recent one. If several cities are listed as places of publication, use the first one. The "UP" after "Oxford" in the example below represents "University Press." The word *Print* at the end of the entry indicates the medium of publication.

Lewis, C. S. *The Allegory of Love: A Study in Medieval Tradition*. New York:

Oxford UP, 1936. Print.

Book with no known author

If the work is anonymous, begin the entry with the title.

Sir Gawain and the Green Knight. Trans. Keith Harrison. New York: Oxford UP,

1998. Print.

Book with more than one work by an author

When you include more than one work by an author, substitute three hyphens for the author's name after the first citation. Arrange the entries in alphabetical order by title.

Jewett, Sarah Orne. *A Country Doctor*. New York: Garret, 1970. Print.

---. *A White Heron and Other Stories*. Boston: Houghton, 1886. Print.

Book with two or three authors

Reverse the name of the first author only.

Berry, Lester V., and Melvin Van den Bark. *The American Thesaurus of Slang:*

With Supplement. New York: Crowell, 1947. Print.

Translation

Salih, Tayeb. *Season of Migration to the North*. Trans. Denys Johnson-Davies.

London: Heinemann, 1969. Print.

Multivolume work

If you refer to just one volume of a multivolume set, indicate the volume you use, as in the first example. If you use all the volumes, indicate how many volumes the set contains, as in the second example.

Richardson, Samuel. *Clarissa; or, the History of a Young Lady*. Vol. 4. London:

Everyman, 1932. Print.

Richardson, Samuel. *Clarissa; or, the History of a Young Lady*. 4 vols. London:

Everyman, 1932. Print.

Book with more than three authors, several editions, and one of several volumes

Using "et al." saves you from listing all the other authors of the work.

Spiller, Robert E., et al. *Literary History of the United States*. 4th ed. rev. Vol. 1.

New York: Macmillan, 1974. Print.

Introduction, preface, foreword, headnote, or an afterword

Charvat, William. Introduction. *The Last of the Mohicans*. By James Fenimore

Cooper. Boston: Riverside, 1958. iii–xiv. Print.

Magarshack, David. Afterword. *The Death of Ivan Ilych and Other Stories*. By

Leo Tolstoy. New York: Signet, 1960. 295–304. Print.

Anonymous introduction, headnote, or article in an anthology of literature

"The Middle Ages to ca. 1485." Introduction. *Norton Anthology of English*

Literature. Ed. M. H. Abrams et al. 7th ed. Vol. 1. New York: Norton, 2000.

1–22. Print.

Book by a corporate author

Sometimes works may not be written by individual authors but by groups, whose members are not named. Such groups—commissions, associations, committees—are "corporate authors." The corporate author in the example below is the Modern Language Association.

Modern Language Association. *MLA Handbook for Writers of Research Papers*.

7th ed. New York: MLA, 2009. Print.

Edition of an author's work

In this example, Arthur Mizener is the editor of this edition of Trollope's *The Last Chronicle of Barset*. The abbreviation "ed." for "editor" or "edition" should be capitalized if it comes after a period, as it does here.

Trollope, Anthony. *The Last Chronicle of Barset*. Ed. Arthur Mizener. Boston:

Riverside, 1964. Print.

Book with one or more editors

Add an "s" to the abbreviation "ed." if the book is edited by more than one person.

Drabble, Margaret, ed. *The Oxford Companion to English Literature*. Rev. ed.

New York: Oxford UP, 1995. Print.

Suleiman, Susan R., and Inge Crosman, eds. *The Reader in the Text: Essays on*

Audience and Interpretation. Princeton: Princeton UP, 1980. Print.

Article in a reference book

For familiar reference works, especially ones that undergo frequent revision, you need not give complete publishing information. Give the author's name (if known), the title of the article, the title of the reference work (italicized), the edition number, and the date of publication. If the entries are listed alphabetically, there is no need to give volume or page numbers. For less familiar references books, as in the second example, give full publication information.

"La Fontaine, Jean de." *The New Encyclopaedia Britannica: Macropaedia*.

15th ed. 1987. Print.

"Blank Verse." *The New Princeton Encyclopedia of Poetry and Poetics*. Ed. Alex

Preminger and T. V. F. Brogan. Princeton: Princeton UP, 1993. Print.

Definition from a dictionary

For dictionary definitions, give a specific definition if you cite one out of several.

"Metamorphosis." Def. 1b. *Webster's New Collegiate Dictionary*. 1981. Print.

Work in a collection or anthology

Akhmatova, Anna. "Requiem." *Anna Akhmatova: Selected Poems*. Trans.

D. M. Thomas. New York: Penguin, 1988. 87–96. Print.

Christie, Agatha. "The Dream." *Detective Stories from the Strand Magazine*.

Ed. Jack Adrian. New York: Oxford UP, 1992. 21–43. Print.

Jackson, Shirley. "The Lottery." Literature: Reading, Reacting, Writing. Ed. Laurie

G. Kirszner and Stephen R. Mandell. Compact 3rd ed. Fort Worth: Harcourt,

1997. 261–69. Print.

Lyon, Thomas J. "The Literary West." *The Oxford History of the American West.*

Ed. Clyde A. Milner, II, Carol A. O'Connor, and Martha A. Sandweiss. New

York: Oxford UP, 1994. 707–41. Print.

Montaigne, Michel de. "Of Cannibals." Trans. Donald Frame. *The Norton*

Anthology of World Masterpieces: The Western Tradition. Ed. Sarah

Lawall and Maynard Mack. 7th ed. Vol. 1. New York: Norton, 1999.

1933–42. Print.

Porter, Katherine Anne. "Old Mortality." *The Old Order: Stories of the South.*

New York: Harcourt, 1969. 107–82. Print.

An illustrated book

For illustrated books, put either the author or illustrator's name
first, depending on the emphasis you want to give.

Milne, A. A. *Winnie-the-Pooh.* Illus. Ernest H. Shephard. New York: Dutton,

1961. Print.

Shephard, Ernest H., illus. *Winnie-the-Pooh.* By A. A. Milne. New York: Dutton,

1961. Print.

Graphic narratives

If the author and artist of a graphic narrative are the same person,
give the same information as you would for any nonperiodical print
publication.

Porcellino, John. *Diary of a Mosquito Abatement Man.* Minneapolis, MN:

La Mano, 2005. Print.

For graphic narratives that are highly collaborative, put the
name or names of the contributors you want to emphasize first.

Gaiman, Neil, writer. "Calliope." *The Sandman: Dream Country.* Art by Kelley

Jones and Malcolm Jones III. New York: DC Comics, 1995. 10–34. Print.

Hale, Nathan, artist. *Rapunzel's Revenge.* Written by Shannon Hale and Dean

Hale. New York: Bloomsbury, 2008. Print.

Book with missing information

If a book has missing publication information, give as much as
you can. Use abbreviations like *n.p.* (no place of publication given;

no publisher indicated), *n.d.* (no date of publication given), and *n. pag.* (no pagination given).

Vader, D. "Breathing Exercises." *Deepening Your Voice in Ten Easy Lessons.*

N.p: GalaxyFFA, n.d. N. pag. Print.

A book published before 1900

You may, when citing a book published before 1900, omit the name of the publisher and use a comma (rather than a colon) after the place of publication.

Scott, Sir Walter. *Kenilworth.* Chicago, 1890. Print.

Sample Entries for Periodical Publications in Print

Unlike books, "periodical" publications appear at regular intervals—daily, weekly, monthly, quarterly, annually. They include newspapers, magazines, and scholarly journals.

Scholarly Journals

In the entry shown below, *"American Literary History"* is the journal, "15.4" are the volume and issue numbers, "2003" is the year of publication, "753–81" are the page numbers, and "Print" is the publication medium. Note that you give page numbers for the entire article, not just for the ones you cite. If the journal gives only the volume or issue number, include just that (before the date).

Leverenz, David. "Trachtenberg, Haskell, and Livingston, Inc." *American Literary*

   History 15.4 (2003): 738–47. Print.

Weekly or biweekly magazine

Dubus, Andre. "Witness." *New Yorker* 21 July 1997: 33–36.

McCarter, Jeremy. "Tony Kushner's Day." *Newsweek* 8 June 2009: 64-68. Print.

Monthly magazine

Malone, Michael. "Books in Brief." *Harper's* June 1977: 82–84. Print.

Book review in a magazine

Blake, Patricia. "Gingerly Removing the Veil." Rev. of *Josephine Herbst*, by

   Elinor Langer. *Newsweek* 3 Sept. 1984: 80. Print.

Article in a newspaper

When citing newspaper articles, indicate if possible the edition of the paper ("late edition," "national edition," "city edition"). The reason is that the content of articles may vary from edition to edition. The edition is usually indicated in the newspaper's masthead. The letter and number at the end of each citation indicate the section of the paper and page number. A plus sign shows that the article continues on another page.

Coneroy, Herman. "*David Copperfield* Revisited." *New York Times* 19 Aug. 1962,

late ed.: F23. Print.

Weeks, Linton. "Stanley Kunitz, 95, Becomes Poet Laureate for a New Century."

Washington Post 29 July 2000: C1+. Print.

Sample Entries for Web Publications

The documentary formats for computer resources continue to evolve along with the resources themselves. The seventh edition of the *MLA Handbook for Writers of Research Papers* (2009) is the source for the guidelines below, but even these will change as technology evolves.

The nature of Web sites presents challenges for handling and documenting them. They differ from materials in print. The *MLA Handbook* says that whereas "readers seeking a cited print publication can be reasonably assured that a copy in a local library will be identical to that consulted by the author, they can be less certain that a Web publication will be so" (181). Since Web sites can change at any time and since people can gain access to them in different ways, any "version of a Web source is potentially different from any past or future version and must be considered unique" (181). Such qualities shape the *Handbook*'s recommendations for handling and citing Web materials. Writers should, for example, record not just publication information about Web sites they use, but the dates they visited the sites. And lest these sites change or even disappear, writers are well-advised to download or print materials they use from them (183).

One technological advance that makes citing Web publications simpler is that search engines can find Web cites by titles, not just URLs (addresses). The *MLA Handbook* now recommends, therefore, that Web addresses (URLs) be dropped from citations. If you feel that the URL is necessary, place it at the end of the citation in angle brackets. Give the complete address, including *http*:.

> Liu, Alan. Home Page. *Voice of the Shuttle: Electronic Resources for the Humanities.* Dept. of English, U of California, Santa Barbara, n.d. Web. 3 June 2009. <http://vos.ucsb.edu>

When you are faced with the sometimes puzzling problem of documenting electronic resources, keep in mind the reasons to document *anything*: You want to verify the existence and reliability of your resources. You want to help readers find these resources. You want to show that you have conscientiously sifted through the relevant evidence and opinion. So, if you are confused about how to document a resource, use common sense. Give the information necessary to accomplish the above goals.

Nonperiodical works that appear only on the Web
These cites are "nonperiodical" in that they are not published on a regular schedule. They, furthermore, appear only on the Web. They include sites owned and maintained by individuals, newspapers, magazines, universities, radio and television stations, and other organizations.

For these sites, supply the following information in this order:

- Author's name (if available)
- Title of the work (italicized if independent; in quotation marks if part of a larger work)
- Title of the overall Web site (italicized)
- Version or edition (2nd. ed., 4th. ed., Rev. ed., etc., if given)
- Publisher or sponsor of the site. If not available, use *n.p.*
- Date of publication (day, month, and year; if not available, use *N.d.*)
- Medium of publication (*Web*)
- Date of access (the date you used the service; day, month, year)

> Churchyard, Henry. Home page. *Jane Austen Information Page*. N.d. Web.
>
> 29 July 2004.
>
> "Courtly Love." *Encyclopaedia Britannica Online*. Encyclopaedia Britannica,
>
> 2004. Web. 3 August 2009.
>
> Liu, Alan, ed. Home page. *Voice of the Shuttle*. Dept. of English, U of California,
>
> Santa Barbara, n.d. Web. 13 February 2009.
>
> Müller, Stephan. Home Page. *The Big Web-Site about Milan Kundera*. N.p.,
>
> 2000. Web. 24 March 2009.

Nonperiodical works that appear in print

The most prominent example of this kind of publication is e-texts, books, articles, and works of literature that have been scanned into a database. For these sources, provide the following:

- Information about the print versions. (See "Sample Entries for Print Materials" above for guidelines on citing print publications.) Leave out the word *Print* as the medium of publication.
- Title of the database or Web site (italicized)
- Medium of publication (*Web*)
- Date of access (day, month, year)

Keats, John. "La Belle Dame sans Merci." *The Poetical Works of John Keats.*

London: Macmillan, 1884. N. pag. *Bartleby.com.* Web. 28 Aug. 2000.

"Milan Kundera." *European Writers.* N.p.: Gale, n. date. N.p. *Literature Resource*

Center. Web. 16 June 2009.

Sidney, Mary, Countess of Pembroke. "The Doleful Lay of the Fair Clorinda."

Colin Clout's Come Home Againe. Ed. Edmund Spenser. N.p.: n.p, 1595.

N. pag. *Women Writers Online.* Web. 16 June 2009.

Periodical works published only on the Web

These sites include magazines and scholarly journals that are published regularly—once a week, once month, once a quarter, once a year. Provide the following information:

- The same information as for articles in print, except that you leave off the word *Print* as the medium of publication.
- The medium of publication (*Web*)
- The date of access

Beukema, Taryn. "Men Negotiating Identity in Zadie Smith's *White Teeth.*" *Post-*

colonial Text 4.3 (2008): n. pag. Web. 15 August 2009.

Erle, Sibylle. "Blake, Colour and the Truchsessian Gallery: Modelling the Mind

and Liberating the Observer." *Romanticism and Victorianism on the Net.* 52

(2008): n. pag. Web. 25 October 2009.

Periodical works published within online databases

Some databases include the entire contents of print periodicals published in the past. These periodicals typically include articles, reviews, editorials, letters to the editor, poems, short stories. Include the following:

- Information about the printed version of the text. Omit the word *Print* for the medium.
- Title of the database (italicized)
- Medium of publication (*Web*)
- Date of access (day, month, year)

Chamberlain, Kathleen. "The Secrets of Nancy Drew: Having Their Cake and

Eating It Too." *The Lion and the Unicorn* 18.1 (1994): 1–12. *Project Muse.*

Web. 2 Jan. 2009.

Murphy, Mary Jo. "The Secret of the 3 Black Robes" [Sonia Sotomayor

influenced by Nancy Drew]. *New York Times* 31 May 2009, late ed. east coast:

WK3. *ProQuest.* Web. 20 Oct. 2009.

Sample Entries for Other Nonprint Sources

Portable databases published periodically on CD-ROM or DVD-ROM. For CD-ROMs and DVD-ROMs that are continually updated, give as much of the following information as you can find:

- Author's name (if known)
- Publication information for the printed source
- Medium of publication (CD-ROM, DVD-ROM)
- Title of the database (italicized)
- Name of the vendor (if different from the publisher or organization that supplies information in the publication)
- Publication date of the database

Dolan, Marc. "The (Hi)story of Their Lives: Mythic Autobiography and 'The

Lost Generation.'" *Journal of American Studies* 27 (1993): 35–56. CD-ROM.

America: History and Life on Disc. ABC-Clio. 1996.

Earthman, Elise Ann. "Creating the Virtual Work: Readers' Processes in

Understanding Literary Texts." Conference on College Composition and

Communication. Seattle, Washington, 17 March 1989. CD-ROM. *ERIC.*

SilverPlatter. June 1996.

Princeton Review Cracking the SAT with DVD. New York: Random, 2006. DVD-ROM.

Portable databases not published periodically on CD-ROM or DVD-ROM. These databases are published only once, like books. Provide as much of the following information as is given or is relevant:

- Author or editor's name (if given)
- Title of the publication (in quotation marks or italics)
- Name of editor or editors (if relevant)
- Edition (if given)
- Place of publication
- Name of the publisher
- Date of publication
- Name of vendor (if different from the publisher) plus the date of publication
- Medium of publication (CD-ROM or DVD-ROM)

Hallam, Walker. *Molière.* Boston: Twayne, 1990. CD-ROM. Boston: DiscLit,

1992.

Johnson, Samuel. *A Dictionary of the English Language on CD-ROM.* Ed. Anne

McDermott. Cambridge: Cambridge UP, 1996. CD-ROM.

"Mingle." *The Oxford English Dictionary.* 2nd ed. Oxford: Oxford UP, 1992.

CD-ROM.

Whitman, Walt. *Walt Whitman for Windows.* Ed. Ed Folson and Kenneth

M. Price. Woodbridge, CT: Primary Source Media, 1997. CD-ROM.

E-mail message
For e-mail messages, give the following information:

- The name of the writer
- The title of the posting, if any (in quotation marks)
- The recipient of the posting
- The date of the message
- The medium of delivery (*E-mail*)

Finney, Jack. "Re: Time travel fiction." Message to Jonathan Albright.

11 Oct. 2004. E-mail.

Interview
The basic information for interviews is (1) the interviewee's name, (2) the title or nature of the interview and the interviewer (if known), and (3) the place and date of the interview. The first entry below

indicates that Fred Rogers was interviewed on the radio program *All Things Considered* by Noah Adams. If you personally interviewed someone, your citation would look like the second entry.

Rogers, Fred. Interview by Noah Adams. *All Things Considered*. Natl. Public

Radio. WFDD, Winston-Salem. 19 Feb. 1993. Radio.

Trillin, Calvin. Personal interview. 2 October 2004.

Lecture, speech, address, or reading

For oral presentations, give as much of the following information as possible: (1) the speaker's name, (2) the title or nature of the lecture, (3) the meeting and sponsoring organization, and finally (4) the place and date.

Gay, Geneva. "Ethnic Identity in a Diverse Society: The Challenge for Education."

Temple University, Philadelphia. 30 Mar. 1993. Speech.

Stoner, Hugh. Class lecture. English 368: English Romantic Poetry. University of

North Carolina at Greensboro. 20 Jan. 2008. Lecture.

Television or radio program

Since radio and television programs are collaborative, you can arrange the information according to your emphases.

- The name of one or more of the collaborators
- The title of the episode (in quotation marks)
- The title of the program or series (in italics)
- The network (CBS, NPR)
- The call letters and city of the local station
- The date of broadcast
- The medium of reception (*Radio, Television*)

Keillor, Garrison, narr. and perf. *A Prairie Home Companion*. Public Radio Intl.

WVTF, Roanoke, 11 July 2009. Radio.

"Mistaken Identity." *Millennium: Tribal Wisdom and the Modern World*. Narr.

Adrian Malone. WUNC, Chapel Hill. 12 Feb. 1992. Television.

Romeo and Juliet. By Sergei Prokofiev. Perf. Sterling Hyltin and Robert Fairchild.

New York City Ballet. Chor. Peter Martins. Live from Lincoln Center. UNCTV,

Chapel Hill, 21 May 2009. Television.

Sound recording

For commercially available recordings, provide as much of the following information as you can find:

- The name of whichever person involved in the recording you want to emphasize, such as the performer, the composer, the performing group, or the conductor
- The title (in quotation marks or italics)
- The title of the recording (if different from the above)
- The artists (if different from the person named first)
- The manufacturer
- The year of issue. If you don't know this, put *n.d.* ("no date")
- The medium (CD, LP, audiotape, audiocassette).

Dale, Jim, narr. *Harry Potter and the Deathly Hallows.* By J. K. Rowling. New York:

Random House, 2007. Unabridged. Landmark Audiobooks, 2007. CD.

Holbrook, Hal, narr. "Journalism on Horseback." *Mark Twain Tonight.*

Columbia, n.d. LP.

McKennitt, Loreena. "The Lady of Shalott." Written by Alfred Tennyson. Music

by Loreena McKennitt. *The Visit.* Warner Brothers, 1991. CD.

Thomas, Dylan. "Fern Hill." *Dylan Thomas Reads A Child's Christmas in Wales*

and Five Poems. Caedmon, 1952. LP.

Film or video recording

When citing films, arrange the initial information according to your emphases:

- The title (in italics). If, however, you want to emphasize one of the collaborators who made the film, you can begin with that person's name (Alfred Hitchcock, Frank Capra, Cary Grant, etc.).
- One or more of the collaborators, such as director, writer, performers, costume designer, and producers
- The distributor
- The date (year of release)
- The medium

Crete and Mycenae. Prod. and dir. Hans-Joachim Horsfeld. Kartes Video Commu-

nications, 1986. Film.

Star Wars. Dir. George Lucas. Prod. Gary Kurtz. Screenplay by George Lucas.

Music by John Williams. Perf. Mark Hamill, Harrison Ford, Carrie Fisher,

Peter Cushing, and Alec Guiness. Twentieth Century-Fox, 1977. Film.

FREQUENTLY USED ABBREVIATIONS

Abbreviations save space. You will run into them when you read essays and books about literature, and you may want to use them yourself. Here is a brief list. For a much longer list, see *The MLA Handbook*. In general, there are no spaces or periods in abbreviations made up of capital letters. The major exception is abbreviations of names (such as J. K. Rowling). Abbreviations consisting of lower case letters have periods but no spaces. The many exceptions include *mph* and *rpm*.

abbr.	abbreviation
adapt.	adapter, adaptation, adapted by
anon.	anonymous
app.	appendix
b.	born
BC	before Christ
BCE	before the common era
bibliog.	bibliographer, bibliography
c., ca.	*circa*, "about" (usually used with dates when the exact date is not certain—for example, ca. 1594)
cap.	capital, capitalize
CE	common era
cf.	*confer*, "compare" (not the equivalent of "see")
ch., chs.	chapter, chapters
chor.	choreographer
comp.	compiler
d.	died
def.	definition
ed., eds.	edited by, editor, editors
esp.	especially
e.g.	*exempli gratia*, "for example"
et al.	et alii, "and others"
etc.	*et cetera*, "and so forth"
i.e.	*id est*, "that is"
l., ll.	line, lines
misc.	miscellaneous
MS, MSS.	manuscript, manuscripts
narr.	narrator, narrated by
NB	*nota bene*, "note well"
n.d.	no date of publication

n.p.	no date of publication
n.pag.	no pagination
P	press
p., pp.	page, pages
par.	paragraph
perf.	performer, performed by
pt.	part
qtd.	quoted
rev.	revised by, revision; review or reviewed by (for reviews, use *review* where *rev.* might be confused with *revision* or *revised by*)
rpt.	reprint, reprinted
sec., sect.	section
trans.	translated by
U, UP	University, university press (in documentation)
URL	uniform resource locator
vol., vols.	volume, volumes
wk.	week
yr.	year

SAMPLE RESEARCH PAPER

The following sample student research paper illustrates the use of the MLA documentary style as well as the principles of the argumentative research essay. As in this paper, the first page of your paper should have your name and course information in the upper-left corner, the title centered just below this information, and the text just below the title. The *MLA Handbook* says that you do not need a title page, but ask your instructor for his or her preference. Usually, you do not need a title page. If you have endnotes, place them on a new page immediately following your text. Put your Works Cited list after the endnotes, beginning on a new page. For more detailed instructions on the format of your paper, see Chapter 10.

Harold Wright

Professor Helen May

English 105–06

12 April 20–

The Monster's Education in Mary Shelley's *Frankenstein*

Education is a prominent endeavor in Mary Shelley's

Frankenstein. Nearly all the major characters—Walton, Victor,

Elizabeth, Henry, Safie, and the monster—are at school or

searching for knowledge. Victor's education leads to the best

known event of the novel, his creation of a human being. But the

similarity of the monster to Mary Shelley herself suggests that she

uses the monster, and especially his education, to express ideas

that were close to her heart.

I

The monster's education begins immediately after his

creation. His creator, Victor Frankenstein, while at school in

Germany, learns how to bring dead tissue back to life. He

assembles a creature from body parts, but when he awakens it,

he shrinks from it in horror and runs away. Two years later, the

monster, now "grown up," meets Victor in the Alps and tells him

his story.

Although the monster's education is improbably rapid,

Shelley makes clear that it follows the pattern of any person's

growth from infancy to adolescence. To establish the normality

of the monster's growth and education, she drew upon two

works she read while writing *Frankenstein*: John Locke's *Essay*

Concerning Human Understanding (1690) and Rousseau's

Discourse on the Origins of Human Inequality (1755). The monster's childhood fits the pattern of Rousseau's noble savage, who must learn how to survive in the wilderness by trial and error. And he acquires knowledge according to Locke's theory that everything people learn originates from sensations (Woodbridge pars. 15–17).

The first stage of the monster's education begins at his birth and continues into his "childhood." Just after he is "born" he is like any baby, completely innocent, empty of knowledge, registering only sensations. Gradually he moves into a kind of early childhood by learning to feel hot and cold, to experience fear and pleasure, to walk, eat, sleep, and clothe himself. His initial encounters with human beings are not happy. The first person who sees him runs shrieking away. He learns from them how unfair and hurtful people can be. When he ventures into a village, the townspeople pelt him with rocks and chase him out. After wandering cold and hungry around the countryside, the monster comes upon a cottage with a lean-to shed attached to it. He crawls into the shed and makes it his home for the next year (Shelley 98–101).

The second stage of his education, a kind of adolescence, takes place here. The cottage is occupied by the De Laceys, a family of political exiles from France. The family consists of an old, blind father, a son, a daughter, and, somewhat later, the son's fiancée, the daughter of a Turkish businessman. Through a chink in a window, the monster observes and listens to them. He is deeply impressed by this family, because, although they are poor, they love and care for one another. Fearing that his appearance might frighten them, he keeps out of sight. But in imitation of them, he acts with kindness. At night, he piles firewood outside their door and shovels snow from their pathways. The more he observes them, the more he yearns to join their warm family circle (101–09).

His opportunity comes, he thinks, when the fiancée arrives. Since the fiancée cannot speak their language and knows nothing about Europe, the family begins to teach her. As they do, the monster becomes her co-student. This, the third stage of his education, is something like a college education. The monster is astonishingly adept. He learns French more quickly than Safie, the fiancée. He studies European history, economics, and politics. He reads Goethe's *The Sorrows of Young Werther,* Plutarch's *Lives*, and Milton's *Paradise Lost* (109–123). As a result, he begins to think about who he is: "My person was hideous and my stature gigantic. What did this mean? Who was I? What was I? Whence did I come? What was my destination?" (123).

His education climaxes when he decides, finally, to reveal himself to the family and beg them to accept him as one of their own. One day, with fear and trepidation, while the rest of the family is away, he visits the blind father. At first all goes well. The monster explains, "I have good dispositions; my life has been hitherto harmless and in some degree beneficial; but a fatal prejudice clouds their [people's] eyes, and where they ought to see a feeling and kind friend, they behold only a detestable monster" (128). The father responds eagerly and recognizes in the monster a kindred spirit: "I also am unfortunate; I and my family have been condemned, although innocent; judge, therefore, if I do not feel for your misfortunes" (128). The monster weeps in gratitude.

But when the others return, they view the monster with horror. The daughter faints, Safie runs out of the cottage, and the son beats the monster with a stick. Two days later, the monster returns, finds the De Laceys gone, and burns the cottage to the ground. Shortly thereafter, when the monster rescues a little girl, he completes his education. Instead of expressing gratitude, the girl's companion shoots and wounds him. The monster then vows revenge on all humankind. From this point onward, he becomes what he is most famous for being—a killer (123–135).

II

Mary Shelley's childhood and education parallel the monster's in striking ways. She was born 30 August 1797 to two of the most notorious political radicals of their day. Her father, William Godwin, was a social critic, philosopher, political reformer, and novelist. Her mother, Mary Wollstonecraft, was the first feminist author. Together, they condemned tyrannical governments and enthusiastically supported the French Revolution. They shared a passionate and deeply satisfying relationship. Neither believed in marriage, but when Wollstonecraft became pregnant, they married to protect the child. Ten days after Mary's birth, Wollstonecraft died from natal complications (Spark 3–11).

Mary grew up in a large and busy family, consisting of Godwin's new wife, Jane Clairmont, a stepsister, stepbrother, half-sister, and half-brother. Although her brothers went to the best schools, she had no formal education. Instead, she was taught at home by her father, her stepmother, and tutors. She read from her father's large library. She listened to the conversation of famous visitors, like William Wordsworth, Charles Lamb, and William Hazlitt. Once she hid behind the sofa to hear Samuel Taylor Coleridge recite "The Rime of the Ancient Mariner" (Spark 13).

By the time Mary was a teenager, relations with her family had become strained. She didn't get along with her stepmother, and her father distanced himself from her. To escape tensions at home, she made several extended visits to friends in Scotland. It was after one of these that she met the poet Percy Shelley, who had become a frequent visitor in her father's house. He was five years older than Mary, already married, and father of one child with a second on the way. He and Mary fell in love and began a passionate affair. After stormy opposition from her family, they ran away together to Europe in July 1814. Percy was twenty-one years old. She was sixteen and had just discovered that she was pregnant (Spark 28–29).

Until Percy's death in 1822 from a boating accident, the couple lived a difficult, often tumultuous life together. After they "eloped," her father condemned her and refused to see or write to her for three and a half years. She and Percy were almost always in financial difficulty, often, at first, having no place to stay so that they slept outdoors or in barns (Spark 28–29). Giving birth and caring for babies dominated her relationship with Percy. She was pregnant five times until Percy's death. She had two miscarriages, the second of which almost killed her. Two of her children died as infants, and only one survived to adulthood.

Amidst these difficulties, Mary wrote *Frankenstein*. To create the novel, she drew upon the huge amount of reading she had done during this period, the conversations she had with Percy

Wright 6

and their friends, her mother and father's writings, and her own
experiences. She began the novel in July 1816 and finished it by
May 1817. It was published in January 1818 (Spark 56–60).

III

The difficulties of Mary's own education and coming of age
gave rise to the ideas she embedded in the story of the monster's
education. The first of these ideas is that children who are
abandoned or neglected by their parents can become "monsters."
Ellen Moers argues that Mary's experience of continual pregnancy,
childbirth, childcare, and child death led her to write about a
careless and inept scientist who gives birth, so to speak, to a
misformed child. Moers calls *Frankenstein* a "birth myth" (140).
The novel is "interesting, most powerful, and most feminine" in
its "motif of revulsion against newborn life, and the drama of
guilt, dread, and flight surrounding birth and its consequences,"
especially in its dealing "with the retribution visited upon
monster and creator for deficient infant care" (142). Mary thus
writes a "fantasy of the newborn as at once monstrous agent of
destruction and piteous victim of parental abandonment" (148).

As a daring and anxious creator of life, Mary is similar to
Victor. But her childhood experiences, gifts, and education link
her also to the monster. Like the monster, she felt "abandoned"
by her parents, first, at childbirth by her mother, by her father
when he remarried, and then when she ran away with Shelley
(Sunstein 34, 114). "Obviously," Emily Sunstein says, "the monster
created from corpses reflects the primitive Mary Shelley: her guilt
at being her mother's killer-reincarnation, her rage that her father
abandoned her, and her resentment of her half brother, William"

(131). Like the monster, Mary grew up rapidly and was extremely young when she took on the responsibilities of adulthood. Like the monster, she had to pick up an education by "looking on." Like the monster, she was precocious, a rapid learner. Like the monster, she was something of an outlaw, stepping across the border of conventional female morality. Like the monster, she was scorned and exiled.

Mary transfers her feelings of parental victimization to the monster. Upon his first meeting with Victor, he holds Victor accountable for mistreating him: "Remember that I am thy creature; I ought to be thy Adam, but I am rather the fallen angel, whom thou drivest from joy for no misdeed" (95). Victor reluctantly agrees: "For the first time, also, I felt what the duties of a creator towards his creature were, and that I ought to render him happy before I complained of his wickedness" (97). The monster compares the happy De Lacey family to his own lack of family: "But where were my friends and relations? No father had watched my infant days, no mother had blessed me with smiles and caresses" (115). At the end of his story, the monster once again accuses Victor of failing as a parent: "You endowed me with perceptions and passions and cast me abroad an object for the scorn and horror of mankind" (133).

IV

The second idea in *Frankenstein* suggested by Mary's life is that, like bad parents, an unjust society can create monsters. Her main source for this idea probably originated with her parents' beliefs about the French Revolution. In her *An Historical and Moral View of the Origin and Progress of the French Revolution* (1794),

Wright 8

Wollstonecraft responds to conservative critics of the French

Revolution, like Edmund Burke, who labeled the revolutionaries

"monsters" (Sterrenburg 153). Wollstonecraft, Lee Sterrenburg

says, "admits that rebels are monsters. But she resolutely insists

that . . . they are the products of oppression, misrule, and

despotism under the *ancien régime*. The lower orders are driven

to rebellion" (162).

The monster embodies Wollstonecraft's belief that social

rebels are formed by society. At birth the monster is innocent.

As he begins his education, he wants to do good deeds and to

have loving relationships. But the failure of society (Victor, the De

Laceys, other people) to accept him, love him, and treat him fairly

causes him to become a monster. He tells Victor, "I was benevolent

and good; misery made me a fiend" (95–96). After the De Laceys

drive him out of the cottage and the little girl's companion shoots

him, he feels "the oppressive sense of injustice and ingratitude"

of the people who have hurt him and vows "eternal hatred

and vengeance to all mankind" (135). "I am malicious," he says,

"because I am miserable" (138). As Sterrenburg states, "The

Monster proves a very philosophical rebel. He explains his actions

in traditional republican terms. He claims he has been driven

to rebellion by the failures of the ruling orders. His superiors

and protectors have shirked their responsibilities toward him,

impelling him to insurrection" (161).

Although the monster is just one person, and an unusual

one, at that, Mary extends her social criticism to include others.

She does so by means of his education. Through his and Safie's

reading of Volney's *Ruins of Empires*,[1] he hears about the tragic

history of human societies: "For a long time I could not conceive

Wright 9

how one man could go forth to murder his fellow, or even why

there were laws and governments; but when I heard details

of vice and bloodshed, my wonder ceased and I turned away

with disgust and loathing" (114). The De Laceys reveal that

society is unfair to all but a few citizens: "I heard of the division

of property, of immense wealth and squalid poverty, of rank,

descent, and noble blood. . . . I learned that the possessions

most esteemed by your fellow creatures were high and unsullied

descent united with riches" (115).

The De Laceys, Safie, Justine Moritz, and the monster are all

victims of an unjust society. So, too, Mary no doubt believed, were

the oppressed workers of her own day. While she was writing

Frankenstein, England suffered from an economic depression

that caused widespread unemployment and hunger among

workers. These conditions led workers to hold protest rallies that

sometimes ended in violence. The worst of these occasions was

the "Peterloo" riot of 1819, when 80,000 people demonstrated in

St. Peter's Fields in Manchester for political reform and were fired

upon by soldiers. Eleven people were killed and 400 injured. The

government's response to such protests was unsympathetic, harsh,

and repressive (Lerner 786). In Mary's mind, the monster could

have been any of these workers, driven to rebellion by poverty,

hunger, and the meanness of powerful people.[2]

V

The third idea suggested by Mary's life is that women, too,

are made monstrous by society. Sandra Gilbert and Susan Gubar

hold that Mary saw herself as a monster because women are

taught to feel like monsters: "As we argued earlier, women have seen themselves (because they have been seen) as monstrous, vile, degraded creatures, second-comers, and emblems of filthy materiality, even though they have also been traditionally defined as superior beings, angels, better halves" (240).

Mary got a taste of this attitude when she learned about her mother's life and ideas. A year after Wollstonecraft's death, Godwin published his *Memoirs of the Author of A Vindication of the Rights of Woman* (1798), in which, Emily Sunstein says, "he revealed the details of her intimate life, which comparatively few had known about: her love for Fuseli, her liaison with Imlay, her premarital affair with him—'stripping his dead wife naked,' said Robert Southey" (19). As a result, the conservative press ruthlessly attacked Godwin and her, calling her a "lascivious whore" (Sunstein 20).

Mary read Godwin's *Memoirs* when she was fourteen, along with *A Vindication of the Rights of Woman* (1794), Wollstonecraft's best-known book, and her other works. Fully aware of the press's charges against her mother, Mary became a fierce partisan of Wollstonecraft's feminist beliefs. She "worshiped" her mother, according to Sunstein, "both as rational intellectual and romantic heroine" (53). Through her mother's writings and actions, Mary saw that women who advocate and practice liberation are labeled "monsters."

The monster's embodiment of women is most visible in his education. In *A Vindication of the Rights of Woman*, Wollstonecraft declared the equality of the sexes and demanded equal rights for women. She argued that the key to women's sharing of power with men is education. Yet Mary, although extremely able as a student, did not go to school. Her brothers and husband went, but not she. And there was probably no college or university at the time that would have accepted females as students. Instead, like the monster, Mary did much of her learning on her own. As if to call attention to her identity with the monster, she shows him reading the same things that she had read under Percy's tutelage. The similarity of their reading program leads Gilbert and Gubar to claim that Mary and the monster are "parented, if at all, by books" (239).

VI

The similarity of Mary's life to the monster's, then, suggests that, through neglect and mistreatment, three groups can be turned into "monsters"; children, citizens, and women. If the monster's experience is anything to go by, education, though exciting, only adds to their monstrousness. It makes them more aware of their alienation and unjust treatment. "Increase of knowledge," the monster tells Victor, "only discovered to me more clearly what a wretched outcast I was" (125). Furthermore, education drives them toward vengeance rather than acceptance: "My sufferings were augmented also by the oppressive sense of the injustice and ingratitude of their infliction. My daily vows rose for revenge—a deep and deadly revenge, such as would alone compensate for the outrages and anguish I endured" (135).

But the monster's education is also our education. Just as he learned by looking over Safie's shoulder, we learn by looking over his. Mary Shelley perhaps hoped that if we, her readers, shared the monster's education, we might help prevent the creation of monsters—by caring for our children, by treating people fairly, and by establishing just societies.

Wright 12

Notes

[1]One of Shelley's sources for the scene wherein the
monster learns about the history of human vice is *Pygmalion et
Galatée* (1803), a play by Stéphanie-Félicité Ducrest de Saint-
Aubin, Comtesse de Genlis. In this play, a pure and innocent
character, Galatea, is, like the monster, "awakened" to life fully
grown. When an old servant fills her in on human history, she is
shocked by revelations of human meanness and misery (slavery,
tyranny, extreme distance between rich and poor, treachery). This
play, Burton Pollin maintains, "helped to suggest the device of
awakening and the actual injustices of society with which both
naive intellects become acquainted" (101).

[2]Elizabeth Bohls claims that Mary extends her social
criticism to imperialism. Safie, as a Turk and Christian, and the
monster, as the alienated outlaw, represent colonized peoples
(32). After reading Volney's book, they both lament the "genocide
of the American Indians" (29). The monster's exclusion from
happy middle class families like the Frankensteins and the De
Laceys, "is inseparable from, in fact depends on, the violence
their civilization does to those whom its structure of value needs
to exclude and condemn" (29). In the monster's expressions of
alienation, we "hear the anguish of a colonized self who has
internalized the values that judge him forever deficient" (32).

Wright 13

Works Cited

Bohls, Elizabeth A. "Standards of Taste, Discourses of 'Race,' and
the Aesthetic Education of a Monster: Critique of Empire in
Frankenstein." *Eighteenth-Century Life* (Nov. 1994): 23–36.
Print.

Gilbert, Sandra M., and Susan Gubar. *The Madwoman in the Attic:
The Woman Writer and the Nineteenth-Century Literary
Imagination.* New Haven, CT: Yale UP, 1979. Print.

Lerner, Robert E., Standish Meacham, and Edward McNall Burns.
Western Civilizations: Their History and Their Culture. 11th
ed. New York: Norton, 1988. Print.

Moers, Ellen. *Literary Women: The Great Writers.* Garden City, NY:
Anchor Books, 1977. Print.

Pollin, Burton R. "Philosophical and Literary Sources of
Frankenstein." *Comparative Literature* 17.2 (Spring 1965):
97–108. Print.

Shelley, Mary. *Frankenstein: Or, The Modern Prometheus.* New
York: Signet Classic (New American Library), 1965. Print.

Spark, Muriel. *Mary Shelley.* New York: Dutton, 1987. Print.

Sunstein, Emily W. *Mary Shelley: Romance and Reality.* Boston:
Little, Brown, 1989. Print.

Woodbridge, Kim. "Mary Shelley and the Desire to Acquire
Knowledge: Demonstrated in the Novel Frankenstein."
Mary Shelley and Frankenstein. N.d. Web. 24 Nov. 2004

Comments on the Research Paper

In the first paragraph—the introduction—the author states his purpose: to use Mary Shelley's life as a means of identifying important ideas in *Frankenstein*. He indicates that he will focus on one part of the novel, the section about the monster's education. Although he does not state his purpose in the form of a question, we can infer the question that lies behind his purpose: How might the monster's education apply to the real world? Put another way, what ideas might Shelley have wanted to convey in her story about the monster's education?

The body of the paper is structured by three answers to this question. First, neglectful parents can turn children into monsters. Second, unjust societies can turn citizens into monsters. Third, prejudiced societies can turn women into monsters. Each of these claims constitutes a major unit of the paper. Within each unit the author draws upon details from the novel, information about Mary Shelley's life, and opinions of critics to explain and support his claims.

In the final paragraph, the author's conclusion, he restates his three major claims. This summary, the first sentence of the paragraph, is his thesis. He then uses the thesis to make a conjecture about what his line of thought adds up to, how the monster's education might apply to people today. Throughout the paper, he follows MLA procedure for introducing facts and testimony in his text. He includes two explanatory notes, which he places at the end of the paper. His parenthetical references refer clearly to the sources in the Works Cited list. The author uses Roman numerals to indicate the major units of the paper. These help readers keep track of his line of thought and give places to "rest" along the way.

Notice that for all the author's inclusion of secondary sources, the paper is nonetheless his argument, his creative investigation of the meaning of the novel. He never presents facts and other people's opinions as ends in themselves, but rather as support for his own ideas. As such, his paper is a fine model of a research essay about literature.

Checklist for Documentation and Research

- Plan a research paper that uses secondary sources to develop and help support your interpretation of a work or works of literature.

- Use the library and computers to locate resources in books, journals, newspapers, databases, and Internet sites.

- Evaluate the quality of any Internet sites you consult.

- In your paper, give proper credit to all primary and secondary sources you include.

- Give credit in your text (parenthetical references) and in a Works Cited section, located at the end. Follow correct documentary style.

12

Taking Essay Tests

So far, this book has dealt with essays written outside the classroom. Tests and examinations, however, are work you do in class, usually within a given time frame. When your instructor tests you, he or she wants to know two things: how familiar you are with the course material (the literature, the instructor's lectures, the secondary material you may be required to read) and how creatively you can think about this material. Tests fall into two categories—objective and essay. Sometimes, the instructor may include questions or assignments from both categories on the same test.

Objective versus essay tests. Objective tests ask you to account for, explain, and identify details about the course material. Essay tests ask you to state your ideas about literary works and to support those ideas with facts and reasoning. Some essay tests call for short, one-paragraph essays; some call for long essays. The same methods for writing out-of-class essays apply to test essays, short or long. Your test essays are arguments: They should have a thesis and should try to convince an audience of the validity of that thesis. They should use sound logic and apt illustrations. Equally important, because of time limits, they need good organization.

Performance on tests. Perhaps the most important general consideration to keep in mind is that your grade will depend on how well you *perform* on a particular assignment, not simply on how much

363

you know. You may know the material very well, but if you do not perform well, your grade will not reflect the abundance or quality of your knowledge. The following guidelines should help you perform well on essay tests.

GUIDELINES FOR TAKING ESSAY TESTS

1. **Prepare thoroughly.**
   a. First, learn the facts of the work or works on which you are being tested. Know who the characters are, what they do, and what happens to them, as well as the specifics of setting, and so forth. When you are taking the test, you should know the details so well that they emerge from your memory almost automatically. This subliminal knowledge saves your creative energy for dealing with interpretive problems the instructor gives you. If you have to slowly dredge up facts from your memory, you lose time for interpretation.
   b. Systematically review the key issues relevant to the works, literary periods, or genres covered by the test. A wise first step is to review the aspects of the works the instructor has emphasized in class. Then ask questions about the works, as you would for finding essay topics. Here, however, cover a range of important questions. Focus on the elements of literature. How does the author handle setting, characterization, theme, point of view, and so forth. If the test covers a number of works, consider ways in which the works are linked. Assume that your instructor will ask you to compare works, noting similarities and differences among them.
   c. When you review class notes, do so *along with* a review of the literary works. Reviewing your notes on the instructor's class comments will help you pinpoint important aspects of the works and help you anticipate test questions. Remember, however, that memorizing class notes is no substitute for reviewing the works themselves. The two go together.

2. **Understand the assignment.** When you get the test, carefully read all of the assignments before you begin writing. If you do not understand any of them, ask the instructor to explain more fully. Sometimes instructors unintentionally write ambiguous assignments. You have a right to know exactly what you are supposed to do.

3. **Plan your answer.**
   a. *Think through* your answer by making a short, topical outline. Making an outline frees you from worrying about relevance and completeness while you write. Instead, once you have planned your answer and jotted down an outline of your plan, you can devote your writing time to a creative develop-ment of each main point. If you have fifty minutes to write an essay, ten minutes making an outline is time well spent. Your outline might look something like this:

   Thesis (state it in a phrase)

   Claim # 1 (state it in a phrase)
      Supporting facts (list several)

   Claim # 2
      Supporting facts

   Claim # 3
      Supporting facts

   b. Cross through items on your outline that do not fit the topic.
   c. Arrange the remaining items in a logical order. Descending order of importance is probably best. That way, if you run out of time, you will have covered the most important items.
   d. Once you have edited your outline, you are ready to write. If you think of additional items to cover, add them in the appro-priate place to your outline.

4. **Respond directly to the assignment.** One or two sentences at the beginning of the essay and at strategic places throughout should do the job. This way the instructor will know that you have kept the assignment in mind and that you have tried to deal with it. Your direct response to the assignment is the thesis of your essay and therefore should usually come near the beginning or end of your essay. Note the following example:

   Assignment: Huck tricks Jim into believing that he dreamed they were separated in the fog. But Jim finally sees the trick for what it is. What does Huck learn from Jim's reaction?

   Direct Response: Huck learns that Jim has feelings and dignity just as white people do.

The complete answer, of course, would explain and illustrate this point, but the direct response connects the whole answer to the assignment. Without a direct response, your answer may seem irrelevant.

5. **Write on one side of the page.** Writing on both sides of the page is messy and hard to read (ink bleeds through). Also, the instructor might overlook what's on the back side, especially if it is just a few sentences. To avoid these problems, write on one side of the page. Do this even if you use blue books.

6. **Add inserts when necessary.** It is acceptable, after you have read your answer through, to add new material. This is another reason to write on only one side of the page. If the new material is short, write it in the margin, with an arrow to indicate where it fits. If the new material is long, write the words "insert (see the back of this page)" in the margin, accompanied with the arrow, and write the new material on the back of the page. You could also write the new material on a separate page.

7. **Write clear, simple, and correct prose.** The limited time and the pressure of the occasion make some mechanical slips likely, but strive to avoid them. Be wary of serious errors such as sentence fragments, ambiguous pronoun references, and subject–verb disagreements. If your handwriting is normally difficult to read, take care to make it legible.

8. **Develop your answer thoroughly.**
   a. State claims that respond directly to the assignment. Often, these claims will serve as topic sentences for paragraphs.
   b. Offer specific details from the works that support and illustrate your claims.
   c. Represent the work or works adequately. The more thoroughly and appropriately you relate the work to your claims (and thus to the assignment), the better your answer will be.
   d. Your answer is an argument. Back up claims with evidence. Show your readers, do not just tell them.

9. **Be creative.** Some instructors want you to reproduce what they have said in class. Studying for their tests is straightforward. Just memorize what the instructor has said and paraphrase it on the test. The more perfect your reproduction, the better your grade. Other instructors, however, want more—and they design their tests to get more. They want *your* thinking, not just their own. They want your creativity. But how can you be creative on tests? The answer is—think for yourself! Here are some ways to do so.

a. Use the instructor's points, but provide your own facts from the works. This shows that you are doing more than just memorizing lectures. It shows that you have thought through and applied the instructor's ideas on your own.

b. Make your own claims. Although instructors try to cover the most important aspects of a work, limited class time makes it impossible for them to cover every aspect, even all the important ones. There are usually plenty of other claims to be made. Study the work yourself, and come up with your own claims. Read what others have said about the work and discover claims that way. Do not neglect claims made by the instructor, but make other claims as well.

c. Describe and take a stand on controversies—disagreements about meaning—in works of literature. Instructors often enjoy presenting controversies for class discussion. You can dip into them yourself by reading criticism of the works you are studying. Understanding literary controversies can sharpen your perception of the work. Showing your awareness of them and taking a stand on them will demonstrate your creative involvement with the work.

d. Be detailed in your support and illustration of points. The more details you provide, the clearer your creative involvement becomes, especially if you include details you have noticed on your own.

SAMPLE TEST ESSAYS

All of the following essays respond to the assignment below. The writers had about twenty minutes to write their essays.

> **ASSIGNMENT:** *Explain the possible symbolic meanings of the rocking horse in D. H. Lawrence's "The Rocking-Horse Winner."*

Essay 1 (A Mediocre Essay)

Paul seems desperately to want his mother to love him. He senses that somehow she disapproves of him, that he stands in her way of achieving happiness. He seeks solace in the rocking horse. She has told him that "luck" means having money, so he rides the horse to get money. He hopes that by giving his mother money, he can buy his way into her heart.

But, unfortunately, when he gives her an enormous sum of money, she is even more unhappy than before. Paul returns to the rocking horse to get more money for her. He frantically rides the horse one last time. But although he wins the jackpot, he dies from overexcitement and exhaustion.

Comments on Essay 1

Although this essay has good qualities, it is nonetheless mediocre because it does not directly address the assignment. It describes the action of the story accurately. It is clearly written. Its organization is easy to follow. It seems to have the assignment vaguely in mind, but nowhere does it say what the rocking horse symbolizes. The instructor may guess what the writer has in mind, but he or she cannot know for sure. The essay also omits important details. The writer does not say, for example, how Paul uses the horse to win money. The instructor may wonder whether the writer has carefully read the story.

Essay 2 (A Good Essay)

Paul's mother claims that she is "unlucky," and she explains to Paul that being unlucky means having no money. But the details of the story suggest that Paul's family does have money, because they live very well. The family has the trappings of wealth—a nurse, a large house, comfortable furnishings, and a gardener. The mother, then, isn't really poor but is obsessed with money. Her children sense this obsession. Most sensitive of all is Paul, who hears voices saying, "There must be more money." As a result, Paul sets out to win his mother's love by being "lucky." His means of achieving luck and thus his mother's love is the rocking horse. He finds that by riding the horse hard enough, he can predict winners of horse races. The rocking horse, then, symbolizes the love his mother has withheld from him. He even experiences something like the ecstasy of love when riding the horse to a winner. But his plan fails when his gift of 5,000 pounds only makes his mother's greed greater. He then becomes so desperate for love that he rides the rocking horse to his death.

Comments on Essay 2

This is a good essay. It not only accurately recounts details from the story, it also directly responds to the assignment: "The rocking horse, then, symbolizes the love his mother has withheld from him."

And it relates all the details cited from the story to that response. In other words, the details become "evidence." Because it deals directly with the assignment, it treats the story more specifically and thoroughly than does essay 1.

Essay 3 (An Excellent Essay)

The rocking horse symbolizes many things in "The Rocking-Horse Winner." Paul's mother complains that she has no money, and she tells Paul that to be "lucky" is to have money. Paul is very impressed by what she says and decides to prove to her that he is lucky. He wants also to stop the voices in the house that incessantly demand more money. He feels that the rocking horse can take him where luck is. Sure enough, when he rides the rocking horse and it takes him "there," he can predict the winners of horse races and make a great deal of money. So one thing the rocking horse symbolizes is luck, which, in turn, means money.

But the rocking horse also seems to represent a second idea. Paul's uncle says after Paul dies that Paul is better off being dead than living in a world where he had to ride a rocking horse to find a winner. The implication is that Paul was using the rocking horse to get what his mother never gave him: her love. So the rocking horse also symbolizes Paul's need for love and his parents' failure to give him love.

Finally, the rocking horse symbolizes success. When Paul rides the rocking horse far enough, it brings him financial success. But this success is only ironic, for it never brings him the "success" he desperately wants—his mother's love—and in the end it brings him death. Lawrence seems to suggest that some kinds of success are better than others; it is better to be loved than to be rich.

Comments on Essay 3

This is an excellent answer. Like essay 2, the essay responds to the assignment directly, and it plausibly and logically connects details of the story to its points. But it is more detailed and creative than essay 2. The writer makes a strong case for the complexity of the rocking horse as symbol and, by so doing, points to the multiple meanings and richness of the story. Its final sentence ties the whole essay together by suggesting an overall meaning for the story.

Checklist for Taking Essay Tests

Preparation

- Know exceedingly well the details in works covered by the test.

- Review key issues of interpretation raised by the instructor, students, and critics.

- Ask your own interpretive questions about the work. Anticipate questions that might appear on the test.

- Study class notes while reviewing the works.

Before You Begin Writing

- Understand the assignment.

- Make a rough outline of your essay.

While You Write

- Respond directly to the assignment.

- Write on one side of the page.

- Insert afterthoughts and corrections where necessary.

- Write clearly.

- Cover the assignment thoroughly.

- Support claims with evidence from the works.

- Be creative.

13

Sample Essays

This chapter contains four sample essays: one on a poem, one on a short story, one on a play, and one on a novel. All essays about literature are different. Interpretive questions vary enormously from essay to essay; authors employ different methods of answering them. These essays, then, are not models to be slavishly imitated. They do, however, embody the main points of this book: that essays about literature are interpretations, that they address explicit or implicit questions, that their theses answer those questions, and that, as arguments, they employ sound logic and well-supported claims. Except for the final essay (on a novel), the full texts of the works featured in these essays appear in the Appendix.

ESSAY ON A POEM

George Cannon

Professor Landsdown

English 251–10

12 February 20—

Point of View in Edwin Arlington Robinson's

"Richard Cory"

Yvor Winters, an American critic, condemns Edwin Arlington

Robinson's poem "Richard Cory" for containing "a superficially

neat portrait of the elegant man of mystery" and for having a

"very cheap surprise ending" (52). It is true that because Richard

Cory fits the stereotype of "the man who has everything," his

suicide at the end is surprising, even shocking. But the poet's

handling of point of view makes the portrait of Richard Cory only

apparently superficial and the ending only apparently "cheap."

In the second line of the poem, we learn that the speaker

is not an omniscient narrator, but someone with a limited view

of things. He is one of the "people" of the town (38). It is as if

he has cornered a visitor on a sidewalk somewhere and is telling

him about a fellow townsman whose suicide has puzzled and

troubled him. He cannot understand it, so he talks about it.

Throughout this speaker's narration, we learn a lot about him

and his peers and how they regarded Richard Cory.

Clearly they saw him as something special. The imagery of

kings and nobility ("crown," "imperially slim," and "richer than

a king") permeates their conception of Richard Cory. To them he

had the bearing and trappings of royalty. He was a "gentleman,"

a word that suggests courtliness as well as nobility. He had good

Cannon 2

taste ("he was always quietly arrayed"). He was wealthy. He had good breeding (he was "admirably schooled in every grace"). He "glittered when he walked," suggesting, perhaps, that he wore jewelry and walked with confidence.

Because of this attitude, the speaker and his peers placed themselves in an almost feudal relationship to Cory. They saw themselves as "people on the pavement," as if they walked on the ground and Richard Cory somehow walked above them. Even if he did not literally walk above them, they saw him as "above" them socially. They seemed to think it unusual that he was "human when he talked." The word *human* suggests several things. One is that the people saw Cory as somehow exempt from the problems and restrictions of being a human being (thus "human") but that when he talked, he stepped out of character. Another is that he, who was so much above them, could be kind, warm, and thoughtful (another meaning of "human"). They were so astonished by this latter quality that when he did such a simple and obvious thing as say "Good-morning," he "fluttered pulses."

In the final stanza, the speaker brings out the most important differences between the people and Richard Cory. Most obvious is that he was rich and they were poor; they "went without the meat, and cursed the bread." But another difference is suggested by the word *light*: "So on we worked, and waited for the light." *Light* in this context most apparently means a time when things will be better, as in the expression "the light at the end of the tunnel." But another meaning of "light" is revelation. Light has traditionally symbolized knowledge and truth, and it may be that this is the meaning the speaker—or at least

Cannon 3

Robinson—has in mind. If so, another difference that the people saw between Richard Cory and themselves was that Cory had knowledge and understanding and they did not. After all, they had no time to pursue knowledge; they needed all their time just to survive. But Richard Cory did have the time. He was a man of leisure who had been "schooled." If anyone would have had the "light"—a right understanding of things—then Richard Cory would have been that person.

Although Robinson does not tell us why Richard Cory killed himself, he leaves several hints. One of these is the assumptions about Richard Cory held by the narrator and the "people." Cory may have been a victim of their attitude. The poem gives no evidence that he sought to be treated like a king or that he had pretensions to nobility. He seems, in fact, to have been democratic enough. Although rich, well-mannered, and tastefully dressed, he nonetheless came to town, spoke with kindness to the people, and greeted them as if they deserved his respect. Could he have wanted their friendship?

But the people's attitude may have isolated Richard Cory. Every time he came to town, they stared at him as if he were a freak in a sideshow (lines 1–2). In their imagination, furthermore, they created an ideal of him that was probably false and, if taken seriously by Richard Cory, would have been very difficult to live up to. Cory did not, at least, have the "light" that the people thought he had. His suicide attests to that. He was, in short, as "human" as they; but, unlike them, he lacked the consolation of fellowship. Ironically, then, the people's very admiration of Richard Cory, which set him apart as more than human and isolated him from human companionship, may have been the cause of his death.

Cannon 4

Had Robinson told Cory's story as an omniscient narrator, Winters's complaint about the poem would be justified. The poem would seem to be an attempt to shock us with a melodramatic and too-obvious irony. But Robinson has deepened the poem's meaning by having one of Cory's fellow townspeople tell his story. This presentation of Cory's character, his relationship to the townspeople, and his motives for suicide open up the poem to interpretation in a way that Winters does not acknowledge or explore.

Works Cited

Robinson, Edwin Arlington. *Tilbury Town: Selected Poems of Edwin Arlington Robinson*. New York: Macmillan, 1951. Print.

Winters, Yvor. *Edwin Arlington Robinson*. Norfolk: New Directions, 1946. Print.

Note: Normally, the Works Cited list would appear on a separate page, but we print it here, right after the essay, to save space.

ESSAY ON A SHORT STORY

Long 1

Blake Long

Prof. Johnson

English 212–04

3 April 20—

Montresor's Fate in Edgar Allan Poe's "The Cask of Amontillado"

Montresor, the narrator of Edgar Allan Poe's story "The Cask of Amontillado," tells the story not to us but to someone else.

Long 2

We see this in the first two sentences: "The thousand injuries of Fortunato I had borne as I best could, but when he ventured upon insult I vowed revenge. You, who so well know the nature of my soul, will not suppose, however, that I gave utterance to a threat" (167). In the story, Montresor reveals that fifty years ago he murdered Fortunato and no one found out. He committed the perfect crime. Why would he be telling anyone about it now?

Details in the story suggest that Montresor's listener is a priest and that the story is a confession. If this is correct, Montresor's motive for telling the story would be to gain absolution for his sin. Montresor is the right age to worry about the fate of his soul. At the time of the crime, he had to be old enough to live through Fortunato's "thousand injuries" and worldly wise enough to plan his complicated revenge. Let's say he was about thirty. Fifty years have passed, so Montresor is now about eighty. Death is staring him in the face. His categorization of the listener as someone who "so well" knows "the nature of my soul" points to someone whose calling is to care for souls— a priest. The final line of the story—*In pace requiescat!*—echoes the words a priest would say at the end of a service for the dead: "May he rest in peace." A priest would know these words as a pious expression. Montresor perhaps thinks that the priest will take them as an expression of remorse, as if, after much reflection, Montresor is sorry for what he did and now wishes "peace" for Fortunato in the afterlife. In his own mind, Montresor might also be applying the phrase to himself: "Since I am about to die, may I rest in peace. And I will if this priest will only absolve me."

Long 3

If the listener is indeed a priest, will he do this, grant
Montresor absolution? Since the story ends before the listener
speaks, Poe leaves it to us to imagine the ensuing scene. What
will the priest decide? In order to answer this question, we need
to judge two things: the magnitude of Montresor's crime and his
attitude toward it.

First, did Fortunato deserve to die? A priest might be
willing to grant absolution if Montresor had been an instrument
of justice. Maybe Fortunato had done terrible deeds but escaped
the law. In that case, Montresor's crime would have visited just
retribution upon Fortunato. From what we see of Fortunato,
he is not especially likable. He is so egotistical that he goes
on a wild goose chase just to prove his superiority to Luchresi,
his rival in wine connoisseurship. He pooh poohs his ill-health
with macho bravado, as if he is above mortal limitations. His
pretense of not knowing Montresor's family crest (171) reveals
his disdain for people. His drunkenness and costume—that of
a fool—underscore his boorishness and stupidity. All of these
qualities support Montresor's claim that Fortunato is guilty of
committing "injuries" and "insults." But does someone deserve
to die for being boorish and stupid? Montresor doesn't say what
the injuries are, but they don't seem to have harmed him greatly.
He is still alive, still the owner of a palazzo, still a person of high
station. His unwillingness to specify what Fortunato did makes
us suspicious that Fortunato wounded Montresor's pride rather
than caused him serious harm. The punishment Montresor dishes
out seems to far outweigh the "injuries" and "insults" of which
Fortunato stands accused.

Long 4

Well, okay, Montresor went too far. Perhaps he realizes
that now. Does he show contrition for killing Fortunato? If so,
the priest might grant him absolution. No, Montresor does not.
The tone of his narrative reflects pride in his cleverness, not
sorrow for his deed. Presenting his plan for revenge as a
kind of game, he states the "rules" at the beginning:
"A wrong is unredressed when retribution overtakes its
redresser. It is equally unredressed when the avenger fails to
make himself felt as such to him who has done the wrong"
(167). He proceeds to gloat about how clever he was in getting
Fortunato to go down into the catacombs. Montresor is an
astute psychologist. He knows that if he plucks the strings of
Fortunato's vanity, Fortunato will keep on walking. All he has
to do is mention Luchresi and Fortunato's cold, and Fortunato
will keep going. Montresor revels in telling how he sadistically
needled Fortunato about his cold by calling attention to the
nitre and dampness. Montresor also enjoys his little jokes.
When Fortunato says he "shall not die of a cough," Montresor
replies "True—true" (170). When Fortunato asks him if he is
a Mason, Montresor assures him he is and pulls out a trowel
(172). After Montresor enchains Fortunato, he says, "Once more
let me *implore* you to return" (173).

Montresor does exhibit some behavior that might
suggest feelings other than self-congratulation. Fortunato's
screams give Montresor pause: "For a brief moment I hesitated,
I trembled" (174). But he trembles from fear of discovery, not
contrition. When Fortunato appeals to Montresor's sense of

divine mercy ("*For the love of God, Montresor!*"), Montresor
blows him off: "'Yes,' I said, 'for the love of God!'" (175). The
only hint of remorse comes when, after hearing the bells on
Fortunato's costume, Montresor says, "My heart grew sick" (175).
In his heart of hearts, Montresor may be revolted by his
crime. But this recognition never reaches the surface of his
consciousness. Instead, he attributes his feeling to "the
dampness of the catacombs" (175). His concluding statement—
"For the half of a century no mortal has disturbed (Fortunato's
bones)"—seems like pride of accomplishment rather than
anything close to remorse.

On two counts, then, Montresor fails the test for
absolution: His crime was not justified and he expresses no
remorse for committing it. We might join the priest here in
saying, "May you fry in hell!" But a final twist in the story
is that Montresor has already, for fifty years, been in hell, a
mental hell. He knows the details of this story so well that we
surmise he has replayed it in his mind, like a movie, over and
over for years and years. Now he wants a different story, one of
ascent: ascent to heaven. The story he will get, however, is one
of descent: deeper and deeper into the earth, past the remains
of the dead, through cold and damp, ending at his own crypt.
He may not have realized it at first, but surely he now knows
that his story was not just about Fortunato's descent to death,
but about his own as well. His final descent will be to the
eternal punishments of hell.

Long 6

Work Cited

Poe, Edgar Allan. "The Cask of Amontillado." *Complete Works of*
Edgar Allan Poe. Ed. James A. Harrison. Vol. 5. New York:
Fred De Fau, 1902. Print.

ESSAY ON A PLAY

Briner 1

Carolyn Briner

Prof. Hesterman

English 104–12

12 September 20—

The Meaning of Physical Objects in

Susan Glaspell's *Trifles*

In most performances of plays, the audience sees physical
objects on stage—the sets and props that locate the action in
time and space. The title of Susan Glaspell's play, *Trifles,* calls
attention to the importance of such objects. Most of them are
the "trifles" that mark the extreme difference between the way
the male and female characters value women's work. They are
also the evidence in the impromptu trial enclosed by the play:
Mrs. Wright is charged with murdering her husband; the county

attorney is the prosecutor; Mr. Hale and the sheriff (Mr. Peters) are the witnesses; and the women, Mrs. Hale and Mrs. Peters, are the jury. We, the audience, join the women as jurors. Like them, we piece together Mrs. Wright's character and her past by discovering what the physical objects mean.

       The action of the play takes place in Mrs. Wright's kitchen. The characters have arrived the day after Mr. Hale discovered Mr. Wright's body. The men have come to find evidence to prove that Mrs. Wright strangled her husband with a rope. They have brought the women along, not to help them find evidence but to gather items to take to Mrs. Wright in jail. The key exchange, which names the play and sets the trial in motion, occurs near the beginning:

> COUNTY ATTORNEY. (to the SHERIFF) You're convinced that there was nothing important here—nothing that would point to any motive.
>
> SHERIFF: Nothing here but kitchen things.
>
> COUNTY ATTORNEY. (after noticing spilled preserves in the cupboard.) Here's a nice mess.
>
> MRS. PETERS:. (to Mrs. Hale) Oh, her fruit; it did freeze. (to the County Attorney) She worried about that when it turned so cold. She said the fire'd go out and her jars would break.
>
> SHERIFF. Well, can you beat the women! Held for murder and worryin' about her preserves.
>
> COUNTY ATTORNEY. I guess before we're through she may have something more serious than preserves to worry about.

HALE. Well, women are used to worrying over trifles.

COUNTY ATTORNEY. And yet, for all their worries, what
would we do without the ladies? (notices the dirty hand
towel.) Dirty towels! (kicks the pans under the sink.) Not
much of a housekeeper, would you say, ladies?

MRS. HALE. (stiffly) There's a great deal of work to be done
on a farm. (38)

In this exchange, the men dismiss the very evidence that
is crucial to the case, evidence that establishes Mrs. Wright's
guilt and her motive. This evidence—objects the men label as
"trifles" —shows three things about Mrs. Wright. First, it shows
that Mrs. Wright was a hard worker and fine craftsperson.
The men don't understand this, since, as the passage above
indicates, they undervalue women's work and conclude that
Mrs. Wright was "a bad housekeeper." But the objects in the
kitchen, as the women know, tell a different story. The broken
jars of preserves represent Mrs. Wright's hard work and skill.
"She'll feel awful bad," Mrs. Hale says, "after all her hard work
in the hot weather. I remember the afternoon I put up my
cherries last summer" (39). An expert herself, Mrs. Hale holds
the one good jar to the window and sees that it's all right.
Equally telling are the loaf of bread, covered with a cloth,
waiting to be placed in the breadbox, and the quilting pieces
the women find in her sewing basket. "It's log cabin pattern,"
Mrs. Hale says. "Pretty, isn't it?" The sewing is "nice and even"
(41). The kitchen has been Mrs. Wright's domain. As playgoers,
we view its objects—stove, table, breadbox, loaf of bread, jar of
cherries, cupboard, sewing basket, quilting pieces—and

see them as the tools of her craft and the products of her
hard work.

The second thing that physical objects show about
Mrs. Wright is that she led a difficult life with her husband.
Even Mr. Hale knows that Mr. Wright was indifferent to his wife:
"I didn't know as what his wife wanted made much difference
to John" (36). Mrs. Hale admits that Mr. Wright was "good" in
that he abstained from drinking, kept his word, and paid his
debts. But "he was a hard man, Mrs. Peters. Just to pass the
time of day with him—(shivers) Like a raw wind that gets to the
bone" (42). Coldness is the dominant atmosphere of the play
and represents the Wrights' life together. At the beginning, we
are told that the night before the temperature was below zero
(36). Ironically, the object that signifies coldness is the stove.
Although the stove is constantly referred to, it never seems
adequate to heat the house, to make it warm and cosy. When
Mrs. Peters returns from the front room, she says, "My, it's cold
in there" (40). When the men come from upstairs, the County
Attorney says, "Frank's fire didn't do much up there, did it?"
(41). Mr. Wright was stingy and did not talk much. The house
is "down in a hollow" where "you don't see the road" (42).
There was no telephone in the house. The severity of Nebraska
winters, the isolation of the house, its location in a low place,
the stingy and obdurate nature of Mr. Wright all make the
house emotionally as well as physically "cold."

The third thing that physical objects show about
Mrs. Wright is her motivation for killing her husband. The
most important objects here are the canary and the birdcage.

Glaspell openly associates Mrs. Wright with the canary. Mrs. Hale says, "She—come to think of it, she was kind of like a bird herself—real sweet and pretty, but kind of timid and—fluttery" (43). Before she married Mr. Wright, she was Minnie Foster, who used to sing (42) and wear pretty clothes (40). But after marrying him, she didn't socialize: "I suppose she felt she couldn't do her part, and then you don't enjoy things when you feel shabby" (40). The canary also represents the children she never had, which Mr. Wright may have denied her. "I wonder," Mrs. Hale says, "how it would seem never to have had any children around. . . . No, Wright wouldn't like the bird—a thing that sang. She used to sing. He killed that, too" (44). The canary's death, Mrs. Peter's speculates, must have caused an alienating "stillness": "When we homesteaded in Dakota, and my first baby died—after he was two years old, and me with no other then—. . . . I know what stillness is" (44).

We can guess that to Mrs. Wright the canary represented the sum total of what she was as Minnie Foster: young, pretty, sweet, lively, a person who took pleasure in singing, in wearing attractive clothes, in other people's company, in hopes for the future. She must have equated Mr. Wright's strangling of the canary to his destroying the Minnie Foster that was her former self. The birdcage, too, represents this violation. Mrs. Hale, upon seeing it, says, "Looks as if someone must have been rough with it." She then immediately connects it to the house: "I don't like this place" (42). The broken birdcage is equivalent to Minnie Foster's violated self.

Briner 6

It is the shell of her privacy, the container of her true self. Mr. Wright breaks into it to find and destroy her. The bird and birdcage, in other words, make clear to the women and to us that Mrs. Wright did in fact kill her husband and that she had a strong motive.

The men, dense as ever, never see any of this. They are literally clueless. From what they say, Mrs. Wright is likely to be acquitted or to get off with a light sentence. They can't find a motive for the crime, and juries, the county attorney says, are easy on women (44). But the women know the truth. They "vote" for acquittal by suppressing the evidence—the dead canary—and by withholding an interpretation of the "trifles" that would make the case against Mrs. Wright.

Their last act is to gather objects to take to Mrs. Wright. In choosing them, they seem almost to communicate with Mrs. Wright, to express their solidarity with her, as if the objects belong to a language that only women know: her apron (for hard work), her jar of cherries (for achievement), her quilting pieces (for work still to do), and her shawl (for warmth).

Work Cited

Glaspell, Susan. *Trifles. Plays by Susan Glaspell*. Ed. C. W. E. Bigsby. Cambridge: Cambridge UP, 1987. Print.

Note: Normally, the Works Cited list would appear on a separate page, but we print it here, right after the essay, to save space.

ESSAY ON A NOVEL

Mary Ann Evans, the author of *Adam Bede,* wrote under the pen name George Eliot. The novel was first published in 1859. The action takes place in 1799 in an English farm village. The events of the novel featured in the essay below are as follows: Hetty Sorrel, a working-class teenager, and Arthur Donnithorne, an aristocrat, fall in love. Not knowing that she is pregnant, he breaks off the relationship. When she can no longer hide her pregnancy, she undertakes an arduous journey in search of him. She fails to find him, gives birth, and, in a confused state of mind, abandons the baby in the woods. After being tried for infanticide and condemned to hang, she gains a reprieve and is transported to Australia. Dinah Morris, a devout Methodist preacher, ministers to her in prison.

Forrest 1

Shalita Forrest

Professor Griffith

English 110–02

2 November 20—

First Love, Lost Love in George Eliot's *Adam Bede*

In George Eliot's *Adam Bede*, I was drawn to Hetty Sorrel. Hetty's first experience of love somewhat resembles my own. Hetty is misunderstood by many of the other characters, but I understood her from the beginning of the book. Hetty is young, in love for the first time, and blinded by love. I know this feeling, because I have been there and experienced a love similar to Hetty's. There are similarities between Hetty's first love and my first love, but we handled our situations in totally different ways.

The first similarity between Hetty and me is the type of men we fell in love with. Hetty and I both loved men who

Forrest 2

could never be completely ours. Hetty is in love with Arthur
Donnithorne, who is on a different social level from her. Arthur
belongs to the aristocracy, and Hetty comes from the working
class. This class difference creates a tremendous barrier between
them. Hetty can never have Arthur. She knows, however, that
Arthur is interested in her: "Hetty had become aware that Mr.
Arthur Donnithorne would take a good deal of trouble for the
chance of seeing her" (99). Despite their class difference, she
welcomes his attentions anyway. I was also in love with a man
who I knew could never be true to one woman. The man I loved
wanted his cake plus his ice cream, too. He had many other
women and was not willing to give them up to be with me. Yet
I pursued him anyway, knowing that it was nothing but trouble,
just as Hetty does.

When you pursue something you know can never be, you
subject yourself to a lot of heartache. Hetty receives a letter from
Arthur, the man of her dreams, telling her that their relationship
has to end, and this crushes her heart. The same thing happened
to me. I was in love and I got a letter saying that we could not
be together because he was not ready for a serious relationship.
Since this was my first love and I had never been rejected like this
before, I hurt more than anything in the world. It was as if the
person I loved took a knife and stabbed me in the heart.

Another way in which Hetty and I are alike is that we
both lost the will to live. In Hetty's case, she travels to find the
man who broke her heart. The journey is not easy for her. Times
get harder, the nights get colder, and her money begins to
disappear. Hetty is so unhappy she wants to kill herself: "It was
because I was so very miserable," she tells Dinah, the Methodist

Forrest 3

minister. "I didn't know where to go . . . and I tried to kill myself before, and I couldn't. O, I tried so to drown myself in the pool, and I couldn't. . . . I went to find him, as he might take care of me; and he was gone, and then I didn't know what to do" (451–52). Hetty has given up on life: "I wished I'd never been born into this world" (452). In my case I was young and didn't know any better. My first love broke my heart, and I did not think that my life could go on without him. I did not believe there was anything to move on to. There were times when I hoped that I would not wake up the next day.

The last similarity between Hetty and me is that we both got pregnant at a very young age. Hetty and I were very young and very naïve. We were just in love; at least, that is what we thought. Not at one time did we ever stop to think about the consequences of sharing ourselves and our hearts with the men we believed we loved. When Hetty gets pregnant she hides it from everybody for months, because she knows it would not be accepted. In her society, getting pregnant out of wedlock is totally unacceptable. Not only can Hetty not tell anyone, she also worries what people will think about her relationship with Arthur: "I daredn't go back home again—I couldn't bear it. I couldn't have bore to look at anybody, for they'd have scorned me" (452). When I got pregnant, I hid it also, because I knew that I would let my family down. I knew that they would be disappointed. I was a very good student with a lot of potential, and I thought that they would only look down on me.

Even though Hetty and I experienced the same first love but lost love, we handled our situations differently. Hetty runs after Arthur when she gets pregnant. She leaves her family

Forrest 4

behind, the family she believes will not help her. Hetty leaves
home to find Arthur, thinking that they can be together: "But it
must be done—she must get to Arthur: oh, how she yearned to
be again with somebody who would care for her!" (371). Hetty
never gives up trying to find Arthur; she never stops to think
about what she is doing. She continues to let herself hurt.

At one point I did leave home, and I did turn my back on
my family, but I had to stop and think about what I was doing.
I was tired of being unhappy. The relationship was too intense.
It caused me to be miserable and never content. I made a very
big decision, and that was to give up and go back home.
I realized that love was not supposed to hurt. Every day with him
I felt the agonizing pain that he was putting me through and
that I allowed myself to go through. I realized that I deserved
better. I knew when to get out, when enough was enough. Hetty
did not have the sense to know when enough was enough.

I turned to my family and friends for support. They helped
me make it through a very rough time in my life. I was only
sixteen years old when I gave birth. Daily, I asked myself, "How
am I supposed to raise a child, when I am just a child myself?"
I realized then that I could no longer consider myself a child.
At that point in my life, I felt I had to take on the responsibilities
of a woman, so that I could be a good mother to my child, and
care for her, support her, and love her as a mother should. My
family and friends made me realize that life goes on and that
I had too much going for myself to give up on life. My family and
friends gave me strength to live and to go on with my life.

Hetty, on the other hand, leaves her child in the woods,
thinking that someone will find it so that she can return home

Forrest 5

and continue as if nothing has happened. Things turn out
badly for Hetty. After Hetty leaves the child, it dies: "I did do
it, Dinah . . . I buried it in the wood . . . the little baby . . . and
it cried . . . I heard it cry . . . ever such a way off . . . all night . . .
and I went back because it cried. . . . I didn't kill it—I didn't kill it
myself. I put it down there and covered it up, and when I came
back it was gone" (451). Hetty does not think that this act will
cause her to spend the rest of her days in prison or to be hanged:
"I thought I should get rid of all my misery, and go back home,
and never let 'em know why I ran away" (452).

I understand the confusion and the sorrow Hetty feels
from lost love. It is a love so deep and consuming that Hetty
cannot make a rational decision about the child she is carrying.
Hetty should realize that the conception of this child will have to
be a symbol of her lost love and to do her best to raise and love
this child as every child deserves. Hetty is overcome with grief for
a man who does not love her. She does not know how to handle
this heartbreak. I, on the other hand, am raising and loving my
child, because she is a part of the man I loved and a part of me,
and just simply because she is my first love!

Work Cited

Eliot, George. *Adam Bede*. Oxford World's Classics. New York:
Oxford UP, 1998. Print.

Note: Normally, the Works Cited list would appear on a separate page, but we print it here, right
after the essay, to save space.

Appendix

POEMS

RICHARD CORY

Edwin Arlington Robinson

Whenever Richard Cory went down town,
We people on the pavement looked at him:
He was a gentleman from sole to crown,
Clean favored, and imperially slim.

And he was always quietly arrayed,
And he was always human when he talked;
But still he fluttered pulses when he said,
"Good-morning," and he glittered when he walked.

And he was rich—yes, richer than a king—
And admirably schooled in every grace:
In fine, we thought that he was everything
To make us wish that we were in his place.

So on we worked, and waited for the light,
And went without the meat, and cursed the bread;
And Richard Cory, one calm summer night,
Went home and put a bullet through his head.
                                        1897

THE DEATH OF THE HIRED MAN

Robert Frost

Mary sat musing on the lamp-flame at the table
Waiting for Warren. When she heard his step,
She ran on tip-toe down the darkened passage
To meet him in the doorway with the news
And put him on his guard. "Silas is back."
She pushed him outward with her through the door
And shut it after her. "Be kind," she said.
She took the market things from Warren's arms
And set them on the porch, then drew him down
To sit beside her on the wooden steps.   10

"When was I ever anything but kind to him?
But I'll not have the fellow back," he said.
"I told him so last haying, didn't I?
'If he left then,' I said, 'that ended it.'
What good is he? Who else will harbor him
At his age for the little he can do?
What help he is there's no depending on.
Off he goes always when I need him most.
'He thinks he ought to earn a little pay,
Enough at least to buy tobacco with,   20

So he won't have to beg and be beholden.'
'All right,' I say, 'I can't afford to pay
Any fixed wages, though I wish I could.'
'Someone else can.' 'Then someone else will have to.'
I shouldn't mind his bettering himself
If that was what it was. You can be certain,
When he begins like that, there's someone at him
Trying to coax him off with pocket-money,—
In haying time, when any help is scarce.
In winter he comes back to us. I'm done."   30

"Sh! not so loud: he'll hear you," Mary said.

"I want him to: he'll have to soon or late."

"He's worn out. He's asleep beside the stove.
When I came up from Rowe's I found him here,
Huddled against the barn-door fast asleep,
A miserable sight, and frightening, too—
You needn't smile—I didn't recognize him—

I wasn't looking for him—and he's changed.
Wait till you see."

"Where did you say he'd been?"

"He didn't say. I dragged him to the house,   40
And gave him tea and tried to make him smoke.
I tried to make him talk about his travels.
Nothing would do: he just kept nodding off."

"What did he say? Did he say anything?"

"But little."

"Anything? Mary, confess
He said he'd come to ditch the meadow for me."

"Warren?"

"But did he? I just want to know."

"Of course he did. What would you have him say?
Surely you wouldn't grudge the poor old man
Some humble way to save his self-respect.   50
He added, if you really care to know,
He meant to clear the upper pasture, too.
That sounds like something you have heard before?
Warren, I wish you could have heard the way
He jumbled everything. I stopped to look
Two or three times—he made me feel so queer—
To see if he was talking in his sleep.
He ran on Harold Wilson—you remember—
The boy you had in haying four years since.
He's finished school, and teaching in his college.   60
Silas declares you'll have to get him back.
He says they two will make a team for work:
Between them they will lay this farm as smooth!
The way he mixed that in with other things.
He thinks young Wilson a likely lad, though daft
On education—you know how they fought
All through July under the blazing sun,
Silas up on the cart to build the load,
Harold along beside to pitch it on."

"Yes, I took care to keep well out of earshot."   70

"Well, those days trouble Silas like a dream.
You wouldn't think they would. How some things linger!

Harold's young college boy's assurance piqued him.
After so many years he still keeps finding
Good arguments he sees he might have used.
I sympathize. I know just how it feels
To think of the right thing to say too late.
Harold's associated in his mind with Latin.
He asked me what I thought of Harold's saying
He studied Latin like the violin   80
Because he liked it—that an argument!
He said he couldn't make the boy believe
He could find water with a hazel prong—
Which showed how much good school had ever done him.
He wanted to go over that. But most of all
He thinks if he could have another chance
To teach him how to build a load of hay—"

"I know, that's Silas' one accomplishment.
He bundles every forkful in its place,
And tags and numbers it for future reference,   90
So he can find and easily dislodge it
In the unloading. Silas does that well.
He takes it out in bunches like big birds' nests.
You never see him standing on the hay
He's trying to lift, straining to lift himself."

"He thinks if he could teach him that, he'd be
Some good perhaps to someone in the world.
He hates to see a boy the fool of books.
Poor Silas, so concerned for other folk,
And nothing to look backward to with pride,   100
And nothing to look forward to with hope.
So now and never any different."

Part of a moon was falling down the west,
Dragging the whole sky with it to the hills.
Its light poured softly in her lap. She saw
And spread her apron to it. She put out her hand
Among the harp-like morning-glory strings,
Taut with the dew from garden bed eaves,
As if she played unheard the tenderness
That wrought on him beside her in the night.   110
"Warren," she said, "he has come home to die:
You needn't be afraid he'll leave you this time."

"Home," he mocked gently.

                       "Yes, what else but home?
It all depends on what you mean by home.
Of course he's nothing to us, any more
Than was the hound that came a stranger to us
Out of the woods, worn out upon the trail."

"Home is the place where, when you have to go there,
They have to take you in."

                     "I should have called it
Something you somehow haven't to deserve."   120

Warren leaned out and took a step or two,
Picked up a little stick, and brought it back
And broke it in his hand and tossed it by.
"Silas has better claim on us you think
Than on his brother? Thirteen little miles
As the road winds would bring him to his door.
Silas has walked that far no doubt to-day.
Why didn't he go there? His brother's rich,
A somebody—director in the bank."

"He never told us that."

                     "We know it though."   130

"I think his brother ought to help, of course.
I'll see to that if there is need. He ought of right
To take him in, and might be willing to—
He may be better than appearances.
But have some pity on Silas. Do you think
If he'd had any pride in claiming kin
Or anything he looked for from his brother,
He'd keep so still about him all this time?"

"I wonder what's between them."

                     "I can tell you.
Silas is what he is—we wouldn't mind him—   140
But just the kind that kinsfolk can't abide.
He never did a thing so very bad.
He don't know why he isn't quite as good
As anyone. He won't be made ashamed
To please his brother, worthless though he is."

"I can't think Si ever hurt anyone."

"No, but he hurt my heart the way he lay
And rolled his old head on that sharp-edged chair-back.
He wouldn't let me put him on the lounge.   150
You must go in and see what you can do.
I made the bed up for him there to-night.
You'll be surprised at him—how much he's broken.
His working days are done; I'm sure of it."

"I'd not be in a hurry to say that."

"I haven't been. Go, look, see for yourself.
But, Warren, please remember how it is:
He's come to help you ditch the meadow.
He has a plan. You mustn't laugh at him.
He may not speak of it, and then he may.
I'll sit and see if that small sailing cloud
Will hit or miss the moon."   160
                    It hit the moon.
Then there were three there, making a dim row,
The moon, the little silver cloud, and she.
Warren returned—too soon, it seemed to her,
Slipped to her side, caught up her hand and waited.

"Warren," she questioned.

                    "Dead," was all he answered.
                              1914

SHORT STORIES

HILLS LIKE WHITE ELEPHANTS

Ernest Hemingway

The hills across the valley of the Ebro were long and white. On this side there was no shade and no trees and the station was between two lines of rails in the sun. Close against the side of the station there was the warm shadow of the building and a curtain, made of strings of bamboo beads, hung across the open door into the bar, to keep out flies. The American and the girl with him sat at a table in the shade, outside the building. It was very hot and the express from Barcelona would come in forty minutes. It stopped at this junction for two minutes and went to Madrid.

"What should we drink?" the girl asked. She had taken off her hat and put it on the table.

"It's pretty hot," the man said.

"Let's drink beer."

"Dos cervezas," the man said into the curtain.

"Big ones?" a woman asked from the doorway.

"Yes. Two big ones."

The woman brought two glasses of beer and two felt pads. She put the felt pads and the beer glasses on the table and looked at the man and the girl. The girl was looking off at the line of hills. They were white in the sun and the country was brown and dry.

"They look like white elephants," she said.

"I've never seen one," the man drank his beer.

"No, you wouldn't have."

"I might have," the man said. "Just because you say I wouldn't have doesn't prove anything."

The girl looked at the bead curtain. "They've painted something on it," she said. "What does it say?"

"Anis del Toro. It's a drink."

"Could we try it?"

The man called "Listen" through the curtain. The woman came out from the bar.

"Four reales." "We want two Anis del Toro."

"With water?"

"Do you want it with water?"

"I don't know," the girl said. "Is it good with water?"

"It's all right."

"You want them with water?" asked the woman.

"Yes, with water."

"It tastes like licorice," the girl said and put the glass down.

"That's the way with everything."

"Yes," said the girl. "Everything tastes of licorice. Especially all the things you've waited so long for, like absinthe."

"Oh, cut it out."

"You started it," the girl said. "I was being amused. I was having a fine time."

"Well, let's try and have a fine time."

"All right. I was trying. I said the mountains looked like white elephants. Wasn't that bright?"

"That was bright."

"I wanted to try this new drink. That's all we do, isn't it—look at things and try new drinks?"

"I guess so."

The girl looked across at the hills.

"They're lovely hills," she said. "They don't really look like white elephants. I just meant the coloring of their skin through the trees."

"Should we have another drink?"

"All right."

The warm wind blew the bead curtain against the table.

"The beer's nice and cool," the man said.

"It's lovely," the girl said.

"It's really an awfully simple operation, Jig," the man said. "It's not really an operation at all."

The girl looked at the ground the table legs rested on.

"I know you wouldn't mind it, Jig. It's really not anything. It's just to let the air in."

The girl did not say anything.

"I'll go with you and I'll stay with you all the time. They just let the air in and then it's all perfectly natural."

"Then what will we do afterwards?"

"We'll be fine afterwards. Just like we were before."

"What makes you think so?"

"That's the only thing that bothers us. It's the only thing that's made us unhappy."

The girl looked at the bead curtain, put her hand out and took hold of two of the strings of beads.

"And you think then we'll be all right and be happy."

"I know we will. You don't have to be afraid. I've known lots of people that have done it."

"So have I," said the girl. "And afterwards they were all so happy."

"Well," the man said, "if you don't want to you don't have to. I wouldn't have you do it if you didn't want to. But I know it's perfectly simple."

"And you really want to?"

"I think it's the best thing to do. But I don't want you to do it if you don't really want to."

"And if I do it you'll be happy and things will be like they were and you'll love me?"

"I love you now. You know I love you."

"I know. But if I do it, then it will be nice again if I say things are like white elephants, and you'll like it?"

"I'll love it. I love it now but I just can't think about it. You know how I get when I worry."

"If I do it you won't ever worry?"

"I won't worry about that because it's perfectly simple."

"Then I'll do it. Because I don't care about me."

"What do you mean?"

"I don't care about me."

"Well, I care about you."

"Oh, yes. But I don't care about me. And I'll do it and then everything will be fine."

"I don't want you to do it if you feel that way."

The girl stood up and walked to the end of the station. Across, on the other side, were fields of grain and trees along the banks of the Ebro. Far away, beyond the river, were mountains. The shadow of a cloud moved across the field of grain and she saw the river through the trees.

"And we could have all this,' she said. "And we could have everything and every day we make it more impossible."

"What did you say?"

"I said we could have everything."

"No, we can't."

"We can have the whole world."

"No, we can't."

"We can go everywhere."

"No, we can't. It isn't ours any more."

"It's ours."

"No, it isn't. And once they take it away, you never get it back."

"But they haven't taken it away."

"We'll wait and see."

"Come on back in the shade," he said. "You mustn't feel that way."

"I don't feel any way," the girl said. "I just know things."

"I don't want you to do anything that you don't want to do—"

"Nor that isn't good for me," she said. "I know. Could we have another beer? "

"All right. But you've got to realize—"

"I realize, " the girl said. "Can't we maybe stop talking? "

They sat down at the table and the girl looked across at the hills on the dry side of the valley and the man looked at her and at the table.

"You've got to realize, " he said, "that I don't want you to do it if you don't want to. I'm perfectly willing to go through with it if it means anything to you. "

"Doesn't it mean anything to you? We could get along. "

"Of course it does. But I don't want anybody but you. I don't want anyone else. And I know it's perfectly simple. "

"Yes, you know it's perfectly simple."

"It's all right for you to say that, but I do know it."

"Would you do something for me now? "

"I'd do anything for you."

"Would you please please please please please please please stop talking?"

He did not say anything but looked at the bags against the wall of the station. There were labels on them from all the hotels where they had spent nights.

"But I don't want you to," he said, "I don't care anything about it."

"I'll scream," the girl said.

The woman came out through the curtains with two glasses of beer and put them down on the damp felt pads. "The train comes in five minutes," she said.

"What did she say?" asked the girl.

"That the train is coming in five minutes."

The girl smiled brightly at the woman, to thank her.

"I'd better take the bags over to the other side of the station," the man said. She smiled at him.

"All right. Then come back and we'll finish the beer."

He picked up the two heavy bags and carried them around the station to the other tracks. He looked up the tracks but could not see the train. Coming back, he walked through the bar-room, where people waiting for the train were drinking. He drank an Anis at the bar and looked at the people. They were all waiting reasonably for the train. He went out through the bead curtain. She was sitting at the table and smiled at him.

"Do you feel better?" he asked.

"I feel fine," she said. "There's nothing wrong with me. I feel fine."

1927

YOURS

Mary Robison

Allison struggled away from her white Renault, limping with the weight of the last of the pumpkins. She found Clark in the twilight on the twig-and-leaf-littered porch behind the house.

He wore a wool shawl. He was moving up and back in a padded glider, pushed by the ball of his slippered foot.

Allison lowered a big pumpkin, let it rest on the wide floor boards.

Clark was much older—seventy-eight to Allison's thirty-five. They were married. They were both quite tall and looked something alike in their facial features. Allison wore a natural-hair wig. It was a thick blonde hood around her face. She was dressed in bright-dyed denims today. She wore durable clothes, usually, for she volunteered afternoons at a children's day-care center.

She put one of the smaller pumpkins on Clark's long lap. "Now, nothing surreal," she told him. "Carve just a regular face. These are for kids."

In the foyer, on the Hepplewhite desk, Allison found the maid's chore list with its cross-offs, which included Clark's supper. Allison went quickly through the day's mail: a garish coupon packet, a bill from Jamestown Liquors, November's pay-TV program guide, and the worst thing, the funniest, an already opened, extremely unkind letter from Clark's relations up North. "You're an old fool," Allison read, and, "You're being cruelly deceived." There was a gift check for Clark enclosed, but it was uncashable, signed, as it was, "Jesus H. Christ."

Late, late into this night, Allison and Clark gutted and carved the pumpkins together, at an old table set on the back porch, over newspaper after soggy newspaper, with paring knives and with spoons and with a Swiss Army knife Clark used for exact shaping of tooth and eye and nostril. Clark had been a doctor, an internist, but also a Sunday watercolorist. His four pumpkins were expressive and artful. Their carved features were suited to the sizes and shapes of the pumpkins. Two looked ferocious and jagged. One registered surprise. The last was serene and beaming.

Allison's four faces were less deftly drawn, with slits and areas of distortion. She had cut triangles for noses and eyes. The mouths she had made were just wedges—two turned up and two turned down.

By one in the morning they were finished. Clark, who had bent his long torso forward to work, moved back over to the glider and looked out sleepily at nothing. All the lights were out across the ravine.

Clark stayed. For the season and time, the Virginia night was warm. Most leaves had been blown away already, and the trees stood unbothered. The moon was round above them.

Allison cleaned up the mess.

"Your jack-o'-lanterns are much, much better than mine," Clark said to her.

"Like hell," Allison said.

"Look at me," Clark said, and Allison did.

She was holding a squishy bundle of newspapers. The papers reeked sweetly with the smell of pumpkin guts.

"Yours are *far* better," he said.

"You're wrong. You'll see when they're lit," Allison said.

She went inside, came back with yellow vigil candles. It took her a while to get each candle settled, and then to line up the results in a row on the porch railing. She went along and lit each candle and fixed the pumpkin lids over the little flames.

"See?" she said.

They sat together a moment and looked at the orange faces.

"We're exhausted. It's good-night time," Allison said. "Don't blow out the candles. I'll put in new ones tomorrow."

That night, in their bedroom, a few weeks earlier in her life than had been predicted, Allison began to die. "Don't look at me if my wig comes off," she told Clark. "Please."

Her pulse cords were fluttering under his fingers. She raised her knees and kicked away the comforter. She said something to Clark about the garage being locked.

At the telephone, Clark had a clear view out back and down to the porch. He wanted to get drunk with his wife once more. He wanted to tell her, from the greater perspective he had, that to own only a little talent, like his, was an awful, plaguing thing; that being only a little special meant you expected too much, most of the time, and liked yourself too little. He wanted to assure her that she had missed nothing.

He was speaking into the phone now. He watched the jack-o'-lanterns. The jack-o'-lanterns watched him.

1983

THE CASK OF AMONTILLADO

Edgar Allan Poe

The thousand injuries of Fortunato I had borne as I best could, but when he ventured upon insult I vowed revenge. You, who so well know the nature of my soul, will not suppose, however, that I gave utterance to a threat. At *length* I would be avenged; this was a point definitely settled—but the very definitiveness with which it was resolved precluded the idea of risk. I must not only punish but punish with impunity. A wrong is unredressed when retribution overtakes its redresser. It is equally unredressed when the avenger fails to make himself felt as such to him who has done the wrong.

It must be understood that neither by word nor deed had I given Fortunato cause to doubt my good will. I continued, as was my wont, to smile in his face, and he did not perceive that my smile now was at the thought of his immolation.

He had a weak point—this Fortunato—although in other regards he was a man to be respected and even feared. He prided himself on his connoisseurship in wine. Few Italians have the true virtuoso spirit. For the most part their enthusiasm is adopted to suit the time and opportunity, to practice imposture upon the British and Austrian *millionaires*. In painting and gemmary, Fortunato, like his countrymen, was a quack, but in the matter of old wines he was sincere. In this respect I did not differ from him materially;—I was skilful in the Italian vintages myself, and bought largely whenever I could.

It was about dusk, one evening during the supreme madness of the carnival season, that I encountered my friend. He accosted me with excessive warmth, for he had been drinking much. The man wore motley. He had on a tight-fitting parti-striped dress, and his head was surmounted by the conical cap and bells. I was so pleased to see him that I thought I should never have done wringing his hand.

I said to him—"My dear Fortunato, you are luckily met. How remarkably well you are looking to-day. But I have received a pipe of what passes for Amontillado, and I have my doubts."

"How?" said he. "Amontillado? A pipe? Impossible! And in the middle of the carnival!"

"I have my doubts," I replied; "and I was silly enough to pay the full Amontillado price without consulting you in the matter. You were not to be found, and I was fearful of losing a bargain."

"Amontillado!"

"I have my doubts."

"Amontillado!"

"And I must satisfy them."

"Amontillado!"

"As you are engaged, I am on my way to Luchresi. If any one has a critical turn it is he. He will tell me—"

"Luchresi cannot tell Amontillado from Sherry."

"And yet some fools will have it that his taste is a match for your own."

"Come, let us go."

"Whither?"

"To your vaults."

"My friend, no; I will not impose upon your good nature. I perceive you have an engagement. Luchresi—"

"I have no engagement;—come."

"My friend, no. It is not the engagement, but the severe cold with which I perceive you are afflicted. The vaults are insufferably damp. They are encrusted with nitre."

"Let us go, nevertheless. The cold is merely nothing. Amontillado! You have been imposed upon. And as for Luchresi, he cannot distinguish Sherry from Amontillado."

Thus speaking, Fortunato possessed himself of my arm; and putting on a mask of black silk and drawing a *roquelaire** closely about my person, I suffered him to hurry me to my palazzo.

There were no attendants at home; they had absconded to make merry in honor of the time. I had told them that I should not return until the

---

*A long cloak

morning, and had given them explicit orders not to stir from the house. These orders were sufficient, I well knew, to insure their immediate disappearance, one and all, as soon as my back was turned.

I took from their sconces two flambeaux, and giving one to Fortunato, bowed him through several suites of rooms to the archway that led into the vaults. I passed down a long and winding staircase, requesting him to be cautious as he followed. We came at length to the foot of the descent, and stood together upon the damp ground of the catacombs of the Montresors.

The gait of my friend was unsteady, and the bells upon his cap jingled as he strode.

"The pipe," he said.

"It is farther on," said I; "but observe the white web-work which gleams from these cavern walls."

He turned towards me, and looked into my eyes with two filmy orbs that distilled the rheum of intoxication.

"Nitre?" he asked, at length.

"Nitre," I replied. "How long have you had that cough?"

"Ugh! ugh! ugh!—ugh! ugh! ugh!—ugh! ugh! ugh!—ugh! ugh! ugh!—ugh! ugh! ugh!"

My poor friend found it impossible to reply for many minutes.

"It is nothing," he said, at last.

"Come," I said, with decision, "we will go back; your health is precious. You are rich, respected, admired, beloved; you are happy, as I once was. You are a man to be missed. For me it is no matter. We will go back; you will be ill, and I cannot be responsible. Besides, there is Luchresi—"

"Enough," he said; "the cough is a mere nothing; it will not kill me. I shall not die of a cough."

"True—true," I replied; "and, indeed, I had no intention of alarming you unnecessarily—but you should use all proper caution. A draught of this Medoc will defend us from the damps."

Here I knocked off the neck of a bottle which I drew from a long row of its fellows that lay upon the mould.

"Drink," I said, presenting him the wine.

He raised it to his lips with a leer. He paused and nodded to me familiarly, while his bells jingled.

"I drink," he said, "to the buried that repose around us."

"And I to your long life."

He again took my arm, and we proceeded.

"These vaults," he said, "are extensive."

"The Montresors," I replied, "were a great and numerous family."

"I forget your arms."

"A huge human foot d'or, in a field azure; the foot crushes a serpent rampant whose fangs are imbedded in the heel."

"And the motto?"

"*Nemo me impune lacessit.*"*

"Good!" he said.

The wine sparkled in his eyes and the bells jingled. My own fancy grew warm with the Medoc. We had passed through long walls of piled skeletons, with casks and puncheons intermingling, into the inmost recesses of the catacombs. I paused again, and this time I made bold to seize Fortunato by an arm above the elbow.

"The nitre!" I said; "see, it increases. It hangs like moss upon the vaults. We are below the river's bed. The drops of moisture trickle among the bones. Come, we will go back ere it is too late. Your cough—"

"It is nothing," he said; "let us go on. But first, another draught of the Medoc."

I broke and reached him a flagon of De Grâve. He emptied it at a breath. His eyes flashed with a fierce light. He laughed and threw the bottle upwards with a gesticulation I did not understand.

I looked at him in surprise. He repeated the movement—a grotesque one.

"You do not comprehend?" he said.

"Not I," I replied.

"Then you are not of the brotherhood."

"How?"

"You are not of the masons."

"Yes, yes," I said; "yes, yes."

"You? Impossible! A mason?"

"A mason," I replied.

"A sign," he said, "a sign."

"It is this," I answered, producing from beneath the folds of my *roquelaire* a trowel.

"You jest," he exclaimed, recoiling a few paces. "But let us proceed to the Amontillado."

"Be it so," I said, replacing the tool beneath the cloak and again offering him my arm. He leaned upon it heavily. We continued our route in search of the Amontillado. We passed through a range of low arches, descended, passed on, and descending again, arrived at a deep crypt, in which the foulness of the air caused our flambeaux rather to glow than flame.

At the most remote end of the crypt there appeared another less spacious. Its walls had been lined with human remains, piled to the vault overhead, in the fashion of the great catacombs of Paris. Three sides of this

*No one attacks me with impunity.

interior crypt were still ornamented in this manner. From the fourth side the bones had been thrown down, and lay promiscuously upon the earth, forming at one point a mound of some size. Within the wall thus exposed by the displacing of the bones, we perceived a still interior crypt or recess, in depth about four feet, in width three, in height six or seven. It seemed to have been constructed for no especial use within itself, but formed merely the interval between two of the colossal supports of the roof of the catacombs, and was backed by one of their circumscribing walls of solid granite.

It was in vain that Fortunato, uplifting his dull torch, endeavored to pry into the depth of the recess. Its termination the feeble light did not enable us to see.

"Proceed," I said; "herein is the Amontillado. As for Luchresi—"

"He is an ignoramus," interrupted my friend, as he stepped unsteadily forward, while I followed immediately at his heels. In an instant he had reached the extremity of the niche, and finding his progress arrested by the rock, stood stupidly bewildered. A moment more and I had fettered him to the granite. In its surface were two iron staples, distant from each other about two feet, horizontally. From one of these depended a short chain, from the other a padlock. Throwing the links about his waist, it was but the work of a few seconds to secure it. He was too much astounded to resist. Withdrawing the key I stepped back from the recess.

"Pass your hand," I said, "over the wall; you cannot help feeling the nitre. Indeed, it is very damp. Once more let me *implore* you to return. No? Then I must positively leave you. But I must first render you all the little attentions in my power."

"The Amontillado!" ejaculated my friend, not yet recovered from his astonishment.

"True," I replied; "the Amontillado."

As I said these words I busied myself among the pile of bones of which I have before spoken. Throwing them aside, I soon uncovered a quantity of building stone and mortar. With these materials and with the aid of my trowel, I began vigorously to wall up the entrance of the niche.

I had scarcely laid the first tier of the masonry when I discovered that the intoxication of Fortunato had in a great measure worn off. The earliest indication I had of this was a low moaning cry from the depth of the recess. It was not the cry of a drunken man. There was then a long and obstinate silence. I laid the second tier, and the third, and the fourth; and then I heard the furious vibrations of the chain. The noise lasted for several minutes, during which, that I might hearken to it with the more satisfaction, I ceased my labours and sat down upon the bones. When at last the clanking subsided, I resumed the trowel, and finished without interruption the fifth, the sixth, and the seventh tier. The wall was now nearly upon a level with my breast. I again paused, and holding the flambeaux over the mason-work, threw a few feeble rays upon the figure within.

A succession of loud and shrill screams, bursting suddenly from the throat of the chained form, seemed to thrust me violently back. For a brief moment I hesitated, I trembled. Unsheathing my rapier, I began to grope with it about the recess; but the thought of an instant reassured me. I placed my hand upon the solid fabric of the catacombs, and felt satisfied. I reapproached the wall; I replied to the yells of him who clamoured. I re-echoed, I aided, I surpassed them in volume and in strength. I did this, and the clamorer grew still.

It was now midnight, and my task was drawing to a close. I had completed the eighth, the ninth and the tenth tier. I had finished a portion of the last and the eleventh; there remained but a single stone to be fitted and plastered in. I struggled with its weight; I placed it partially in its destined position. But now there came from out the niche a low laugh that erected the hairs upon my head. It was succeeded by a sad voice, which I had difficulty in recognizing as that of the noble Fortunato. The voice said—

"Ha! ha! ha!—he! he! he!—a very good joke, indeed—an excellent jest. We will have many a rich laugh about it at the palazzo—he! he! he!—over our wine—he! he! he!"

"The Amontillado!" I said.

"He! he! he!—he! he! he!—yes, the Amontillado. But is it not getting late? Will not they be awaiting us at the palazzo, the Lady Fortunato and the rest? Let us be gone."

"Yes," I said, "let us be gone."

"*For the love of God, Montresor!*"

"Yes," I said, "for the love of God!"

But to these words I hearkened in vain for a reply. I grew impatient. I called aloud—

"Fortunato!"

No answer. I called again—

"Fortunato!"

No answer still. I thrust a torch through the remaining aperture and let it fall within. There came forth in return only a jingling of the bells. My heart grew sick; it was the dampness of the catacombs that made it so. I hastened to make an end of my labour. I forced the last stone into its position; I plastered it up. Against the new masonry I re-erected the old rampart of bones. For the half of a century no mortal has disturbed them. *In pace requiescat!**

1847

*May he rest in peace.

PLAY

TRIFLES

Susan Glaspell

The first performance of the one-act play Trifles took place at the Wharf Theater, Provincetown, Massachusetts, on 8 August 1916. Susan Glaspell played the part of Mrs. Hale.

Characters

George Henderson (County Attorney)   Mrs. Peters
Henry Peters (Sheriff)   Mrs. Hale
Lewis Hale (a neighboring farmer)

SCENE: *The kitchen is the now abandoned farmhouse of* JOHN WRIGHT, *a gloomy kitchen, and left without having been put in order—unwashed pans under the sink, a loaf of bread outside the bread-box, a dish-towel on the table—other signs of incompleted work. At the rear the outer door opens and the* SHERIFF *comes in followed by the* COUNTY ATTORNEY *and* HALE. *The* SHERIFF *and* HALE *are men in middle life, the* COUNTY ATTORNEY *is a young man; all are much bundled up and go at once to the stove. They are followed by the two women—the* SHERIFF's *wife first; she is a slight wiry woman, a thin nervous face.* MRS. HALE *is larger and would ordinarily be called more comfortable looking, but she is disturbed now and looks fearfully about as she enters. The women have come in slowly, and stand close together near the door.*

COUNTY ATTORNEY. *(rubbing his hands)* This feels good. Come up to the fire, ladies.

MRS. PETERS. *(after taking a step forward)* I'm not—cold.

SHERIFF. *(unbuttoning his overcoat and stepping away from the stove as if to mark the beginning of official business)* Now, Mr. Hale, before we move things about, you explain to Mr. Henderson just what you saw when you came here yesterday morning.

COUNTY ATTORNEY. By the way, has anything been moved? Are things just as you left them yesterday?

SHERIFF. *(looking about)* It's just the same. When it dropped below zero last night I thought I'd better send Frank out this morning to make a fire for us—no use getting pneumonia with a big case on, but I told him not to touch anything except the stove—and you know Frank.

COUNTY ATTORNEY. Somebody should have been left here yesterday.

SHERIFF. OH—yesterday. When I had to send Frank to Morris Center for that man who went crazy—I want you to know I had my hands full yesterday. I knew you could get back from Omaha by today as long as I went over everything here myself—

COUNTY ATTORNEY. Well, Mr. Hale, tell just what happened when you came here yesterday morning.

HALE. Harry and I had started to town with a load of potatoes. We came along the road from my place and as I got here I said, "I'm going to see if I can't get John Wright to go in with me on a party telephone." I spoke to Wright about it once before and he put me off, saying folks talked too much anyway, and all he asked was peace and quiet— I guess you know about how much he talked himself; but I thought maybe if I went to the house and talked about it before his wife, though I said to Harry that I didn't know as what his wife wanted made much difference to John—

COUNTY ATTORNEY. Let's talk about that later, Mr. Hale. I do want to talk about that, but tell now just what happened when you got to the house.

HALE. I didn't hear or see anything; I knocked at the door, and still it was quiet inside. I knew they must be up, it was past eight o'clock. So I knocked again, and I thought I heard somebody say, "Come in." I wasn't sure. I'm not sure yet, but I opened the door—this door *(indicating the door by which the two women are still standing)* and there in that rocker—*(pointing to it)* sat Mrs. Wright.
(They all look at the rocker.)

COUNTY ATTORNEY. What—was she doing?

HALE. She was rockin' back and forth. She had her apron in her hand and was kind of—pleating it.

COUNTY ATTORNEY. And how did she—look?

HALE. Well, she looked queer.

COUNTY ATTORNEY. How do you mean—queer?

HALE. Well, as if she didn't know what she was going to do next. And kind of done up.

COUNTY ATTORNEY. How did she seem to feel about your coming?

HALE. Why, I don't think she minded—one way or other. She didn't pay much attention. I said "How do, Mrs. Wright it's cold, ain't it?" And she said, "Is it?"—and went on kind of pleating at her apron. Well, I was surprised; she didn't ask me to come up to the stove, or to set down, but just sat there, not even looking at me, so I said, "I want to see John." And then she—laughed. I guess you would call it a laugh. I thought of Harry and the team outside, so I said a little sharp: "Can't I see John?" "No," she says, kind o' dull like. "Ain't he home?" says I. "Yes," says she, "he's home." "Then why can't I see him?" I asked her, out of patience. "'Cause he's dead," says she. "*Dead?*" says I. She just nodded her head, not getting a bit excited, but rockin' back and forth. "Why—where is he?" says I, not knowing what to say. She just pointed upstairs—like that *(himself pointing to the room above)* I got up, with the idea of going up there. I walked from there to here—then I says, "Why, what did he die of?" "He died of a rope round his neck," says she, and just went on pleatin' at her apron. Well, I went out and called Harry. I thought I might—need help. We went upstairs and there he was lyin'—

COUNTY ATTORNEY. I think I'd rather have you go into that upstairs, where you can point it all out. Just go on now with the rest of the story.

HALE. Well, my first thought was to get that rope off. It looked . . . *(stops, his face twitches)* . . . but Harry, he went up to him, and he said, "No, he's dead all right, and we'd better not touch anything." So we went back down stairs. She was still sitting that same way. "Has anybody been notified?" I asked. "No," says she unconcerned. "Who did this, Mrs. Wright?" said Harry. He said it business-like—and she stopped pleatin' of her apron. "I don't know," she says. "You don't know?" says Harry. "No," says she. "Weren't you sleepin' in the bed with him?" says Harry. "Yes," says she, "but I was on the inside." "Somebody slipped a rope round his neck and strangled him and you didn't wake up?" says Harry. "I didn't wake up," she said after him. We must 'a looked as if we didn't see how that could be, for after a minute she said, "I sleep sound." Harry was going to ask her more questions but I said maybe we ought to let her tell her story first to the coroner, or the sheriff, so Harry went fast as he could to Rivers' place, where there's a telephone.

COUNTY ATTORNEY. And what did Mrs. Wright do when she knew that you had gone for the coroner?

HALE. She moved from that chair to this one over here *(pointing to a small chair in the corner)* and just sat there with her hands held together and looking down. I got a feeling that I ought to make some conversation, so I said I had come in to see if John wanted to put in a telephone, and at that she started to laugh, and then she stopped and looked at me— scared. *(the* COUNTY ATTORNEY, *who has had his notebook out, makes a note)* I dunno, maybe it wasn't scared. I wouldn't like to say it was. Soon Harry got back, and then Dr. Lloyd came, and you, Mr. Peters, and so I guess that's all I know that you don't.

COUNTY ATTORNEY. *(looking around)* I guess we'll go upstairs first—and then out to the barn and around there. *(to the* SHERIFF*)* You're convinced that there was nothing important here—nothing that would point to any motive.

SHERIFF. Nothing here but kitchen things.

(The COUNTY ATTORNEY, *after again looking around the kitchen, opens the door of a cupboard closet. He gets up on a chair and looks on a shelf. Pulls his hand away, sticky.)*

COUNTY ATTORNEY. Here's a nice mess.

(The women draw nearer.)

MRS. PETERS. *(to the other woman)* Oh, her fruit; it did freeze. *(to the* LAWYER*)* She worried about that when it turned so cold. She said the fire'd go out and her jars would break.

SHERIFF. Well, can you beat the women! Held for murder and worryin' about her preserves.

COUNTY ATTORNEY. I guess before we're through she may have something more serious than preserves to worry about.

HALE. Well, women are used to worrying over trifles.

(The two women move a little closer together.)

COUNTY ATTORNEY. *(with the gallantry of a young politician)* And yet, for all their worries, what would we do without the ladies? *(the women do not unbend. He goes to the sink, takes a dipperful of water from the pail and pouring it into a basin, washes his hands. Starts to wipe them on the roller-towel, turns it for a cleaner place)* Dirty towels! *(kicks his foot against the pans under the sink)* Not much of a housekeeper, would you say ladies?

MRS. HALE. *(stiffly)* There's a great deal of work to be done on a farm.

COUNTY ATTORNEY. To be sure. And yet *(with a little bow to her)* I know there are some Dickson county farmhouses which do not have such roller towels.

> *(He gives it a pull to expose its length again.)*

MRS. HALE. Those towels get dirty awful quick. Men's hands aren't always as clean as they might be.

COUNTY ATTORNEY. Ah, loyal to your sex, I see. But you and Mrs. Wright were neighbors. I suppose you were friends, too.

MRS. HALE. *(shaking her head)* I've not seen much of her of late years. I've not been in this house—it's more than a year.

COUNTY ATTORNEY. And why was that? You didn't like her?

MRS. HALE. I liked her all well enough. Farmers' wives have their hands full, Mr. Henderson. And then—

COUNTY ATTORNEY. Yes—?

MRS. HALE. *(looking about)* It never seemed a very cheerful place.

COUNTY ATTORNEY. No—it's not cheerful. I shouldn't say she had the homemaking instinct.

MRS. HALE. Well, I don't know as Wright had, either.

COUNTY ATTORNEY. You mean that they didn't get on very well?

MRS. HALE. No, I don't mean anything. But I don't think a place'd be any cheerfuller for John Wright's being in it.

COUNTY ATTORNEY. I'd like to talk more of that a little later. I want to get the lay of things upstairs now.

> *(He goes to the left, where three steps lead to a stair door.)*

SHERIFF. I suppose anything Mrs. Peters does'll be all right. She was to take in some clothes for her, you know, and a few little things. We left in such a hurry yesterday.

COUNTY ATTORNEY. Yes, but I would like to see what you take, Mrs. Peters, and keep an eye out for anything that might be of use to us.

MRS. PETERS. Yes, Mr. Henderson.

> *(The women listen to the men's steps on the stairs, then look about the kitchen.)*

MRS. HALE. I'd hate to have men coming into my kitchen, snooping around and criticising.

> *(She arranges the pans under sink which the LAWYER had shoved out of place.)*

MRS. PETERS.   Of course it's no more than their duty.

MRS. HALE.   Duty's all right, but I guess that deputy sheriff that came out to make the fire might have got a little of this on. *(gives the roller towel a pull)* Wish I'd thought of that sooner. Seems mean to talk about her for not having things slicked up when she had to come away in such a hurry.

MRS. PETERS.   *(who has gone to a small table in the left rear corner of the room, and lifted one end of a towel that covers a pan)* She had bread set.

(Stands still.)

MRS. HALE.   *(eyes fixed on a loaf of bread beside the bread-box, which is on a low shelf at the other side of the room. Moves slowly toward it)* She was going to put this in there. *(picks up loaf, then abruptly drops it. In a manner of returning to familiar things)* It's a shame about her fruit. I wonder if it's all gone. *(gets up on the chair and looks)* I think there's some here that's all right, Mrs. Peters. Yes—here; *(holding it toward the window)* this is cherries, too. *(looking again)* I declare I believe that's the only one. *(gets down, bottle in her hand. Goes to the sink and wipes it off on the outside)* She'll feel awful bad after all her hard work in the hot weather. I remember the afternoon I put up my cherries last summer.

> *(She puts the bottle on the big kitchen table, center of the room. With a sigh, is about to sit down in the rocking-chair. Before she is seated realizes what chair it is; with a slow look at it, steps back. The chair which she has touched rocks back and forth.)*

MRS. PETERS.   Well, I must get those things from the front room closet. *(she goes to the door at the right, but after looking into the other room, steps back)* You coming with me, Mrs. Hale? You could help me carry them.

> *(They go in the other room; reappear, MRS. PETERS carrying a dress and skirt, MRS. HALE following with a pair of shoes.)*

MRS. PETERS.   My, it's cold in there.

> *(She puts the clothes on the big table, and hurries to the stove.)*

MRS. HALE.   *(examining the skirt)* Wright was close. I think maybe that's why she kept so much to herself. She didn't even belong to the Ladies Aid. I suppose she felt she couldn't do her part, and then you don't enjoy things when you feel shabby. She used to wear pretty clothes and be lively, when she was Minnie Foster, one of the town girls singing in the choir. But that—oh, that was thirty years ago. This is all you was to take in?

MRS. PETERS. She said she wanted an apron. Funny thing to want, for there isn't much to get you dirty in jail, goodness knows. But I suppose just to make her feel more natural. She said they was in the top drawer in this cupboard. Yes, here. And then her little shawl that always hung behind the door. *(opens stair door and looks)* Yes, here it is.

(Quickly shuts door leading upstairs.)

MRS. HALE. *(abruptly moving toward her)* Mrs. Peters?

MRS. PETERS. Yes, Mrs. Hale?

MRS. HALE. Do you think she did it?

MRS. PETERS. *(in a frightened voice)* Oh, I don't know.

MRS. HALE. Well, I don't think she did. Asking for an apron and her little shawl. Worrying about her fruit.

MRS. PETERS. *(starts to speak, glances up, where footsteps are heard in the room above. In a low voice)* Mr. Peters says it looks bad for her. Mr. Henderson is awful sarcastic in a speech and he'll make fun of her sayin' she didn't wake up.

MRS. HALE. Well, I guess John Wright didn't wake when they was slipping that rope under his neck.

MRS. PETERS. No, it's strange. It must have been done awful crafty and still. They say it was such a—funny way to kill a man, rigging it all up like that.

MRS. HALE. That's just what Mr. Hale said. There was a gun in the house. He says that's what he can't understand.

MRS. PETERS. Mr. Henderson said coming out that what was needed for the case was a motive; something to show anger, or—sudden feeling.

MRS. HALE. *(who is standing by the table)* Well, I don't see any signs of anger around here. *(she puts her hand on the dish towel which lies on the table, stands looking down at table, one half of which is clean, the other half messy)* It's wiped to here. *(makes a move as if to finish work, then turns and looks at loaf of bread outside the breadbox. Drops towel. In that voice of coming back to familiar things.)* Wonder how they are finding things upstairs. I hope she had it a little more red-up up there. You know, it seems kind of sneaking. Locking her up in town and then coming out here and trying to get her own house to turn against her!

MRS. PETERS. But Mrs. Hale, the law is the law.

MRS. HALE. I s'pose 'tis. *(unbuttoning her coat)* Better loosen up your things, Mrs. Peters. You won't feel them when you go out.

> *(*MRS. PETERS *takes off her fur tippet, goes to hang it on hook at back of room, stands looking at the under part of the small corner table.)*

MRS. PETERS. She was piecing a quilt.

> *(She brings the large sewing basket and they look at the bright pieces.)*

MRS. HALE. It's log cabin pattern. Pretty, isn't it? I wonder if she was goin' to quilt it or just knot it?

> *(Footsteps have been heard coming down the stairs. The* SHERIFF *enters followed by* HALE *and the* COUNTY ATTORNEY.*)*

SHERIFF. They wonder if she was going to quilt it or just knot it!

> *(The men laugh, the women look abashed.)*

COUNTY ATTORNEY. *(rubbing his hands over the stove)* Frank's fire didn't do much up there did it? Well, let's go out to the barn and get that cleared up.

> *(The men go outside)*

MRS. HALE. *(resentfully)* I don't know as there's anything so strange, our takin' up our time with little things while we're waiting for them to get the evidence. *(she sits down at the big table smoothing out a block with decision)* I don't see as it's anything to laugh about.

MRS. PETERS. *(apologetically)* Of course they've got awful important things on their minds.

> *(Pulls up a chair and joins* MRS. HALE *at the table.)*

MRS. HALE. *(examining another block)* Mrs. Peters, look at this one. Here, this is the one she was working on, and look at the sewing! All the rest of it has been so nice and even. And look at this! It's all over the place! Why, it looks as if she didn't know what she was about!

> *(After she has said this they look at each other, then start to glance back at the door. After an instant* MRS. HALE *has pulled at a knot and ripped the sewing.)*

MRS. PETERS. Oh, what are you doing, Mrs. Hale?

MRS. HALE. *(mildly)* Just pulling out a stitch or two that's not sewed very good. *(threading a needle)* Bad sewing always made me fidgety.

MRS. PETERS. *(nervously)* I don't think we ought to touch things.

MRS. HALE. I'll just finish up this end. *(suddenly stopping and leaning forward)* Mrs. Peters?

MRS. PETERS. Yes, Mrs. Hale?

MRS. HALE. What do you suppose she was so nervous about?

MRS. PETER. Oh—I don't know. I don't know as she was nervous. I sometimes sew awful queer when I'm just tired. (MRS. HALE *starts to say something, looks at* MRS. PETERS, *then goes on sewing)* Well I must get these things wrapped up. They may be through sooner than we think. *(putting apron and other things together)* I wonder where I can find a piece of paper, and string.

MRS. HALE. In that cupboard, maybe.

MRS. PETERS. *(looking in cupboard)* Why, here's a bird-cage. *(holds it up)* Did she have a bird, Mrs. Hale?

MRS. HALE. Why, I don't know whether she did or not—I've not been here for so long. There was a man around last year selling canaries cheap, but I don't know as she took one; maybe she did. She used to sing real pretty herself.

MRS. PETERS. *(glancing around)* Seems funny to think of a bird here. But she must have had one, or why would she have a cage? I wonder what happened to it.

MRS. HALE. I s'pose maybe the cat got it.

MRS. PETERS. No, she didn't have a cat. She's got that feeling some people have about cats—being afraid of them. My cat got in her room and she was real upset and asked me to take it out.

MRS. HALE. My sister Bessie was like that. Queer, ain't it?

MRS. PETERS. *(examining the cage)* Why, look at this door. It's broke. One hinge is pulled apart.

MRS. HALE. *(looking too)* Looks as if someone must have been rough with it.

MRS. PETERS. Why, yes.

(She brings the cage forward and puts it on the table.)

MRS. HALE. I wish if they're going to find any evidence they'd be about it. I don't like this place.

MRS. PETERS. But I'm awful glad you came with me, Mrs. Hale. It would be lonesome for me sitting here alone.

MRS. HALE. It would, wouldn't it? *(dropping her sewing)* But I tell you what I do wish, Mrs. Peters. I wish I had come over sometimes when she was here. I—*(looking around the room)*—wish I had.

MRS. PETERS.   But of course you were awful busy, Mrs. Hale—your house and your children.

MRS. HALE.   I could've come. I stayed away because it weren't cheerful—and that's why I ought to have come. I—I've never liked this place. Maybe because it's down in a hollow and you don't see the road. I dunno what it is, but it's a lonesome place and always was. I wish I had come over to see Minnie Foster sometimes. I can see now—*(shakes her head)*

MRS. PETERS.   Well, you mustn't reproach yourself, Mrs. Hale. Somehow we just don't see how it is with other folks until—something comes up.

MRS. HALE.   Not having children makes less work—but it makes a quiet house, and Wright out to work all day, and no company when he did come in. Did you know John Wright, Mrs. Peters?

MRS. PETERS.   Not to know him; I've seen him in town. They say he was a good man.

MRS. HALE.   Yes—good; he didn't drink, and kept his word as well as most, I guess, and paid his debts. But he was a hard man, Mrs. Peters. Just to pass the time of day with him— *(shivers)* Like a raw wind that gets to the bone *(pauses, her eye falling on the cage)* I should think she would 'a wanted a bird. But what do you suppose went with it?

MRS. PETERS.   I don't know, unless it got sick and died.
    (She reaches over and swings the broken door, swings it again, both women watch it.)

MRS. HALE.   You weren't raised round here, were you? (MRS. PETERS shakes her head) You didn't know—her?

MRS. PETERS.   Not till they brought her yesterday.

MRS. HALE.   She—come to think of it, she was kind of like a bird herself—real sweet and pretty, but kind of timid and—fluttery. How—she—did—change. *(silence; then as if struck by a happy thought and relieved to get back to everyday things)* Tell you what, Mrs. Peters, why don't you take the quilt in with you? It might take up her mind.

MRS. PETERS.   Why, I think that's a real nice idea, Mrs. Hale. There couldn't possibly be any objection to it, could there? Now, just what would I take? I wonder if her patches are in here—and her things.
    (They look in the sewing basket.)

Mrs. Hale. Here's some red. I expect this has got sewing things in it. *(brings out a fancy box)* What a pretty box. Looks like something somebody would give you. Maybe her scissors are in here. *(Opens box. Suddenly puts her hand to her nose)* Why—(Mrs. Peters *bends nearer, then turns her face away*) There's something wrapped up in this piece of silk.

Mrs. Peters. Why, this isn't her scissors.

Mrs. Hale. *(lifting the silk)* Oh, Mrs. Peters—it's—
(Mrs. Peters *bends closer.*)

Mrs. Peters. It's the bird.

Mrs. Hale. *(jumping up)* But, Mrs. Peters—look at it! It's neck! Look at it's neck! It's all—other side to.

Mrs. Peters. Somebody—wrung—its—neck.
(Their eyes meet. A look of growing comprehension, of horror. Steps are heard outside. Mrs. Hale slips box under quilt pieces, and sinks into her chair. Enter Sheriff and County Attorney. Mrs. Peters rises.)

County Attorney. *(as one turning from serious things to little pleasantries)* Well ladies, have you decided whether she was going to quilt it or knot it?

Mrs. Peters. We think she was going to—knot it.

County Attorney. Well, that's interesting. I'm sure. *(seeing the birdcage)* Has the bird flown?

Mrs. Hale. *(putting more quilt pieces over the box)* We think the—cat got it.

County Attorney. *(preoccupied)* Is there a cat?
(Mrs. Hale glances in a quick covert way at Mrs. Peters.)

Mrs. Peters. Well, not now. They're superstitious, you know. They leave.

County Attorney. *(to Sheriff Peters, continuing an interrupted conversation)* No sign at all of anyone having come from the outside. Their own rope. Now let's go up again and go over it piece by piece *(they start upstairs)* It would have to have been someone who knew just the—
(Mrs. Peters sits down. The two women sit there not looking at one another, but as if peering into something and at the same time holding back. When they talk now it is in the manner of feeling their way over strange ground, as if afraid of what they are saying, but as if they can not help saying it.)

Mrs. Hale. She liked the bird. She was going to bury it in that pretty box.

MRS. PETERS. *(in a whisper)* When I was a girl—my kitten—there was a boy took a hatchet, and before my eyes—and before I could get there—*(covers her face an instant)* If they hadn't held me back I would have *(catches herself, looks upstairs where steps are heard, falters weakly)*—hurt him.

MRS. HALE. *(with a slow look around her)* I wonder how it would seem never to have had any children around. *(pause)* No, Wright wouldn't like the bird—a thing that sang. She used to sing. He killed that, too.

MRS. PETERS. *(moving uneasily)* We don't know who killed the bird.

MRS. HALE. I knew John Wright.

MRS. PETERS. It was an awful thing was done in this house that night, Mrs. Hale. Killing a man while he slept, slipping a rope around his neck that choked the life out of him.

MRS. HALE. His neck. Choked the life out of him.

(Her hand goes out and rests on the bird-cage.)

MRS. PETERS. *(with rising voice)* We don't know who killed him. We don't know.

MRS. HALE. *(her own feeling not interrupted)* If there'd been years and years of nothing, then a bird to sing to you, it would be awful—still, after the bird was still.

MRS. PETERS. *(something within her speaking)* I know what stillness is. When we homesteaded in Dakota, and my first baby died—after he was two years old, and me with no other then—

MRS. HALE. *(moving)* How soon do you suppose they'll be through, looking for the evidence?

MRS. PETERS. I know what stillness is. *(pulling herself back).* The law has got to punish crime, Mrs. Hale.

MRS. HALE. *(not as if answering that)* I wish you'd seen Minnie Foster when she wore a white dress with blue ribbons and stood up there in the choir and sang. *(a look around the room)* Oh, I wish I'd come over here once in a while! That was a crime! That was a crime! Who's going to punish that?

MRS. PETERS. *(looking upstairs)* We mustn't—take on.

MRS. HALE. I might have known she needed help! I know how things can be—for women. I tell you, it's queer, Mrs. Peters. We live close together and we live far apart. We all go through the same things—it's all just a different kind of the same thing. *(brushes her eyes, noticing the bottle of fruit, reaches out for it)* If I was you, I wouldn't tell her her fruit was gone. Tell her it ain't. Tell her it's all right. Take this in to prove it to her. She—may never know whether it was broke or not.

MRS. PETERS. *(takes the bottle, looks about for something to wrap it in; takes petticoat from the clothes brought from the other room, very nervously begins winding this around the bottle. In a false voice)* My, it's a good thing the men couldn't hear us. Wouldn't they just laugh! Getting all stirred up over a little thing like a—dead canary. As if that could have anything to do with—with—wouldn't they laugh!

(The men are heard coming down stairs.)

MRS. HALE. *(under her breath)* Maybe they would—maybe they wouldn't.

COUNTY ATTORNEY. No, Peters, it's all perfectly clear except a reason for doing it. But you know juries when it comes to women. If there was some definite thing. Something to show—something to make a story about—a thing that would connect up with this strange way of doing it—

(The women's eyes meet for an instant. Enter HALE from outer door.)

HALE. Well, I've got the team around. Pretty cold out there.

COUNTY ATTORNEY. I'm going to stay here a while by myself. *(to the SHERIFF)* You can send Frank out for me, can't you? I want to go over everything. I'm not satisfied that we can't do better.

SHERIFF. Do you want to see what Mrs. Peters is going to take in?

(The LAWYER goes to the table, picks up the apron, laughs.)

COUNTY ATTORNEY. Oh, I guess they're not very dangerous things the ladies have picked out. *(Moves a few things about, disturbing the quilt pieces which cover the box. Steps back)* No, Mrs. Peters doesn't need supervising. For that matter, a sheriff's wife is married to the law. Ever think of it that way, Mrs. Peters?

MRS. PETERS. Not—just that way.

SHERIFF. *(chuckling)* Married to the law. *(moves toward the other room)* I just want you to come in here a minute, George. We ought to take a look at these windows.

COUNTY ATTORNEY. *(scoffingly)* Oh, windows!

SHERIFF. We'll be right out, Mr. Hale.

(HALE goes outside. The SHERIFF follows the COUNTY ATTORNEY into the other room. Then MRS. HALE rises, hands tight together, looking intensely at MRS. PETERS, whose eyes make a slow turn, finally meeting MRS. HALE's. A moment MRS. HALE holds her, then her own eyes point the way to where the box is concealed. Suddenly MRS. PETERS throws back quilt pieces and tries to put the box in the bag she is wearing. It is too big. She opens box, starts to take bird out, cannot touch it, goes to pieces, stands there helpless. Sound of a knob turning in the other room. MRS. HALE snatches the box and puts it in the pocket of her big coat. Enter COUNTY ATTORNEY and SHERIFF.)

COUNTY ATTORNEY. *(facetiously)* Well, Henry, at least we found out that she was not going to quilt it. She was going to— what is it you call it, ladies?

MRS. HALE. *(her hand against her pocket)* We call it—knot it, Mr. Henderson.

(CURTAIN)

1916

Glossary

Accentual meter Meter based on the number of stressed syllables per line. See **meter.**

Accentual-syllabic meter A metrical pattern based on the number of stresses and the number of syllables per line. Accentual-syllabic is the most typical metrical pattern in English poetry. It is marked by repeated units (feet) such as iambs, trochees, anapests, dactyls, and spondees. See **meter.**

Aesthetic quality of literature The "beauty" of a work; aspects that give pleasure, brought about by its form.

Allegory A kind of literature in which concrete things—characters, events, and objects—represent ideas.

Alliteration The repetition of consonant sounds at the beginning of words or at the beginning of accented syllables: "the <u>w</u>oeful <u>w</u>oman <u>w</u>ent <u>w</u>ading <u>W</u>ednesday."

Allusion A reference within a work to something outside the work, such as historical people and events, mythological and biblical figures, places, and other works of literature.

Analogy A statement that claims the similarity of things that are basically different. See **figurative language.**

Analysis The examination of the parts of something in order to discover the relationships among them and the meanings suggested by those relationships.

Anapest   A metrical foot consisting of two unaccented syllables followed by an accented syllable: overwhélm. See **foot** and **meter**.

Anaphora   Repetitions of phrases at the beginning of lines of poetry. A device characteristic of biblical free verse. See **free verse** and **biblical free verse**.

Antagonist   The opponent, whether human or otherwise, of the protagonist. See **protagonist**.

Approximate rhyme   Words that are close to rhymed: "book-buck," "watch-match," "man-in." See **rhyme**.

Archetypal criticism   Literary criticism that brings to light and explores the implications of repeated patterns (archetypes) in works of literature, such as the hero, the scapegoat, the journey, death and rebirth, and the Promethean rebel.

Argument   A line of thought that uses inductive and deductive reasoning to support claims and develop a thesis. See **essay**.

Argumentative structure of essays   The inductive and deductive reasoning that underlies an essay's line of thought. See **inductive reasoning, deductive reasoning,** and **argument**.

Assonance   The repetition of vowel sounds followed by different consonant sounds: "O the groans that opened to his own ears."

Atmosphere   The emotional response—such as fear, happiness, foreboding, and tension—that the audience and sometimes characters have to the setting and events of a work.

Attitudinal irony   A person's belief that reality is one way when, in fact, it is very different. See **irony**.

Ballad   A poem that is meant to be sung, that tells a story, and that is arranged in ballad stanzas. *Folk ballads* are anonymous and intended to be sung aloud. *Literary ballads* are written for publication by known authors. See **ballad stanza**.

Ballad stanza   A four-line stanza of poetry, traditional to ballads, that typically has four stresses in lines one and three and three stresses in lines two and four. The rhyme scheme is usually abcb. See **rhyme scheme, ballad,** and **common meter**.

Biblical free verse   Free verse influenced by translations of the Hebrew Bible (Old Testament), featuring long lines, anaphora (repeated phrases at the beginnings of lines), end-stopped lines, musical language, and an elevated tone. See **anaphora** and **free verse**.

Biographical criticism   Literary criticism that shows the relationship between authors' lives and their works of literature.

Blank verse   Iambic pentameter with no end rhyme. See **meter, iamb, foot,** and **pentameter.**

Brainstorming   A strategy for generating ideas by allowing the mind to flow where it will while it focuses on a problem, topic, or work of literature.

Caesura   A strong pause in a sentence, used as a rhythmic and thematic device in lines of poetry. See **meter** and **rhythm.**

Canon   The unofficial collection of works of literature that critics deem worthy of admiration and study.

Center of consciousness   See **central consciousness.**

Central consciousness   The sole character through whose mind we experience a narrative as rendered in the third person limited point of view. See **point of view.**

Character   The people in narratives and dramas.

Characterization   The presentation and development of the traits of characters in drama and narrative fiction.

Chronological organization of facts   In an essay, the presentation of facts in a work of literature in the order in which they occur in time. See **spatial organization of facts.**

Climax   The point in a narrative where the conflicts reach a peak of intensity and are resolved or will soon be resolved. See **Freytag pyramid.**

Comedy   A subgenre of drama that, among other things, provokes laughter and, through exaggeration and incongruity, depicts ludicrous situations, appearances, and behavior. See **tragedy.**

Common meter   Ballad meter adapted for hymns, consisting of four lines rhyming abcb or abab. Lines one and three have four stresses; lines two and four have three. Also called *hymn meter.* See **ballad stanza.**

Complex characters   See **round characters.**

Complex sentence   A sentence containing independent and subordinate (dependent) clauses. See **simple sentence.**

Connotation   The subjective, emotional associations that a word has for one person or a group of people. See **denotation.**

Consonance   The repetition of final consonant sounds that are preceded by different vowel sounds: "The bea_st_ climbed fa_st_ to the cre_st_." Consonance is also called *half-rhyme.*

Conventions   Devices of literature, such as stock characters, omniscient point of view, end-rhyme, and symbolism, that an audience easily recognizes and accepts.

Couplet   A two-line stanza of poetry whose lines are the same length and have the same end rhymes. See **rhyme scheme.**

Dactyl   A metrical foot consisting of one accented syllable followed by two unaccented syllables: róyalty. See **meter** and **foot.**

Database   An electronic resource—on a compact disc or on the Internet—that provides, among other things, works of literature and information about them.

Deconstruction   A theory of language, developed by Jacques Derrida and based on the linguistics of Ferdinand de Saussure, that rejects certainty of meaning in linguistic communications, including especially literature. To "deconstruct" a work of literature is to expose its contradictory ideas and thus its lack of meaning.

Deductive reasoning   A form of logic based on claims. The major premise (a general claim) and minor premise (a claim about a specific instance of the general claim) lead to a conclusion. The three together make up a syllogism. See **syllogism, inductive reasoning,** and **argumentative structure of essays.**

Defamiliarization   The concept, developed by Russian Formalists, that authors change familiar aspects of communication so that they are "unfamiliar." Literature, they claimed, is different from other communications because it contains such unfamiliar, "strange" qualities. See **foreground.**

Denotation   The object or idea—the referent—that a word represents. See **connotation.**

Dénouement   See **falling action.**

Dependent clause   See **subordinate clause.**

Descriptive language (imagery)   Representations of physical details that appeal to the senses.

Dialogue   The words characters speak to one another.

Diction   An author's choice of words.

Dimeter   A line of poetry consisting of two metrical feet. See **meter** and **foot.**

Drama   A genre of literature that is meant to be performed. It features characters, setting, and plot and is acted out on a stage.

Dramatic irony   Statements and beliefs by characters that the audience knows to be false or that signal meanings the audience knows but the characters do not. See **irony.**

Dynamic characters   Characters who change during the course of drama and narrative fiction. See **static characters.**

Elements of literature   Conventions that make up works of literature, such as characterization, plot, regularized rhythm, sound devices, metaphor, and setting. See **conventions.**

Embedded stories   Narratives that appear within a narrative or drama and that often seem to digress from the main plot.

End rhyme   Rhymed words that appear at the ends of lines of poetry. See **rhyme.**

End-stopped lines   A line of poetry that has a definite pause at the end. See **line** and **enjambment.**

Enjambment   The continuance of a phrase from one line of poetry to the next so that there is no pause at the end of the line. See **line.**

Enthymeme   A syllogism with one of the premises—usually the major premise—missing: "Anna Karenina is fascinating because she is so complex." The missing premise here—the main premise—is that all people who are complex are fascinating. See **syllogism.**

Epigraph   A pertinent quotation placed at the beginning of a work or unit (for example, a chapter) within the work. Usually an epigraph comments on or reflects the contents of the work or unit.

Epiphany   A term invented by James Joyce to mean a sudden feeling of revelation experienced by a character in a work of literature.

Essay   A piece of writing that is relatively brief, that adheres to rules of usage typical of mainstream publications, that develops an argument—a line of thought—whose purpose is to persuade a general audience of the validity of the author's claims, and that is unified by a thesis. See **usage, argument, general audience for essays,** and **thesis of an essay.**

Ethos   The image that speakers and writers project of themselves in their speaking or writing.

Events   Things that happen in a narrative or drama–actions, statements, thoughts, and feelings.

Experiential quality of literature   A kind of "truth" in works of literature that causes an audience to feel, emotionally and intellectually, a concept or situation, such as racism, triumph, injustice, rejection, true love, and transformation.

Exposition   Throughout a narrative, the narrator's explanation of the conflict. See **Freytag pyramid.**

Expressiveness in literature   The presentation in works of literature of authors' personalities, emotions, styles, tastes, and beliefs.

Extended metaphor   An analogy extended throughout an entire poem or a major section of a poem. See **analogy, metaphor,** and **simile.**

External conflicts Conflicts that take place outside characters—between characters or between characters and physical realities, such as storms, earthquakes, extreme heat, hostile terrain, and machines. See **internal conflicts.**

Facts in works of literature "Facts" consist of anything in the work: details about places and characters, word sounds, rhythm, characterization, physical description, the passage of time—anything.

Falling action The events in a narrative that occur after the climax and lead to the end. Another word for "falling action" is *dénouement*. See **Freytag pyramid.**

Feminine rhyme Rhymed sounds that have two or more syllables: "<u>subtle</u>-re<u>buttal</u>," "de<u>ceptively</u>-per<u>ceptively</u>." See **rhyme.**

Feminist criticism Literary criticism that studies the representation of women and issues that concern women in works of literature. See **gender criticism.**

Fiction Generally thought of as a prose narrative that includes made up (invented) materials. More specifically, "fiction" refers to the invented material itself and the stylization of materials so that the audience knows they are different from reality.

Figurative language Generally, the conscious departure from normal or conventional ways of speaking. More specifically, tropes such as metaphor and simile. See **trope, metaphor, simile,** and **analogy.**

First person point of view In narrative fiction, the telling of a story by a character in the story who refers to himself or herself in the first person, as "I."

Fixed forms Stanzas and whole poems that conform to traditional patterns and rules. See **rhyme scheme** and **nonce forms.**

Flat characters Characters with one or two traits who can be described in a short phrase. Another term for flat characters is "simple" characters. See **round characters** and **stock characters.**

Folk ballad See **ballad.**

Foot A unit of rhythm in a line of poetry. See **meter.**

Foreground The method of giving prominence to something in the work of literature that makes it different from everyday use. See **defamiliarization.**

Form The ordering of a work of literature so that it has structure, induces pleasure, and is recognizable as a genre or subgenre. See **aesthetic qualities of literature.**

Formal structural divisions in plays Units, such as acts and scenes, that playwrights or editors indicate. See **structural divisions in plays.**

Frame stories   Narratives that "surround"—provide a frame for—other narratives in the work. An example is the account of the pilgrims in Chaucer's *Canterbury Tales*, who agree to tell one another tales as they walk to Canterbury.

Free verse   Poetry without meter. See **meter, biblical free verse,** and **imagist free verse.**

Freewriting   A strategy for generating ideas by writing without stop for a brief period on a topic, problem, or work of literature.

Freytag pyramid   A diagram, developed by Gustav Freytag, that illustrates the typical plot pattern of a five-act tragedy and of most works of fiction.

Gaps in a work   Information left out of a work that the audience usually completes with its imagination.

Gender criticism   An outgrowth of feminist criticism, literary criticism that deals with all matters related to gender in works of literature: heterosexuality, homosexuality, male–female roles, role playing, politics, dress. See **feminist criticism.**

General audience for essays   Anyone who might be interested in the author's topic and who genuinely wants to learn from the essay.

Genre   A type or kind of literature, identifiable by the presence of easily recognizable conventions. Very broad genres include fiction, drama, poetry, and the essay. Subgenres of drama include tragedy, comedy, tragicomedy, farce, and theater of the absurd. Subgenres of fiction include science fiction, detective, gothic, western, fantasy, and spy. Subgenres of poetry include sonnet, ode, villanelle, and haiku.

Haiku   A poem, originating in Japan, that typically has three lines, with five syllables in the first, seven in the second, and five in the third—a total of seventeen syllables. The haiku also refers to nature, to a specific event, to actions in the present, and to a particular season of the year. See **fixed forms.**

Half-rhyme   See **consonance.**

Heptameter   A line of poetry consisting of seven metrical feet. See **meter** and **foot.**

Hexameter   A line of poetry consisting of six metrical feet. See **meter** and **foot.**

Historical criticism   Literary criticism that studies how historical events, intellectual beliefs, and cultural patterns relate to works of literature.

Hymn meter   See **common meter.**

Hypertext   A World Wide Web database that contains *links*—highlighted phrases that connect (link) to other databases.

Iamb A metrical foot, consisting of an unaccented syllable followed by an accented syllable: abóve. The iamb is the most used and "natural" foot in English poetry. See **foot** and **meter.**

Iambic pentameter A line of poetry consisting of five iambic feet. See **foot, iamb, meter,** and **blank verse.**

Imagery **a.** Descriptions of physical phenomena that appeal to one or more of the senses. **b.** Figurative language, such as metaphor and simile. See **trope, descriptive language,** and **figurative language.**

Imagist free verse Free verse that abandons the grandiose style of biblical free verse for shorter lines, enjambment, subtle rhythms, colloquial language, understatement, and a realistic depiction of human experience. Also called "meditative," "private," and "conversational" free verse. See **free verse** and **biblical free verse.**

Implied author Wayne C. Booth's concept of an idealized "author" who manifests himself or herself in a work of literature. The implied author may be similar to but is distinct from the real author.

Incremental repetition The repetition of phrases, lines, and even whole stanzas. Most of the repetitions include subtle variations that advance the story. Incremental repetition is a traditional device of ballads, especially ones featuring dialogue between two characters. See **ballad.**

Independent clause See **simple sentence.**

Inductive reasoning A form of logic based on observing specific instances of something and drawing conclusions about them. See **argumentative structure of essays** and **deductive reasoning.**

Informal structural divisions in plays Units not identified by the playwright but that nonetheless have a self-contained quality. See **structural divisions in plays** and **formal structural divisions in plays.**

In medias res Latin for "in the middle of things." A plot that begins in the middle of a story and that uses flashbacks to reveal events that occur prior to the beginning. See **plot** and **story.**

Internal conflicts Conflicts that take place within the minds of characters.

Internal rhyme Rhymed words that occur within a line of poetry or that appear close together in prose. See **rhyme.**

Interpretation The process of examining the details of something in order to make sense of it. Interpretation of literature involves analyzing individual works in order to discover "meaning" in them—how elements cohere inside the works, how the works connect to realities outside the works.

Intertextuality The formal, thematic, and historical relationship of works of literature to other works of literature. See **conventions** and **genre.**

Irony   The obvious contrast between appearance and reality. See **verbal irony, situational irony, attitudinal irony, dramatic irony.**

Line   One or more words arranged in a line (on a horizontal plane). Line is the most immediately visible structural unit of poetry. See **enjambment** and **end-stopped lines.**

Literary ballad   See **ballad.**

Literary criticism   The analysis and interpretation of works of literature.

Literary theory   The study of the nature of literature and strategies for analyzing it.

Literature   A form of communication, oral and written, that includes some or all of the following elements: language, fiction, truth, aesthetic appeal, and intertextuality.

Marxist criticism   Literary criticism that explores how works of literature reflect the theories of Karl Marx or that examines literature from the perspective of Marx's ideas.

Masculine rhyme   Rhymed sounds that consist of one stressed syllable: "mán-rán," "detéct-corréct." See **rhyme.**

Mask wearing   A character's pretense to be something he or she is not.

Meaning in literature   At its most basic level, the sense of words and sentences. More broadly, "meaning" is the signification, purpose, or underlying truth of something in the work or of the work as a whole.

Metaphor   In general, any analogy. More specifically, metaphor is a statement that claims a similarity between things that are essentially unlike and that omits the comparative words *like* and *as:* "My love is a red, red rose" rather than "My love is like a red, red rose." See **analogy, simile,** and **figurative language.**

Meter   A regular and repeated pattern of rhythm in a line of poetry. Meter (from the Greek word for "measure") can be based on (measured by) the duration of syllables (quantitative meter), the number of syllables per line (syllabic meter), and the number of stresses per line (accentual meter). The most typical meter in English poetry is accentual-syllabic: stresses and syllables per line. Accentual-syllabic meter is arranged by units (feet) such as iambs, trochees, anapests, dactyls, and spondees. See **foot.**

Monometer   A line of poetry consisting of one metrical foot. See **meter** and **foot.**

Moral center   A character in a work of literature who seems to embody the author's (or implied author's) concepts of right belief and conduct.

Narrated monologue   Characters' thoughts in their own words but presented by narrators in the past tense and third person. See **reported thought, quoted monologue,** and **stream of consciousness.**

Narratee   The person or persons who read or listen to a narrative.

Narrative   A story, told by a narrator, featuring characters who act, think, and talk.

Narrative fiction   A narrative that includes made-up events. See **narrative.**

Narrator   The teller of a story. The narrator can be a person or a medium (images, bodily movements, music) that conveys the story.

New criticism   Literary criticism that deemphasizes the value of biography and history for interpreting literature and that instead focuses on the form and unity of works of literature.

New historicist criticism   Literary criticism that endeavors to show how authors and their works of literature are products of their culture. Influenced by Ferdinand de Saussure's linguistics, new historicist critics see culture and all of its products, including literature, as similar to language.

Non sequitur   A conclusion that is unwarranted by—does not follow from—facts or verifiable claims. The literal meaning is "it does not follow."

Nonce forms   Stanzas and whole poems that conform to no traditional patterns or rules. See **fixed forms.**

Octameter   A line of poetry consisting of eight metrical feet. See **meter** and **foot.**

Octave   A stanza consisting of eight lines. See **stanza.**

Onomatopoeia   The use of words that sound like what they mean ("buzz," "boom," "hiss," "fizz," "pop," "glug").

Ottava rima   A stanza of poetry that has eight lines and rhymes abababcc. See **stanza** and **rhyme scheme.**

Overstatement   A type of verbal irony that exaggerates the nature of something while meaning the opposite. See **verbal irony.**

Pastoral poetry   Poetry that includes such conventions as a peaceful rural setting, carefree shepherds, beautiful maidens, eternal spring, pleasant weather, an absence of harsh difficulties, talk of love, and a witty use of language.

Pattern poetry   See **visual poetry.**

Pentameter   A line of poetry consisting of five metrical feet. See **meter** and **foot.**

Personification   An analogy that attributes human qualities to something not human: Old Man Winter, Father Time, Mother Nature. See **metaphor.**

Petrarchan sonnet A form of sonnet, named for its inventor Francesco Petrarch, whose typical rhyme scheme (abbaabba/cdecde) divides it into an octave (the first eight lines) and a sestet (the final six lines). See **sonnet.**

Phenomenology The study of the essential structures of consciousness. The philosophical movement *phenomenology*, founded by the German philosopher Edmund Husserl (1859–1938), influenced reader-response criticism.

Plagiarism The presentation of other people's ideas, work, and facts as one's own.

Plot An aspect of narrative and drama consisting of three things: first, the author's arrangement of events, which we experience as we read, hear, or witness the work. Second, the connection of events by cause and effect, which gives rise to conflict. Third, devices the author uses to engage us emotionally and intellectually (such as pacing, rising action, climax, surprise, intense conflict, suspense, and foreshadowing). See **events** and **story.**

Plot line In a narrative or drama, a single chain of events linked together by cause and effect. There may be more than one plot line within a narrative or drama. See **events** and **plot.**

Poetry A genre of literature that combines conventions that convey ideas (diction, speakers, imagery, symbolism), musical devices (rhythm, word sounds), structural arrangements (lines, stanzas), and sometimes visual qualities.

Point of view In narrative fiction, the narrator's relationship to the world of the work. The location (point) from which the narrator sees (views) everything in the narrative and from which the narrator tells the story. See **third person omniscient point of view, third person limited point of view, third person objective point of view,** and **first person point of view.**

Primary research The study of something by means of firsthand investigation.

Primary sources The objects of primary research. For the study of literature, most primary sources are the works of literature themselves: short stories, novels, poems, epics, romances, plays, etc. See **secondary sources.**

Private symbols Objects whose symbolic meaning is unique to one writer. See **symbol** and **public symbol.**

Probable actions In narrative and drama, events and their consequences that seem plausible.

Prose The ordinary speech of people. See **poetry** and **prose poetry.**

Prose poetry   Prose that has some of the qualities of poetry, such as nuanced diction, rhythmical devices, imagery, and internal rhyme.

Protagonist   The main character of a narrative.

Psychobiography   Biographies that apply Freudian theories of the mind to the lives and works of authors.

Psychological criticism   Literary criticism that attempts to explore the psychological implications of works of literature. In the twentieth century, the theories of Sigmund Freud heavily influenced this movement.

Public symbols   Objects whose meanings the general public would recognize. See **symbol** and **private symbol.**

Quantitative meter   See **meter.**

Quatrain   A unit of poetry consisting of four lines.

Queer theory   The study of practices and modes relevant to gays and lesbians, including cross dressing, bisexuality, and transsexuality.

Quoted monologue   The thoughts of characters rendered in the characters' own words. See **reported thought, narrated monologue,** and **stream of consciousness.**

Reader-response criticism   Literary criticism that focuses on how readers respond to literature and especially how readers, in the act of reading, help create works of literature.

Referent   The thing to which a word refers.

Reflector   See **central consciousness.**

Repetitions   Repeated actions, patterns of behavior, and thoughts that call attention to characters' traits and beliefs.

Reported thought   The thoughts of characters as rendered by narrators in the narrators' own words. See **quoted monologue, narrated monologue,** and **stream of consciousness.**

Research paper   An essay (research essay) that incorporates research in order to support the author's line of thought about a work or works of literature.

Rhetoric   The art of persuasion.

Rhetorical structure of an essay   All the aspects of an essay that makes it persuasive. These include its prose style, its tone, its beginning, its reasoning, its location of thesis, its organization of key claims, its support of claims, and its ending.

Rhythm   One of the characteristic features of poetic language. See **meter.**

Rhyme   The repetition of the last accented vowel of words and the sounds that follow: slów-grów, Máy-dáy. See **masculine rhyme, feminine rhyme, internal rhyme, end rhyme,** and **approximate rhyme.**

Rhyme scheme   Any pattern of end rhyme. End rhyme is a traditional method of organizing stanzas and poems. Rhyme scheme is indicated by letters. Ballad stanzas, for example, typically rhyme abcb (the second and fourth lines rhyme). See **rhyme** and **end rhyme.**

Rising action   The intensification of conflict in a narrative, leading to ("rising" toward) a climax. See **Freytag pyramid.**

Round characters   Characters who have multiple personality traits, who resemble the complexity of real people. "Complex" characters.

Scanning   The marking of accented and unaccented syllables in lines of poetry. See **meter.**

Scenic narration   Telling an event in real time, so that reading or hearing the event takes about as long as the event to take place. Scenic narration usually features dialogue. See **summary narration.**

Secondary research   The examination of studies other people have made of something.

Secondary sources   For literary studies, resources that provide information about authors and works of literature. These include such things as books, articles, oral presentations, and Web sites. See **primary sources.**

Sestet   A unit of poetry consisting of six lines.

Sets   Objects that represent the physical setting of a play.

Setting   The physical, sensuous location of the action, the time in which the action occurs, and the social environment of the characters.

Shakespearean sonnet   A form of sonnet, named after its most famous practitioner. The typical rhyme scheme (abab/cdcd/efef/gg) divides the poem into three quatrains (four lines each) and a couplet. See **sonnet.**

Simile   A statement that claims the similarity of things that are essentially unlike and that uses the comparative words *like* or *as:* "My love is as fair as a dove." See **analogy, trope, metaphor,** and **figurative language.**

Simple characters   See **flat** characters.

Simple sentence   The basic independent clause that constitutes a sentence, usually following the order of subject-verb (Jane loves) or subject-verb-object (Jane loves Joe). See **complex sentence.**

Situational irony   A situation that differs from what common sense indicates it is, will be, or ought to be. See **irony.**

Sonnet   A form of poetry that consists of fourteen lines of iambic pentameter and conforms to one of two patterns of end rhyme: Shakespearean sonnet (abab/cdcd/efef/gg) and Petrarchan sonnet (abbaabba/cdecde). See **Shakespearean sonnet, Petrarchan sonnet,** and **fixed forms.**

Spatial organization of facts   In an essay, the presentation of facts from a work of literature as they appear in the work. See **chronological organization of facts.**

Spenserian stanza   A nine-line stanza of poetry, invented by Edmond Spenser, that rhymes ababbcbcc. See **stanza.**

Spondee   A metrical foot consisting of two accented syllables: bréak, bréak. See **meter** and **foot.**

Stable situation   The end of a narrative, where all or most of the major conflicts have been resolved. See **Freytag pyramid.**

Stanza   In a poem, a unit of lines set apart from other units by spaces. A stanza can encompass the whole poem (for example, a sonnet) or part of the poem (for example, a ballad). Stanzas are often organized by patterns of end rhyme, such as ballad stanza, ottava rima, couplet, and Spenserian stanza. Poems with stanzas are "strophic." Poems without stanzas are "stichic." See **rhyme scheme.**

Static characters   Characters who do not change throughout a narrative or play. See **dynamic characters.**

Stichic poems   See **stanza.**

Stock characters   Flat (simple) characters that are easily recognized conventions in dramas: the wily servant, the pretentious doctor, the gullible simpleton, the young lovers, the old cuckold.

Story   Everything that happens in a narrative and a play, arranged in chronological order. See **plot** and **events.**

Stream of consciousness   The presentation of characters' preconscious or prespeech thoughts as an apparently incoherent "stream." See **reported thought, quoted monologue,** and **narrated monologue.**

Strophic poems   See **stanza.**

Structural divisions in plays   Units, such as acts and scenes, that are self-contained and that can be distinguished from other units in the play. See **formal structural divisions in plays** and **informal structural divisions in plays.**

Structuralism   A method of analyzing literature, arising from the linguistics of Ferdinand de Saussure, that focuses on similarities between the structure of language and the structure of literature.

Structure in works of literature   The way the parts of a work are organized into a coherent whole.

Style   The way writers and speakers use language.

Subgenres   Kinds of literature that have the typical features of a broad genre (like fiction, drama, and poetry) but that have further, more specific features. Detective fiction, for example, is a subgenre of fiction.

Subject   Something a work of literature seems to be about—genuine love, political integrity, financial corruption, bravery under fire, leadership. See **theme.**

Subordinate clause   Phrases within a sentence that do not stand alone as sentences, and that are "dependent" on the independent clause of the sentence. See **simple sentence.**

Subtext in a play   The unspoken but discernible meanings of the written words, especially of the dialogue.

Summary narration   The narration of events and repeated actions that happen over time. Reading a summary narration takes much less time than for the events to occur: "For two years, Marcia attended concerts at Carnegie Hall, hoping against hope to see Raymond." See **scenic narration.**

Syllabic meter   See **meter.**

Syllogism   A unit of reasoning consisting of two claims that support a third claim. The two supporting claims are called *premises* and the third claim is called a *conclusion.*

Symbol   An object, event, or character that signifies an abstract idea or ideas. The symbol's meaning is often interestingly vague, suggestive rather than precise. See **private symbols** and **public symbols.**

Symbolism   The use of symbols in a work.

Syntax   Sentence structure; the way words go together to make sentences. See **simple sentence** and **independent clause.**

Testimony   Interpretive statements by literary critics that authors of research papers use to support their own lines of thought. See **research paper.**

Tetrameter   A line of poetry consisting of four metrical feet. See **meter** and **foot.**

Theme   An idea about the human condition that the audience extracts from works of literature. A theme is what the work seems to say about a subject. See **subject.**

Thesis of an essay   The main claim of the essay, the one idea that unifies the essay.

Third person limited point of view   In narrative fiction, the telling of a story by an apparently all-knowing ("omniscient") narrator who enters the mind of only one character. The narrator refers to all the characters in the third person, as "he" and "she."

Third person objective (dramatic) point of view   In narrative fiction, the telling of a story by an apparently all-knowing ("omniscient") narrator who enters the mind of no characters. We learn about characters from the outside, just as we do when watching a play–thus the term "dramatic." The narrator refers to all the characters in the third person, as "he" and "she."

Third person omniscient point of view   In narrative fiction, the telling of a story by an apparently all-knowing ("omniscient") narrator who enters the minds of more than one character and who refers to all the characters in the third person, as "he" and "she."

Tone   A narrator's or writer's predominant attitude toward a subject. The subject can be a place, event, character, or idea.

Topoi   Traditional patterns of thought, identified by Aristotle as *topoi*, "places" to discover meaning and to develop ideas. Topoi include definition, structure, process, cause and effect, and comparison.

Tragedy   A subgenre of drama that, according to Aristotle, contains conventions such as a larger-than-life hero whose flaw brings about a precipitous fall and whose fate elicits pity and fear in the audience. See **comedy.**

Trimeter   A line of poetry consisting of three metrical feet. See **meter** and **foot.**

Trochee   A metrical foot consisting of an accented syllable followed by an unaccented syllable: lóvely. See **foot** and **meter.**

Trope   Generally, the extension of the meanings of a word beyond its literal meaning. More specifically, a trope is an analogy such as metaphor and simile. See **figurative language, metaphor, simile,** and **analogy.**

Truth in literature   The reflection in works of literature of aspects of the world outside the works.

Turn   A point in a poem when the poet shifts from one meaning or mood to another. The turn in a Shakespearean sonnet typically occurs from the first twelve lines to the couplet. The turn in a Petrarchan sonnet takes place between the octave and sestet.

Typical characters   Characters that typify real people.

Understatement   A form of verbal irony that minimizes the nature of something while meaning the opposite. See **verbal irony.**

Unreliable narrators   Narrators or "centers of consciousness" whose judgments and rendering of facts are untrustworthy.

Unstable situation   The introduction of conflict at the beginning of a plot. See **Freytag pyramid.**

Usage   The way English is used in mainstream publications, such as newspapers, magazines, books, advertisements, financial reports, business reports, and scholarly journals.

Verbal irony   A statement that says the opposite of what one means. See **irony.**

Villanelle   A traditional form of poetry, originating in Italy and France, that has nineteen lines and six stanzas. Each stanza except the last has three lines; the last has four. The rhyme scheme is aba, aba, aba, aba, aba, abaa. The first and third lines of the poem are repeated throughout: the first line at the end of stanzas two and four, the third line at the end of stanzas three and five. At the end of the poem, these two lines form a couplet.

Visual poetry   Poetry that must be seen as well as heard in order to be fully understood. Visual poetry is also called *pattern poetry.* Visual poetry has traditionally taken the appearance of recognizable objects like angels' wings, love knots, hearts, crosses, animals, stars, and labyrinths.

Writing process   The steps authors go through in order to write an essay: inventing, drafting, revising, and editing.

Credits

Appendix

Index of Concepts
and Terms

Index of Critics, Authors, and Works

453